History of Congleton

History of Congleton

Published to celebrate the 700th
anniversary of the granting of the
charter to the town

Edited by
W. B. Stephens

Published for the
Congleton History Society
by
Manchester University Press

Published by
Manchester University Press
316–324 Oxford Road
Manchester M13 9NR

SBN 7190 1245 7

7101

Printed in Great Britain by
Butler & Tanner Ltd
Frome and London

Congleton History Society Committee

President   Sir Randle Baker Wilbraham Bt.

Chairman   Mr. R. W. Beardmore

Hon. Secretary   Mr. J. F. Sebire

Hon. Treasurer   Mr. F. S. Cartlidge

Committee   Miss Joan P. Alcock
Miss M. Cinnamon
Mrs. E. H. Gilmour
Mr. J. Colin Jones
Mr. D. H. Mottram
Mr. P. Timmis Smith
Mr. R. G. Whiston

Representing Congleton Borough Council   His Worship the Mayor
Alderman W. H. Semper
Alderman D. Charlesworth
Councillor F. Heapy
Councillor C. Pedley
Councillor S. Davies
Councillor A. R. Saywell

Co-opted   Mr. J. C. Hopkins

The Committee wish to place on record their thanks to Mr. B. B. Brown and Mr. D. Daniel, who helped in the formation of the Society as Hon. Treasurer and Hon. Solicitor respectively.

Contents

List of Plates

Acknowledgements are due where and as indicated above. Except where otherwise stated, the photographs are by the late Mr. K. Benson.

List of Figures

Acknowledgements are due where and as indicated above. For the map of the 1960s (based on an adaptation of the O.S. by Geographia Ltd.), permission to reproduce is acknowledged to *J. Burrow & Co.*, *Geographia* and *H.M.S.O.* Permission for the 1837 map is also acknowledged to *H.M.S.O.*

Abbreviations

Add. Ch.—Additional Charter
Add. MS.—Additional Manuscript
Berisfords—Berisfords, The Ribbon People (1958 edition)
Borough accounts—Borough account books (Congleton Town Hall)
Borough Charters—Collection of deeds and other documents in three volumes (Congleton Town Hall)
B.M.—British Museum
Borough Order Bk.—Borough Order (or Minute) Book (Congleton Town Hall)
C 66—Chancery, Patent Rolls (P.R.O.)
C 146—Chancery, Ancient Deeds, Series C (P.R.O.)
Cal. Chart. R.—Calendar of Charter Rolls
Cal. Close R.—Calendar of Close Rolls
Cal. Fine R.—Calendar of Fine Rolls
Cal. Inq. Post Mortem—Calendar of Inquisitions Post Mortem
Cal. Pat. R.—Calendar of Patent Rolls
Cal. S.P. Dom.—Calendar of State Papers Domestic
Cat. Anc. Deeds.—Catalogue of Ancient Deeds
Chester Arch. Jnl.—Journal of the Chester and North Wales Architectural, Archaeological, and Historical Society
Cong. Chron.—Congleton Chronicle
C.R.O.—Cheshire Record Office
Davies, *Macclesfield*—C. S. Davies, *History of Macclesfield* (1961)
Dir. Ches.—Directory of Cheshire
DL 1—Duchy of Lancaster, Equity Proceedings, Pleadings (P.R.O.)
DL 3—Duchy of Lancaster, Equity Proceedings, Depositions and Examinations, Series I (P.R.O.)
DL 7—Duchy of Lancaster, Inquisitions Post Mortem (P.R.O.)
DL 10—Duchy of Lancaster, Royal Charters (P.R.O.)
DL 25—Duchy of Lancaster, Deeds, Series L (P.R.O.)
DL 29—Duchy of Lancaster, Ministers' Accounts (P.R.O.)
DL 30—Duchy of Lancaster, Court Rolls (P.R.O.)
DL 37—Duchy of Lancaster, Chancery Rolls (P.R.O.)
DL 42—Duchy of Lancaster, Miscellaneous Books (P.R.O.)
D.N.B.—Dictionary of National Biography
E 40—Exchequer, Treasury of Receipt, Ancient Deeds, Series A (P.R.O.)

E 42—Exchequer, Treasury of Receipt, Ancient Deeds, Series AS (P.R.O.)

E 117—Exchequer, King's Remembrancer, Alienation Office Accounts, Church Goods (P.R.O.)

E 134—Exchequer, King's Remembrancer, Depositions taken by Commission (P.R.O.)

E 179—Exchequer, King's Remembrancer, Tax Rolls, etc. (P.R.O.)

Earwaker—J. P. Earwaker, *East Cheshire* (1877)

Ec. H.R.—Economic History Review

Ed. 7—Ministry of Education, Public Elementary School Files Preliminary Statements (P.R.O.)

Ed. 16—Ministry of Education, Local Education Authorities, Supply Files (P.R.O.)

Ed. 19—Ministry of Education, Local Education Authorities, Code Files (P.R.O.)

Ed. 21—Ministry of Education, Public Elementary School Files (P.R.O.)

Ed. 35—Ministry of Education, Secondary Education, Institution Files (P.R.O.)

Ed. 99—Ministry of Education, Premises Survey Files, Accountant General Department (P.R.O.)

EDA, EDP, EDV—Chester Diocesan Records (C.R.O.)

E.H.R.—English Historical Review

*E.P.N.S.—*English Place Names Society

Harl. MS—Harleian Manuscript

Head—R. Head, *Congleton Past and Present* (1887)

H.M.C.—Historical Manuscripts Commission

H.O. 45—Home Office, Correspondence, Registered Papers (P.R.O.)

H.O. 48—Home Office, Law Officers' Reports and Correspondence (P.R.O.)

H.O. 129—Home Office, Census Papers, Population Schedules 1841, 1851 (P.R.O.)

H.O. 107—Home Office, Census Papers, Ecclesiastical Returns, 1851 (P.R.O.)

Jnl.—Journal

Min. P.C.—Minutes or *Reports of the Committee of Council on Education, with appendices,* Parl. Paper—followed by session

NGR—National Grid Reference

Ormerod—G. Ormerod, *History of Cheshire* revised and edited by T. Helsby (1882)

Parl. Paper—Parliamentary Paper

P.C.C.—Somerset House, Prerogative Court of Canterbury

P.R.O.—Public Record Office

QDL—Quarter Sessions Records, Land Taxes (C.R.O.)
QDP—Quarter Sessions Records, Deposited Plans (C.R.O.)
Rec. Soc. L. & C.—Record Society of Lancashire and Cheshire
Record Comm.—Record Commission
Rep. Boundaries Comm.—*Report of the Royal Commission on Municipal Corporation Boundaries,* Parl. Paper (1837), xxvi
Rep. Handloom Weavers (1834), (1835)—*Reports of the Select Committee on Handloom Weavers' Petitions,* Parl. Papers (1834), x; (1835), xiii
Rep. Handloom Weavers (1840)—*Report of the Royal Commission on Handloom Weavers,* pt IV, Parl. Paper (1840), xxiv
Rep. Handloom Weavers (1841)—*Report of the Royal Commission on Handloom Weavers,* Parl. Paper (1841), x
Rep. Mun. Corps.—*Report of the Royal Commission into the Government of Municipal Corporations in England and Wales* (1835), xxvi
Rep. Silk Manufacture (1818)—*Report of the Select Committee on the Petitions of Ribbon Weavers and Silk Manufacturers,* Parl. Paper (1818), ix
Rep. Silk Trade (1831–2)—*Report of Select Committee on the present state of the Silk Trade,* Parl. Paper (1831–2), xix
Rep. Tech. Instr. (1884)—*Report of Select Committee on the present state of Technical Instruction,* Parl. Paper (1884), xxxi
RG 4—Registrar General, Non Parochial Registers, Authenticated, Main Series (P.R.O.)
RG 6—Registrar General, Authenticated Registers, Society of Friends (P.R.O.)
RG 9—Registrar General, Census Schedules, 1861 (P.R.O.)
SC 2—Special Collections, Court Rolls (P.R.O.)
SC 11, 12—Special Collections, Rentals and Surveys (P.R.O.)
T.H.S.L.C.—*Transactions of the Historic Society of Lancashire and Cheshire*
T.L.C.A.S.—*Transactions of the Lancashire and Cheshire Antiquarian Society*
Trans.—*Transactions*
V.C.H.—*Victoria County History*
Yates—S. Yates, *History of Congleton* (1820)

Note on Contributors

Joan P. Alcock, M.A. is Senior Lecturer in History at Battersea College of Education.

J. B. Blake, M.A. works for Granada Television, and was formerly Research Assistant at the History of Parliament Trust.

E. A. G. Clark, M.A., PH.D. is Principal Lecturer in Geography at Newland Park College of Education.

Robert W. Dunning, B.A., PH.D., F.S.A. is editor of the *Victoria History of Somerset*.

Norah Fuidge, M.A. is Research Assistant to Professor Sir John Neale at the History of Parliament Trust.

M. W. Greenslade, M.A., F.S.A. is editor of the *Victoria History of Staffordshire*.

David Iredale, M.A., PH.D. was formerly an archivist in the North Riding.

J. Colin Jones, M.A. is Senior English Master at Stansfield Technical High School, Burslem.

P. Timmis Smith is a practising architect in Congleton and lecturer on local history and archaeology.

W. B. Stephens, M.A., PH.D., F.S.A. is Lecturer in Education in the University of Leeds, and was formerly the Deputy General Editor of the *Victoria County Histories*, at the Institute of Historical Research, University of London.

F. H. Thompson, M.C., M.A. is Assistant Secretary of the Society of Antiquaries, and was formerly Curator of the Grosvenor Museum, Chester, and Lecturer in History in the University of Manchester.

W. H. Semper, B.A. is Senior History Master at Sandbach School, and has been twice Mayor of Congleton.

Editorial Note

Congleton received its first charter at some time between 1272 and 1275. The Congleton History Society was founded in 1964, under the presidency of Sir Randle Baker Wilbraham, High Steward of the Borough, by a group of interested citizens with the express purpose of promoting the publication of a new history of the town, to mark its seven centuries as a borough. I was approached by founding members of the Society and agreed to undertake the organization of the writing of such a history and to edit it. I was fortunate to be able to bring together a team of contributors consisting partly of local historians, and partly of historians with connexions with Cheshire or interest in its history. The forethought of the committee and the enthusiasm and hard work of both the contributors and of the committee members have made it possible for this new history to be tackled in a thorough manner and without undue haste.

This is not the first history of Congleton to be published, and it lays no claim to being definitive. Two notable histories of the borough have preceded it—those of Samuel Yates and of Richard Head. Head's *Congleton Past and Present*, published in 1887, was a considerable work which will continue to be consulted by those interested in the history of the borough. Indeed Head's history is now a primary source since he printed extracts from Congleton records later destroyed by fire. It has not, however, been possible to include in the present volume all the information that was in Head's work for, in the first place, a great deal of new evidence has become available in recent years and this has naturally been emphasized. Secondly, about a century of town history has passed since Head wrote and this has deserved detailed treatment. For these reasons topics dealt with exhaustively by Head, such as the manorial history and the history of the Established Church, have here received briefer treatment than aspects of the town's history with which he dealt less extensively, such as economic history and the history of nonconformity. This volume is primarily concerned with the history of the ancient borough of Congleton but although Buglawton was not incorporated in the borough until the present century, it was physically so much a part of the town before that that several aspects of its previous history are touched on. Since the nineteenth-century fire Congleton has had only a small collection of borough records. The work of the various contributors has, however, revealed that records relating to Congleton's history, though dispersed, are more numerous than was at first thought, and there is certainly scope for further more detailed work to be undertaken. No history is ever the last word.

Too many people in Congleton and elsewhere have given help for all to be mentioned here by name, although it has been possible to draw attention in notes to chapters to some who have assisted particular contributors. Here I should like to acknowledge the great assistance I and the contributors have received from the committee and other members of the Society. Thanks are also due to the late Mr. Kenneth Benson for taking many of the photographs reproduced in the volume, to the Rector of Astbury, and the Vicar of St. Peter's for making church records available, to Mr. J. Robertshaw of Robert H. Lowe and Co. for the use of records and photographs, to Mr. J. M. Dodgson of University College, London, for information on place-names, to the Goldsmiths' Librarian of the University of London and to Miss Joan Gibbs for housing Congleton records for use by myself and by contributors in the London area, to Mr. A. J. Condliffe, the Editor of the *Congleton Chronicle*, and his staff for making their valuable files available, for providing certain photographs, and for assistance in many other directions, to Mr. W. J. Varley for permission to reproduce an illustration from his *Cheshire before the Romans*, to Miss Muriel Cinnamon and sixth-form pupils of Congleton County Grammar School for Girls for work on church registers and in collecting newspaper cuttings, to the late Mr. Jack Mee and Mr. H. Lawton, successive Town Clerks of Congleton, and their department, and to other borough officials, for making available the official Congleton archives and for help in other ways, to Lord Congleton for permission to consult his family records, to the Congleton Council of Churches and its Secretary, Mr. A. Gilmour, for organizing a census of church attendance in March 1968, to Mrs. C. C. L. Browne of Salisbury, and Mr. George Foden of Congleton for the loan of books, to Dr. G. Hornung of Leeds University for reading part of the text, to the officers of the many libraries and record depositories used in the compilation of the book, to local ministers of religion, members of congregations, and to local firms and others for information freely given. Above all I must express my gratitude to the contributors not only for their co-operation in the organization and presentation of their own chapters, but also for their great assistance to myself and to each other in the many problems involved in the compilation of the book. Finally, grateful acknowledgement must be made to the Corporation of Congleton for its generous support towards the cost of publication.

W. B. S.

University of Leeds,
November, 1968

I The Archaeology of the Congleton Area

by F H Thompson

Congleton lies at the eastern edge of the rolling Cheshire plain at the foot of the southern reaches of the Pennines. Most of the township's huge area of twenty-six hundred acres lies between two and four hundred feet above sea level, but rises gently eastwards towards the hills. Men founded the settlement on the hillside south of the Dane and the Daneinshaw (or Dane-in-Shaw) brook where springs and wells provided water. A medieval diversion of the Dane later provided extensive meadowland between town and river, and the rich soil of the area once provided sustenance for thick oak woods. By 1700, however, the area of woodland had considerably diminished. Geologically, the position of Congleton is interesting in that it stands near the junction of the Triassic marls and sandstones underlying the Cheshire plain to the west with the older Carboniferous formations of sandstones, grits and shales[1] which rise to the east. The Triassic formation is, however, overlain by glacial sands, gravels and clays and the plain west of the railway is broken into numerous small hills and deep valleys; east of the railway, however, the Carboniferous rocks emerge sharply from this overlying drift and rise to a height of over 1,000 ft above sea level, with individual peaks at the Cloud, Congleton Edge and Mow Cop. These foothills of the Pennines serve as protection against cold winds from the east but are also encountered by the more frequent moist winds from the west; thus, the area has the damp but mild climate characteristic of east Cheshire. Geographically, the other main feature of the area is the Dane which rises on

Axe Edge, near Buxton, and debouches into the plain at Bosley, north-east of Congleton. In the earlier part of its course it is a clear swift stream flowing through steep-sided wooded valleys, but it becomes more sluggish on entering the plain, and after passing through Congleton (where it must have been a major factor in the town's origin) adopts a meandering course until it joins the Weaver at Northwich.

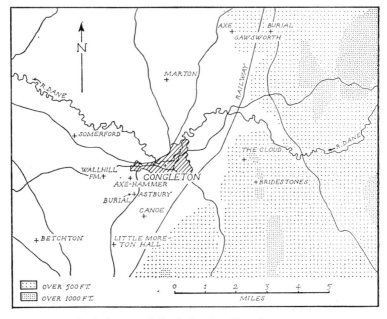

Archaeological sites and finds in the Congleton area

For much of the town's history we rely on the written evidence left behind by countless generations of men. Congleton's story would not, however, be complete without an attempt to collect the evidence for the earliest presence of man in the area. In so doing we abandon history for prehistory, being forced to turn from documentary evidence to those few material traces of human existence which have survived the accidents of time. But Congleton itself had no independent existence at this remote time and it would be unduly restrictive merely to consider the evidence from the area of the later town. We shall then speak of the Congleton 'area' without precisely defining what that area is and discuss, in chronological order, a number of sites and finds of archaeological interest.

The archaeological monument of the Congleton area which ranks first in both time and importance is the Neolithic chambered tomb known as the Bridestones.[2] It belongs in general to a so-called 'megalithic culture' characterized by the practice of collective burial in stone-built chambers beneath mounds of earth and stone, monuments which are widely distributed over the western parts of the British Isles. They were built by groups of settlers from what may be broadly called Atlantic Europe who, in common with others crossing the Channel to settle in southern England, introduced the revolutionary idea of farming to this country, the population of which had hitherto depended on hunting, fishing and food-gathering for survival. The tombs themselves can be classified, on structural and geographical grounds, into groups of which one of the larger ones is the so-called Clyde-Carlingford group;[3] this is centred on the northern end of the Irish Sea and takes its name from the main concentrations around Carlingford Lough in northern Ireland and the Clyde in Scotland. The distinguishing features of the group are the segmented gallery forming the actual chamber and the forecourt which probably served as the scene of pre-burial ritual.

It is to this group that the Bridestones belong, although far enough removed from the main distributions to be considered an outlier. Its remains lie approximately three miles east of Congleton, just inside the county boundary, at a height of 900 ft above sea level.[4] The monument has lost much of its original structure, even since 1766 when it was first described. Today there exists the chamber, composed of gritstone slabs, divided internally by a transverse slab which originally had a circular 'porthole'; at the east end a massive upright adjoins the south side of the chamber and this, with two or three isolated smaller stones, are all that survive of the original crescentic façade enclosing the forecourt. The 1766 description indicated a semi-circular façade of six or eight uprights, placed about 6 ft apart, and two stones placed in the forecourt at a point where there was a scatter of charcoal; two more uprights adjoined the eastern angles of the chamber, which itself had been covered with slabs, giving an internal height of about 6 ft; it had a rubble floor on which rested a layer of charcoal and fragments of burnt

bone; the porthole in the transverse slab was stated to be 19½ in.
in diameter; the remains of two other (perhaps lateral) chambers
are mentioned but without any precise indication of position,
while there was said to have been a massive stone cairn (possibly
trapezoidal) once covering the whole complex but this had been
robbed for roadmaking and other purposes.

The excavation of 1936–7 did not produce any startling new
evidence but served to confirm and clarify the early description.
The chamber measures approximately 16 ft long internally and
5 ft wide, and is divided about halfway by the transverse slab
mentioned above. The forecourt immediately east of the chamber
was found to be roughly paved with small rounded blocks of
gritstone, while one survivor of the pair of stones in the forecourt was located 21 ft east of the chamber entrance; a spread
of charcoal, as mentioned in 1766, was found to the north, from
the surface of which came a small flint blade and scraper. As a
result of the excavation, a limited amount of restoration was
carried out, leaving the monument in the state in which it can
be seen today, although there has been some encroachment of
undergrowth.

So little evidence in the way of actual Neolithic objects has
been recovered from the Bridestones that it is impossible to use
this approach in order to date the tomb, and instead we must
consider its construction and evidence of date afforded by
similar monuments elsewhere. In general, it has been suggested
that the Clyde-Carlingford culture appeared first in Scotland
and only later in Ulster, where it may have arrived direct from
the Continent or by colonization from Scotland. The Bridestones tomb can be compared with Irish examples and may
itself represent an isolated burial-place of Continental farmer-
settlers moving north up the Irish Sea or a secondary movement
across the Irish Sea from Ulster. In either case, it belongs to the
somewhat later stage of population movements beginning before
3000 B.C. and continuing throughout the third millennium; a
central date of *c.* 2500 B.C. gives a very approximate indication
of when the Bridestones may have beeen built. The tomb may
have continued in use for a long time, successive cremations
being inserted into the chamber until, for some reason, no more
took place and the cairn was erected over the burial-place. We
do not know how much cremated bone was present and in any
case this particular method of disposing of the dead makes it

difficult to say much about numbers; but the total cannot have been great, perhaps between ten and 50, or one family and its descendants. They were not, however, completely isolated since other farmers were settling, on the evidence of more chambered tombs, on the limestone hills of the Peak District to the east.

Any attempt to explain the structural features of the Bridestones, for example the curved façade enclosing the forecourt, the porthole, and so on, is bound to enter on very debatable ground. Some writers have argued for a sexual symbolism in the

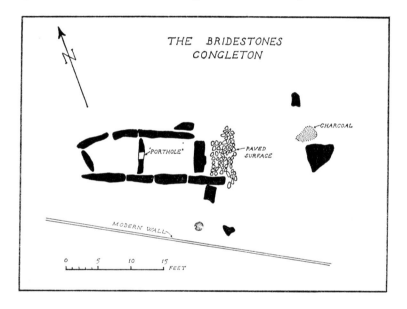

presence of 'male' and 'female' stones in the portals and forecourts of chambered tombs; equally, the porthole, burial chamber and the contracted attitude in which some undisturbed inhumations are found in megalithic tombs may point to some such concept as a return to the womb. On the other hand, where a porthole appears in conjunction with cremation burials, it is possible that the idea of an exit for the souls of the dead may be involved. But, clearly, it will never be possible to arrive at the truth in matters of this kind.

A discovery in 1966 of outstanding importance was of a late Neolithic burial at Fool's Nook, Gawsworth, which in certain of its features foreshadows the burial practices of the subsequent Bronze Age. It consisted of a round barrow or burial mound, five miles north-east of Congleton and just west of the main road from Macclesfield to Leek (the A523);[5] it stands on high ground just below the 550 ft contour and to an observer in the valley through which the main road runs would appear to be on the crest—a common practice.[6]

The mound is quite small with a diameter of 50 ft and was found to be composed of sand with a small stone cairn 6 ft in diameter at the centre, set in a D-shaped pit. A wartime gun-position had been built into one side of the mound and had destroyed part of the cairn but had fortunately just missed the burial which the cairn had originally marked. The evidence for this was a long-necked beaker with which was associated a flint knife, while other worked flints were also recovered. The acid soil had destroyed all the skeletal remains so it is impossible to say whether this was a cremation or inhumation, but it was most probably the latter. The beaker, an exceedingly rare find for the counties immediately west of the Pennines, is 6 in. high and made in a buff, rather coarse ware. The decoration is principally executed with a square-toothed comb and consists (from the rim downwards) of a narrow zone of lattice pattern separated by a cordon from a zone of vertical lozenges which in turn is separated by another cordon from a zone of horizontal lozenges extending to the base. The cordons are themselves decorated with a wedge-shaped point to give a notched effect. The burial must represent an outlier from the main distribution of long-necked beakers to the east and a date of *c*. 1600 B.C. can be very tentatively suggested.[7] Further excavation, until 1968, has located more burials on a secondary position on the edge of the mound; these are later in date, being early Bronze Age cremations with and without urns.

For our other evidence of Neolithic activity in the Congleton area we turn to something which stands at the opposite extreme to the Bridestones, at least in size. This is a polished flint axe from Gawsworth, between Congleton and Macclesfield, said to have been found in the Church Field during ploughing.[8] These implements are spread widely over Britain and their presence may be due to one of at least two causes. It is generally accepted that they were intended for use in tree-felling in order to clear suitable ground for agriculture, so that they may have been lost

a The Gawsworth Beaker (height 6 in.), *b* the Astbury Urn (height 7½ in.),
c the Betchton Cremation Group (urn approx. 14 in. high)

a

b

c

The Bridestones, interior of burial chamber

The Betchton Pygmy Cup base and side views (max. diameter $3\frac{1}{4}$ in.)

during this activity, particularly where they occur on lighter soils or in proximity to actual settlements. On the other hand, it is possible that they were lost in the course of transport from production centres to Neolithic settlement areas; we know that there was a brisk trade, particularly in stone axes, between so-called 'axe-factories' and the newly established farming communities. The Gawsworth axe has been geologically determined as a flint of possibly Yorkshire or Lincolnshire origin,[9] which is itself interesting, since the main production centres were the chalk formations of south-east England.[10] But the precise significance of the Gawsworth axe must remain an open question.

It is convenient at this point to mention three other stone implements of a different type, since they provide a convenient link with the ensuing Bronze Age (*c.* 1600 B.C. onwards). These are perforated axe-hammers, more massive than the flint or stone axes of the Neolithic, but probably also used for tree-felling, perhaps in conjunction with wedges. One comes from Cocks Moss Wood, near Marton, about two and a half miles north of Congleton,[11] the second from the vicinity of Moreton Old Hall, three miles south-west of the town,[12] and the third, an unfinished implement, was found in 1966 at Padgbury Farm, Padgbury Lane, one mile west-south-west of Congleton.[13] Of more significance for Bronze Age settlement, however, are the barrows or burial mounds of the area which, in the absence of actual habitations, provide the evidence for the presence of a local population. The ritual of collective burial had been largely abandoned towards the end of the Neolithic and instead we find single inhumations, frequently beneath barrows such as the recent example from Fool's Nook, Gawsworth. This became the norm in the Early and Middle Bronze Age, with cremation substituted for inhumation and the remains placed in a container, the so-called collared urn. Both the ritual and the pottery are thought to denote the resurgence of a latent native tradition incorporating features borrowed from successive immigrant cultures.[14]

The interesting point about Bronze Age burials in east Cheshire is that they now appear on soils such as gritstone and sand which had been largely ignored by their Neolithic predecessors, who had preferred, for instance, the limestone of the Peak District (on the assumption again that burials represent settlement in the vicinity). It has been suggested that this may have been the result of climatic change, a decrease in rainfall which made the limestone areas too arid, but in that case the sands of the Central Ridge of Cheshire, around Delamere for instance, which show a scatter of burials, would have been equally uninviting.[15] In fact, round barrows were apparently still being built on the limestone of the Peak District and their spread to other areas may well have been the result of a general increase in population; the semi-nomadic communities of the time, still relying as much on hunting as on farming for their subsistence, would need large areas to exercise their skills.

In the vicinity of Congleton groups of barrows are recorded from Twemlow (the -*low* ending is in itself significant since it frequently denotes the presence of a burial mound or mounds), Withington and Capesthorne Hall, all on an arc of approximately six miles radius extending from the north-west to the north of Congleton itself, but nothing is known of the burials within.[16]

Another unexplored barrow is recorded from Somerford, three miles west-north-west of Congleton.[17] On the other hand, there are two instances where the urn and burial have survived but the original barrows (if these existed) have disappeared. The first is a collared urn and cremation from Astbury, one mile south-west of Congleton, once preserved in St. Mary's Church but now in the Grosvenor Museum, Chester. The burial was actually found in 1941, by a strange coincidence in the excavation of a new grave in an extension to the churchyard on the west side of the main road from Congleton to Newcastle-under-Lyme (the A34); the precise find-spot was approximately 150 yards due west of the junction of the main road and the side-road leading to the church.[18] There were no surface indications of a barrow but this may have been levelled by earlier ploughing or other activities. The urn itself was found in an upright position with its base 2 ft below the surface, resting on the sand subsoil. It contained fragments of cremated bone including teeth and there were anatomical indications that they probably belonged to an adult woman of below middle age.

The vessel itself is a quite small (7½ in. high) and neat example of the collared urn, the collar and neck being ornamented with five and three rows respectively of whipped cord impressions, so arranged as to form a herring-bone pattern. The decoration and presence of formal traits, for example the convexity of the collar, place it in what has been called the Primary Series of collared urns.[19] Dating is, of course, a very approximate business in the case of these urns, but a central date of *c.* 1500 B.C. is tentatively suggested.

The other burial was found at Betchton, about five miles south-west of Congleton, during building operations in 1928; the position was approximately 100 yards west of Betchton House, just to the north of Love Lane which here skirts a small but steep-sided valley.[20] As in the case of the Astbury burial, the subsoil was glacial sand and there was again no indication of a mound, but this could possibly have been levelled by continuous ploughing. The cremation was contained in a large collared urn, of which only the upper part was recovered, and was accompanied by a miniature vessel or pygmy cup and a perforated bone pin. The fact that only the upper part of the urn survived suggests that it may have been inverted so that the base was removed by ploughing. The diameter at the rim is $9\frac{1}{2}$ in. and restoration suggests a height of approximately 14 in. The collar is decorated with zones of alternately horizontal and nearly vertical whipped cord impressions, demarcated at top and bottom by continuous horizontal impressions; below the lower line appear short vertical whipped cord impressions and these have also been used on the internally bevelled rim. Analysis of the decorative and formal features suggests that the urn may belong to the Secondary Series and should be dated to *c.* 1400 B.C. at the earliest.[21]

The pygmy cup is a neat biconical vessel decorated with a chevron pattern of incised parallel lines demarcated by a single and double horizontal lines at top and bottom respectively; the internally bevelled rim also bears two horizontal lines. The base is decorated with a six-rayed star with two concentric rings surrounding a central depression. Around the star is a zone of obliquely radiating lines bounded by inner and outer rings. Finally, the side of the vessel is pierced by two small holes just over 1 in. apart, at a point immediately below the carination. The star motif can be compared with similar examples noted on the base of certain Irish Bronze Age vessels.[22]

The bone pin, found with the cremated bones, was just over 3 in. long; it was bluntly pointed, slightly curved and approximately circular in section except at the head, which was flat, squared off, and perforated. Perforated bone points of this kind appear in Neolithic contexts, particularly those cultures described as Secondary Neolithic which developed from the interaction of native and immigrant peoples; it is possible that they served as pendants.[23] No anatomical identification was made of the cremation itself but it was said to include fragments of the skull, long bones, etc.

To sum up, the evidence of burials points to a fairly intensive occupation of sandy soils in the Congleton area, though these were possibly outliers from an even more intensively occupied area centred on Macclesfield[24] and extending east onto the gritstone formations. As some of the burials were accidentally recovered and were possibly never marked by barrows, there is the chance that known sites only form a proportion of the total and the Early and Middle Bronze Age population of north-east Cheshire may have been larger than we suppose. As so often in Britain, there is no trace of actual habitations and this may indicate the use of tents or temporary shelters by a population relying more on hunting than on settled farming. This would mark the revival of a traditional economy and be one more example of the persistent insular character of many prehistoric cultures in Britain.

For the ensuing Late Bronze Age, beginning probably some time after 1000 B.C., there is no burial evidence in our area; instead, there is the occasional occurrence of bronze weapons and implements, singly or in groups, as evidence for the presence of their owners. From Betchton again there is recorded a small socketed spear-head, only 5 in. in length;[25] the blade is leaf-shaped and just above the mouth of the socket are two holes. Such holes have often been thought to hold a rivet securing the spear-head to the wooden shaft but Continental evidence suggests that a leather thong was used instead, so that, even if the tip of the shaft snapped on impact, the spear-head would remain attached to the shaft itself.[26]

But the most notable discovery relating to this period comes from Congleton itself, that is the small personal hoard belonging to a Late Bronze Age hunter or warrior and consisting of two socketed bronze spear-heads with their bronze butts and a socketed bronze axe (see fig.).[27] They were found in 1925, in close proximity to one another at a depth of 3–4 ft during the digging of foundations for the school in New Street. In greater detail, the objects (now preserved in Congleton Public Library, with the exception of the shorter bronze butt, which is missing) were as follows: (1) a spear-head, 15½ in. long, with a slender leaf-shaped blade in which appear two crescentic or lunate openings on either side of the midrib;[28] the socket continues, circular in section, to within 2 in. of the point and would have held the shaft firmly, being secured by a rivet passing through

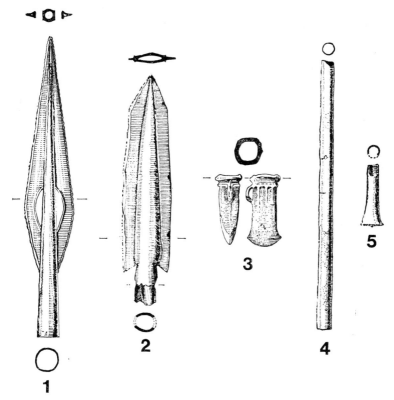

The Congleton Hoard

holes placed 2 in. above the socket mouth; (2) a second spear-head, at least 12 in. long, of the barbed type[29] in which the midrib again runs hollow nearly to the point but changes from a circular cross-section to a flattened ellipse level with the barbs; immediately below the barbs two holes appear in the socket, not for a rivet but for a stout bronze peg (still surviving in certain examples), the ends of which projected to the same distance as the barbs; it is clear that the spear-head cannot have been riveted directly to the shaft and Professor Hawkes has argued[30] that it was not merely attached by a leather thong, like the Betchton spear-head, but that a separate wooden butt-piece was pegged into the socket, slotted into the tip of the wooden shaft and then secured by a thong which ran round the ends of the bronze peg; on impact, the head would stay sticking in the target while the heavy shaft would fall loosely but still be attached by the thong and so serve as an encumbrance in the manner of a harpoon; (3) a socketed axe, $3\frac{1}{2}$ in. long, the mouth of the socket being approximately square and both faces being decorated with three short vertical ribs; a single loop served to secure the axe to its handle by means of a thong; (4) and (5) two tubular bronze butts, presumably from the shafts of the two spear-heads; one is almost 14 in. long with a diameter of $\frac{11}{16}$ in. and has a rivet-hole $8\frac{3}{4}$ in. from the base which is closed by a small concave disc of bronze, while the other is a broken tube just over 3 in. long with a diameter of $\frac{9}{16}$ in. but expanding to 1 in. at the base which is again closed by a bronze disc.

The hoard, then, represents the personal gear of one man and the association of these two types of spear-head with a socketed axe is extremely valuable for Late Bronze Age chronology in Britain, while the bronze butts can be related to Continental prototypes to give an absolute date of eighth century B.C. in this country.[31] Professor Hawkes would argue that the objects are the equipment of a fighting man: the barbed spear with its heavily weighted butt was used first to impede the enemy, the second spear as a thrusting weapon to dispatch him, and the axe to administer the *coup-de-grâce* if he was still found to be breathing. Compelling though this picture is, however, it is fair to suggest that the same technique might have been equally well applied to the pursuit of large mammals in the Cheshire countryside. After all, Wildboarclough is only eight miles north-east of Congleton!

Of the ensuing Iron Age, from *c.* 550 B.C., there is nothing which can be claimed with certainty from the Congleton area. However, in 1923 a dug-out canoe was found at Ciss Green Farm,[32] approximately three-quarters of a mile south of Astbury Church, and is now preserved in Manchester Museum. Such craft are notoriously difficult to date in isolation and, where they have been found in association with actual objects, can be shown to occur over a period extending from the Neolithic to at least the Middle Ages.[33] Recent research has, however, placed some at least within the Early Iron Age[34] and in the absence of any evidence for date of the Astbury boat it may be that its use fell within the last five hundred years B.C.

It was actually found during gravel digging in the bed of a small stream known as Dairy Brook, but it seems probable that originally there was a lake in the area. Before drainage there seem to have been numerous lakes and peat bogs in east Cheshire (such as Congleton Moss, one and a half miles east of Astbury, for instance), where such craft would have proved particularly useful. The Astbury boat belongs to Group I in the Fox classification,[35] that is rectangular punt- or trough-shaped vessels. One end was broken off at the time of discovery and probably 2 ft should be added to the existing length of almost 11½ ft; it is square in section with parallel sides and a width of 1 ft 8 in. The end which is complete shows a broad flat extension and there are two holes in the sides, presumably for oars.

The other monument in our area for which an Early Iron Age date has sometimes been claimed is the earthwork on the Cloud, three miles east-north-east of Congleton and three-quarters of a mile north-north-east of the Bridestones. It was at one time included in the small number of hill-forts to be found in Cheshire[36] but has since been excluded.[37] Its position is not actually on the summit but on a spur pointing to the south-west and just above the 900 ft contour; this need not by itself disprove an Iron Age date but is suggestive. The enclosure itself, about three and a half acres in area internally, is rectangular with the corners orientated approximately to the points of the compass; the sides are noticeably straight and the single bank and ditch of which they are composed are too slight to be of any military value. Altogether there are ample reasons for not accepting it as an Iron Age hill-fort and the suggestion that it is possibly a plantation enclosure of comparatively recent date may well be true.[38]

Again, there is little definite evidence for Roman occupation in the area and this may not be unconnected with the lack of Iron Age settlement. King Street, the Roman road which runs from Wilderspool through Middlewich to Chesterton, north of Newcastle-under-Lyme, runs well to the south of Congleton, while a road between Middlewich and Buxton, running north of the town, remains no more than a hypothesis.[39] There is an early record of a small group of coins from 'Howey Lane', Congleton, including one of Commodus (A.D. 176–92), but none survives.[40] However, a coin of Diocletian (A.D. 284–305) was recovered just north of Park Lane in 1959.[41]

A site claimed as Roman and about which one would wish to know more was first observed in 1725 but had been largely destroyed by 1744.[42] It was said to be at 'Wallfield' near Congleton which led Watkin to suppose that it was at Hulme Walfield, north of the town, although the 1744 account refers to 'the adjoining village of Astbury', which is, of course, south of Congleton. Watkin claimed to have seen traces of it in 1874 when, curiously, he says that the site is in the parish of Astbury. His companion then was J. P. Earwaker who argued that 'Wallfield' was 'Wall Hill' (presumably Wallhill Farm, two miles west of Congleton on the Sandbach road—the A534).[43] The 1725 account certainly speaks of it as 'near the principal farm house' and this led another writer to place it at Loachbrook Farm, also on the Sandbach road but one and a half miles west of Congleton.[44] Amid this welter of conflicting suggestions it becomes difficult to decide with certainty about the position of the site. However, it is interesting to note that at Wallhill Farm the main road turns sharply through a right angle but its original line is continued by a track running through Bent Farm to Astbury, a route which perhaps crosses Congleton Edge at Nick-i'-th'-Hill. In the other direction, it is possible to detect a road running through Brereton Green to the known Roman site at Middlewich (*Salinae*). The character of the site remains to be considered. The 1725 account describes it as a parallelogram enclosing an area of about 60 acres, defined by a single bank and ditch and with the angles facing the cardinal points of the compass. What are called 'military roads' leave the two long sides, one towards Astbury and one towards Middlewich, features which would accord well with the line of the road described in the previous paragraph. An earthwork of this size, its shape, and the ease with which it was destroyed all suggest a temporary Roman site such as a marching camp of the early phases of the conquest.

Fieldwork in the area[45] has located a possible earthwork at Bent Farm and slighter indications on the hill west of Wallhill Farm; in fact, the latter site gives a much better prospect over the surrounding country, the hilltop offers a large, relatively flat area, and at the northern end there are faint indications of a levelled rampart. During 1967 sections were cut through the Bent Farm earthwork mechanically.[46] The results were not entirely conclusive but there was evidence of a V-shaped ditch of military type and a levelled rampart, although the lack of datable finds means that a Roman date is not yet entirely certain. More work is needed but at least it would not be wise to dismiss the site as the writer once did.[47]

Of post-Roman settlement in the Congleton area there is so far no archaeological evidence at all. Anglo-Saxon penetration into the district was presumably slow and piecemeal as compared, say, with that into the Peak District of Derbyshire. Not until the late Saxon period, with the appearance of the so-called 'round-shaft' crosses in the west Pennines,[48] do we find any physical indication of Mercian control of this area. It is interesting to note that there is preserved in Astbury church a semi-circular fragment of pink sandstone with scroll decoration which could conceivably have come from such a cross, as well as two stones with Anglo-Saxon foliage decoration which are possibly architectural fragments. There is thus some small evidence for an early church at Astbury, although the style of the decoration suggests that it could just as easily have been after 1066 as before. But of the Dark Ages in Congleton between the Roman and late Saxon periods our knowledge remains truly dark except for the evidence of place-names, and this is discussed in the later chapter dealing with place-names.

Notes

[1] The geology of the area is described in *The Geology of the Country around Macclesfield, Congleton, Crewe and Middlewich* (Geological Survey Memoir, 1968).

[2] The fullest description, including an account of the 1936–7 excavation, is in *T.L.C.A.S.*, liii, 14–31; shorter accounts appear in G. E. Daniel, *Prehistoric Chamber Tombs of England and Wales* (1950), 83 and fig. 24,1; S. Piggott, *Neolithic Cultures of the British Isles* (1954), 181; W. J. Varley, *Cheshire before the Romans* (1964), 28–32. See fig. and plate in this vol.

[3] Piggott, *op. cit.*, 152–92.

[4] NGR SJ/906622.

[5] NGR SJ/915696.

[6] The credit for its discovery belongs to Mr. G. Rowley of Macclesfield and he was assisted in its subsequent excavation by Mr. D. Bethell of Macclesfield. The writer is indebted to Mr. Bethell for showing him the site

in Nov. 1966, and to him and Mr. Rowley for permission to give details here.

7 P. Ashbee, *The Bronze Age Round Barrow in Britain* (1960), 120–2, 135–8. See plate, 'Gawsworth Vase'.
8 NGR SJ/895697. *Procs. of the Prehistoric Soc. of East Anglia*, i, 236. Now in the possession of Mr. R. Richards, Gawsworth Old Hall.
9 By Prof. F. W. Shotton, Birmingham University.
10 Piggott, *op. cit.*, 36–45.
11 NGR SJ/859674. W. Shone, *Prehistoric Man in Cheshire* (1911), 38; W. J. Varley and J. W. Jackson, *Prehistoric Cheshire* (1940), schedule II and fig. 26.
12 Varley and Jackson, *ibid.* and fig. 3,1.
13 NGR SJ/841624. Now in Congleton Public Library; cf. *Cong. Chron.*, 17 June 1966.
14 Ashbee, *op. cit.*, espec. Ch. X.
15 Cf. Varley, *op. cit.*, 70–2.
16 Varley and Jackson, *op. cit.*, schedule V and fig. 29.
17 NGR SJ/812645. Inf. from records at Grosvenor Museum, Chester.
18 NGR SJ/844616. *T.L.C.A.S.*, lix, 155–60. See plate, 'Astbury Vase'.
19 *Procs. Prehistoric Soc.*, xxvii, 263–306. The Astbury urn is no. 198 in the list (p. 298).
20 NGR SJ/793591. *Chester Arch. Jnl.*, xxxiii, 40–4.
21 The writer is indebted to Dr. Ian Longworth for this comment. See plate.
22 E.g. J. Abercromby, *The Bronze Age Pottery of Great Britain and Ireland* (1912), i, pl. L, 332a (food vessel from Down). See plate.
23 Piggott, *op. cit.*, 334, 360.
24 Varley and Jackson, *op. cit.*, fig. 29; to the examples shown there should be added another burial from Macclesfield found in 1960 (*Chester Arch. Jnl.* xlviii, 43), again apparently unmarked by a barrow.
25 Cf. Varley and Jackson, *op.cit.*, 106 and fig. 21,4; it is now in Warrington Museum.
26 For the precise method of attachment, cf. *Procs. Prehistoric Society*, xxxi, 371–2 and fig. 2a.
27 *Antiquaries Jnl.*, vii, 62–4; Varley, *op. cit.*, fig. 29.
28 Class V in the Greenwell-Brewis classification; cf. *Archaeologia*, lxi, 439–72.
29 Class VI in the Greenwell-Brewis classification.
30 *Procs. Prehistoric Soc.*, xxxi, 371–3 and fig. 2, b and c.
31 *Ibid.*, 373.
32 NGR SJ/848605. *Antiquaries Jnl.*, iv, 64.
33 *Antiquaries Jnl.*, vi, 121–51, 127–8.
34 *Procs. Prehistoric Soc.*, xxiv, 82–4.
35 *Antiquaries Jnl.*, vi, 132–3, figs. 3 and 4.
36 Varley and Jackson, *op. cit.*, schedule VI and fig. 29.
37 Ordnance Survey, *Map of Southern Britain in the Iron Age* (1962).
38 The site is discussed in *T.L.C.A.S.*, lxxii, 9–46 (cf. 10–11).
39 F. H. Thompson, *Roman Cheshire* (1965), 22.
40 *Ibid.*, 105, based on W. T. Watkin, *Roman Cheshire* (1886), 311.

[41] Inf. Grosvenor Museum, Chester, records.

[42] Watkin, *op. cit.* 298–9, citing the original MS refs.

[43] NGR SJ/827625. *Ibid.* and p. 74; *T.H.S.L.C.*, xxix, 83–5.

[44] NGR SJ/834630. Thomas Cooper, *Remarks respecting the Ancient British and Roman Encampments and the Bridestones at or near Congleton, Cheshire, and other matters of Antiquarian Interest in the Neighbourhood* (1893), 6n. This pamphlet was brought to my notice by J. F. Sebire Esq.

[45] By Dr. G. D. B. Jones and the writer, November 1966.

[46] Under the supervision of Dr. Jones.

[47] Thompson, *op. cit.*, 102.

[48] T. D. Kendrick, *Late Saxon and Viking Art* (1949), 68–76.

II *Medieval Congleton*

by J B Blake

It is not easy to imagine what Congleton looked like in the early Middle Ages for there are no plans or maps. Written evidence, however, notably the fine series of local deeds (or 'charters') preserved in the town hall, does help to create a picture of the borough. Dominating most medieval towns and villages was the church and by the end of the fourteenth century Congleton possessed two places of worship although the parish church was at Astbury. One was the Lower Chapel, evidently a small chapel built on the crossing of the river and therefore often called the Bridge Chapel. The town records[1] provide ample illustration of the extent to which the Church influenced the life of the borough and the zeal of the burgesses in donating land and money to the upkeep of the Bridge Chapel. In 1413, for example, when Reginald Brodok granted land to the mayor and his successors in the office, he made it a condition of the grant that the profits of the property should be devoted to the maintenance of the Lower Chapel or the bridge itself. A clause was inserted into the deed to say that Brodok could reclaim the land if these conditions were not fulfilled. In 1423 John Latham bequeathed certain lands in the 'Netherfield' for the upkeep of the Bridge Chapel, and in the following year Ralph Pedley granted an annual rent of 1s 6d for repair work to the chapel. The influential Moreton family were particularly wealthy benefactors; in 1437 Roger left a sum of 3s 4d in his will for the upkeep of the chapel, and in 1465 another Roger Moreton granted half a burgage which produced an annual rent of 3s 4d for its repair.[2]

The date of the construction of the second place of worship

in Congleton, the Upper or Higher Chapel, is not known but it, too, figures prominently in the bequests of the leading burgesses. It was certainly there by 1418 when Emma de Theteswall left lands, tenements and rents to the mayor for its maintenance. Four years later Margery Becheton granted the third part of a burgage to the mayor for the repair of the stone bridge and the chapel.[3] Similarly, in 1453, John Childerly gave over his rights in a burgage in Congleton so that the profits could be used for the maintenance of the Higher Chapel.

Many of the streets of Congleton in this period were conventionally named. The most important thoroughfare was probably West Street and it is referred to in many surviving medieval deeds. It was mentioned in grants of 1392 and 1403, while in 1437 Richard Hadfield received a gift of a burgage in the street and an acre in Colay field.[4] The importance of the mill at Congleton presumably led to the naming of Mill Street mentioned in documents of 1405.[5] The through road was the Highway, later known as the King's Way, leading to Astbury. It followed the course of the later Wagg Street and Mill Street. As early as 1347 Ralph Moreton granted to 'Thomas the lead-beater' a piece of land in the borough which led from the Highway to the smithypost and then to Congleton, while in 1454 the mayor, Hugh Moreton, confirmed a lease of a piece of land situated near the Highway to Alexander Lathom.[6] Two other ways referred to in medieval deeds were the Moorway in 1393 and the Holway in 1442.[7] A major street in the town, Dog Lane, is first mentioned in a conveyance of 1463. There was a park at Congleton in the late thirteenth or early fourteenth century. A road called Park Lane is referred to in a grant of land in 1457 and 1459, and again in 1477 when the mayor, William Smith, leased a burgage near Park Lane.[8] Details of some of these streets are contained in the chapter on place-names below.

The public secular buildings of medieval Congleton were apparently few in number. The mill was doubtless the most important and with it the bakehouse and the meldhall (mentioned as early as 1361)[9] which was perhaps a granary or an adjunct to the mill or the bakehouse where meal or dough may have been mixed. Close to the meldhall was a 'Stonehall'. This was certainly built by 1404 when Richard Denys and Adam Denys released their claim to it to Alexander Denys, and in the following year Alexander himself granted an annual rent of 5*s* from it. It was said to be situated near the town cross. The town or market cross was a common feature of any medieval village and such a cross is often referred to in surviving Congleton deeds. The earliest reference to it at Congleton is in 1385 when Thomas Givelock sold a piece of land next to the cross to John Benet. A new cross may have been erected about the year 1500 and decorated with the national and borough arms.[10] Another public building, the Moot Hall, probably the early town hall of Congleton, was in a bad state of repair in 1425–6 and a sum of £2 was spent on roofing the building, purchasing nails and shingles, and for paying the men engaged in the work; in 1436–7 beams for the roof were paid for.[11] In 1427–8 about £1 was spent on making windows for a building known as the *Aula Placitorum*[12] (Hall of Pleas), perhaps the place where the manorial court was held and maybe identical with the Moot Hall. Leading out of the town was the stone bridge over the river; it had been constructed by 1407 when money was granted for its repair by Thomas Hassall.

Surrounding the settlement at Congleton were the fields which were so vital a part of the economic life of the period. In 1342 there is mention of a piece of land called Shawfield. A particularly important piece of land was the Overwestfield, the high land from Crossledge to Windy Bank up to the Brownswolds. In 1407 Peter Swetham granted half an acre there to Roger Swetham, and in 1437 the mayor of Congleton, Roger Moreton, confirmed a grant to Peter Hilton of half a burgage and half an acre of land in that field, the profits of which were to be expended on the upkeep of the Bridge Chapel. This may have been the same field as the Overfield where Thomas Lathom purchased land from Reginald Brodok in 1425. In 1412 an indenture mentioned an acre of land in Holwayfield, and in 1433 the same field is recorded again. Other pieces of land surrounding the borough included the 'Flaskes' which had been leased by the lord of the manor as early as 1296–7, and which was leased by William Stanley, steward of Halton, to Hugh Moreton in 1414–15 for a period of twenty-one years, and the wood of Wharleighbank (Whateley Bank) which features prominently in the manorial accounts and in 1411 was leased by the king to Arthur and Roger Swettenham (perhaps the same as Roger Swetham, above) for twenty years.[13] The 'Flaskes' derives from the Cheshire word 'flaskes' or lakes and refers to the two Black Lakes behind the present Girls' Grammar School.

Medieval Congleton was thus a small settlement consisting of a few streets and a few public buildings. Little is known of the size of the population. It may have been as few as twenty or thirty inhabitants at the time of the Domesday Book (1086), although by 1311 the village had apparently grown to some 400 people. It possibly expanded still further before the mid-fourteenth century, but the evidence of the fifteenth-century records suggests the advent of a temporary decline which was to continue until the more prosperous Tudor era.[14]

The Lords of the Manor
The origins of the earldom and county palatine of Chester are closely linked with the great Mercian rebellion of 1069 after William I's invasion of England and his occupation of the lands of Earl Edwin. The rebellion led to the ruthless harrying of northern England in which the counties of Cheshire and Yorkshire were devastated both as a punishment for the uprising and as a warning against future revolt. The safeguarding of Cheshire was then entrusted in 1070 and 1071 to an important Flemish lord, Gherbod. For some unknown reason, however, he resigned this command within a year of his appointment and left England, probably without ever having exercised his new position. As a replacement William I appointed Hugh, the son of Richard le Goz, viscount of Avranches, as earl of Chester. Hugh apparently had not come to England with the Conqueror in 1066 but may have arrived in the December of the following year.[15]

The lands and possessions of the earl of Chester in 1086 as revealed in Domesday Book show how powerful a figure Hugh had become in that region for the whole of Cheshire was placed under his lordship. Contrary to the general practice of granting scattered pieces of land to the barons, the area was allocated as a solid block of territory. This was doubtless intended to protect the north-west of England, especially against the raids of the Welsh. The only other landowner in Cheshire was the bishop of Chester. Domesday Book shows that before the Norman conquest Congleton was held by Earl Godwin but in 1086 it was in the possession of a lay tenant of Earl Hugh, one Bigot, who has been identified as Bigot de Loges, who witnessed Hugh's charters to Chester Abbey and was the owner of three manors in the earl's fief in Suffolk. Bigot de Loges was allocated some thirteen manors in Cheshire, namely Lea Newbold, Thornton-le-Moors, Mobberley, Norbury, Siddington, North Rode, Sandbach, Sutton, Wimboldsley, Weaver, a part of Alderley and Farndon, and Congleton itself. The fief was a scattered one, perhaps deliberately to prevent a tenant of the earl consolidating his estates and thereby presenting a territorial threat to Hugh. Bigot de Loges's fief never became recognized as a barony, and its subsequent history is somewhat confused. It seems that the greater part of the fief afterwards formed the basis of the fee of Aldford which was created about 1130 and which included the manor of Gawsworth. In the period 1136–46 there occurs a reference to a Hugh, son of Bigot, possibly a son of Bigot de Loges, receiving the grant of Gawsworth from Ralph, earl of Chester. In the reign of Henry II (1154–89) the lord of this fee was Robert de Aldford, who married Mary, daughter of Richard fitzEustace, fifth baron of Halton. Nothing further is known of the descent of this fee until early in the thirteenth century when the manor of Gawsworth was said to have been in the possession of Richard de Aldford who then granted it to Herbert and Lucy Orreby. Congleton was apparently part of this Aldford fee until the reign of King John.[16]

Richard de Aldford died about 1213 and the Aldford fee passed into the possession of Sir John de Arderne who may have been the younger son of Eustace Arderne of Watford (Northants.). Probably about 1220 John Arderne obtained by deed a grant of the whole of the fee of Aldford, including Congleton, from Ralph Blundeville, earl of Chester.[17] It seems probable that Sir John Arderne had married Margaret, the daughter and heiress of Richard de Aldford and that this grant from the earl of Chester was only a formal ratification of his right to the fee which he had acquired through marriage.

Sir John de Arderne died at some date prior to 1238 and was succeeded by his son, Walkelyn Arderne, a substantial military figure of the period. As early as June 1237 he had been ordered to deliver the castles of Chester and Beeston in Cheshire to Henry de Aldithelegh and for a greater part of his life Walkelyn was engaged in Welsh affairs. In 1245 he received royal letters of protection for his assistance in munitioning the castle of Deganwy (Caernarvonshire), and he was constable there in the following year. In 1250 he received a royal mandate to inspect the condition of the castles of Deganwy and Dyserth (Flints.). His military service, however, was not confined to Wales. In 1253 he crossed to Gascony in the company of the king, and by the following year he had been granted the custody of the castle of Montcuq in the Dordogne. In 1254 he was referred to as a marshal of the king's household when he acted as an escort for a delegation coming to meet the king at Bordeaux. Later in life he was to reward a servant of his, Robert Camville, by releasing him of his rent for property in Old Withington because of his service in Gascony. Walkelyn Arderne had returned to England by February 1255 when he was sent on royal service to Wallingford. He was active in Scotland in the September of that year and was again employed in the Welsh Marches by November 1256.[18]

Walkelyn's long service to the Crown did not go unrewarded. He had married Agnes, the daughter of Philip de Orreby, and by this marriage he came into possession of the manors of Elford in Staffordshire, Alvanley, Upton, and other manors in Cheshire, and in 1254 he received a royal grant to hold a market and fair and have free rights of warren at Aldford, Alderley, Elford and also at Normanby in Lincolnshire. Walkelyn also owned property in Norbury, Torkington, Offerton, Withington and a part of Marton and Sherston which had been leased to Robert Stokepond, and Knutton in Staffordshire.[19] It seems unlikely that he ever came to Congleton and certainly no record has survived of such a visit, and presumably the land was leased to a sub-tenant. Arderne died about the year 1268 and Peter Arderne succeeded to his extensive property. Peter himself died in 1292 but about 1269 he settled the manor of Congleton on his eldest son John and his wife Margaret, daughter of Griffin ap Madog, lord of Bromfield. The reason for the settlement is not clear but it is perhaps significant that shortly afterwards, in January 1271, Peter received royal letters of protection for a period of four years to enable him to go on a crusade to the Holy Land.[20]

John Arderne could hardly have been in possession of Congleton for any length of time for it passed during his lifetime to Henry de Lacy, earl of Lincoln, who granted the first borough charter to the burgesses of Congleton. The actual date of this charter remains undiscovered but it was probably granted between the latter part of the year 1272 (when Henry de Lacy was invested with the earldom of Lincoln) and May 1275 by which time one of the witnesses of the charter, Sir Robert de Stokeport, was dead. Stokeport last appears as a witness in July 1274 and he may have died shortly after that date.[21]

The Lacy interest in Cheshire can be traced back to the end of the twelfth century when the sixth constable of Chester and baron of Halton was John, the son of Richard fitzEustace by Aubreye, heiress of the Lacy estates. John was killed at the siege of Tyre in 1190. He was succeeded as constable of Chester by his son Roger who held Halton and also inherited the Lacy manors of Clitheroe and Pontefract in 1194 through his grandmother. Afterwards he assumed the name of Lacy.[22] Roger died in 1212 and he was succeeded by his son, Sir John Lacy, who became the eighth constable of Chester and was created earl of Lincoln in 1232. Sir John died in 1240 and his son Edmund, who was still a minor at the time of his father's death, eventually became the ninth constable of Chester. Edmund died in July 1257 leaving an only son Henry, third earl of Lincoln. Henry did not come of age until January 1272 and he was not knighted until October 1272 on the occasion of the wedding of Edmund, earl of Cornwall, and it may have been about this time that he received the full investiture of his earldom.

From the time of Henry's first charter to the burgesses of Congleton, the manor appears to emerge from the obscurity of the previous two centuries and much more information is available for the remaining two hundred years of the medieval period. Perhaps a symptom of this growing importance was the royal visit of Edward I to Congleton on 6 October 1278, which was sandwiched between two days at Stafford. Several deeds have survived from this period and they make it possible to identify some of the sub-tenants of Henry Lacy. In 1281-2, for example, Thomas Pulford acknowledged Lacy's right to a tenement and some land in the borough and in return received a grant for life of a tenement and four acres of land, which formerly had been in the possession of Adam Barker, together with property in Astbury.[23] Benedict, the son of Walter Stanley, was the owner of a substantial amount of property in Congleton; between 1280 and 1285 he purchased a total of 44 acres of wasteland although he was later to release his rights to this land to John Stanley, rector of Astbury.[24] Henry de Lacy himself received grants of land in Denbighshire for his assistance in subduing the Welsh in a campaign in 1282 and 1283, and it may have been two of his retainers, Vivian and Adam, who were rewarded with grants of ten acres of wasteland in Congleton in 1283 for their 'homage and service'.[25]

Henry de Lacy had two sons, both of whom died in childhood. In or before October 1294, therefore, when his only surviving child by his first marriage, Alice, then aged about thirteen, was married to Thomas of Lancaster, the nephew of Edward I, Henry's estates in Cheshire and Lancashire were surrendered to the king so that they could be granted to Thomas and Alice after the death of Henry and his wife, Margaret.[26] Henry de Lacy died in February 1311. The formal inquest revealed that the castle and lands of Halton pertained to the constableship of Chester together with Runcorn, Whitley, Moore, Thelwall and Congleton. Henry's heir, Alice, was said to be aged twenty-eight. In May 1311, however, the king's escheator for Cheshire, Hugh le Mercer, was ordered to deliver to Henry Lacy's second wife and widow, Joan, various lands in Cheshire including Congleton, Whitley, Runcorn and Moore. This property had been assigned to Joan by Edward II, together with other lands, as dower of her husband's lands.[27] One of Joan's sub-tenants at this time was one John de Porta, chaplain, who granted his property in Buglawton and Congleton, which he had originally received from Alexander Denys, to Thomas Denys in 1319–20.[28]

The year 1322 was a dramatic one in English history for it marked the execution of Henry Lacy's son-in-law, Thomas of Lancaster, cousin of Edward II. For much of the reign of Edward II Lancaster had been in opposition to the Crown or the royal household. By 1312 he was prepared to use force and raided Newcastle-upon-Tyne, just failing to capture the king and his favourite, Peter Gaveston. He eventually succeeded in having Gaveston executed in 1312, and, despite various attempts to reconcile him with the king, he was again in open rebellion in 1321–2 when he was defeated at Boroughbridge. He was executed at Pontefract in March 1322.

Edward II must have wasted no time in taking possession of the lands of Thomas of Lancaster. On 5 April 1322 William Tatham, parson of Halton, was appointed to receive the profits and produce of the castles and lands which had belonged to

Thomas, including Halton itself, Whitley and Congleton. On the following day, Gilbert Singleton received a royal appointment to keep Congleton, Whitley and other lands formerly in the custody of John Travers. In May Singleton was referred to as keeper of the castle of Halton and the manors of Congleton and Widnes when he received a royal mandate to make an assessment of the value of these lands and to summon those tenants who were obliged to do homage for them. In the following September he was obliged to distrain those who had not done homage for their property.[29]

The enemies of Thomas of Lancaster, notably the Dispensers, were to reap solid territorial gains following his execution. His widow Alice had been imprisoned and she remained in disgrace until July when Halton and a large part of her property elsewhere in England was restored to her. But on 22 July 1322 she was compelled to release her right in the reversion of Congleton, Whitley and Runcorn to the king and the younger Dispenser who received a grant of the constableship of Chester and other property held in dower by Joan, the widow of Henry de Lacy. On the following day Joan confirmed the grant to Sir Hugh Dispenser the younger, for the term of her life, of the manor of Congleton together with Whitley, Runcorn and other property.[30]

In 1326, however, the Dispensers fell from power. Joan de Lacy had already died, at some date prior to 27 October 1322.[31] Alice had left her husband, Thomas of Lancaster, in 1317 or 1318 and she eventually married Sir Ebulo Lestraunge, probably in the autumn of 1322, but certainly by December 1324 when Ebulo and Alice granted Halton to Hugh Dispenser for life.[32] After the death of Lestraunge in 1335 Alice married Sir Hugh de Freyne in February 1336 but he died in the following September. Alice herself died in October 1348 but despite her three marriages she had no immediate heir.[33]

Since 1322 Thomas of Lancaster's brother, Henry, who had not been directly involved in the rebellions of the reign of Edward II, had been endeavouring to regain control of the family estates. A petition from Henry asking the king to restore to him Halton and the manor of Congleton has survived and probably dates from the period just following the fall of the Dispensers.[34] In 1348, following the death of Alice, Henry's son, Henry, finally obtained possession of these lands and in 1349 he became earl of Lincoln. As constable of Chester and lord of Halton he made an exhaustive claim to certain liberties in Cheshire including his right to hold Congleton as a free borough. He claimed also that he and the burgesses there should be free of toll, passage and other dues in the city of Chester and in addition the right to have a weekly market on Saturday and an annual fair on St. Martin's day in the winter, and to have a view of frankpledge (that is a right to deal with petty criminal offences) three times a year.[35]

Henry died in 1361. He had no son to succeed him, and the king divided his vast possessions between his two daughters, Maud, then aged twenty-two, and Blanche, aged fourteen. Blanche, who had been married to the king's son, John of Gaunt, two years earlier received the manors of Halton, Runcorn, Moore, Whitley, Kelsall, Bidston, Widnes and Congleton, together with other property to the total value of some £313.[36]

John of Gaunt died in February 1399. His son and heir by his first marriage to Blanche was Henry Bolingbroke who became king as Henry IV, in the September of that year. Accordingly the property of John of Gaunt, including Congleton, passed into the possession of the Crown as part of the duchy of Lancaster, and there it remained for the rest of the medieval period. There is little further to add to a study of the descent of the manor of Congleton. Henry V later placed a large part of his estates in feoffment for the purpose of his will which was drawn up on 24 June 1415, before his departure to France. Those invested with the fief included Henry Chichele, archbishop of Canterbury, who on 22 July received a grant of the manors of Widnes, Congleton and other property. The feoffees then conveyed the estates in their keeping to the king for a period of twelve years.[37] The lands then remained in royal hands, although in 1473 Elizabeth, wife of Edward IV, apparently obtained the castle of Halton, and the manors of Moore, Runcorn, Whitley and Congleton, together with the right of appointment to the office of the bailiwick of the manor of Halton.[38]

The Economic Life of the Manor

Cheshire was a comparatively poor and remote county at the time of the Domesday survey of 1086. The income from all the manors in Cheshire amounted to little more than £200 a year and, even allowing for the devastation caused by the harrying of the north by William I, it seems that the value even in 1066 had been less than £300.[39] Only twelve manors in the area of modern Cheshire, however, were valued in 1086 at £12 or more. Only four places had more than thirty recorded individuals (usually heads of families), and east of the River Weaver only five settlements had over ten such recorded individuals. Even if a multiplier of five is used to take into account the families, the population of most of the manors was extremely small and possibly the total population of the county was only some 11,000.

The original reasons for holding the Domesday survey still remain a matter of controversy, but it was presumably designed to assist not only in ascertaining the amount at which each estate should be assessed for tax purposes but also in determining the legal ownership of the property in question and in recording royal rights, throughout the country.[40] The entry for Congleton reads as follows:

> The same Bigot holds Cogeltone. Godwine held (it). There is one hide that pays geld. There is land (enough) for four ploughs. There are two there with two villeins and four bordars. There is wood (land) one league long and one wide and two hays there. It was waste and he found it so. Now it is worth four shillings.[41]

The entry is brief but it does throw valuable light on the economic life of Congleton at that time. Domesday records the harrying of the north by William I and many folios of the Cheshire account provide evidence of the widespread devastation of the region. Congleton itself had apparently been laid waste either by the earlier raiding of the Welsh or by the forces of William for it was in this condition that Bigot de Loges inherited the property. By the time of Domesday, however, the land was slowly recovering and its value had increased to 4s. The estate remained undercultivated despite this partial recovery for there was a deficiency in plough-teams, and only two were in operation instead of four. This was a common feature in eastern Cheshire because of the large amount of waste that existed there, and it was only in the more prosperous west of the county that the number of plough-teams equalled the number of plough-lands. Cheshire was a heavily wooded region and perhaps as much as two-fifths of the county was forest. The area around Congleton was largely wooded and there were two hays, enclosures for catching wild animals. The settlement at Congleton was evidently a small one with a probable population of only some thirty inhabitants.[42]

After the valuable evidence provided by the Domesday survey, Congleton disappears into the mists of obscurity for a long period and not until the time of Henry de Lacy is evidence of economic growth forthcoming. Doubtless there was growth and expansion although it was apparently slow and by no means at a uniform rate, but by the time of Henry's death in 1311 many changes had taken place. The very fact of the granting of the charter to the burgesses of Congleton suggests its growing importance and this is confirmed by the inquisition post mortem taken on Lacy's lands in Cheshire. This revealed that Congleton then consisted of 80 burgages, 80 acres of arable land, a watermill, and a market, signs of a flourishing settlement with a possible population of some 400 inhabitants; it was said to be worth £15 4s a year.[43]

By the later thirteenth century there were thus two administrations in Congleton—the manor and the borough. Some glimpses of the economic organization of the manor are provided by a series of manorial accounts which survive from the end of the thirteenth century. The intricacies of medieval accountancy, however, are such that it is only with difficulty that tentative deductions about the varying fortunes of the manor of Congleton in the Middle Ages can be made. It will perhaps be interesting to illustrate what is revealed through a detailed examination and explanation of the accounts which show how a medieval bailiff (the agent in charge of a manor) accounted to his employer, the lord of the manor. The general purpose of the manorial account was to enable the higher officials of the duchy to estimate whether the lord's lands were yielding him the maximum income that could be obtained. The structure of the account remained virtually constant throughout the medieval period, and it was submitted annually at Michaelmas. There were two sides to the account, the receipt side and the expense side. On the receipt side of the account there were five main entries or sources of income: arrears, assized or established rents, leases, issues of the manor and the income from the manorial courts.

The arrears were the amounts in which the bailiff was in

debt on the previous year's accounts. They formed a regular part of the account and were not considered to be an unusual feature. The annual amount of arrears fluctuated considerably from as much as some £47 in 1397–8 to as low as £1 6s 8d in 1402–3, but from the beginning of the reign of Henry VI (1429) it seems to have increased rapidly. Arrears rose from some £33 in 1425–6, to some £48 in 1438–9, £63 in 1440–1, and finally over £146 in 1458–9. There was a partial recovery in the reign of Edward IV (1461–83) but the arrearage reached more than £149 in the last year of his reign, suggesting perhaps a gradual breaking up of the old manorial system.[44]

The second feature of the receipt side of the manorial account consisted of the rents of assize which included the rents both of the tenants who held their lands by custom and of those who held by written charter. In 1295–6 these rents totalled some £28 11s and they increased steadily to over £30 9s in 1304–5 and to £30 16s 1½d in 1361–2. This last rent remained the basic rent of assize for the rest of the period although from time to time certain additions were made: for example, a rent of a halfpenny from Thomas Whelok for a waste place in Market Street next to the meldhall was added in 1378–9, 2s rent from a cottage next to the fulling mill was included in 1436–7, and an extra shilling from the plot of land called 'Byflete' was added in the same year.[45]

Unfortunately these rents of assize cannot be taken at face value for they were charged to the bailiff whether or not he actually collected them. In order to get an accurate picture of the value of these rents it is necessary to subtract from the annual total the so-called 'decays of rent' which in fact appear on the other side of the account, the expense side. These decays consist of both the rent of lands which were no longer tenanted and which were in the lord's hand, and also decreases in rent since the original rental was compiled. In other words, instead of reductions in rent being accepted and subtracted from the total of the rents of assize, they were placed under the decays of rent and added to as further rent reductions took place. In the reign of Richard II (1377–99) these allowances on rents which could no longer be collected were quite small; they consisted in 1382–3, for example of 3s 4d from a garden, 6d from a fishpond and 2s from a cottage next to the fulling mill. But by 1421–2 they had become more considerable and then in-

cluded a further 2s from four and a half acres of land formerly
owned by Mathew Rode, 3d from a burgage once in the tenure
of Thomas Willebay, 1s 3d from a burgage of Thomas Whelok,
and 1s from the property of William Frith, all of which were
then in the king's hands presumably because he was unable to
find new tenants. It was also found impossible to collect the rent
of 7s due from the pasture of Moss Hey. From 1436 to 1446 these
decays in rent varied from some 13s down to some 7s but they
again increased to over 13s in 1452-3, to over £1 in 1457-8, and
to over £2 5s in 1465-6 as more and more rents became un-
collected including the toll of the fair and market.[46]

Another important source of income for the lord of the manor
of Congleton was the leases or 'farms' of land and services.
Originally parts of the manor, known as the demesne, had been
worked by the lord or his agent and not leased like the rest of
the estate. By 1295-6, however, this area of some 27½ acres was
being leased for an annual sum of £2 11s 5d. In 1304-5 (then
26 acres and 3 roods) it was worth only £1 15s 8d a year, but
by 1356-7 it had been extended to 31 acres and 1 rood when it
was leased for 14 years at an annual rent of £2 5s. The value of
the land continued to increase, by 1392-3 reaching £3 6s 8d.
In 1436-7 the lands were worth £3 1s 9d a year when they were
stated to consist of the following: a plot of land called 'Houghteth' next to the River Dane, land in Strongford and Whitley,
land called Greater and Lesser 'Tyrwhyn', land called 'Halmede', land in Whatley and in 'Halleland' called the Park, and
land in 'Davenhees'. Halmede and Halleland were probably
pieces of land attached to the Moot Hall. The rent for the
demesne land remained at this rent until 1444-5 when it increased by a penny.[47]

Also an important source of revenue for the lord of Congleton was the farm (or rent) of the watermill. There is a reference
to such a mill in the original charter of Henry de Lacy to the
burgesses of Congleton when it was stated that the inhabitants
could grind their corn 'to the twentieth grain provided the mill
is sufficient'; that is, the charge for grinding corn was fixed at a
twentieth of the amount to be ground.[48] In 1295-6 the mill was
said to be worth £8, but by 1356-7, when it was leased to Roger
Mortimer, the annual rent was £10 6s 8d. Its value increased to
£12 in 1361-2. When the lessees were Richard de Moreton,
Adam Atkinson and Richard Eygnon, who held it for six years

D

from 1369–70, the terms of the lease included an agreement that the lord of the manor should provide the wood and the iron necessary for the maintenance of the mill, while the lessees were to supply the millstones. This period would appear to have been the most important in the history of the mill for by 1378–9 it was valued at only £6 13*s* 4*d*. It then became joined with the lease of the fair, market, the meldhouse and the bakehouse when they were all leased to Thomas Whelok and William Nesfield for a period of 20 years for a total annual payment of £9 6*s* 8*d*.

A new agreement was entered into in 1397–8. A cottage next to the bakehouse and a garden attached to the meldhall were added to the lease of the mill and the rest of the property when they were leased to Hugh Moreton for 30 years for a rent of £10 a year. The lord of the manor agreed to keep the bakehouse and the cottage in good repair while Moreton was granted wood in order to keep the mill on the Dane in full working order. Despite these long leases the evidence suggests that the value of the mill continued to decrease throughout the fifteenth century. It was valued at £8 in 1417–8 but only £6 13*s* 4*d* in 1428–9, when it was leased to John Yate for 20 years. This process of decline was aided by a natural catastrophe in the middle of the century when the River Dane flooded its banks causing great devastation in the town and destroying the mill, still valued then at £6 13*s* 4*d* a year. On 29 June 1451 the king, as lord of the manor, ruled that the mayor and burgesses of Congleton could use the mill rent free for a period of ten years and after that for a decreased rent of £1 6*s* 8*d*, that they could change the course of the river and construct another channel, and that they could build up to three water, wind or horse mills. In the following November, however, the king discovered that other mills were being erected without his authority and that they were curtailing his profits. He therefore instructed the duke of Buckingham, steward of Congleton from 1451 to 1454, not to allow any other mills to be built in the area or any person to grind their corn at new mills.[49]

The accounts show that the toll of the fair and the market of Congleton provided a regular supply of revenue for the lord of the manor. In 1282 Henry Lacy had received permission to hold a weekly market on Saturdays at Congleton and two annual fairs there at the feasts of the Holy Trinity and St.

Martin.[50] In 1295–6 the fair and market were worth 10s to Henry de Lacy, but this had increased to £1 10s by 1304–5. They were leased for an annual payment of £1 in 1356–7 and this remained the fixed sum until 1378–9 when they became part of a general lease, together with the mill and the meldhouse. The value of the fair and market, like that of the mill, declined throughout the fifteenth century. In 1417–18, together with the meldhouse, the bakehouse, a cottage and a garden, they were leased for a sum of £2 13s 4d a year. Steps were taken to remedy the situation for in 1430 Henry VI granted a licence for an annual fair at Congleton at the feast of the Apostles Philip and James together with the one held at the feast of St. Martin. By 1450–1 the lease was worth £1 6s 8d but in 1474–5 the toll of the fair and the market and a piece of land called 'Ragge' were leased for as little as 5s.[51]

There is little trace of medieval industrial development in the manorial accounts but one important source of income was a quarry called 'Milstonbergh' situated in Congleton Wood. It provided supplies for local use but it was also a source for the surrounding areas. In 1370–1 John Burgh, the bailiff of Whitley, spent £1 16s on the purchase and transport of two millstones from Congleton for the water mill at Whitley; it was ordered that two of the best grindstones were to be carried to the castle of Halton in 1378–9, and a further two millstones were to be sent to Whitley, Halton and Runcorn in 1397–8. The lord of the manor did not work the quarry himself. It was leased to Richard Brodok for three years in 1356–7 for an annual payment of 13s 4d. It was worth £1 2s 4d in 1365–6, £1 in 1369–70, and £1 4s 4d in 1372–3, when it was leased to William Bacoun, Richard Bacoun and Thomas Stonehewer for six years. The same three men obtained a ten-year lease of the quarry in 1377–8 for a rent of £2 a year which was increased to £2 2s by the end of the fourteenth century. It was still being leased at the same rent in 1423–4 when Roger Stonehewer, Richard Kelyng and Thomas Grant obtained a six-year grant, and it was worth £2 1s in 1428–9. But its value also declined towards the end of the fifteenth century and it was said to be worth nothing in 1475–6 and only 3s 4d in 1477–8.[52]

A group of buildings closely connected with the provision of bread to the inhabitants of the manor was also regularly leased throughout this period. The meldhouse fetched an annual rent of £1 for a period of thirteen years in 1361–2, but in 1378–9, as we have seen, it was amalgamated in the lease of the bakehouse, a cottage and house, and the water mill. In 1417–18 the meldhouse, the bakehouse, the attached buildings and the toll of the fair and market were leased for £2 13*s* 4*d*. But in the second half of the fifteenth century their value was considerably reduced; they were worth only £1 6*s* 8*d* in 1460–1 and as little as 4*s* in 1473–4.[53]

Two pieces of pasture land were also leased by the lord of the manor. Moss Hey was leased for 4*s* in 1356–7 and for 5*s* in 1392–3. It was leased for 20 years in 1391–2 to Hand del Cliff and again for a similar period to Philip del Yate in 1410–11. The 'Flaskes' was leased for 2*s* in 1296–7 but had disappeared from the manorial accounts by 1356–7. A fishpond, presumably leading off the Dane, was leased for 6*d* in 1361–2, and for 1*s* in 1397–8 and for the rest of the medieval period. A turbary, a piece of land where turf or peat could be dug for fuel, was leased for 1*s* 6*d* in 1356–7 and for 6*s* 8*d* in 1364–5.[54]

Congleton also had a cloth fulling mill although it never attained the importance of the corn mill. The date of the erection of the fulling mill is not known, but it may well have been built in Henry de Lacy's time for it was usually a profitable investment for the lord of the manor. It was worth £1 12*s* 2*d* in 1361–2, but in the following year its value had increased to £2 6*s* 8*d* when it was leased to Roger and William Walker. This would appear to mark the height of its importance for it had disappeared from the manorial account roll by 1369–70.[55]

To summarize, the receipt side of the manorial account is concerned with the revenue of the manor from the rents of assize and the leases of land buildings and services. Before the profits to the lord of the manor can be estimated, however, the expenses side of the account must be examined.

The first major expense item was the payment of the wages of the bailiff, the lord's representative in the manor. This payment was originally fixed at 6*s* 8*d* a year in the time of Henry de Lacy but it rose steadily throughout the medieval period. By 1385–6 he was getting £1 6*s* 8*d*. From the reign of Henry V onwards it became an occasional practice to award the bailiff for his services with a special increment of 6*s* 8*d*. The wage reached £2 in 1444–5.[56]

Grants of money to individuals were sometimes included on

the expense side of the account. In 1295-6 Sir Nicholas Leyburn and Robert de Leyburn were each paid £5 by Henry de Lacy, and they both received £10 in 1304-5. Following Lacy's death, however, a mandate was issued in July 1311 to examine this grant and to see whether it should be confirmed.[57]

The principal expense item of the lord of Congleton was the repairing and the maintenance of his property. Small repairs included the making of hedges round a garden in 1295-6, the repairing of houses in 1294-5 which cost 8*d*, and a payment of 4*s* 9*d* in 1304-5 to six men of Halton for marking the bounds of the waste of Congleton. But the major items of expense were closely linked with those assets of the manor which were leased. In 1361-2 the sum of £1 1*s* 8*d* was spent on the purchasing of stakes, the hewing of brushwood, and payment for carriage and labour for the repairing of the millpond. The corn mill itself was regularly in need of repair throughout this period. The sum of over £1 10*s* was spent in 1365-6 on the repairing of a wheel of the mill and the wages of the hired carpenter, and in the following year the mill dam was repaired, the wheel and the cog-wheels were replaced, and a new beam was purchased. In 1369-70, some £3 7*s* was spent on the wages of labourers employed in felling timber in Whateley Bank and carrying it to the pond, and also for digging a new pond, while in 1372-3 over £4, a large sum, was laid out on repairs to the dam. The fulling mill was also in need of repair on occasion and in 1369-70 it was found necessary to spend £2 15*s* 3*d* to remedy the faults. In 1379-80 the meldhall was repaired at a cost of 3*s* 11*d* which included the wages of a carpenter and the purchasing of nails. The bakehouse, too, regularly featured on the expense side of the account, the largest repair bill found being in 1430-1 when £3 2*s* 4*d* was spent on purchases of timber, nails, beams, and for the carriage of these materials.[58]

The final item on the expense side of the account consisted of the amounts in actual cash handed over to the treasurer of Halton. These amounts[59] varied quite considerably from year to year. Occasionally, as in 1446-7, 1460-1 and 1469-70, it seems that nothing was handed over to the treasurer, and the payments were as low as £11 in 1449-50. The largest amounts handed over were more than £76 in 1450-1 and over £69 in 1433-4. There were also miscellaneous payments made to the estate receiver or his agents who came on occasion to

Congleton to take away quantities of spare cash owing to them. The accounts show that, after all payments had been made, the auditors would total the expense side of the account and usually an arrearage would be discovered which would be carried over to the following year's account.[60]

To obtain any precise idea of how far the manor of Congleton was a source of profit to the lord is difficult. Rents remained largely unchanged, and the accounting totals often only vary because of the accumulation of arrears. Nevertheless certain trends are evident. In 1361–2 the gross income of the manor (the total of rents, leases of all kinds, profits of the court, profits of demesne lands, and profits of the fair and market) was £53 6s 2d while the total expenses for that year were £1 15s; the profit for that year was then £51 11s 2d. At the turn of the fourteenth and fifteenth centuries profits were about £45–£46.[61] It is already apparent, however, after dealing with the individual items of the account, that from the mid-fifteenth century the value of Congleton declined. What was affecting the economy is not clear. There may have been a decrease in population; unfortunately no subsidy (tax) returns, which might have given a clue to the population trend, have survived, but the evidence of longer leases may suggest the encouragement of lessees because of the lack of tenants. Whatever the reason, the evidence of the accounts reveals that decays in rent increased after 1452–3, the profits of the mill were severely affected by the town flooding in 1450 although a decline had already begun before that date, revenue from the fair and market shrank after 1450–1, the quarry declined in importance, and the profits of the manorial courts were severely reduced after 1449–50. By the reign of Edward IV (1461–83) the annual profit of the manor was only about £35.

The Social Life of the Manor

Northern England throughout the medieval period was a turbulent area and doubtless Cheshire was no exception. Certainly several examples of violence at Congleton or connected with its inhabitants have survived. In 1321 Adam Denys of Congleton was accused of travelling to Newcastle-under-Lyme with a gang of some 500 men and stealing a quantity of linen, 10s-worth of woollen cloth, money, oats and victuals while one of his followers was said to have stolen a brass pot.[62]

In 1394 Thomas Willaboy was pardoned for the death of Robert Gardene who had been murdered at Congleton four years previously.[63] A more sinister case came to light in 1431–2, following a declaration made by Hugh Marshall of Congleton. He maintained that while on a visit to Nottingham he had been approached by three men who told him that his deceased uncle had held property in Northwich and asked him to sign a release to them of these 'wich houses' (buildings in which brine was evaporated for salt making). Bribery was first tried. Sir William de Hulme offered Hugh two nobles to sign the release of the property but he refused 'leste hit were myscheve to me or my saule or to any of my frendes'. Sir William and two of Hugh's uncles, Robert and Thomas Latham, then used menaces but again without success. Finally forgery was attempted. Geoffrey Starkey brought a letter ostensibly from Hugh's deceased uncle saying that the deeds should be handed over, but when Marshall saw the letter he realized that his uncle could not have written it for 'there were none of the usual tokens'. Despite all their efforts he refused to sign the release, but instead released his interest to Roger Starkey of Northwich.[64] Another case of possible local violence occurred in April 1457 when John Mainwaring, deputy steward of Congleton, Hugh Moreton, mayor of Congleton, and others were appointed to arrest John Davenport, but the offence is not known.[65]

Henry de Lacy's charter to the burgesses of Congleton had proclaimed that if the bailiffs of the borough caught a suspected felon they could hold him for three days in the stocks if they so desired and then they were to deliver him to the castle at Halton.[66] Congleton had its own court with a view of frankpledge (that is a right to deal with petty criminal offences) although its independent position did not go unchallenged. Among the surviving local records preserved in Congleton town hall is a letter from John Pelham, steward of the south part of the duchy of Lancaster from 1405 to 1413, to some unknown person. Pelham stated that certain officials had ordered the mayor and the bailiffs of Congleton to appear at other courts than their own which was contrary to their charter and he commanded them to cease this practice. Friction continued, however. Another letter has survived addressed to Sir Thomas Stanley, one of the justices of Chester and treasurer of the duchy of Lancaster. The mayor of Congleton had complained to the king that the burgesses had been sued by actions of trespass at Chester and they had been commanded to appear at courts outside their franchise. Stanley was ordered to investigate the position and to ensure that any suits of this nature were withdrawn.[67]

The authorities at Congleton were obviously very jealous of attempts to limit the power of their court. An excellent series of manorial court rolls has survived from 1377 onwards, providing much information of the proceedings of this court. It was mainly concerned with ensuring fair dealing especially with regard to the assizes of bread, and in weights and measures. Medieval burgesses were convinced that all bakers gave false weight and charged too highly for their bread. The assize of bread was an attempt to regulate the weight of bread according to the price of wheat, so loaves became smaller as the price of corn rose.[68] At certain intervals throughout the year the bailiffs of Congleton had to ascertain whether the assize was being properly kept and all infractions were punished. In 1367-8 Henry Baxter was fined 6d for breaking the assize of bread; in 1369-70 fines totalled £1 11s 8d; in 1384-5, Robert and Henry Baxter, bakers, were fined 2s and in 1450-1 Agnes Preston, Katharine Moreton, Agnes Green and Margaret del Cliff were each fined 6d.[69] The assize of ale was an attempt to regulate the price of beer according to the price of wheat, barley and oats. Two ale-tasters were appointed at Congleton to ensure that good ale was brewed, but the assize proved difficult to keep, to judge from the large number of inhabitants who were fined in the courts. In 1379-80 a total of 12s 3d was collected from various men for breaking the assize and in 1384-5 Hugh Latham and Hugh del Dene, ale-tasters, accounted for 9s 6d from various breakers of the assize. Offences against the assize of meat also figured prominently in the court rolls. In 1357-8 William Levestone, William Alot, Philip del Yate and William del Yate, butchers of Congleton, were fined a total of 3s 2d, and in 1384-5 Philip del Yate and William Coget were also accused of breaking the assize of meat. Indeed the regularity of all these offences suggests that the fines were little more than licensing fees rather than punishments for a specific offence.[70]

The court was not only concerned with offences against the various assizes. It imposed fines or exacted payments for permission to take over the lands of a deceased relative or friend.

It also dealt with cases of violence; thus in 1379-80 Richard Astby was fined 6*d* for assaulting William Morton; in 1384-5 Ralph Morton was fined 1*s* for an attack on Thomas Brodhok, and in the same year certain fishermen were fined for catching trout in the River Dane.[71] The revenues of the manorial court formed an important part of the income of the lord of the manor. The profits varied from year to year[72] but from the mid-fifteenth century onwards they gradually declined in value and indeed from 1457-8 onwards no revenue at all was obtained from the court, a result of the decline of the importance of the manor in the economy.

Evidence of a general dissatisfaction with the state of Cheshire may be seen in a tour of the region in 1476 undertaken by the council of the duchy of Lancaster. The council desired to see how the duchy estates were being administered and endeavoured to enforce better order in the county. Its recommendations for Congleton are of particular interest. These ordained that no man dwelling in the town was to be retained as an armed follower by any other person, nor should he attend on anyone but the king or his deputy, Lord Stanley, steward of Congleton; in particular, Sir William Brereton and John Davenport were not to attempt to recruit retainers in the area, presumably a bid to stop private feuding. No one was allowed to bear bills or spears within the town, and the smiths were forbidden to manufacture these weapons. Finally the council suggested that a new building should be erected on the site of the old Moot Hall, probably the town hall of Congleton, containing five shops and a prison-house beneath it, while above it should be a hall where the king's court could be held.[73]

The Borough of Congleton

The charter of Henry de Lacy had stated that 'our burgesses ... may choose by themselves a mayor and catchpole and tasters of ale and shall present them openly in the sitting of our great court there on the Tuesday following the feast of St. Michael and our bailiff shall take their oath of faithful service to the lord and community'. This charter had been granted at some date between 1272 and 1275 but the first recorded name of a mayor was Philip son of Richard who held the office in 1318. From then until the end of the medieval period it is possible to compile a fragmentary list of the holders of this office. As one might expect from such a small community as Congleton, certain families gained a predominance in the municipal life of the borough. One such family were the Moretons. William was mayor in 1341–2, Roger in 1367–8, 1369–70, 1375–6, 1387–8, another William in 1397–9 and 1404–5, Richard in 1425–6, another Roger in 1437–8 and 1441–2, and Hugh in 1453–4 and 1456–7. Philip Green, who in 1424 purchased a tenement, a homestead, a garden, fourteen acres of land, an acre of meadow, and an acre of wood, was mayor in 1408–9, 1412–13, 1414–15, 1416–17, 1421–2, and again in 1435–6, while Hugh Green was mayor in 1440–1, 1445–6, 1452–3, 1459–61, 1462–3, and 1467–9. The Yate family were also prominent with Richard being mayor in 1391–2 and Robert in 1401–2, 1409–10, and 1420–1. The evidence from the list of mayors[74] suggests a community governed by a tightly knit group of a few influential families.

The economic life of the borough was doubtlessly closely linked with that of the manor, but it is possible to obtain some idea of the various occupations of the inhabitants of Congleton. Perhaps the wealthiest men in the town were the merchants. In Henry de Lacy's charter the burgesses had been allowed to form 'a merchant gild with all liberties and free customs to the same gild belonging'. Presumably the chief article of trade was cloth and, as has been noted, there was a fulling mill on the Dane. The Green (Grene) family, which supplied many mayors of the borough, was closely connected with trade. In 1445 Philip Green was called a mercer, perhaps a dealer in textile goods, and seven years later Hugh Green was also referred to as a mercer. Another mercer was Thomas Green who witnessed a deed in 1446.

The woollen-cloth industry was obviously an important one in this period, for many of the burgesses were connected with it. A member of the Green family, Hugh, was referred to as a draper in 1448 and 1454, and two prominent members of the Moreton family, William (who witnessed deeds in 1452 and 1456) and Hugh (who leased a meadow near the Dane in 1455), were also drapers. Another draper, John Barker, was mentioned in 1468. One of the most influential families in Congleton at this time was the Yate family. In 1398 Robert Yate was appointed a yeoman of the Crown receiving a daily wage of 6*d* for life; but other members of the family were closely linked with the cloth industry. John del Yate was a glover, probably a maker of woollen gloves, and another John was called a weaver in 1409. Wealthy craftsmen included the carpenter Thomas del Mason, who was granted a tenement in Park Lane and a plot of land in 1436 on condition that he allotted 3s each year for the maintenance of the Upper Chapel of Congleton, and the barker John Barker who was leased half an acre of land near the 'Horslyppe' in 1459. Another industry employing Congleton inhabitants was bell-making; in the last decade of the fifteenth century an order was placed for three bells, three clappers, six gudgeons and three baldricks to be obtained from Green's foundry. There were also the numerous butchers, bakers and innkeepers who figure so prominently in the court rolls.

Of the individual wealth of these burgesses little evidence is available. Their wills, however, can be useful in assessing their relative financial standing, and two particularly interesting ones have survived from the medieval period. Emma de Theteswall's will was made in 1418 and proved in 1419. She bequeathed to her daughter a tenement together with the adjoining lands and buildings and a garden and a barn. Ralph Theteswall was granted an acre of land extending above Lambardslone with a meadow, and Philip Theteswall received an acre and a rood of land in Wellescroft and half an acre under Paynesbrook. John de Galmo was bequeathed a piece of land in Congleton. The second will, that of Thomas Chell (or Chelle), was drawn up on the feast of the Holy Innocents, 1442. His financial bequests included the grant of a shilling to each of the chapels of St. Mary at Astbury and the Upper Chapel of Congleton and to the altar of St. Katharine's at Astbury, while the sum of 10s was left for the maintenance of the parish church of Astbury. He bequeathed half a burgage with the buildings attached to it to William and Alice Johnson together with an acre of land lying near 'Lambert's Loone' (Lane) and half an acre in the Over-westfield. To his daughter Alice he left a croft near Holway brook. They may not have been as wealthy as some of the mercers of Congleton, but both Emma de Theteswall and Thomas Chell seem to have been of some financial standing. The population of Congleton may have declined in the fifteenth century but they were not poverty stricken if one can judge from their wills and the consolidation of property evident in the local deeds.

Notes

1   Unless otherwise stated inf. is drawn from the collection of Borough charters (vols. i–iii).
2   For the Bridge Chapel see also p. 208–9.
3   B.M., Add. Ch. 37013.
4   B.M., Add. Chs. 48890–1.
5   B.M., Add. Ch. 37006.
6   B.M., Add. Ch. 37005. See p. 334n.
7   B.M., Add. Ch. 37004; Borough charters.
8   B.M., Add. Chs. 37014–5.
9   DL29/4/27.
10 Head, 5.
11 DL29/6/62.
12 DL29/6/64.
13 B.M., Add. Chs. 37007, 37008, 37011, 72344; P.R.O., E40/14805; *Cat. Anc. Deeds*, iv, A8724; v, A11204.
14 This theme is developed below in the section on the economic life of the manor.
15 G. Barraclough, *The Earldom and County Palatine of Chester*, (1953), 9; see also *History* ns, xxviii, 46.
16 *Domesday Survey of Cheshire*, ed. J. Tait (Chetham Soc., lxxv), 87, 187; B.M., Harl. MS. 2074, fol. 184; R. Richards, *Manor of Gawsworth* (1957), 7; Ormerod, ii, 754; iii, 547; Earwaker, ii, 549; *A Medieval Miscellany for D. M. Stenton*, ed. P. M. Barnes and C. F. Slade, Pipe Roll Soc. for 1960 (1962), 31; *Sir Christopher Hatton's Book of Seals*, ed. L. C. Loyd and D. M. Stenton (1950), 96.
17 B.M., Harl. MS. 2074, fol. 13; Earwaker, i, 462.
18 *Cal. Pat. R.1232–47*, 188, 464, 487; *1247–58*, 70, 213, 235, 274, 283, 298, 304–5, 309, 316–17, 320, 323–4, 338, 341–2, 345–8, 378, 402; *Cal. Close R. 1251–60*, 241, 341, 389; Earwaker, ii, 371.
19 C146/9824; *Cal. Pat. R. 1247–58*, 339; *Cal. Inq. Post Mortem*, i, no. 125; *Cal. Chart. R.*, i, 452.
20 B.M., Harl. MSS. 2079, fol. 15; Ormerod, ii, 97; *Cheshire Sheaf*, 3rd ser., vol. 20, 310–11; Earwaker, i, p. 462; *Cal. Inq. Post Mortem*, ii, 181, 189, 284, 360, 762, 782; iii, 8, 44; *Cal. Pat. R. 1266–72*, 588.
21 A. Ballard and J. Tait, *Borough Charters, 1216–1307* (1923), p. xl; *Chartulary of Chester Abbey*, ii, ed. J. Tait (Chetham Soc., lxxx), 432. See Appendix A, p. 336.
22 *V.C.H. Lancs*, i, 300, 319.
23 *Cheshire County Rolls*, ed. R. Stewart Brown (Chetham Soc., lxxxiv), 40.
24 Earwaker, i, 6. For the history of the Stanleys see *T.H.S.L.C.*, cv, 49; *Cheshire Sheaf*, xix, 17.
25 DL 25/L.67, 68; P.R.O., *Dep. Keeper's Rep.*, xxxv, 11.
26 *Cal. Chart. R.*, ii, 455–6.
27 *Cal. Inq. Post Mortem*, v, 164; *Cal. Close R. 1307–13*, 315; P.R.O., *Dep. Keeper's Rep.*, xxxvii, 101.
28 *Ibid.*, xxviii, 36.

29 *Cal. Fine. R. 1319–27*, 115, 116, 126, 149, 173; *Cal. Pat. R. 1321–4*, 161; *Cal. Close R. 1323–7*, 140.
30 *Cal. Pat. R. 1321–4*, 181, 182, 194; *Cat. Anc. Deeds*, i, A198; DL 10/170.
31 *Cal. Inq. Post Mortem*, vi, 371.
32 E 42/253; DL 10/239; *Cal. Pat. R. 1324–7*, 63.
33 *Cal. Inq. Post Mortem*, ix, 95.
34 P.R.O., Ancient Petition 2766; R. Somerville, *Duchy of Lancaster* (1953), 34. A Congleton landowner at this period was John Domville, senior, who in 1343 granted to Richard del Crosse all his lands in Upton, Bernston, Wylaston, Buglawton and Congleton. (*Talbot Deeds, 1260–1682*, ed. E. E. Barker, Rec. Soc. L. & C., ciii, no. 49.)
35 DL 42/1/fol. 47.
36 *Cal. Fine R. 1356–68*, 164; H. J. Hewitt, *Medieval Cheshire* (Chetham Soc., lxxxviii), 26; W. Beamont, *An Account of the Rolls of the Honour of Halton*, (1879), 18.
37 *Cal. Pat. R. 1413–16*, 356; *Cal. Close R. 1413–19*, 385.
38 P.R.O., *Dep. Keeper's Rep.*, xxix, 89.
39 This paragraph is based on Barraclough, *op. cit.*, 12, and *Historical Atlas of Cheshire*, ed. D. Sylvester and G. Nulty (1958), 18–22.
40 R. W. Finn, *Domesday Inquest* (1961), 16.
41 *Domesday Survey of Cheshire, op. cit.*, 87, 187.
42 *Domesday Geography of Northern England*, ed. H. C. Darby and I. S. Maxwell (1962), 330–92.
43 *Cal. Inq. Post Mortem*, v, 164. The estimated population is obtained by using a multiplier of five. See *Ec. H. R.* 2nd ser. ix, 420–32.
44 Figures from DL 29/4/24–9/115.
45 DL 29/1/1; 1/2; 6/72; 801/16.
46 DL 29/4/39, 40; 5/58; 6/72, 73, 75, 77, 78, 79, 85, 89; 8/97, 107.
47 DL 29/1/2; 801/16; 4/27; 28; 6/72; 7/78.
48 Ormerod, iii, 36.
49 DL 29/1/1; 801/16; 4/26, 30, 35; 5/56; 6/65; 7/86, 89, 90, 92; DL 37/10/45; 19/11; 20/23; Head, 36; Yates, 111.
50 B.M., Harl. MS. 2074, fol. 202; *Cal. Chart. R.*, ii, 260; Ormerod, iii, 35–36.
51 DI 29/1/1, 2; 801/16; 4/35; 5/46, 56; 6/72; 7/92; 8/107; Head, 35.
52 DL 29/801/16; 2/29; 4/31, 35; 5/46; 6/65; 8/107, 109: SC 2/155/84.
53 DL 29/4/26, 35; 5/46; 6/72.
54 DL 29/1/1; 801/16; 4/27; 5/43, 49, 51.
55 DL 29/4/26; 5/46.
56 DL 29/1/1; 801/16; 4/39, 40; 6/64; 7/78.
57 DL 29/1/1/, 2; *Calendar of Chancery Warrants, 1244–1326*, 367.
58 DL 29/1/1, 2; 4/26, 28, 29, 30, 32; 6/67.
59 DL 29/16/201–54.
60 For a discussion of these manorial accounts see *E.H.R.*, xlii, 180–200.
61 DL 29/728/11987–8.
62 T. Pape, *Medieval Newcastle-under-Lyme* (1928), 76.
63 *Cal. Pat. R. 1391–6*, 426.
64 *H.M.C.*, ii, 18–19.
65 P.R.O., *Dep. Keeper's Rep.*, xxxvii, 186.

66 Ormerod, iii, 36n; R. S. Brown, *The Sergeants of the Peace in Medieval England* (1936), 21; F. J. C. Hearnshaw, *Leet Jurisdiction in England* (1908), 264.

67 The letter is undated but the list of witnesses suggests that it was probably written between 1445 and 1449.

68 For a discussion of this, see P. Studer, *The Oak Book of Southampton*, ii, pp. xxi–xxix; *Ec. H. R.* 2nd ser. ix, 332–42.

69 DL 30/1/24; 2/25, 33.

70 *Statutes at Large*, i, 23; DL 30/1/21; 2/29, 33; 5/63.

71 DL 30/2/29, 33.

72 Bases on annual accounts 1294–5 to 1454–5 in DL 29 and DL 30, and (for 1396–7) SC 2/155/84. For 1457–1455 there are nil returns.

73 *T.H.S.L.C.*, cvx, 6–8; Edward had already agreed upon a grant of £40 to the mayor of Congleton for the building of a new gaol: DL 37/30/m.19.

74 See Appendix B.

III *Tudor and Stuart Congleton*[1]

by W B Stephens
& Norah Fuidge

Our knowledge of the topography of Congleton increases in Tudor times. Little is known before 1485 apart from the names of a few fields, streets and buildings like the chapel, the bridge, the mill and the moot hall, and that crofts lined Park Lane, Moor Lane and West Street. The map of the town *c.* 1500 (see p. 46) is based on the evidence of place-names. The town accounts, available from the mid-sixteenth century, add to our knowledge. In 1555, for example, it is noted that Crossledge was the slum area of the town, where the poorest inhabitants lived. The 'great bridge . . . upon Mossley Moss and the Edge' (Daneinshaw Bridge) is mentioned, and another boundary of the town is referred to as the 'bridge upon the West Heath and the Marsh', probably at Fol Hollow. A document of 1593 provides the legal bounds of the borough, and the town accounts show what areas were actually in use. The Brownswolds, between Fol Hollow and Banky Fields, were by then town property and in 1595 several persons were caught illegally ploughing there. The same sort of illegal ploughing took place along Padbridge Lane and West Heath and at the hollow known as Babslack next to Loachbrook. In other words, the wolds or woodlands of the Brownswolds were now being cut down for the plough, and the outermost heathland of West Heath was being brought into cultivation. The fact that it was being done illegally, like the illegal turning out of swine along the Loachbrook and Biddulph Brook, suggests that the population may have been slowly getting too large for the available land within the town.

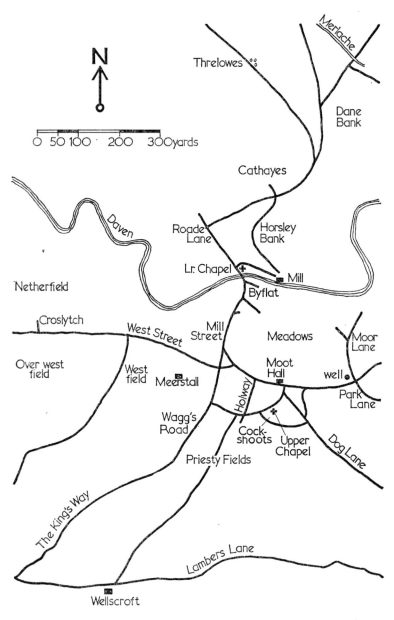

N

0 50 100 200 300 yards

Merlache

Threlowes

Dane Bank

Cathayes

Daven

Roade Lane

Horsley Bank

Netherfield

Lr. Chapel

Mill

Byflat

Croslytch

West Street

Mill Street

Meadows

Moor Lane

Over west field

West field

Meerstall

Moot Hall

well

Park Lane

Holway

Wagg's Road

Cock-shoots

Upper Chapel

Dog Lane

Priesty Fields

The King's Way

Lambers Lane

Wellscroft

Congleton about 1500

Meadows between the town and the Dane, cleared of minor houses by the flood of 1451, and not built on till after 1840, indicate the overriding importance of stock husbandry at this time. The proliferation of leather trades in late Tudor and Stuart Congleton, discussed below, is witness of this, and so is the town's continued concern with keeping the stock wells and ordinary wells clean. In 1588, for example, 'viewers of wells' were appointed by the town, and in 1589 strong warnings were given to those who piled their 'muck or manure' in the town streets.

The wooded areas round the town took on a great importance towards the end of the sixteenth century. The chief sources of timber were the Lambert's Lane area and at Cathayes behind Daisy Bridge. Padgbridge Lane was also well wooded. The streets of the town were increasingly being repaired with stone which came from Congleton Edge and was brought down Dog Lane. General repairs were made to roads leading into the town; in 1593 it was noted that the inhabitants of the town 'have from tyme to tyme when needed repaired and made amends to the Queen's Highway leading from Congleton to-wards Morton unto the new Crofft footwaie', that is as far as the borough boundary.

Two areas of the town which were strictly controlled were the Town Wood or Acre Wood and Overwestfield. In 1584 it was ordered 'that no-one shall fodder cattle by night in the Overwestfield' and in the same year people were forbidden to cut timber in the Town Wood across the Dane or to let animals stray there.

Further topographical information is provided by the 1593 account of the town boundaries. Fields were fairly small, and, except on West Heath, all were surrounded by hedges. Their names are rarely given but occasionally a marl-pit is mentioned. One would have expected many ponds to have been noted, but, with the exception of the 'Waters' opposite the present Castle Inn and the two great lakes behind the present Girls' Grammar School, they are conspicuous by their absence. On West Heath the boundary was marked by a series of stones, not by hedges. Later the marsh at Astbury appears to have shrunk consider-ably, for in 1731 it became possible to drive a road from Fol Hollow to West Heath.[2]

All the evidence of streets named in available records suggests

E

that any population growth during Tudor and Stuart times made few demands on the land available for housing in the town. There is no evidence of any dwelling beyond Crossledge in the one direction and the junction of Lawton Street and Park Lane in the other. By 1641 low-quality dwellings existed in Moody Street for the poor, and the existence of an inn called the *Dragonne* in Wagg Street suggests a possibility of housing there; but clearly most people lived in Chapel Street, Mill Street, West Street, High Street and Lawton Street. The richer people perhaps occupied the large houses facing the road, and poorer people the courts behind them. Often stables, too, lay behind the larger houses, so the picture we get is of a town crammed fairly tightly along the sides of its streets, with all available land given over to farming. Camden, in 1586,[3] noted that the centre of the town was watered by the 'little river Howty', so one would expect the highest density of population there.

Economic and Social Structure

Towards the end of the seventeenth century Richard Blome described Congleton as 'a large and noted town'.[4] It is difficult, however, to estimate the actual size of the population of the town in this or the preceding century, or to analyse very exactly its social structure. The records of the subsidy tax collected in 1524–5, often used for such purposes,[5] have not survived for Congleton, and a diocesan report on the number of households in each parish and chapelry, made in 1563, is rather unsatisfactory for Congleton. It returned 853 households for Astbury parish, and 16 for Congleton.[6] Clearly 16 is too small a figure for Congleton, and the Astbury figure must include a high proportion of Congleton households. If there were an average of four persons per household, then there would have been about 3,400 persons, and if three per household, about 2,550, in the whole of Astbury parish including Congleton and Buglawton: but an estimate of population in Congleton a century later suggests that these figures are rather high.

In 1660 a poll tax was levied on all but the poorest adult inhabitants. The tax-roll for Congleton[7] lists 506 individuals, consisting of 155 married men, 237 single persons and widows and 114 other individuals, some of them widows, others men whose marital state is not indicated. If we assume that of these

114, say half were married, then we arrive at a rough total of 718 adults in Congleton. If we follow the seventeenth-century statistician, Gregory King, and assume that 40 per cent of the population were children, we obtain an approximate total population for Congleton at the time of the Restoration of about 1,200, plus an unknown number too poor to pay 1s a head or per married couple.

A hearth tax imposed in 1668 shows that there were then 349 houses in the town, including the dwellings of those exempt from the tax on grounds of poverty.[8] If there were four persons per household a population of 1,400 is suggested. It seems reasonable to suppose, therefore, that in the early years of Charles II's reign Congleton supported something in the region of 1,200–1,400 souls.

Evidence for the social structure of this community is, as with population figures, more useful for the later seventeenth century than for earlier periods. In 1568 about 140 persons (including wives and some children) were of sufficient importance to be allotted by name seats in the chapel 'according to estate and degree'.[9] Poorer inhabitants were merely to sit as they came in. Presumably the 140 were those able to pay pew rents and perhaps included people as unimportant as minor tradesmen. They were not necessarily persons of great wealth. In 1592 a list of those agreeing to pay a proportion of the minister's salary numbered 80 persons of whom only 35 agreed to pay more than 1s a quarter, only 15 over 2s, and only 9 above 5s.[10] This suggests that in Elizabeth I's reign there was a community of active citizens within the borough of whom a small group was considerably wealthier than most others.

Tudor tax returns where they exist tend to confirm this picture, which would anyway be expected of most towns of the time. In 1545–6, for example, 16 Congleton men were assessed for tax. Of these Richard Grene, several times mayor, was rated highest—on goods valued at £35 a year. James Rode (Rood) paid on £21, Thomas Comberback on £20, and the rest were assessed on goods of between £5 and £14. When a voluntary contribution was raised by the king in the following year, Grene, Rode and Comberback were the only three Congleton men named: it is clear that they were the wealthiest men in the town in the mid-sixteenth century. In the latter half of the century Greens, Rodes (Grene, Rode, Roode are alternatives) and

Spencers seem to have been among the dominant families, heading, for example, the list of seven Congleton men paying tax in 1595.[11] But some taxpayers were quite humble men. One of those rated in 1595, John Hobson (d. 1613), was an alderman and a farmer. At his death he left goods worth £51, including 9 cattle, a pig, 6s 8d worth of dung and £4 in growing corn, all of which was cancelled out by debts and funeral expenses.[12] Even so the number of taxpayers was always well below the number of town council members (of whom there were twenty-four), and the active rulers of the town thus included in their number many who never appeared on tax returns.[13]

In the early years of Charles II's reign a more definite picture emerges of the social make-up of Congleton. The poll tax of 1660 was graded according to ability to pay, so that it can be utilized to provide a rough indication of the spread of wealth in the town.[14] The following table is based on the return:

Congleton Poll Tax, 1660

Amount paid	Number of payers	Approx. percentage of all payers
10s and above (i.e. worth £25 p.a. and above)	12	2 ⎫
4s 10d–8s 10d (over £10–£21)	16	3 ⎬ 5
2s 5d–4s (over £5–£10)	30	6 ⎫
2s (worth £5 p.a.) (£5)	56	11 ⎬ 17
1s (single persons) ⎱ (less than	237	47 ⎱ 78
1s (married men) ⎰ £5)	155	31 ⎰
	506	100

The same broad-based narrow-apexed social pyramid, suspected for the sixteenth century, is revealed for the seventeenth. It is clear that the very top Congleton group, able officially to 'dispend in lands, leases, money, stock', and so on, £25 a year or more, can have numbered only 2 per cent of the population and the well-off (£10 p.a. and above) altogether only about 5 per cent. Those who paid 10s tax or above—the top 2 per cent—included Matthew Bateson (30s), who had been of sufficient standing to be given control over the manor of Congleton when it was sequestrated by Parliament,[15] Mrs. Penelope Bradshaw (perhaps a relative of the regicide), who was reputed to have '£1,500 to her person', and Thomas (18s) and Richard Parnell (16s), members of a family later to become important in the town and elsewhere. Richard and his brother Tobias were the leaders of the Parliamentary party in Congleton. Richard was a mercer or draper and lived in a large five-hearthed house, probably formerly his father's, next to the town hall.[16] John Hobson, who paid 16s on the basis of land worth £40 a year, had ancestors who had held important office in the town since the sixteenth century. A royalist, he had been set aside by the Commonwealth government when elected mayor in 1658, only to become, after Cromwell's death and before the Restoration, mayor in 1659–60.[17] He was a tanner, and though owning books worth 10s had to attest his will with a mark. Yet his goods were valued at £96 at his death in 1667 and included a carpet in the parlour and a 'pair' of virginals.[18] Other members of the most affluent group of citizens included Richard Grene (12s), mayor 1627–8, 1631–2, called 'gent', and perhaps a master carpenter,[19] John Henshaw (12s), who had been mayor in 1642–3 and had been a republican in the war,[20] and John Walker (10s), a skinner, and also a former mayor who had raised a royalist company in Congleton to help in the siege of Nantwich.[21] Another was George Ford who paid 12s for the tax. His career gives some indication of the sort of life led by a citizen at this time. He was apprenticed to Ralph Hammersley, mercer, in 1617,[22] and 20 years later became a member of the town council. He was royalist mayor in 1641–2 and 1643–4, and though he seems to have lain low in the second civil war he evidently continued in his allegiance to the Crown. At the Restoration in 1660 he became alderman and mayor within a fortnight, gathering round him the old royalist members of the corporation. By trade he was a mercer owning a shop in Congleton and trading at Macclesfield market.[23] At his death in 1666 his household goods were valued at £65 and his trading stock (cloths, thread, buttons and the like) at £121. His house consisted of his shop, a room over it (presumably the best room), an attic room, four rooms used as bedrooms, a kitchen and a back kitchen, a buttery and a hall.[24] Congleton had no merchant princes and this level of living was probably typical of the upper crust of the town's society.

In the next 3 per cent (paying less than 10s but above 4s and so worth £10–£21 p.a.) were those like William Moxon, described as 'gent.' (8s), William Bayley (perhaps the mayor in 1702–3) (6s 5d), William Drakeford (6s), a tanner and common councilman in 1637,[25] Ralph Stubbs (6s) perhaps the same Ralph Stubbs, 'citizen and merchant tailor of London' whose will dates from 1661,[26] and Roger Pointon (8s), mayor in 1653–4, who was a shoemaker.[27]

The 17 per cent who comprised those paying between 2s and 4s (and so worth between £5 and £10) were clearly very much less wealthy. It is equally certain, however, that they included men of standing in the community. Ralph Hammersley, for example, paid 2s, yet he was a council member in 1637[28] and mayor in 1665–6, and was a mercer by trade.[29] William Knight, a tanner,[30] a former mayor and fined as a royalist delinquent in the war,[31] paid 4s; James Lingard, mayor in 1625–6, and a skinner,[32] paid 2s 5d; John Rood, a tanner and common councilman in 1637[33] and Thomas Rood, another tanner, both probably of the well-known local family, both paid 2s, as did William Harding, draper, and mayor in 1672–3. William Drakeford (2s), a farmer, with house and gardens in Dog Lane, had goods and money owing to him at his death in 1671 of £155, including £10 in ready money.[34]

Those who paid 1s (worth less than £5 p.a.), the vast bulk (78 per cent) of the population, comprised tradesmen of varying degrees, apprentices and labourers, and probably ranged in wealth from those on the brink of poverty to those in fairly comfortable circumstances. Below them, an unrecorded group of those too poor to pay even 6d a head existed. Its size can only be guessed at. Information culled from the hearth-tax returns of Charles II's reign, however, gives a clue as well as reinforcing the picture of the rest of the community provided by the poll tax. A hearth tax of 1668[35] gives details of all the houses in Congleton. There were 349, of which 245 had only one hearth. Of these 112 were occupied by people too poor to pay the tax— probably they housed a large proportion of widows, widowers, spinsters and aged couples. Another 62 houses had 2 hearths, and one of these was exempt on grounds of poverty. Of the 42 other houses 23 had 3 hearths, 9 had 4, and only 10 had between 5 and 7. Thus 32 per cent of households were officially regarded as poor, and another 56 per cent, with only one or two fireplaces, must have been mostly those of labourers or of small craftsmen. These people were certified as not possessing land or goods worth more than £10, and the houses themselves were officially not worth more than £1 a year.[36]

Of the top 12 per cent of households—those with 3 or more hearths—at least two were inns (the two houses with 7 hearths each), including the *Swan*.[37] The other inn, then owned by Ellen Roe, widow of Thomas Roe, is unnamed, but was in Lawton Street. In 1661 it consisted of a dining room and other rooms including those picturesquely called the Red Chamber, the Cocke Chamber, the Bell Chamber, the Half Moon, the Rose, the Mermaid, the Ram, the 'Flowertyluce', the Bull and the Spreadeagle.[38]

There were thus only some 40 private houses in the town with more than two hearths, and only 17 (5 per cent) with more than three. In 1673 there were 18 houses (including inns) with four or more hearths.[39]

It is not possible to find out the occupations of all the upper groups of Congleton society, but some can be discovered. It is clear that some men, even of the humbler classes, owned land. In 1572, for example, the four chief taxpayers in Congleton were all assessed on land rather than goods, in 1605–6 four of the ten assessed paid on land, and in 1626–7 eight of the twelve assessed.[40]

Some Congleton men were obviously farmers and nothing else. This was so, for example, of alderman John Hobson (d. 1613), mentioned above, of Roger Spence, gent. (d. 1614), who left a small flock of sheep, pigs and poultry; John Rode alderman (Rood), who on his death in 1640 had cattle, sheep, barley and wheat in store, and wheat, rye and oats in the fields, and whose goods were valued at £86; and of William Drakeford (d. 1671) who left two cows, two heifers and corn in store and in the ground. On the whole they do not appear to have been large landowners, and generally speaking farming was a part-time occupation of many Congleton tradesmen albeit in a small way. John Slater, a plasterer (d. 1602), left 3 sheep, Thomas Roe, the innkeeper (d. 1661), left cattle and pigs and owned land about the town, George Ford, the mercer (d. 1666), owned Priesty Fields, and left wheat and barley, Matthew Lowndes (d. 1668), a shoemaker, had a barn and stable and kept pigs and a few cattle, John Stubbs, a glover (d. 1668), had land and an orchard as well as a turbary on Mossley Moss, John Passe, a shoemaker, left £36 worth of animals, corn and farming equipment, and was leasing land including arable fields.[41] So while few men were farming on a large scale Congleton and the surrounding fields must have contained plenty of cattle, pigs, a few sheep, as well as growing corn. Its inhabitants were by no means urbanized in the modern sense.

Nevertheless while land was owned or leased and farming indulged in, the ruling class in Congleton was generally engaged in trade, often in various branches of the leather trade. Some mercers, drapers, skinners and tanners among the more substantial taxpayers in 1660 have already been noted. Thomas Hanford, who had a four-hearth house in 1664, was a butcher,[42] and may thus have been connected with skinning.

In the sixteenth and early seventeenth centuries the same dominance of the leather trades had been evident. One of the chief taxpayers in 1594–5, James Hankynson, was a shoemaker.[43] Ralph Stubbs, important enough to be a juryman in 1593,[44] was also a shoemaker.[45] William Newton, taxed in 1626–7, mayor in 1623–4 and 1636–7, was a shoemaker,[46] and in the 1650s another of the same name, perhaps his son, was a glover,[47] and yet another William Newton also a glover.[48] One of these whose will was proved in 1654 left several closes of land in Congleton, houses and a shop.[49] Thomas Parnell, made a freeman in 1669, was also a shoemaker.[50] Thomas Spencer, mayor in 1656, apprenticed his two sons as a shoemaker and a tanner,[51] and was probably in the leather trade himself.

This analysis of the leading groups in Congleton bears out Blome's report of 1673 that Congleton's inhabitants 'make great store of leather gloves, purses, and points',[52] and it is quite clear that the leather trades did indeed dominate economic activity in the town as a whole. Of the 75 persons whose trade is recorded in the 1660 poll tax 40 were engaged in these crafts or trades.[53] Similarly a list of those taking the freeman's oath between May 1655 and July 1664 includes eight shoemakers, and the only other crafts claiming four or more entries were glovemaking, tanning and farming. Three tailors were listed, and several crafts had two representatives—mercers, weavers (one a silk and the other a coverlet worker) and smiths. The single entries included a carpenter, barber, pointer, cooper, tallow chandler, currier, salter, feltmaker, ironmonger, glazier and chapman. In addition there were the various tradesmen connected with food supplies.[54] Congleton men evidently liked their drink: in 1584 no fewer than 42 alehouse keepers (including several widows) received licences.[55]

The earliest reference to bell founding in Congleton occurs in the later fifteenth century, and this is mentioned above.[56] By the early seventeenth century the old Lower Chapel at the bridge, no longer employed for religious purposes, was partly used as a bell foundry. George Lee, the first known lessee, cast a bell for Nantwich at Congleton in 1608,[57] though Henry Oldfield may have begun the foundry some years earlier. Oldfield, a famous craftsman throughout the eastern and midland counties, certainly cast two bells in 1595 for the Upper Chapel at Congleton. Other members of the family paid rent for the old chapel foundry up to about 1677, after which it may have gone out of business. In the eighteenth century it was used as a poorhouse, and was finally pulled down in 1814.[58]

Congleton traders, including those in the leather crafts, appear to have had little working capital or stock. Francis Spencer, a tanner, who died in 1642, left stock of some 90 hides varying in value from 8*s* to 18*s* each; Alexander Green (d. 1667), another tanner, left goods valued at £268 including 10 dickers of leather and hides worth £64. His tools, however, were valued at only 10*s*. John Glover, mercer, in 1669 had household goods and stock including such goods as tobacco, spices, sugar and currants, as well as cloth, lace, buttons and thread to the value of £52; Thomas Hull, another shopkeeper dealing in tobacco, dried fruits, sugar and the like, left stock and debts owing to him valued at £64 in 1665. The stock of George Ford, mercer (d. 1666), worth £121, has already been noted.

But such large stocks were unusual. Most traders were clearly more humble. Randle Somerville, a shoemaker, left stock of leather worth only £3 13*s* 4*d* and his tools were valued at 6*s* 8*d* when he died in 1627. John Hobson, tanner, and mayor 1660–1, left only £10 in leather, tools and other professional goods; Matthew Lowndes, a shoemaker, appears to have had no stock at all at his death in 1668; John Stubbs, a glover, who died in the same year, left goods worth only £7, and his ready cash, clothes and working tools were worth together only 10s.[59]

Yet Congleton was clearly the most important community in its immediate vicinity, and the most industrial. The poll tax of 1660 indicates that in Buglawton, Astbury and Sandbach most of the inhabitants were farmers and farm labourers, although Sandbach had a few shoemakers. The following table[60] gives some idea of the relative importance of these places:

	Poll tax 1660 Total paid	Hearth tax 1664 Total paid	Poll tax 1675 Total paid
	(Amounts to nearest £)		
Congleton	66	20	35
Buglawton	16	4	12
Astbury	26	6	18
Sandbach	37	11	27

Nevertheless some of the farmers and landowners in the rural peripheries of the town indulged in agriculture in a bigger way than Congleton men. Christopher Byron, gent., of Buglawton, for example, was clearly richer than most of the townfolk. He paid 22s for the poll tax of 1660 and his goods at his death in 1684 were valued at nearly £500. They included £8 10s in plate and 13 gold sovereigns—items not found in Congleton inventories of the time—and he possessed many more farm animals than was common in the town. William Drakeford (d. 1641), also of Buglawton, was less important, but he too had more cattle than was usual in Congleton itself.[61]

Plague and Poverty

Many Congleton men must of course have been labourers, employed in agriculture and other unskilled work. It was these people and the poorer craftsmen who were hardest hit by any dislocation of life and unemployment. For example, the 'great snow' of 1614–15 caused great hardship, while the winter of 1634–5 saw one of the worst frosts the country had known, with considerable sums being spent to keep roads and waterways open. It took three men to cut ice and snow 'in the rood lands to get passage there', and the river was so heavily frozen that it was difficult to keep the mills working. Though the corporation provided free coal for the most needy inhabitants and employed men to clear the snow from house doors, at least one poor woman, with her child, died. Another of her children was cared for at the town's expense.[62]

'Plague', an eclectic term used to describe several epidemic diseases, and a dreaded scourge, appeared at least three times on a large scale—in 1559, 1603–4, and 1641–2. During the second visitation the corporation laid down stringent regulations to keep Congleton free from the disease. Alehouse keepers were forbidden to give hospitality to travellers from infected areas, while no innkeeper could take in anyone after 10 p.m. unless the caller was well known to him. 'Foreigners' bringing in malt, grain or other supplies had to have certificates that the goods were not from infected places, and to swear that the certificates were genuine. Anyone discovered to have brought in 'foreign' goods against the regulation, or to have received them into his house, could be 'shut up' for 20 days or longer if the authorities saw fit, guard being kept over him and his household.[63]

These measures, however, failed to prevent the arrival of the plague, and the Cheshire magistrates ordered neighbouring townships to send weekly help to relieve the Congleton poor. The total contribution in provisions included '1,000 loaves, 1,000 pails of milk, 50 pails of milk porridge, 150 good cheeses, 50 pieces of beef, 6 flitches of bacon, one great bun, 10 oatcakes, 1,000 puddings, several pear pies, pasty pies, and a gallon of butter.'[64]

Though this outbreak of disease was serious, it seems to have been relatively short. But the third, beginning about December 1641, was much more persistent, and six months later Congleton was still not completely clear. Contemporary documents give a vivid picture of its catastrophic effects. In November watchmen were employed to prevent communication with Nantwich and Newcastle-under-Lyme, where the sickness had already appeared, but by the middle of December Moody Street and surrounding districts were affected. The disease, said to have been carried in a box of clothing, spread quickly. 'Plague stones'—cubical blocks with hollowed tops filled with water for changing money—were used; cats and dogs were killed; the authorities provided not only coal for communal boiling of clothes, but also pitch, tar and frankincense for 'purging' houses, and winding sheets and a 'white nag' to take the corpses to Astbury for burial. Nevertheless the epidemic soon got out of hand. A common grave had to be dug, and men employed to carry the dead bodies there. A payment to one of these is described as 'money which a man so dearly bought by burying the sick'. Francis Stubbs, the chief 'burier', who survived, received 7s a week—or was promised it: as late as 1647 the town paid him £2 arrears. When soon afterwards he died, the corporation voted 10s for his funeral.

The almost complete cessation of trade with the outside world, and the 'shutting up' of infected houses, produced great distress among the poor. Lord Brereton sent 60 loaves; others contributed money; neighbouring districts sent over £40; and in all £75 or more was spent by the town on poor relief, including provision of coal during what was apparently another hard winter. Yet the numbers of 'clamorous poor', declaring that they had not received their rightful share of the dole, increased to such an alarming extent that to satisfy their demands, even temporarily, the mayor was forced to borrow £20 from Alderman Walker. In May 1642 a public fast was proclaimed, and a collection taken in Congleton chapel, but this produced only 4s.

Even in ordinary times there was a perennial problem of poverty and the need to provide relief. Congleton was fortunate in having several substantial charities, the details of which were inscribed on the walls of the courtroom in the town hall. For example, by her will in 1622, Lady Elizabeth Booth gave £2 10s a year to be distributed weekly on bread to the Congleton poor, and the same sum to those at Astbury: the local authorities in each place added 2s a year to the total for their own district. The bread was to be provided from the interest on £100 bequeathed by the will to the mayor and corporation of Congleton, who 'should from year to year let out and lend the same to honest young tradesmen at 5 per cent interest, who were freemen of the borough and carrying on some trade therein'. No single loan was to be for more than £10, and the money had to be repaid within three years. After this gift had been taken over by the Charity Commissioners, a judgment of 1864 decided that £50 of the bequest belonged by law to Astbury, though Congleton maintained that 'never within the memory of man' had Astbury claimed it.

At about the same time as Lady Booth's grant, a surgeon, Dr. William Dean, left the rents of two houses in Congleton High Street to be used to provide clothes for the poor. In addition he bequeathed land on Mossley Moss, and two sittings in Congleton chapel, to the corporation for relief of distress—a bequest totalling £60 a year or more. In 1622, 'William Parnell, gentleman, gave by will, payable off lands in Buglawton, an annuity of £8, £2 whereof to the minister of Congleton, 14*s* for aldermen's breakfasts, and to be distributed in money and bread, the yearly sum of £5 6*s*'. Other contemporary bequests included Ralph Stubbs's £2 12*s* a year for weekly bread distribution, payable from 'Chappel House, situated near the church', and from a close of land called Upper Riddings in Congleton: an additional 8*s* was to be paid annually to the mayor and aldermen to be spent as they deemed fit.

Details have survived as to how one charity, that of Joan Davis, in 1651, was spent. The benefactress, whose connection with Congleton is not stated, is described as 'of London'. At first sight it looks as if the intention of the bequest—£50 'for the use of the poor of Congleton'—was not carried out by the corporation, who 'disbursed £25 to Alderman Richard Parnell for money laid down for the mace'. An additional £15 went to Parnell, as 'left to him in the mayoralty of Alderman Hollyday', and £10 'in part of a bond of £30', so that 'the whole £50 came to the hands of Alderman Richard Parnell, now mayor'. However, this does not seem to have been misappropriation of funds. The suggested explanation that the town borrowed the money, paying £2 10*s* annual interest to the poor, is almost certainly correct: this was still being done in the nineteenth century.

Bequests for the regular relief of paupers, and the sums collected through the statutory poor rate, did not cover unusual expenses such as medical treatment or the care of orphans. At various times the borough authorities paid doctors—for example, to 'set a poor wench's broken leg', and 'to salve a boy left at the great stone'; while a local woman, 'little Bess', regularly received money for tending the sick. In 1660 or the following year Bess Alvison (probably the same woman), was caring for 'Samon's boy, 14 days sick of smallpox'. Sometimes clothes were provided, as in the case of an orphan, Daniel

Sherman: 'two yards of cloth to make Sherman's child a coat of, 4s. Two shirts, thread and making of them, and for some buttons for him, 2s 4d'. Congleton people leaving the town, perhaps to work elsewhere, occasionally received grants: 'To Margaret, the daughter of Richard Rogers, by consent at her going to London, 3s.'

Caring for their own poor was not by any means the corporation's only charitable commitment. There was a constant stream of travellers with passes (genuine or forged) allowing them to claim relief from towns and villages on the road. 'Four poor Irish people', who 'had lost £500 by Turkish pirates', were helped. Barbary corsairs were still occasionally operating off Ireland and Cornwall, but the word 'Turk' was sometimes used as a general term denoting a pirate of unknown origin. A large number of paupers claimed to have been ruined by their attacks, such as the 'Irish gentlewoman whose husband had been a sheriff in Ireland and had suffered great losses by the Turks', and the 'two several companies' in 1661 who had 'passes from the commissioners at Westminster and had been prisoners to the Turks'. However, travellers wanting help were often more specific, and their stories reflect the political troubles of the period. In March 1623, two soldiers 'brought a pass from Bohemia or those countries', and two others, presumably also returning from the wars in Germany, a certificate from 'Pawlesgreeave'. The writer of the town accounts, evidently not well up in German dignitaries, seems to have been doubtful if this was a person or a place. On occasion even a traveller's nationality defeated him: 'Bestowed upon two outlandishmen who came with licence out of foreign lands to have had a collection in our chapel'. Early in Charles I's reign two poor men received relief 'who were robbed upon the seas by the Dunkyrks (i.e. pirates from Dunkirk), and all they had taken from them', and one of the worst abuses of the time appears soon afterwards in the 'poor soldier who had a pass from the Prince of Orange to travel into his native country, being pressed from Plymouth'. He may have deserved his 8d, but it is difficult to believe in another successful beggar at about the same time— 'a poor maid who had served under the King of Sweden'. There is a later reflection of the Thirty Years' War in 1636: 'Bestowed upon a poor minister that came forth of the Palatinate, being constrained to forsake his country and was in great want and could never a word of English'. He received a shilling, the same amount as the 'poor maid'. It is surprising to find a 'poor Spaniard' and a 'poor Frenchman' being given money at the beginning of the Civil War, but the 'company of poor Jewish people' helped in 1652 is a reminder that the Commonwealth government, so intolerant in many ways, was generous to an often persecuted race. 'Three soldiers much wounded in Jamaica' passed through Congleton in 1657; not long after Charles II's marriage to Catherine of Braganza, 'a traveller . . . came out of Portingall'; while about 1667 the town made a contribution to 'seven persons that had been taken by the Dutch'.

The Civil War and its aftermath, of course, produced great distress, and disabled men often needed relief—like the 'two sick soldiers that came from Wouster battle', and were given a shilling 'towards bringing them into Lancheshire'. Such pathetic refugees appeared as, for example, the woman whose husband had been 'slain by Prince Rupert' at Liverpool, or the Westmorland man whose house had been burnt by the Earl of Derby's army. As to the 'Shrewsbury gent. lately robbed in the north by the moss troopers and worth £480 taken from him', questions that might occur to a modern reader do not seem to have worried the apparently gullible Congleton authorities. Perhaps 'moss troopers' evoked painful memories: at any rate the sufferer received the almost unprecedented sum of 2*s* 6*d*.

Ireland provided a constant trickle, during the Civil War period rising to a flood, of needy poor passing through Cheshire, but there were paupers from the immediate neighbourhood also, like the 'old woman whose husband was killed in a marl-pit'. Occasionally, the town clerk, his memory perhaps failing him over details, recorded alms simply to 'a poor creature' or 'a poor and fit object of pity'. The poor-law stipulation that those unable to work should return to their own parish led to great hardship as well as to disputes between local authorities. Towards the end of Elizabeth's reign a shillingsworth of bread and drink was 'bestowed upon four cripples carried in carts and barrows, to avoid the town of them'. Gipsies appear only very rarely in Congleton records, but in 1612 or 1613 the corporation made a contribution to 'the captain of the Egyptians which had a pass'.

Amusements

There was, however, a lighter side to life. During the late sixteenth and early seventeenth centuries, groups of actors under the patronage of some magnate were often paid for performing at Congleton. The King's, Queen's and Prince of Wales's men, and those of James I's daughter, Elizabeth, played fairly regularly, receiving 10s or £1 a visit, and there are notices of other troops of players belonging to the Earls of Derby and Worcester, the Lord Admiral, Lords Mountegle, Dudley and Strange. In November 1623 a performance was cancelled at short notice 'by reason they [the players] were sent for by the prince in haste'. Sunday seems to have been a favourite day for plays, but by 1632 the Puritans on the corporation were evidently opposing this: some unspecified actors received 6s 8d 'towards their charges, in regard Mr. Deputy Wagge and the two justices would not suffer them to play on the Sabbath Day'. No payments to travelling players have been found after 1635.

Congleton citizens do not appear to have done much acting themselves during the period, though in 1589 there was a 'Lord of Misrule' in the town, perhaps connected with the wakes. The only recorded dramatic performance was around Shrovetide in 1621 when a musician from Chester twice came to Congleton, charging £1 a visit, first to play while 'the scholars' (perhaps from the grammar school) acted. No details of the performance are given, apart from the fact that the 'scholars' borrowed a canopy from Brereton for the occasion. It may have been the same entertainment which was given at the musician's second appearance, when 'the townsmen played their play on Mr. Green's court at the entreaty of Mr. Oldfield'.

Several medieval customs lingered on, as, for example, the rushbearing, which took place on special feast days. The bells rang early in the morning to rouse the inhabitants, who came out to meet the procession of gaily dressed young men and women carrying garlands of flowers to decorate the chapel, with fresh rushes to strew the floors of the principal pews. The visitors, often from the marshy valleys near Buglawton, were headed by a piper and other musicians. After a short religious service, with much psalm or hymn singing, the celebration continued with wine and cakes, dancing and merrymaking.

Puritan disapproval seems to have put a stop to the rushbearing about the middle of the seventeenth century.

Another 'popish' ceremony, which went on in a degraded form for nearly 300 years, was that of 'ringing the chains'. In medieval times, on the vigil of 1 August at midnight, the beginning of the feast of St. Peter ad Vincula, the Congleton 'wake' commenced (altered in 1752 by the change of the calendar to the first Sunday after 12 August). Three acolytes danced through the town wearing leather belts containing loose bullet clappers. When the din had awakened the citizens, the chief officer of the feast proclaimed the wake at St. Peter's cross, exhorting everyone to keep it religiously. After the Reformation the belts came into the hands of a family of chimney sweeps, whose profane proclamation at the Cross henceforward encouraged the townsfolk to drink as much good ale as possible during the wake. Finally a nineteenth-century town clerk, Dr. John Wilson, called to adjudicate following fights between two rival sets of claimants to the belts, bought out both sides for 10*s* each, had the belts and bells cleaned and mended, and presented them to the town. They are still kept at the town hall.[65]

During the Tudor and early Stuart reigns the wake, together with the town fairs, gave the borough authorities a good deal of work in controlling merrymakers. Watchmen's wages appear regularly in the accounts at festival times: in 1636 'four men who did look after rogues and harlots on May Day' received 2*s* between them. The two outstanding sports were bearbaiting and cockfighting. Bearwards seem to have been well paid, often up to £3 or £4 a visit. A well-known Cheshire one, Ralph Shelmerdine, often came to Congleton, and on one occasion 'the King's Majesty's bears' were in the town for the week after Whitsuntide. A rude verse current in the neighbourhood claimed that

> Congleton rare, Congleton rare,
> Sold the Bible to pay for a bear

but the townspeople indignantly denied this, insisting that all they had done, faced with a crisis owing to a bear's death just before the wake, was to lend the bearward 16*s* towards a replacement—money saved to buy a Bible and temporarily kept in the town chest.

F

Congleton was a recognized local centre for cockfights, neighbouring gentry visiting the town for 'cockings' which might last, as at the 'great cockfight' of May 1601, for several days, or sometimes for a full week. The cockpit near the school was regularly repaired before festivals, probably at the instigation of the schoolmaster, who directed the fighting, reclaiming all runaway cocks as his perquisite. Though during the puritan period Congleton had fewer bearbaitings and cockfights (the authorities frowning on the gambling and the disorder that attended them), the Restoration saw a quick revival: in 1670 the borough paid over £2 5*s* for wine, ale and 'symnells bestowed on the gentlemen at the cocking', in addition to nearly £2 given to the visitors in purses.

The corporation often entertained magnates and their ladies with banquets, or gave them presents of money, sugar, sweetmeats, ribbons, gloves or Congleton points. The high steward's visits were generally celebrated in this manner, together with those of justices on their way to the Chester assizes, or of Parliamentary commanders such as Sir William Brereton. Earl Rivers, high steward from 1657, sent the town a buck at least once a year, and a communal feast, often at the *Swan*, was celebrated with wine, beer and 'bisketts'. Sometimes large sums were spent on gifts and entertainments—for example a visit from the high steward cost as much as £9. Entertainers from the households of great men might perform on these occasions, as when in 1620 one of the Earl of Derby's servants came to 'show feats of activity'.

At special times the bells were rung, the standard payment for the ringers being 6*s* to 8*s*. The recorded wages begin with Elizabeth's accession day, 17 November, and continue through 'the King's holiday' (5 November) to the anniversary of Charles II's coronation. The ringers performed also on St. George's day and at other specified times—in 1657 on 'the day that the proclamations were made at the Cross', and in June 1666 'for the victory we got at sea'—a reference to the naval war with the Dutch.

Local Government

During the sixteenth century Congleton men were afforded some protection by the town's position as part of the barony of Halton in the duchy of Lancaster. The duchy court continually intervened over cases of indictment of Congleton townspeople before the Chester assizes, contrary to Henry de Lacy's charter (confirmed by an injunction of Henry VIII). The duchy court also strongly supported Congleton traders' perennial dispute with the town of Macclesfield over their liability to pay toll there.[66] Nevertheless the growth in Congleton's population and prosperity appears to have stimulated a desire for a greater measure of control over its own affairs. Thus while in this period both duchy and borough officials continued to exercise their functions in Congleton the importance of the duchy and the manor gradually receded into the background.[67]

In the early sixteenth century the rights of the steward of the honour of Halton, who presided at the court leet—by then attached to the borough rather than the manor[68]—and those of the mayor exercised in the mayor's court or court of assembly (originally held every three weeks but by 1589 apparently at regular two-monthly intervals)[69] were not clearly defined. Serious confrontation, however, apparently did not arise while the steward, as one of the landed gentry, remained of considerably higher social status than the average mayor. An incident in 1553,[70] however, while it may be taken as an example of rivalry between two neighbouring gentry, is perhaps indicative of local feeling too. In that year the townsmen found a champion in Sir William Brereton, who upheld their cause against the steward, his fellow magistrate, Sir John Savage. Savage claimed the right to choose, at the first court leet held after Michaelmas Day, two 'triers' from among the aldermen[71] and burgesses. These were to empanel a jury of twelve 'discreet, substantial and indifferent burgesses' to elect the mayor, afterwards presenting him before the steward, who administered the oath of office. Brereton challenged this system of election by claiming to have been legally elected as mayor, and accusing Savage and his deputy steward of refusing to tender the mayoral oath to him. The Queen appointed commissioners to look into the matter, and each side called numerous witnesses who all appealed, vaguely enough, to 'our ancient charters' and to the customary procedure 'during the memory of man'. Apparently no one in Congleton had a clear picture of what Henry de Lacy's charter meant in practice, now that the court leet had become a borough rather than a manorial court.[72]

To Savage's accusations that Brereton had brought some 40 of his followers, including the 'meanest sort of burgesses', with him, and carried out the so-called election in the absence of the steward and of James Rode, the outgoing mayor, the defendant's witnesses alleged that Rode, an adherent of Savage, had left the court, taking some of the aldermen with him, and refusing to accept responsibility for anything further that might happen there. Those remaining in the hall then carried on with the election, Brereton being chosen despite his own nomination of Sir Edward Fitton. Since no responsible person was present to administer the oath, the Brereton faction came to the succeeding court, where Fitton presented Sir William as mayor. On the deputy steward's refusal to swear him, Brereton or Fitton (witnesses' stories differ as to which) persuaded the bailiff, John Smith, one of their supporters throughout, to do so. During these proceedings, a duchy of Lancaster injunction[73] was handed to Brereton, forbidding him in the Queen's name to 'meddle any further' with the mayoralty, but he 'put it into his bosom' unread, according to his deposition 'thinking and supposing it had been a process to appear'. However, after taking the oath he discovered his mistake, and urged the deputy steward to proceed to a new election. The harassed deputy played for safety by declaring that he could not find enough burgesses to form a jury, and adjourning the court, despite claims by the opposing faction that there were 30 or 40 qualified persons present. This left the borough in administrative confusion, since Brereton had not been confirmed as mayor by Savage (who apparently wanted James Rode re-elected) and no further election had taken place.

Following the commissioners' report, the duchy court gave judgment that, in future, resident burgesses only were to choose one of themselves as mayor, to whom the steward of Halton or his deputy should administer the oath. A mayor was to live in the town for his whole period of office, the chancellor and court of the duchy to be arbitrators in any case of absence leading to local complaints. The steward was to continue to preside at the court leet and court baron. The final sentence of the judgment stated that nothing in the court order was to be interpreted as prejudicial to the steward's 'lawful liberty or privilege', so long as he exercised his powers in accordance with 'the liberties and privileges contained within the charter' of Henry de Lacy.

Since this seems to beg the whole question of exactly what the town's privileges were, it is not surprising that many later sixteenth-century cases of conflicting claims between stewards or the duchy's manorial bailiffs, and the corporation, came before the duchy courts.[74]

Witnesses in the Marian suit gave such contradictory evidence that it is not easy to discover what actually happened. However, it seems obvious that though Brereton (whose election was finally disallowed) had unconstitutionally taken matters into his own hands, he had received strong support from a body of townsmen who found Savage's abuse of his position intolerable. Evidence that as steward Sir John had continually chosen his closest followers as 'triers' to empanel the jury for the election was borne out by extracts from the court rolls or assembly books, and there is no doubt that during his period of office there had been considerable corruption.

At all events a step towards greater freedom from the duchy was taken in 1584 when a charter granted by Elizabeth I reconstructed the ruling body of Congleton, making it much more independent than it had been before. The corporation, established as the 'mayor and commonalty', was to be self-perpetuating and to have the right to own and grant property, to plead and be impleaded, to make by-laws and to enforce them, and to have a common seal.[75] Congleton's freedom from duchy control was thus increased. In the following year the right of Congleton traders to exemption from toll in all markets and fairs in England was confirmed.[76]

James I's charter of 1625, however, established in detail the borough constitution which was to serve until 1835,[77] in particular reducing the power of the steward and turning him from a duchy into a borough official.

The charter declared Congleton 'for ever a free borough of itself', with a body corporate composed of the mayor, eight aldermen and sixteen capital burgesses—these last to be chosen by the mayor and aldermen, for life or good conduct: aldermanic vacancies were to be filled from their number. A high steward, 'a person of high repute and special eminence', was to be elected by the corporation, after the death of Sir Thomas Savage, named in the charter as the first holder of the office, and of his son and heir Sir John Savage, who was to succeed him. Later high stewards during the seventeenth century included other members of the Savage family, Earl Rivers, and the lawyer and regicide, John Bradshaw.

Among the other town officials were two serjeants. The first, who received an annual fee of 26s 8d, was appointed by the serving mayor, and was responsible among other things for the town gaol, while the second, generally called the catchpole, who served writs and processes, was nominated by the whole corporation: he does not appear to have been paid regular wages. There was also a constable, and four overseers (not to be confused with the overseers of the poor), who seem to have been mainly in charge of financial matters. At least from the mid-seventeenth century, each of them supervised the drawing up of the mill accounts for one quarter of the year.

Several other officials received regular salaries. Those of the minister and schoolmaster are not always easy to calculate, since the positions were sometimes held jointly and sometimes by separate men: qualifications and relative scarcity value may explain apparent variations in stipend. In 1595, 'Mr. Broster, minister and schoolmaster', received £3 6s 8d a quarter, but in the early years of Charles II's reign the schoolmaster alone was paid £4 for the same length of time, and the minister about £6 5s. The schoolmaster could theoretically expect £16 a year, but in practice, since this sum was the produce of burgages and lands bequeathed by benefactors to the school, the corporation as trustees frequently absorbed the rents, paying the schoolmaster what they pleased. Shortage of borough funds often forced ministers and teachers to accept payment partially in corn, or by cash instalments. 'Part of his last quarterage' is a frequent entry in the town accounts.[78] Lawyers—the recorder and from time to time an additional legal counsel—received 10s a quarter, the payment being occasionally noted as a 'retaining fee'. The town clerk in the 1580s was paid 6s 8d a quarter, but by the end of Elizabeth's reign this sometimes rose to £2 a year.[79]

Contemporary records have references to minor officials, such as the clerk of the mills, who wrote down details of corn sales by the two mill reeves; ale-tasters; 'old John Stubs', who in 1666 received 5s as 'his Lady Day quarter' wage for mending the streets; and the 'sow-gawter' (i.e. perhaps muzzler), whose domestic circumstances in 1661 make sad reading:

Given by consent to the sow-gawter's wife and two children to seek her husband and trouble the town no more—*2s 6d.*

and immediately below:

Paid the sow-gawter's wife to inter her child—*2s 6d.*

The paternalism of Congleton authorities covered every side of town life, from the inspection of raw materials and articles manufactured or sold, to the enforcement of church attendance, and the licensing of alehouses. Conditions of apprenticeship proved a constant source of trouble, as elsewhere in England, at a time when the whole system was breaking down. Public health regulations included regular inspection of the wells and ponds (one at the end of Lawton Street and two others known as Stockwell and 'Valow's Well') and exhortations to householders to clean the streets before their homes every Saturday evening 'unto the crest or middle of the pavement'. A curfew for servants and all young people came into force at nine in the evening. In addition to fines, and imprisonment in the 'cage' or in the town gaol, punishments were the barbarous ones of the period. Scolds had to wear an iron bridle, and were ducked sitting in the cuckstool: other offenders were stocked, pilloried or whipped through the streets before being taken to the house of correction. The process of law could prove expensive, as for example, in the case of John Foxe, whose crime in 1637 is not specified. Two men received 12*s* 4*d* for watching him 'in his cave' (i.e. probably, 'cage') for four days and five nights; a 'cabin' for him cost 1*s* 4*d*; there were payments of 5*s* for bringing him to the house of correction, smaller sums to the boy who whipped him, and for the use of a horse to tie him to; while sixpenny-worth of powder and shot were provided 'when John Foxe was tended upon the heath, for to prevent further danger'. Added to this was a bill of 1*s* 3*d* for his food while in the serjeant's custody, making over £1 spent on one man's case—and this at a time when the surplus from the mill accounts for the year was little more than £15.[80]

Most of the regular taxes in the borough were paid apparently by special assessment of the burgesses, but the constable, who collected the money, often needed a grant from the town chest to make up the sum required. The terms 'king's rent' (or during the Commonwealth, 'state's rent'), the 'town's rent' and 'rent of the mills' are used frequently in the accounts without further definition, the amounts varying considerably from time to time. The first was probably part of the fee farm, the mill rent being the 26*s* 8*d* levied from the fifteenth century for the use of the mills.[81] A legal case of about 1582–4, concerning the borough's rights to the lands known as Brownswolds and Bye-flat or Byfleet, mentions the rent payable to the Crown bailiff for these, for the town wood, fishing privileges in the river Dane and the alnage of cloth in the borough.

The income entered in the borough accounts for the six-teenth and seventeenth centuries came in large measure from the profits of the corn mills. Not only did Henry VIII in 1521 forbid anyone to erect any other mill 'within the lordship of Congleton', or to grind on any part of the stream there, but the inhabitants were also compelled to grind corn solely at the town mills: the main duty of the two mill reeves was to enforce this rule. Fines for disobedience were relatively heavy: in 1682 Thomas Oakes had to pay 2*s* for offending against the regula-tion. In average years the mill profits amounted to between £25 and £35 a quarter, but there were recurrent bad periods; for example in 1598–9 the annual receipts were under £60, while during the second quarter of 1676–7 only £16 5*s* 7*d* was collected. In 1684, however, one quarter alone showed a profit of nearly £47.[82]

The account books sometimes show additional sources of revenue to the profits of the mills. One such, rents paid to the corporation, is difficult to define in detail. It was never a very satisfactory source during this period. The highest annual sum shown (in 1612) was only £29, and sometimes receipts for rents came to under £3 a quarter.[83] The dues were notoriously diffi-cult to collect: 'and no town's rent hath been received at all', reads a note for the last quarter of 1631. Profits from the three medieval fairs were officially retained by the duchy of Lan-caster, but those of another (apparently introduced by the 1625 charter), 'Goodit' or Good Tide fair on the Thursday before Shrovetide, were allowed to the borough. The tolls from this often reached £3 or £4. The 1658–9 figures break down the amounts collected in toll at the fair:

Taken at the great bridge	—	17*s* 4*d*
At Milstreet end	—	2*s* 9*d*
At Waystreet	— £1	10*s* 7*d*
At Westreet end	—	18*s* 0½*d*

At the stalls	—	4*s* 4½*d*
At Maude (Moody?) Street and Cros(s)e	—	13*s* 1*d*

Out of this total of £4 6*s* 2*d*, twelve toll-gatherers were paid 8*d* each.[84]

Another source of revenue was the making of freemen, a privilege which the town authorities guarded strictly, keeping a virtual monopoly of trade in the hands of the leading inhabitants by charging 'foreigners', especially merchants and craftsmen, high entrance fees. The mayor seems to have had a limited right of granting freedom free of charge, but the corporation sometimes raised large sums by making freemen; for example in 1670–1 Joseph Bickerton (presumably a 'foreigner') was charged £1, but a local man, Robert Knight, only 1*s* 6*d*. This is the lowest amount shown, but as much as £10 was occasionally exacted.[85] An average charge to local people was between 2*s* 6*d* and 7*s* 6*d*. As was normal at the time only freemen could exercise a craft or keep a shop in the town.[86]

Congleton's accounts at this period do not suggest public affluence. In the financial year 1617–18, for example, the town received a little over £101 from mill profits, and apparently only an additional £42 from other sources. Disbursements came to over £25 more than this. The position was probably that if conditions were normal, dues regularly paid and accounts carefully kept, the borough coffers might show a respectable balance at Michaelmas, the end of the mayoral year. But disasters such as an outbreak of plague or an exceptionally hard winter, a national crisis such as the Civil War, or unusual local expenditure on law suits or town buildings, might produce such a substantial deficit that the borough authorities had to borrow at high interest from wealthy Congleton citizens like the Parnell family. The general financial stringency led to close scrutiny of the accounts, even small sums being queried in the assembly: and base money (from which the town seems to have suffered especially during the Civil War period) was noted as a significant loss:

> Lost in receiving coarse twopences for the trained soldiers — 7*s* 6*d*
> Mistaking a brass half-crown — 2*s* 6*d*

During the year 1646–7, 'clipt money' was apparently blamed for a total loss of between £2 and £3.[87]

Congleton and National Events

During the Tudor reigns the inhabitants of Congleton were apparently not seriously involved in national events, though some of them may have been employed, as militia men, in the suppression of the pretenders, Lambert Simnel and Perkin Warbeck, and of the later Pilgrimage of Grace. Happily for the town, however, no large-scale hostilities took place in the immediate neighbourhood. Again, the dissolution of the monasteries seems to have had no direct effect on the borough, the constitutional position of which, complicated though it might be, was not aggravated by difficulties over monastic property. The northern rebels of 1569 were put down before the rising had time to spread to Cheshire, while the peaceful accession of James I involved no trouble with Ireland, Scotland or North Wales—fighting in any of which might have affected Congleton, lying as it did on the main London to Lancashire road.

This comparative isolation from major national problems, however, ended abruptly in the reign of Charles I.[88] The year 1642 was a miserable one for the town. Before the serious outbreak of plague was over, the Civil War had begun, and with Chester holding out as a leading Royalist stronghold, Congleton's geographical position necessarily involved it in the struggle. It has been pointed out that 'what with the quarrelling soldiery, raids on provision, and demands for money, the little borough was almost driven to its last extremity'.[89] Local disturbances began almost at once. Between August 1642 and the end of the year, the town authorities had to pay watchmen 'for their care in quieting the soldiers' and for 'watching the unruly night when the soldiers would have mutinied'. Congleton, where a strong section of the corporation supported Parliament, got into trouble over an early Royalist demand for troops from Cheshire towns. A significant entry in the town accounts reads: 'Given a boy to hold our horses, until we had excused ourselves to the Earl of Derby in sending him no men—2*d*.'

The headquarters of the anti-Royalist forces in Cheshire were at Nantwich, and there was a good deal of desultory fighting in the district from the autumn of 1642. The Parliamentary commander, Sir William Brereton of Handforth, raised money and troops in London, and on 28 January 1643 passed through

Congleton on his way to defend Nantwich against a threatened attack by Sir Thomas Aston's forces. In the spring Prince Rupert advanced to take Nantwich and relieve the hard-pressed garrison at Chester, but after his victory at Lichfield in April he was summoned south by the King, and an uneasy balance of forces remained in Cheshire, Brereton's attempts to reduce Chester and the Royalist commanders' efforts against Nantwich all proving unsuccessful. In November the arrival of Irish troops to join Sir John Byron at Chester put Nantwich in considerable danger, but in January 1644 Sir Thomas Fairfax marched across Delamere Forest in severe frost and snow, joined Brereton and completely defeated the Royalists who were besieging Nantwich. Later that year the battle of Marston Moor was a crushing blow to the King's cause in the north, and though Rupert relieved Beeston Castle in March 1645, a rising in Herefordshire made it impossible for him to reach Chester as he had planned. In September, three months after his final major defeat at Naseby, Charles entered Chester with over 300 horses, but the Parliamentary victory over Sir Marmaduke Langdale at Rowton Heath immediately afterwards deprived the city of all hope of relief, and it surrendered to Brereton in February 1646. Even after this, mopping up operations continued until the end of the year, when Beeston and Lathom House were taken.

During the four years of fighting in Cheshire, the Congleton corporation had its own factional disputes. John Bradshaw, who might have been strong enough to hold the town firmly to the side of Parliament, had shut up his Congleton house, probably in August 1642, and moved to London, leaving two groups of local families to quarrel over borough policy in the almost impossible situation created by the war.[90] Three succeeding mayors (William Knight, John Walker and George Ford), who held office between 1639 and Michaelmas 1642, were strong Royalists, later forced by Parliament to compound for their property as 'delinquents'. John Henshaw, elected soon after the war began, was a supporter of Parliament, but in the following autumn George Ford succeeded him for a second term. However, after this a strong Parliamentary group, led by the brothers Tobias and Richard Parnell, with the town clerk, Jonathan Walley, seems to have controlled Congleton until the fighting was over, though the Cheshire composition papers show that there was still strong Royalist feeling in the borough. John Walker, a skinner by trade, 'did join with the enemy at their *rendezvous* on Knottesford (Knutsford) Heath, and bore arms for them, and was conductor of a company of soldiers there. He ... did at several other times join with the enemy in association and bore arms in Congleton for them, and was one prime occasion of raising a company in Congleton aforesaid for the enemy when Namptwich was besieged.'[91]

The number of the corporation who supported the King was mentioned in 1657 during one of the perennial law suits with Macclesfield about tolls, a witness stating inaccurately that 'the magistrates of Congleton have been for the King',[92] while those of Macclesfield had consistently supported the Parliament. At one time, if witnesses can be believed, Macclesfield men— apparently soldiers quartered in Congleton—had taken the mayor prisoner, and rifled the study of William Drakeford, 'an eminent professor, clerk, and a gentleman of great employment in Congleton, who had many writings and records' about the borough's privileges 'for the most part in his custody and keeping, which were all taken away by the men of Macclesfield'.

Congleton suffered heavily from the extra taxation levied by Charles I and later by Parliament. Demands for ship money (in 1635, £40), and other levies added seriously to the difficulty of balancing town accounts, and sometimes there was open opposition to the exactions. In 1647 the mayor had to disburse £2 2s from the town box 'for quartering of Colonel Jones's troop which was too short, which the outburgesses and some other townsmen would not pay'. Later in the same year the constables were granted 'by consent' £1 'to make up a lay (i.e. levy) to prevent the soldiers coming'. This was not the only amount paid to persuade officers to quarter elsewhere: the largest sum noted for this purpose was in August 1647, when a quartermaster was bribed with £2 to take his men on to New-castle-under-Lyme.

Constant demands for supplies of food or weapons were also an embarrassment. Late in 1642 over £2 worth of beer and bread was sent to Byron, the Royalist commander at Chester, who had served the town with a warrant for '20 pounds' load or thereabouts of provision for his soldiers.[93] Nantwich had to be supplied locally, as far as possible (in 1643 Congleton gave £1 13s 9d for 21 measures of oats sent there), but by October

1645 Brereton was writing urgently to the Parliamentary Committee of Both Kingdoms: 'For provision this county is wholly exhausted, as may appear by the commissary's letter, no supply being as yet afforded us from any of the neighbouring counties.'

Both sides claimed the services of local levies. A quantity of 'points, loaves and beer' bought off a Royalist demand for the 'appearance of all our able men to Northwich, to do service at the works'. But Brereton's troop requirements were heavy, and Congleton had somehow to find and equip men from the town to meet her obligations—at one time six at 8*d* a day for service at Nantwich alone. Parliamentary victories produced yet another problem. Congleton was one of the towns where, as Brereton told the Speaker of the House of Commons, 'we are constrained to command the country to guard and secure prisoners, of which trouble and charge it is humbly desired this country may be eased as soon as may be conveniently'.[94] Billeting of troops, which throughout the Civil War period had been a crippling expense, reached appalling proportions in 1645 and the following year, with prisoners from one after another Royalist stronghold swelling the total. In less than three months of 1646 the borough paid out over £5 for quartering alone, in addition to the equipping of their own local troops and the food and weapons needed for other parts of the county. Even in the following year, with the main fighting over, more than a third of the balance from the mill accounts in the town chest was disbursed for billeting.

The economic dislocation caused during the war years by the vast, though temporary, increase in the population of Cheshire was reflected for some time in higher prices. In April 1648 Tobias Parnell asked for £1 expenses for two days at the assizes on town business since, 'the assizes being at Nantwich, horse and man's meat were at unreasonable rates'. The corporation had also to cope with a number of *ad hoc* orders from the sequestrators, while at the Restoration the notorious parliamentary and republican bias of the town authorities during the later Civil War years laid the borough open to new economic and political demands. The wording of the town mace, inscribed in 1651—'the Freedome of England by God's Blessing Restored'—was ten years later hastily altered by the addition of 'to' before the original words, and of 'C.R. 1661' after them, a change which cost the town £3. This silver-gilt mace is still in use.[95]

It is unlikely that the alteration was approved by the original donor of the mace, the uncompromising Parliamentarian Richard Parnell, who refused to take the oath of allegiance to Charles II. His family first became prominent in the town during the sixteenth century, and in the Civil War period, as happened elsewhere in Cheshire, supported different sides. The first Parnell known to have lived in Congleton, another Richard, was a mercer of Henry VIII's reign.[96] His eldest son, William, a London wax-chandler whose will provided for the dole of money and bread to the Congleton poor, died in 1622, leaving his property in the borough to a younger brother, Thomas, who was resident there and had been elected mayor in 1620. Thomas had four sons, the eldest of whom, William, forfeited all his estates as a Royalist, dying without children in 1646: but the land remained in the family, as it was granted to his brother Tobias, the Puritan alderman, who practised as an apothecary in Congleton. The third brother, Thomas, began as a Royalist, wavered and changed sides, but Tobias was strongly supported throughout by the youngest of the four, Richard (mayor, 1647–8), who presented the borough with its mace. After the Restoration little is known of Richard. Though he had property in Congleton, it is possible that he ceased to live there: he was noted as 'disclaimed' in the 1664 heraldic visitation of Cheshire. However, this is not conclusive evidence. Like many Puritans, he may have considered heraldry 'worldly pomp', and either refused to acknowledge the arms to which his family laid claim, or simply avoided the heralds.[97]

Perhaps the most outstanding seventeenth-century Parnell was Tobias's eldest son, Thomas—a confusingly common Christian name in the family: there were at least six, possibly seven, living at the time. This Thomas, born at Congleton in 1625, was sent to study as a clerk under his father's friend, John Bradshaw, the regicide—probably Congleton's most famous citizen. Bradshaw (whose immediate ancestors came from Marple and Wibersley Halls, Cheshire), had been called to the bar in 1627; he had formerly served for several years in an attorney's office at Congleton. A well-known lawyer in the district, he was elected mayor in 1637, and a few years later became high steward, holding the office until, after a corporation dispute, he resigned in May 1656. Another quarrel broke out over his refusal to surrender the court records and other books, and the borough authorities had to threaten legal action. He had long ceased to live regularly in Congleton: by 1643 he was settled in Basinghall Street, London, with young Thomas Parnell as one of his secretaries.[98]

For the next sixteen years Parnell remained attached to his master, whose career fluctuated with changing governments. Bradshaw returned for a time to his native county in 1647, on his appointment as chief justice of Chester. The war had seriously interfered with the holding of the grand sessions there, but in August 1648 Bradshaw wrote to the mayor of Chester, promising to resume the practice, but to further the city's welfare only so long as the inhabitants carried out Parliament's instructions. After his rise to national importance as president of the court which tried Charles I, he became not only president of the Council of State, but (in July 1649) attorney-general of Cheshire and North Wales and chancellor of the duchy of Lancaster—offices which brought him once more into close touch with Congleton's affairs. Early in 1653 his courage in opposing Cromwell's dissolution of Parliament and the Council of State earned him the Protector's hostility, which was shown in the successful campaign of 1656 to prevent his election to Parliament for the county of Cheshire. Tobias Bridge (or Bridges), Cromwell's major-general for the county, was particularly active against him, and Congleton, where he had recently resigned his stewardship, was presumably one of the towns where the county voters, the 40s freeholders, were subjected to anti-Bradshaw propaganda. Local criticism of Bradshaw had been expressed at an earlier parliamentary election. In November 1645, when he stood as burgess for Newcastle-under-Lyme, a certain Christopher Tomkinson, asked how he would give his vote, was reported as saying, 'Not with Mr. Bradshaw by any means, for I hold Mr. Terrick to be the honester man.' His grounds for this opinion were that 'when Sir Francis Wortley came to Congleton with prisoners', including a relative of Tomkinson's, 'Mr. Bradshaw counselled him "not to part with [them?] without money, for they were able men", and it endangered his kinsman's life'. During the 1645 election campaign Sir William Brereton had strongly supported Bradshaw, condemning 'such labouring and anticipating of voices as did much corrupt the election', and pointing out that the accused was in London at the time when rumour claimed that he had 'joined and advised' the Royalist, Wortley. But by 1656 Bradshaw had antagonized authority, and Cromwell even tried unsuccessfully to deprive him of the attorney-generalship at Chester. Under Richard Cromwell, however, he regained some of his lost influence, dying in October 1659, fortunately for himself, before the Restoration.

In May 1660 Thomas Parnell, in a highly dangerous position as the former servant of a regicide, sued out a pardon,[99] and soon afterwards went to Ireland. There is apparently no record of his returning to England, but he still owned his Congleton property: this was probably managed for him by his brother Tobias, who had taken over their father's business as an apothecary, and was living in the old family house in the town. Thomas, after a distinguished career in Dublin, died in 1685, leaving four children, including a son, John, who became a judge, and was the direct ancestor of the present Lord Congleton.

The year in which Thomas Parnell died was that of James II's accession. The Congleton bells were rung for the new reign and for the birth of a prince (the Old Pretender) in 1688,[100] but the corporation seems to have transferred its loyalty to William and Mary without serious internal faction. Perhaps there were regrets in the town at the execution of the Duke of Monmouth, who had visited Congleton—apparently its only even semi-royal visitor during this period—in 1682, and been lavishly entertained there.[101]

Notes

1 The introductory paragraphs of this chapter are by J. C. Jones. They are based, except where otherwise indicated, on borough accounts, order books and charters (all in Congleton town hall), and DL 29.
2 Astbury Churchwarden's accounts.
3 W. Camden, *Britannia*, ed. Gough, ii. 425.
4 R. Blome, *Britannia* (1673 edn.), 57.
5 Cf. W. G. Hoskins, *Local History in England* (1959), 145.
6 B.M., Harl. MS. 594, fol. 99. It is not clear whether the 16 are included in the 853. The accuracy of this return is doubtful: cf. W. B. Stephens (ed.), *V.C.H. Warwickshire*, viii (1969), 5.
7 E 179/244/30.
8 E 179/86/150. Total given is 348, but on addition appears to be 349.
9 Head, 173–5.

a Nos. 1–3 The Vale, *b* no. 43 Lawton Street

a

b

a

b

[10] Borough Order Bk., 1544–1699, 63. Subsequent citations of Borough Order Bk. refer to this vol.

[11] E 179/85/19; 85/27; 85/75.

[12] C.R.O., Inventory and expense account.

[13] Tax returns and assessments other than those already cited include: E 179/85/10; 85/57; 85/64; 85/66; 85/99; 85/128.

[14] *Ibid.*, 244/30. Among those paying at 10s and above is a 'doctor of physick' rated on rank and not income.

[15] Head, 25.

[16] *Ibid.*, 51n, 87, 109; E 179/86/150.

[17] Head, 108–9.

[18] C.R.O., Inventory.

[19] Head, 178.

[20] *Ibid.*, 87.

[21] *Ibid.*, 51, 88.

[22] Borough Order Bk., 308.

[23] Head, 51n, 82, 108, 115.

[24] C.R.O., Will and inventory of George Ford.

[25] Head, 80. There was a mayor of this name, perhaps his father, in 1610–11 and 1611–12, and several other men of the same name lived in the town. Wm. Drakesford, husbandman, who died in 1671 (C.R.O., Will and Inventory) was probably not the same man.

[26] Head, 230.

[27] Borough Order Bk., 312. Perhaps, however, the mayors were father and son.

[28] Head, 80.

[29] Borough Order Bk., 308.

[30] *Ibid.*, 318.

[31] Head, 51.

[32] Said to be 'of Sandbach'.

[33] Borough Order Bk., 259; Head, 80.

[34] C.R.O., Will and inventory.

[35] E 179/86/50.

[36] Cf. *ibid.*, 86/152 which makes this clear.

[37] Not named in the return, but Roger Kent, the taxpayer listed for 7 hearths, was innkeeper there: Head, 106.

[38] C.R.O., Inventory of Thomas Roe.

[39] E 179/86/155. Four more were recorded in 1674.

[40] *Ibid.*, 85/64; 85/99; 85/128.

[41] C.R.O., Wills and inventories.

[42] Borough Order Bk., 331.

[43] Head, 83.

[44] *Ibid.*, 120.

[45] Borough Order Bk., 83, 90.

[46] *Ibid.*, 309, 323; Head, 241.

[47] P.C.C., Wills, 1654 (300).

[48] Borough Order Bk., 320.

[49] P.C.C., Will, Alchin 300.

[50] Borough Order Bk., 330.

G

51 Borough Order Bk., 321.
52 Blome, *op. cit.*, 57. Points were ties of leather used by men and women to fasten clothes. They were later superseded by buttons.
53 Comprising: 15 shoemakers, 9 tanners, 4 pointers, 7 glovers, 2 curriers, 2 pursemakers, 1 lastmaker.
54 Borough Order Bk., 319–22.
55 *Ibid.*, 87.
56 See p. 41.
57 Jnl. of Wilbraham family, *penes* Sir Randle Baker Wilbraham.
58 Head, 167–9, 182–3; Borough accounts, *passim*.
59 C.R.O., Wills and Inventories.
60 Based on E 179/244/30; 86/145; 86/158. In 1664 Macclesfield paid £21.
61 C.R.O., Wills and inventories.
62 Borough accounts for these years. Unless otherwise stated, information in the following paragraphs is based on these accounts, and Head.
63 DL 30/10/121; Borough Order Bk., 249 ff.
64 B.M., Harl. MS. 2090, fols. 22, 34–6; Head, 71–5.
65 *Cheshire Sheaf*, ii, 36.
66 Head, 36–7; DL 1 *passim* (e.g. 129/G7; 133/G5; 136/G10; 137/R4); Davis, *Macclesfield*, passim.
67 For the subsequent descent of the manor from the barons of Halton to the Shakerleys, see Head, 24–6.
68 *Ibid.*, 45.
69 Borough Order Bk., 1589.
70 Head, 47.
71 The term 'aldermen' is used throughout the case. Though the charter of 1625 was, apparently, the first officially to appoint aldermen, Camden (*Britannia*, 1586 edn.) uses the term and it was evidently in general currency.
72 DL 1/15/R1; 3/67/S5; B.M., Harl. MSS. 844, fols. 7–8; 2074, fols. 119–21.
73 DL 42/96, fol. 81.
74 E.g. DL 1/115/A8; 124/A11; DL 3/27/R2.
75 Head, 36–7.
76 *Ibid.*, 37.
77 B.M., Stowe MS. 796.
78 Head, 237; Borough Accounts, 1595 ff.
79 Borough accounts, 1584–9 *passim*.
80 *Ibid.*, 1636–7, 1645–6 to 1653–4, 1657–8, 1660–1; Yates, 22 ff; Borough Order Bk., 80–2.
81 Head, 37, and see p. 32 above.
82 Borough accounts, *passim*; Borough order Bk. 1592.
83 Borough accounts, 1590.
84 *Ibid.*, 1658–9.
85 Borough Order Bk., 1696.
86 *Ibid.*, 1690; Head, 55.
87 Borough accounts, 1617–47 *passim*.
88 Professor A. M. Everitt was kind enough to read a draft of this section.
89 Head, 89.

⁹⁰ *Ibid.*
⁹¹ *Ibid.*, 88.
⁹² *Ibid.*
⁹³ B.M., Add. MS. 11332, fol. 35.
⁹⁴ *Ibid.*, fol. 59.
⁹⁵ The mace has been displayed at Goldsmiths' Hall and photos are in the guide book to the Palace of Westminster, and in this volume.
⁹⁶ Y. Parnell, 'The Parnell Family' (T/S *penes* the author), 4, 39.
⁹⁷ *Ibid.*, 5,15.
⁹⁸ *D.N.B.*; *Gentleman's Magazine*, lxxxviii (1), 328; Parnell, 'Parnell Family', 25-6.
⁹⁹ Original among Lord Congleton's papers, at time of writing.
¹⁰⁰ Borough accounts, 1685, 1688.
¹⁰¹ *Cal. S.P. Dom. 1682*, 416, 423.

IV *Local Government and Politics since 1700*[1]

by W H Semper

Before the Municipal Corporations Act of 1835

Throughout the eighteenth century, and until the passing of the Municipal Corporations Act of 1835, Congleton was administered under the terms of the charter of 1625. The corporation consisted of the mayor, eight aldermen (including the mayor), and sixteen capital burgesses (or councillors). The mayor was elected at the common hall of the 'Mayor, Aldermen and Capital Burgesses and Freemen', held each Michaelmas (29 September). This was often a formality, though a contest occasionally happened, as in 1724–5, when Thomas Shaw received 65 votes against the 22 cast for John Barlow (who was elected the next year). Each mayor was a J.P. and two of the aldermen were elected to serve with him. Aldermen served for life, and when one died his successor was elected by the mayor and common council from among the capital burgesses, and another capital burgess was elected, again by the council, from among the freemen, 'to exercise office during his natural life', though both aldermen and capital burgesses were removable by the council 'for some offence or offences, default or defaults by them respectively perpetrated, committed or done'. Mayor, aldermen and capital burgesses were required to take an oath to execute faithfully the duties of their office. The council appointed 'an honest and discreet man to be the common clerk'.

There were four ways in which the freedom of the borough could be gained: by birth, confined to the eldest sons of freemen; by apprenticeship, served within the borough; by purchase;

and by gift of the mayor, who claimed the right to appoint one freeman during his year of office. As the fees for enrolment were a principal source of income of the corporation, the compulsion of tradesmen to take it up appears to have been carried to great lengths. In 1724 there were 223 freemen, a figure which had risen by 1834 to 337 resident freemen and 102 non-resident.[2]

The annual meeting of the common hall also appointed the lesser or petty officers of the corporation, who were sworn in before the mayor to perform their duties faithfully. In 1710, for example, there were appointed: 4 burlimen (i.e. inspectors of those who cut new wood), 4 market lookers (i.e. inspectors), 4 scavengers, a tender of the town wood, 4 lookers of the commons, 4 lookers of the wells (on which the town then relied for its water supply), 4 inmate lookers (whose duty was to prevent unauthorized settlement, lest such persons became a charge on the poor rate), 4 swine catchers, 2 leather sealers, 2 fire lookers, 2 overseers of weights and measures, 2 tolltakers for High Street, Wagg Street, West Street, Town Bridge, and Mill Street. There were in addition a bellman and an ale-taster. In 1723 there was added a dog whipper, for in that year it was decided that 'a pack of hounds shall be from henceforth kept within this borough, and the mayor . . . shall be the master thereof'. Each officer took an oath. The scavengers, for example, were required to swear

carefully and diligently to your power oversee weekly, and every week and especially against Sundays that all the streets in this town be swept and made clean and the muck and filth carried away out of the streets that the same be no annoyance unto the passengers. You shall from time to time for this year now in being and to come . . . give warning to the inhabitants in general of this Borough that they and every of them duly sweep and keep clean such parts of the streets before their houses and liberties as to them do appertain and belong—and to the renters of the sweepings of the other parts of the said streets as belong to them to sweep and keep clean under an Order or Bye-Law of the Corporation, and that each and every of them do remove and carry away with as little delay as possible all the Muck Dirt and Filth so swept and collected together—and likewise that you do, at every assembly or meeting of the Mayor, Aldermen and Burgesses of this Town . . . present the Names of all . . . as upon your appointment and warning do not or will not sweep and keep clean the Streets or carry away the Dirt and Sweepings thereof—So help you God.[3]

By the early nineteenth century a local police force existed. Four constables were 'appointed at the latter court leet in December, by the jury'. The mayor's serjeant-at-mace, one special constable and two beadles were also sworn in as peace officers, and six watchmen were appointed under the provisions of a general Act for lighting and watching. In the 1830s this force was found to be 'sufficient, under ordinary circumstances, for the preservation of peace within the borough'.[4]

Apart from fees for admission to freedom, the corporation's income included the profit from the corn mill, for all corn had to be ground there. The following is a balance sheet for a quarter in 1717:

Received	£	s	d
The profits of the Mills the last quarter	30	18	7
Recd. of Mr. Jackson for Tho. Swain's Freedom	2	3	–
Recd. of John Whitehurst his Freedom		10	–
	33	11	7

Expended	£	s	d
Paid the parson his sallary	6	5	–
Paid the Schoolmaster's sallary	4	–	–
Paid Millreeve's sallary		2	6
Paid Clerk's sallary		6	–
Paid Gaoler's sallary		6	–
Paid Thomas Salmon for bread		13	4
Paid the woman for sweeping the church		1	0
Paid Joseph Hackney for bread		12	6
Pd. Matthew Bell for work 7 days and ½ at 2–6, and for other work 3.0.	1	1	9
Pd. Wm. Foden for 4 days work at 2–6		10	0
Given the Poor		5	0
Pd. Mr. Jackson his expenses to Thornicroft and over to Sandbach		2	0
Pd. John Whitehurst his Bill		18	0
	15	3	1
In purse	£18	8	6

The emolument attached to the office of mayor was not very large, and in 1725 he was allowed the tolls of Shrovetide Fair 'towards carrying off the said office of Mayor decently'. As the century wore on a definite sum was fixed, and by 1834 this had risen to £25 10s, 'with eight loads (or 48 bushels) of malt, and an ancient reserved mill-rent of 20s per annum. Upon going out of office, he entertains the corporation and freemen, and the malt is allowed for furnishing ale to the freemen, and at the dinner. About 25 corporators and 200 freemen commonly partake of this hospitality, the cost of which always exceeds the emoluments of the office.'

It is not surprising that office and even freedom were not always sought after. In 1757 it was reported that inhabitants and tradesmen were increasingly making excuses to avoid being made freemen, and freemen excuses to avoid becoming capital burgesses; and capital burgesses were attempting to avoid being made aldermen, and aldermen to avoid becoming mayor or J.P.s. Consequently there was great danger of a want of proper persons to execute these offices. A scale of fines for refusal to accept office or take up freedom was therefore imposed. Refusal to be made mayor bore the penalty of £10, to be made J.P. £5, alderman 13*s* 4*d* a month, capital burgess 6*s* 8*d* a month, and failure to become free 3*s* 4*d* a month.

In 1814, however, it was reported that the average number of new freemen per year for the previous 40 years was only nine.[5] In 1824 the fines for not taking office or freedom were increased to £50, £20, £2 10*s* monthly, £1 5*s* monthly and 12*s* 6*d* monthly. This was a common enough situation, and there was in fact no breakdown of administration.

In an age when a large percentage of the population lived on or below the bread line much of the business of public administration concerned the problems of the poor. The Elizabethan poor law had made it the duty of each parish to support its own poor; and the Settlement Act of 1662 empowered the removal to their parish of legal settlement of persons likely to become a charge to the town. In 1730 the council decided to convert the old Lower Chapel into a workhouse, 'and that the Mill Backside together with the Byflatt shall be enclosed and appropriated to the inhabitants of the said Workhouse'. It was on this workhouse garden that in 1752 John Clayton was empowered to erect the first silk mill in Congleton, but he had to give security that his workmen from other towns and parishes 'shall not gain settlements by his services'. That is to say he had to guarantee that they would not become a burden to the poor rate. Nevertheless the industrial revolution in Congleton did accentuate the problems of poverty for in days of short-time working and unemployment, the relief of the poor became a heavy burden on the better-off inhabitants. Workhouse children were thus indentured as apprentices in the factories allegedly to be taught the trade and 'to receive a shilling every Christmas and sufficient meat, drink, apparel, lodging, washing and all things necessary and fit for an apprentice'.[6] In 1771 there is record of Congleton paying the Warwick authorities money to avoid having a pauper returned to Congleton under the Settlement laws.[7]

Yet by 1820 it could be reported that the money collected on the poor rates had increased more than tenfold since 1750, when it amounted to £300. In 1758 it was said to be about £500. This great increase coincided with the advent of the silk industry and resulted from an influx of poor seeking employment in the mills but not earning sufficient to support themselves.[8] The average amount paid for poor rate for the years 1783, 1784 and 1785 was £703 10s.[9]

Philanthropy no doubt played a part in the provision of poor relief. Nevertheless the fear of bread riots was also a consideration. An incident of 1757 illustrates what might happen. Congleton was then the local market for corn, and owing to bad harvests the farmers using the market raised their prices. One Thomas Jackson, of Trent Hay Farm, near Stoke, returned from market and began agitating in Hanley about the dear prices. Hundreds of potters and colliers assembled one Saturday morning and set off on the march to Congleton, gathering recruits on their way through Burslem and Tunstall. As they marched down the hill into the town the inhabitants were alarmed, but the marchers went straight to the market, seized the stocks of corn, and sold it to the dealers at what they considered a fair price. The money was then handed over to the farmers. Some Congleton folk reported that the farmers had more corn in their barns, so most of the Potteries men went off to look for it. The mayor sent for a Captain York who was in the town with a company of soldiers on a recruiting drive. The Riot Act was read, and twelve ringleaders were arrested and put in the town jail. When the mob returned to find their leaders under lock and key it demanded that they should be released, failing which it would go back to the Potteries for reinforcements, return, and storm the town hall. The mayor refused and the mob left through the snow which had begun to fall heavily. Next day, although the way was deep in snow, over one thousand set off to release their comrades. The town hall was prepared for a siege, with guns peeping through the windows. Nothing daunted the determined potters; they marched resolutely on—and the guns were not fired. Instead, there was a mad rush of the defenders through the back door headed, it is said, by aldermen Martin and Clayton. Only the mayor remained at his post, and he released the prisoners. After receiving refreshment from the Congletonians who sympathized with them, the marchers returned home in triumph.[10] Further corn riots, however, took place in 1759.[11]

The French Revolutionary Wars brought further distress in the form of inflation and unemployment. In 1798 the council voted £100 for the war effort, and 12 guineas to the Congleton Volunteer Association. But there were more immediate causes for alarm. In the severe winter of 1795 food prices soared and there was great distress. The council itself gave 5 guineas in January to subscriptions being raised for relief, and in August another 10 guineas was voted. In 1800 £40 was similarly given. This was in addition to private charity and the amount levied by way of poor rate. This latter was very high for a small borough which in 1801 had only 3,861 inhabitants. In the year ending Easter 1803 the poor rate produced £1,385;[12] expenditure was £1,312 for relief of 195 poor in their own homes, and £169 on 17 poor people in the workhouse. In addition 65 children under 5 were relieved and 130 between 5 and 14 years. Sixty-five people over 60 years of age were among those receiving relief. To offset this expenditure pauper children 'employed in Mr. Pattison's silk-house' earned £76.

By then the old Lower Chapel which had served as a workhouse for so long was tumbling down, and the council decided in 1810 to lease ground on Mossley Moss near Park Lane Head and to erect a new workhouse there.

The end of the Napoleonic Wars did not bring prosperity. A general recession in trade affected local industry and there was much poverty, want, unrest and danger of disturbances. A public meeting held at the town hall in February 1817 with the mayor in the chair, deplored 'the present unrest and the inflaming of the minds of the people by doctrines subversive of all civil government', and promised to do 'the utmost in our power to support the judicial authority to the continuance of Loyalty, Morality and true Religion and to maintain tranquillity and public decorum'. This resolution was sent via the Cheshire M.P.s to Sidmouth, the Home Secretary.

The amount raised for the relief of the poor had increased to over £2,000 a year, which seems a large sum for a township of 4,616 inhabitants, but in addition the poor received help from private organizations such as the 'Benevolent Institution for visiting and relieving poor sick persons and married lying-in women at their own Habitations'. In the year ended August 1819, this society visited and relieved 347 individuals. The 'total number of visits to the abodes of sickness and poverty being upwards of 1,500; and the money thus distributed amounting to £86'.[13] There were, in addition, seven sick clubs, or friendly societies. Congleton was not engrossed entirely with its own distress, however, for in 1805 the council made a donation of £10 to Lloyds Coffee House national fund for the families of deceased servicemen.

Yet it was the regular poor rate which was the mainstay of the poor in times of need. There were always some 20 or 30 permanent paupers on the town books. Such people possibly from old age or sickness could not survive at all without help. By 1820 about 40 people regularly received a pension and 26 asked for help periodically. When the textile trade ran into difficulties many families lost wages and could survive only with poor relief. From 1825 50 paupers claimed a weekly pension, and over 400 asked for casual help. In 1829 there were 540 casual paupers, in 1831–2 561. Poor-relief expenditure rose from £790 in 1828 to £1,520 in 1831–2.[14]

The heavy burden of poor relief no doubt hampered other public enterprises. Nevertheless even during the war years the council did effect some improvements.

In 1784 the old bridge over the Dane, which had fallen into a sad state of disrepair, was pulled down; it was very narrow, and a much wider one capable of taking the wagons of industry was needed. The new bridge was 8 yards wide, 54 yards long, and cost £700.

In 1804 the council decided to build a new town hall and prison and engaged a joiner, John Brown, to build it for the sum of £630. While the work was in progress the council had to hold its meetings in private houses and at various inns, such as the *Golden Lion* and the *Roebuck*.

It was during these war years, too, that steps were taken to widen the narrow streets and then to pave them, and resolutions

such as the following of 21 May 1810 and 11 July 1817 are to
be found in the minutes:

Whereas Mr. John Beckett is now taking down several houses in
Duck Street and adjoining Clay Bank which at the west end of the
said street project very much into the same whereby the same is not
only very narrow and incommodious but also dangerous—It is
unanimously ordered by this assembly that Mr. Beckett and those
interested in the said buildings be applied to and treated with for
the present projecting part to be laid open to the street and also so
much of the other part of the buildings as can be obtained in order
for the widening and improving of the street and greater safety and
accommodation of the public.

It is also ordered that if any person shall hereafter wheel any truck
or wheelbarrow upon any of the flagged or other footways within
this Borough such person shall for every such offence forfeit and pay
to the Mayor for the use of the Corporation the sum of two shillings
and sixpence.

In these war years Mill Street was widened, and Little Street
widened and paved. The inclusion of a small covered market
alongside the 1804 town hall was perhaps prompted by a desire
to lessen congestion in the streets. The four traditional fairs,
Thursday before Shrovetide, 12 May, 13 July, 3 December (by
1888 22 November),[15] no doubt caused great congestion but at
least did not last long. The traditional market, however, was
held every Saturday in the open air of the Market Place and
certainly overflowed into other streets. Farmers and traders set
up wooden stalls to offer foodstuffs and household goods. On
alternate Tuesdays an important cattle market took place. In
1826 the town sought and obtained the right to move the cattle
market from the public street to the market square. The
council was, however, in no position to follow this up for
another generation.

It is evident that the council had overstepped itself in its
activities. To build the new workhouse of 1820 and to defray
the cost of street-widening £150 was borrowed. A new church
bell and the erection of a Sunday school added to expenses.
Rising costs and the fall-off in receipts from the purchase of
freedom (noted above) led to a crisis. In 1814 an investigation
into the borough's finances revealed that the borough's income
was £294, and its expenditure, including interest on a public

debt of £1,170, was £312. The report[16] warned that £300 was needed to pay for further public works already decided on, including the land 'whereon the Malt Kiln stands in Chapel Street so as to widen that street opposite to the Church'.

Twenty years later a royal commision into the government of municipal corporations included Congleton in its investigations. In view of its strictures on the honesty and efficiency of the administration of many boroughs Congleton came off lightly. The commission, reporting in 1834, found that the 'accounts appear to be very regularly kept; but no printing or publication of them in any way takes place. There appears to have been less waste of money in litigation, and more moderation on the part of the law officers of this corporation, than in others of equal revenue. The Charity accounts appear to be kept with great regularity.'[17] The commission outlined the income of the borough. The corporation received money to pay for government in the main from rates levied on all property. The Dane corn mill brought in between £150 and £190 a year. The town wood above the mill brought 'occasional profit to the corporation'. The butchers' stalls in the Shambles and Market House were rented at £118 a year in 1832. In addition the town owned portions of the common and of farmland. The 1798 enclosure award gave certain fields to the corporation for the benefit of the poor and these fields produced £600 rent in 1832. Brownsfold farm of eleven acres yielded £30 rent. Yet the corporation was still in debt, a debt of £6,534 bearing interest of £269. The council had not been deterred by the 1814 report. In 1822 it had paid £740 for land on which Sir Edmund Antrobus built an assembly room at his own expense, while the corporation paid for the erection of a market house.

An era of local government was brought to an end by the subsequent Municipal Corporations Act of 1835 and the Poor Law Amendment Act of 1834. But before turning to these a word about the political side of public life in the eighteenth and early nineteenth-century borough will not be amiss. The division between the dissenters and the Anglicans so evident in the town in the seventeenth century was still strong in the early eighteenth century. At the accession of the first Hanoverian king, George I, in 1714 a trial of strength, joined in the streets, is best described in the words of Yates:

George I was proclaimed, but the Tories would not allow the church bells to be rung. The Whigs, many of whom were Dissenters, on the other hand, rejoiced at the event, and hastened to the church to ring the bells. Some Waggish or mischievous person had secretly tied the fire-bell to one of the other bells, consequently when the merry peal was raised the alarm bell rang also, which occasioned a tumultuous assemblage of the townsmen. On the crowd rushing to the church they found some of the Dissenters busily engaged, on which the Tories buffetted them out of the steeple, and having collected in a large body, they proceeded to the Meeting-house, near the end of Mill-street, where, though the Dissenters made some defence, their opponents finally prevailed, entered the place, which they completely ransacked, carrying away the pulpit and forms to Dane Bridge, where they were destroyed by fire.[18]

The Corporation was always diligent in protecting the rights of the freemen attending the markets and fairs of Cheshire, who by the charter of Henry de Lacy were quit of tolls. In 1729 an agreement was made with Macclesfield for the prevention of future disputes and the preservation of the privileges of the freemen of both towns.

A generation later, in 1745, when the second Jacobite rising included a last attempt to restore the Stuarts, Congleton remained loyal to the house of Hanover. The council in October contributed ten guineas towards the cost of 'raising and paying soldiers within the county of Chester for the defence of his Majesty's person and government'.

Early in December the townsfolk were alarmed by the entry of about 1,300 of the Young Pretender's army, commanded by Lord George Murray. These compelled the mayor to proclaim the Old Pretender King at the market cross. Although they harmed no-one, they billetted themselves freely on the inhabitants, and searched for arms and food before marching away next morning to Leek, receiving no support from the inhabitants of the town.

Other public events of note in this period included the visit of the Prince Regent in 1806. This was the later George IV who in 1826 granted a charter to the borough confirming its privileges. Perhaps even more remarkable than the royal visit, however, were the celebrations which marked the defeat and abdication of Napoleon in 1814. The corporation ordered that 'whereas there are now rejoicings for a general peace throughout Europe and amongst other things an Illumination hath been agreed upon to take place in this Borough on Wednesday the 13th instant on which most glorious occasion it is understood Transparencies and appropriate devices in lamps will be exhibited and employed. Ordered unanimously by this assembly that our Guildhall be decorated with the following device: CROWN, G.R., and word PEACE and also a festoon at the bottom thereof in lamps.'

The Period from 1835 to 1918
The Parliamentary Reform Act of 1832 was followed by other far-reaching measures of reform, two of which directly affected Congleton. The Poor Law Amendment Act of 1834 completely re-organized the administration of poor relief. Locally it was to be administered by elected Boards of Guardians, and neighbouring parishes were to form Poor Law Unions. The Congleton and District Union comprised the parishes and townships of Congleton, Buglawton, Biddulph (until 1893), Astbury, Somerford Booths, Swettenham, Moreton, Hulme Walfield, Somerford, Sandbach, Alsager, Odd Rode, Smallwood, Church Lawton, Betchton, Bradwall, Hassall, Wheelock, Elton, Moston, Tetton, Arclid, Brereton, Church Hulme, Cranage, Blackden, Davenport, Leese, Cotton, Twemlow and Kerminshaw. The workhouse at Mossley was not large enough to cope with the demands made upon it and the guardians were constantly being pressed by the central Poor Law Commission to build another. Various sites in Congleton were suggested, but eventually the new workhouse was built at Arclid in 1844, with a casual ward remaining in Congleton.[19]

At first it was intended that poor relief would now be forthcoming only to those who entered the workhouse as residents, but this rigid regulation gradually waned. In 1864 casual poor could obtain temporary relief in the form of 8 oz. of bread and $3\frac{1}{2}$ pints of milk and water in return for breaking 2 cwt. of stone or picking 3 oz. of oakum.[20] By the beginning of the twentieth century more were being relieved outside the house than in it. In 1906–7, for example, 262 adults and 133 children received indoor relief; but 893 adults and 473 children received relief in their own homes.[21]

The Municipal Corporations Act of 1835 reformed the corporations of 178 boroughs, including that of Congleton, and modern Congleton may be said to have been created by it. The new council was to comprise eighteen councillors and six aldermen. The town was divided into three wards, North, South and West, with six councillors for each ward, two of whom were to retire annually. A councillor thus served for three years and was eligible for re-election. The aldermen were to be elected by the council, to serve for six years, half of their number retiring each third year. The council was to elect the mayor at the annual council meeting, held on 9 November. Candidates for election to the council had to own real or personal property worth £500, or land assessed at £15 or more. The electors were all male occupiers of any house during the current year and two years previously, provided they had been rated to the relief of the poor during the period and had paid all rates by 31 August, except those payable during the preceding six months. A register of electors had to be drawn up, and a burgess list published. Objections to, or omissions of, names had to be submitted to the town clerk, and were heard by a court consisting of the mayor and two elected assessors.

The number of voters was not large, many being disfranchised by the clause about payment of rates. Elections were to be held on 1 November each year, and the elector was required to deliver to the mayor or other presiding officer a voting paper 'containing the Christian names and surnames of the persons for whom he votes, with their respective places of abode and descriptions, such paper being previously signed with the name of the Burgess voting, and with the name of the street, lane or other place in which the property he appears to be rated on the Burgess Roll is situated'. The council was also to elect a town clerk and treasurer, and to pay them a salary. All acts of the council were to be decided by a majority of the members present, one third part of the whole number to be a quorum. Notice of a council meeting was to be given at least three days beforehand, minutes of the proceedings were to be kept, and to be open to inspection by any burgess. Accounts were to be kept, audited and published. Council meetings were to be held at least every quarter; the general business of the corporation was to be carried out by committees, provided that 'the acts of every such committee shall be submitted to the Council for their approval'. Except for minor changes and extensions of the franchise, that system is in use today. One of the committees to be appointed was the watch committee, 'to appoint a sufficient number of fit men to act as constables for preserving the peace by day and by night, and preventing robberies and other felonies'. Congleton was one of the boroughs appointed to hold a commission of the peace, the serving mayor was chairman of the local magistrates.

The Act revolutionized the administration of the borough, and soon two distinct political groups emerged: the Tories, or 'Dear Party', and the Whigs and Radicals, or 'Cheap Party'. The emphasis was not on the services which the council might give to the townspeople, but its duty to prevent extravagant expenditure. As a keen observer of the times noted, 'There never was such a coup as the Municipal Reform Bill has turned out to be. It marshals all the middle classes in all the towns of England in the ranks of reform; aye, and gives them monstrous power, too.'[22] It certainly did so in Congleton. Party politics were now fiercely contested, and at first the Dear Party held a majority on the council. In 1838 a severe trade depression set in, causing more unemployment and distress. The Cheap Party held meetings in the town hall, promising economy, and increased revenue from the sale of timber from the Town Wood, and by an increase in stall rents in the market. They secured a majority in the election of 1839, and at once halved the borough rate, reducing the total sum demanded from £600 to £300. In 1843 they actually promised 'in course of a year or two from the present time the Borough Rate will cease to be imposed'.[23] One of their number, John Latham, was appointed town clerk in 1842.

These were troublesome times, and both the Anti-Corn Law League and the Chartist Movement had their supporters in Congleton. There were riots in 1841 during the parliamentary election for South Cheshire,[24] special constables being enrolled, the Riot Act was read by the mayor, and much disorder prevailed until the yeomanry were called in; though peace was restored 'without damage to property and without injury to life and limb'. The revival of Chartism in 1842 brought far more serious disorders, including what is often referred to as 'the Mob Wakes'.[25] In July meetings, at which lectures of an inflammatory character were given, were held at the Social Institution in Market Street, and were advertised by the town crier (admission 1*d*). During a disturbance of Staffordshire

a The old Town Hall, *b* the present Town Hall

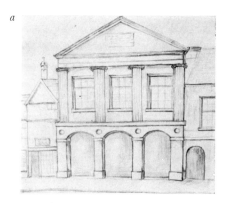

a

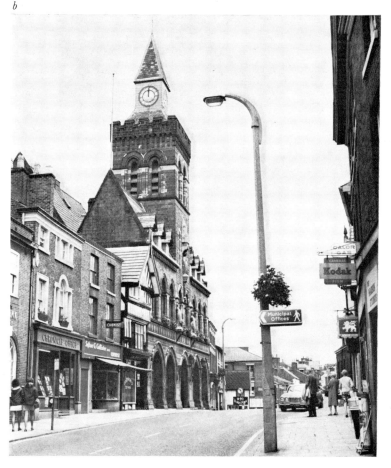

b

a The Congleton Mace, *b* the Mayor's Chain of Office, *c* the Mayoral
Procession

colliers on 16 July two of the ringleaders were arrested, and on 21 July a mob of five or six thousand, mostly unemployed, entered the town and demanded their release. Fortunately they had been previously sent off to Knutsford gaol, yet armed with sticks and bludgeons the invaders demanded food from terrified shopkeepers and householders and attacked the borough head constable. Workers removed plugs from boilers and so completely held up machinery. William Warrington, mayor of Congleton, immediately wrote to the Home Secretary for military help and civil guidance. Less than a month later, on Saturday 13 August, Macclesfield silk weavers on strike or unemployed spent a day in Congleton. A mob of from six to eight thousand people from Macclesfield, Bollington and the manufacturing districts of north Cheshire entered the town. Most of the men were armed with heavy sticks and they walked in military array, ten or twelve abreast, and were preceded by a band of music.

On 15 August early in the morning a company of Congleton strikers went to stir up labourers in neighbouring places. That day the merchants and traders of Northwich appealed for special constables because the Congleton mobs were approaching 'for the purpose of turning out the workmen'. The mob sought recruits throughout the county but did not in fact terrorize any town because a strong force of police was known to be at hand. Congleton shops, however, were looted on the mob's return, and all workplaces had to close.

On 18 August a meeting took place at the Methodist New Connexion chapel. The independent Methodists tended to be radical in politics and leaders of trade union activity. Thomas Berrisford, a local Chartist, led the assembly allegedly with violent words implying he would 'resist the Soldiers with fire arms' notwithstanding the presence of special constables. Indeed so strong did the language of the strikers become that one female orator was chased to Macclesfield afterwards, arrested, imprisoned and tried at the Assizes. Fortunately the magistrates merely lectured Berrisford, or the week might have ended disastrously. But when a woman, Elizabeth Walker from Macclesfield, was heard to say that she hoped God Almighty would open the hearts of the shopkeepers to supply the people, and that 'if they did not supply them they must come to other means', she was arrested. The mayor kept a draper's shop. Sir

H

James Graham, the Home Secretary, took the opinion of the law officers of the Crown, with a view to criminal proceedings against the mayor and magistrates of Congleton for neglect of their duty, but they decided against it. The watch committee did not agree with the views of the Home Secretary, nor was it ready to increase the size of the borough force. In a long memorandum, accepted by the council on 30 November 1842, it declared that it 'cannot speak in terms of too eulogium on the conduct' of the mayor and magistrates; that 370 special constables had been sworn in, and public order maintained; that two extra constables had been appointed, and that the expenditure of £156 a year was sufficient for the protection of life and property and the detection and punishment of offenders within the borough.

Railway construction, despite its economic advantages, added to political and social problems. In 1840 the corporation was disgusted that the proposal to take the Manchester and Birmingham Railway through the town came to nothing. The foundation stone of an immense viaduct intended to carry the line across the town had already been laid, but the company found the cost prohibitive, and the bricks were used to build the houses in Astbury Street and Antrobus Street.[26] In 1845, however, the North Staffordshire Railway Company came into existence; and in 1847 the council was able to thank Mr. E. Kennerley for his efforts in securing the railway within a half-a-mile of the town, giving it 'the advantages of being placed on the great line of railway communication between Manchester and London'.

The Corn Laws were repealed in 1846, but bad trade led to a revival of Chartism in 1848, and the council had to take precautions against 'the possibility of a Riot taking place within the Borough by persons calling themselves Chartists'. The Lord Chancellor was requested to appoint four more J.P.s because of the increasing population. 'There are upwards of one thousand excavators residing within the Borough besides three thousand in the immediate neighbourhood employed in the construction of the North Staffordshire Railway, the greater part of whom are likely to remain for a considerable length of time and some for a permanency.' In this way trouble seems to have been averted.

The municipal election of November 1850 saw the return of

a majority of the Dear Party, which ordered an investigation into the administration of the corporation's finances. On 6 August 1851 a resolution was moved, and carried by eleven votes to ten, that the town clerk should be dismissed. John Wilson was appointed town clerk in his place, an office he held until 1856; he was reappointed in 1867, and held office until 1894 as town clerk, clerk to the justices, deputy high steward and clerk to the common land trustees. John Latham continued to campaign for the Cheap Party, and wrote many scurrilous pamphlets addressed to the burgesses.

Electioneering in those days in Congleton was an exciting and hard-fought contest, when there was no secret ballot. At a public meeting in 1852 one Thomas Lacy affirmed that 'no man in the Old Mill can vote as he likes', a statement confirmed by many others.[27] A Latham pamphlet of 1852 claimed 'we have intimidation, bribery and corruption in their worst forms, used and sanctioned by those whose office and station ought at least to induce a more modest and unblushing use of means. They stand by and see men carried away in a state of helpless drunkenness, to be herded together for a week like swine, to be brought on the Polling Day to record their independent and unbiased votes for the Tories.'[28] This charge was emphasized in 1853: 'I am prepared to admit that if we have this year, as last, the same amount of bribery and coercion, the same disgraceful abduction of voters to the Rudyard Hotel, there to be kept for a week immersed in sottish sensuality and herded together like swine, the exertions of the rightminded among you may for a time longer be frustrated.' Latham's rival, John Wilson, he described as 'the Mayor and Corporation, Town Clerk, Bench of Magistrates, Magistrates' Clerk, Constables, and in fact the whole Body Corporate of the Town of Congleton'.[29] The allegations of bribery and corruption are borne out by an interesting letter written by a young man to his parents on 7 November 1852:

Our party took care to take the initiative in this year's electioneering proceedings, and commenced the 'Bottling System' about a week before the day of the election. We established a sort of colony at Rudyard Lake about 7 miles from this place. We smuggled off to there about a score of voters of slippery character . . . The colonists were provided with roast beef and plum pudding and other kinds of grub gratis, and each had 2s per day allowed to spend in drink and tobacco . . . After the poll the scene which ensued beggars description. Flags were torn down, three or four battles going on at one and the same time amongst the crowd as the contending parties began to intermingle, our party being decorated with red ribbons, theirs with blue. Constables' staves worked away right and left, and many a broken head will serve for a long time to remind its owner of the perils of the day. . . . All the voters, nearly 700, who voted on our side were treated to a substantial feast of English fare.[30]

The Tories certainly made tremendous efforts to secure the election of their candidates and were successful in every ward.[31]

A contemporary journal recalls the excitement of the occasion:

At an early hour the bands and colours of both parties paraded the streets amidst crowds of people; and all business seemed suspended except at those establishments that purveyed creature comforts to the hungry and thirsty. Loud were the cheers and groans that issued as friend or foe alternately drove up. In a short time the band and colours of the Liberals retired. . . . A series of fights had already commenced and when the Radicals found their leaders would not be heard, they commenced a furious and indiscriminate attack upon those about them; broken hats, torn garments, and tattered caps were soon flying in the air with such missives as were obtainable. The police, only eleven in number, did their best to allay the row, without use of their staves; but that soon became necessary and not a few cracked heads was the consequence.[32]

Some election pamphlets were more humorous, such as that published for the elections in November 1863, only part of which can be quoted here:

ENTRIES FOR THE
CONGLETON
MUNICIPAL RACES

The renowned PROFESSOR RAREY WILSON has resumed his practice of training and taming these noble animals, over which he has so much control, with the view of entering them for the coming meeting. As true sportsmen we recommend that all Jockeying should be done away with. We say give each horse his Head, and let him gallop on the course of straightforwardness and leave RAREY to mourn the restiveness of the steeds and the unfavourable state of the course.

THE KILKENNY STEEPLE-CHASE

Two miles and a distance round the Church. WILLIAM WAR-RINGTON, by Liberty out of Poor-Mans-Friend.

This horse claims our attention; he stands sixteen hands high, has a good head and neck, sound legs and powerful puffing pipes. This favourite has been specially trained for this race and will be very hard to beat. GEORGE KENT by Political Freedom out of Every-Man-His-Own Opinion. He is a faithful animal, and is in honourable hands. Long odds are laid on this Nag in the shape of honest votes which are sure to bring him safe to the winning-poll. WILLIAM DEMPSEY: This is a fine powerful Irish horse; he stands in RAREY'S stables. GEORGE FARRINGDON: Just before going to press we received the following tip—that RAREY was then dressing an old sore in this horse and doctoring him up with the view of entering him to run in this race in the name of Goldfinder.[33]

In 1872 the Ballot Act introduced secret voting. A West Ward manifesto exhorted:

> Sound the Timbal over Congleton town,
> Rejoice in your freedom, the Screw is broke down.
> The Ballot you know is the Working Man's friend,
> Then go to the Poll and your Freedom Defend.

As time went on the functions of the council came to be regarded in a new light—less as the trustees of the rates and more as the providers of public services. One aspect of public administration which began to concern the council more and more was that of public health. The council appointed its first health committee in 1846. In 1849 Congleton petitioned for a local board of health under the Public Health Act of 1848,[34] and the following year William Ranger, one of the General Board of Health's inspectors, investigated the sanitary state of the town: unfortunately there seems to be no copy of his report in existence. In 1853, however, the town's application was still being considered.[35] The fact that the health committee, which had lapsed, was reconstituted later in 1853 suggests that the request was granted and that, as in some other boroughs, the council itself was constituted the local board of health. The work of sanitary inspector was carried out first by the Superintendent of Police, but in 1860 a part-time sanitary inspector was appointed. At the same meeting the Park Pool, which had become a nuisance, was considered. The cleansing of this pool posed a problem which was ultimately solved in 1861 by the decision to construct a sewer down Moor Street and Foundry Street to the Dane, and thus diverting the filth from the pool—but into the river. The first part-time medical officer of health,

FELLOW WORKMEN!

If you vote for Messrs. Frost and Titley in the South Ward, or for Messrs. Bradwell and Daniels in the North Ward, or for Messrs. Blackshaw and Lowe in the West Ward, you vote indirectly for John Wilson, "the Soft-soaping Town Clerk," the author of all political jobbery and cursed personal squabbles. John Wilson and his dummies have vigorously opposed every measure of local reform, self and municipal government for the last thirty years, especially the ballot, which he and his party have been so anxious to stifle.

John Wilson and his party formerly compelled you to vote as they liked, upon pain of instant dismissal from employment, *but now you have the long-looked-for ballot, so that they cannot tell how you vote.* So be true to yourselves, and vote independently and fearlessly for

Messrs. WARRINGTON & SHELDON,
(NORTH WARD,)

Messrs. KENT & PICKFORD,
(SOUTH WARD,)

Messrs. BEECH & JOHNSON,
(WEST WARD,)

All men pledged to serve you faithfully, by promoting measures of economy, reform, and usefulness to benefit you and your families.

Election broadsheet

Dr. P. M. Davidson, was appointed in 1873, and served the town till his death in 1917.

The water supply was also a health problem. The contamination of wells often caused typhoid. A scheme to build a reservoir at Timbersbrook was abandoned on grounds of cost. Instead, with the permission of Sir Charles Shakerley, the springs in Forge Wood and the adjoining land were collected and the water pumped to a water-tower 200 ft above the river bed. Mossley and Hightown were supplied with water from Corda Well, situated near to the ridge of Congleton Edge. The waterworks was officially opened in October 1881, an event which inspired a local poet to write about

> This day, to see the Mayor, elate
> With great delight inaugurate
> Our Waterworks, proclaiming them
> This Ancient Borough's diadem
> Each sparkling drop a precious gem.[36]

By 1885, 1,830 houses were supplied with town's water; and in 1888 the medical officer of health could report a considerable decrease in the death rate and the virtual elimination of typhoid.[37]

The fifty years preceding 1914 witnessed great changes in the town, and in retrospect it must be wondered at that the councils of the day accomplished so much, rather than did so little. In 1837 the central streets were reported 'not in a good state of repair', and the outlying roads in the borough were in a wretched condition with cobbles missing and huge holes unfilled.[38] Now, sewers, gas-mains, water-mains were laid throughout the town, and streets widened, paved and lighted. Duck Street, Mill Street, Swan Bank, Brookside, Moody Street, Chapel Street, Lawton Street, Market Street, Kinsey Street, Dane Bridge, Park Street, Thomas Street, Dane Side Walk, Royle Street, Spragg Street, Eaton Bank and Park Road, Shepherd Street, Swan Street, Nelson Street, Howey Lane, Wagg Street, Canal Street and Canal Road, Culvert Street, Bromley Street, Park Lane and West Road were widened and improved. Astbury Street, Lion Street, Davenport Street, Egerton Street, Blake Street, Henrietta Street, John Street, Prospect Street, Parson Street, Garden Street, Silk Street,

Elizabeth Street, Queen Street, Booth Street, Heywood Street, Wallworth Bank, Union Street, Derby Street, Milk Street, Tanner Street and Back Park Street were made up, drained, kerbed, flagged and sewered; and the sewerage works was constructed in 1902, though not all sewers were connected to it. Mill Bridge was again re-constructed in 1888, the carriage-way being widened from 18 ft to 24 ft, and projecting footpaths being added to each side, at a cost of £800.[39]

In the 1850s the corporation had opposed the government's attempts to enlarge and amalgamate local police forces and place them under the control of the Home Secretary, while still leaving the ratepayers responsible for their upkeep. The Police Act of 1856, however, was passed, but a government inspector's report in 1858 that the Congleton force was 'perfectly nugatory for the preservation of peace and the prevention of felonies' was denied by the corporation which continued to defy the Home Secretary. In 1881 the council claimed that although it only had five policemen these were sufficient for 'a borough so quiet and so free from crime.'[40] The report of the Home Secretary in 1889, however, alleged that Congleton was 'now the only borough in England and Wales having a separate force that does not maintain its police in a state of efficiency'. In 1890 the council at last decided to fall into line, and thus to earn the grant in aid. The force thenceforth consisted of a chief constable, two sergeants and eight constables, in uniform for the first time.

Meanwhile during the 1860s three important enterprises were undertaken. The foundation stone of a new town hall was laid in 1864. A bottle containing copies of the *Macclesfield Courier*, *Congleton Advertiser* and *Congleton Mercury*, together with a new florin, shilling, sixpence, threepenny piece, penny, halfpenny and farthing was placed under the stone.[41] The town hall was ceremoniously opened on 11 July 1866.

The town hall complex included a spacious covered market facing the Market Place. In the meantime the 1826 charter had been acted upon, and the growing cattle market was moved from the main street. In 1859 this market was taken to a square behind High Street, and during the next few years the remainder of the stalls followed. The removal of horses, pigs, cows and sheep from High Street certainly eased traffic congestion at weekends but led to a perceptible decrease in market trade. After 1901 the market at the rear of the town hall had its own building owned by a private company. In 1893 the three-day cattle fair, held in the streets, was criticized as 'a nuisance and a danger' and ceased to be held soon after. But the fair, for pleasure and horse sales, survived each 12 May to about 1926. A winter fair in October or November took place for the sale of horses and cattle.[42]

The decision was also taken to embark upon a new municipal enterprise, and in 1866 an Act of Parliament authorized the corporation to buy the gas works from the Congleton Gas and Light Company for £12,500. The gas works had been financed by local industrialists and business men—including William and Charles Vaudrey, Thomas Reade, Charles Barlow, Edward and John Drakeford and Samuel Yates.[43]

The Act permitting the setting up of the works was obtained in 1833 and by it the company had to lay pipes to any premises in Congleton or Buglawton whose owner would instal meters and gas lights.[44] The works were established on land in the meadows south of the Dane opposite the Old Mill. The company supplied gas to premises nearby in 1833-4. The church got gas lighting in 1834. Henry Hogg, far out in Buglawton, had his mill lit in April 1835. Charles Johnson of Wood Street mill and other silk throwsters, despite the depression, invested in lighting from 1835 onwards. Soon the company was paying a regular 5 per cent dividend annually and reduced its tariffs. Large consumers, like the corporation for its street lighting, received a concession rate. But it soon became customary for new buildings such as the Methodist New Connexion chapel to be lit with gas as a matter of course, and ordinary householders followed suit.[45]

The extension of public activity opened a new area for criticism of the borough government. A local paper commented, perhaps with some truth, that the 'corporation was now the surveyors of the highways, the proprietors of the Gas Works and the general curators of the health of the Borough. Everyone who has been crying out against the new Act and against the new town hall and against the expenses attending all these things will now be crying out that the Council does nothing, that the gas is very bad and that the streets and roads are awfully neglected.'[46] The purchase of the gas works, however, turned out to be a very good stroke of business. Not only were gas mains laid throughout the town and a plentiful supply of cheap gas assured, but in 1887 it could be claimed that the 'Gas Works have now borne all the expenses of the Public Lighting of the Town for 18 years, estimated at £9,540 in respect of expenses saved to the Ratepayers on acount of the Public Lamps; to which should be added £50 as a grant to the Park in 1880 and £1,996 13s 11d as a grant to the Highway Account'.[47]

It was in 1865, too, that land was acquired for the provision of a public park which was eventually opened in 1871, covering an area of some 12 acres. Forming a pleasing background and pleasant sylvan retreat of 11 acres was the Town Wood. A new road to the park was made leading through Market Street and accessible from Kinsey Street. There was a bowling green, a croquet lawn and boating on the Dane. The croquet lawn's receipts in 1886 were only £2 3s 4d but boat receipts totalled almost £70.[48]

Meanwhile, local political strife continued unabated, each side, when it secured a majority, unseating the other's aldermen. On several occasions there were contests for the mayoralty at the annual council meeting. In November 1886 the mayor-elect was defeated at the election, but was still elected mayor, and at the same meeting was elected an alderman. Dubious means were still adopted at election-time, as is instanced by the case of the 'prominent inhabitant who, towards the end of the century, was indicted at the Assizes on a charge of bribery and corruption and sentenced to a term of imprisonment at Knutsford. He went round the town on election day with supporters carrying buckets full of halfcrowns which were distributed to the poorer electors and in public houses. On his release from prison the would-be councillor was met and escorted by a cavalcade of supporters in triumph back to Congleton where, it is said, a great crowd welcomed him back.'[49]

An enormous growth of local government activity therefore took place in the latter half of the nineteenth century, much of it during the town clerkship of John Wilson (b. 1810), who held office from 1851 to 1856, and from 1867 to 1894 when he retired to die in 1895. The power he wielded was considerable. A contemporary reported that 'he could hate as intensely as he could love, and no man that I have ever known more deeply resented opposition. Time once was when he held the entire rule of Congleton in one hand and the affection of three-quarters of the population in the other; whilst by the smaller faction perhaps he was hated as deeply as he hated . . . I remember when a child asking who was King of Congleton. I was told "John Wilson".'[50] On his retirement it was correctly remarked how much local government had grown in his period of office.[51] The number of the following corporation committees appointed in 1901 bears this out: highways, sewerage, gas, water, sanitary, park, general purposes, new streets and buildings, watch, and finance; to which an education committee was added after the Education Act of 1902.

There was a lighter side to public life, of course, when pleasure as well as public business was the order of the day. The year 1848, for example, witnessed the fiftieth anniversary of the election of Randle Wilbraham as high steward of Congleton. This was celebrated on 18 October:

The day was ushered in by merry peals from the Bells of St Peter's Church. At eleven o'clock the corporation met. . . . At halfpast twelve o'clock the Marquess of Westminster (the Lord Lieutenant) with Lord Skelmersdale (a brother of Mr. Wilbraham) and other gentlemen accompanied the Mayor (W. Warrington) from his residence to the Town Hall where the Corporation were still in Council assembled when the addresses to the Marquess of Westminster and the High Steward were duly presented. The Mayor then with the Marquess and Lord Skelmersdale preceded by a Band of Music and the Corporation Insignia and followed by the Corporation and a long train of gentlemen walked in procession to St. James' National School Room where the Dejeuner took place, the Assembly Room not being sufficiently large for the purpose.[52]

There were about 250 persons present, and after the meal numerous toasts were proposed and drunk. The high steward was presented not only with an address, but with a gold medal and a deed of endowment for the free education of three boys at the grammar school.[53] This event is commemorated by a marble plaque still in place in the council chamber.

The death of the Duke of Wellington in 1852 was observed by a public memorial service at St. Peter's Church. The Lord Mayor of London visited the town in 1855 and was entertained to a banquet by the corporation, at which 'a special Sack and a Congleton Court Cake' were served. On 7 May 1856, a loyal address was presented to Queen Victoria on the conclusion of the Crimean War, and on 14 June 1859, the town was on holiday for the public parade of a fine Sebastopol gun, eventually put on a stone platform at the foot of Moody Street. David Livingstone visited the town in 1858 and was presented with an address by the corporation, after which he delivered a lecture to a crowded Assembly Room, and another one later to those who had been unable to get in to hear the first.

At the end of his year of office it was the custom in these times for the retiring mayor to entertain his fellow aldermen and councillors, officials and other local dignitaries to dinner—the traditional 'Wine Party'. The menu below for the dinner in 1870 suggests a reason for the reluctance of some councillors to assume office, for the mayoral allowance was still only £25 a year.

TOWN HALL, CONGLETON
ROBERT BEALES, ESQ., M.D. MAYOR
DINNER, OCTOBER 27, 1870

First Course
HARE AND JULIENNE SOUP

Second Course
COD FISH AND FRIED EELS

Third Course
OYSTER PATTIES   STEWED SNIPES
VEAL CUTLETS   LARDED KIDNEYS

Fourth Course
TURKEY   GOOSE   FOWLS   TONGUE
BOILED MUTTON   ROAST BEEF

Fifth Course
PHEASANTS   PARTRIDGES

Sixth Course
PLUM PUDDING   BAKEWELL PUDDING
DAMSON TART   APPLE TART   CHEESE CAKES
LEMON SPONGE   TARTLETTES   JELLY
BLANC MANGE   CUSTARDS

Seventh Course
DESSERT

Wines
HOCK   CLARET
AMONTILLADO SHERRY   GOLDEN SHERRY
CHAMPAGNE   PORT

The Toast List was equally impressive:

> The Queen
> The Earl and Countess of Chester
> The Bishop and Clergy of the Diocese
> The Army, Navy, Militia and Volunteers
> The Mayor and Corporation of Macclesfield
> The High Steward and Lord of the Manor
> (*All proposed by the Mayor*)
> The Mayor of Congleton
> The Magistrates of Congleton and District
> The ex-Mayor
> The Town Clerk (*proposed by John Latham*)
> The Treasurer and Surveyor
> Mr. J. Pearson—his birthday[54]

The pre-war period may be said to have ended on a glorious note with the visit of King George V and Queen Mary to the 'Loyal and Ancient Borough of Congleton' on 23 April 1913, a day when 'brilliant sunshine . . . continued till nightfall', and 'the spontaneous admiration expressed by Her Majesty the Queen of the pretty little town and its surroundings makes us all feel proud'. Queen Mary was pleased to accept three 20-yard lengths of purple-coloured velvet hand-cut at Fred Jackson's Moor Street Mills, and some spun silk which had been woven by Sergt. Sheehan at the Congleton mills of Messrs. Reade and Company. Their Majesties also accepted a packet of Congleton gingerbread made by Maskery and Co. After the departure of the royal party upwards of 200 old people were entertained to tea in the Assembly Room.[55]

The outbreak of the first World War on 4 August 1914 had a profound effect. At Congleton party politics were abandoned, and vacancies on the council were filled by council resolution. Belgian refugees were welcomed, a ladies' working committee and a food control committee were established, precautions against air-raids were adopted. Schemes of development were postponed, and the war years saw the growth of two problems which were to trouble the council for many years—traffic and housing.

The Period from 1918

The years following the first World War have seen some significant developments. In 1918 women of 30, who were ratepayers or wives of ratepayers, received the parliamentary vote. In 1907 women had become eligible for election to borough councils, but no female candidate had appeared in Congleton and the town was little affected by the suffragette movement. In the local government election of 1919 Congleton women seemed reluctant to use their vote, but in 1920, according to a local newspaper, 'the ladies turned up in good numbers, and one of their sex was heard to say, "we were never made so much of before" '.[56] In 1928 the electorate was expanded by the extension of the vote to women of 21 with the necessary qualifications.

The post-war years also saw an increase in the political flavour of local government, and between the wars the gradual eclipse of the Liberal party was a national as well as a local trend. The Labour party became the organ of radicalism. During the years immediately after the war candidates were sponsored in each ward by the Discharged and Demobilized Sailors and Soldiers Association, for whom Frank Dale was successful in North Ward, and W. H. Haddock in the West. By 1922 the composition of the council was 12 Conservatives, 10 Liberals, 1 Labour and 1 Independent. For a time some candidates abandoned the political label, there being as many as 6 Independent councillors in 1925. The economic depression of the 1930s hit Congleton very badly, and the National Unemployed Workers' Movement put forward candidates, one of whom was elected in 1932, though this was the only success of this organization. The Co-operative movement also sponsored candidates, but gradually these last two groups became one with the Labour Party. A fourth ward, represented by one alderman and three councillors, was added to the borough when the urban district of Buglawton was taken in in 1936. The first Labour alderman (F. Barton) was elected in 1936, and the first lady councillor (Mrs. M. Pass) in 1937. In 1937 the council resolved that 'in the future each of the two political parties represented on the Council should alternately be given the opportunity of submitting a nomination for the office of mayor, and that such nomination should then be accepted by the council'. Thus the first Labour mayor (D. Charlesworth) was elected in 1939, and the custom of alternate nomination has continued ever since. The 'Wine Party' was discontinued in that year, and has not been revived.

The composition of the council in 1938 was Conservative 17,

Labour 9 and Independent 2. As in 1914 the outbreak of war in 1939 caused the abandonment of local government elections; vacancies were filled by the council itself acting on the advice of a Home Office circular that 'new councillors to be elected shall as far as possible be persons belonging to the same political party as the outgoing members'.

The problems of post-war reconstruction facing the corporation in 1918 must have seemed well-nigh insuperable. Problems included the town's inadequate housing accommodation, slum clearance, the provision of an additional water supply, street traffic, new sewers and an extension of the sewerage works. The National Unemployed Workers' Movement demanded more public works for the relief of unemployment; angry ratepayers demanded rate reduction. The council did its best, though its first consideration appears to have been to keep the rate as low as possible. This was justified by the fact that by 1929 Congleton was regarded as an area suffering from severe and prolonged unemployment, and in 1936 was designated a 'special area'. No new industries, however, were directed to it by the government.

Today's generation will hardly appreciate the magnitude of the traffic problem. The streets were very narrow and paved with granite blocks, totally unsuited to increasing motor traffic. The noise was excessive, 'shopkeepers serving customers have to shout or wait'.[57] A 'splendid' drinking fountain, paid for by Mrs. Howard of Brereton Hall, had been erected in 1887[58] in the middle of the road at the junction of Swan Bank, Mill Street and Duke Street, all of which had two-way traffic. Vehicles coming into Congleton from Manchester and Macclesfield had to negotiate a very sharp bend at the steepest part of Rood Hill, where there were frequent accidents. Road-widening schemes were adopted at Rood Hill, Mill Street, the bottom of Antrobus Street, Moody Street, Bromley Road and Park Lane. At the dangerous corner on Rood Hill a lighthouse was built in 1924, the only one of its kind in Britain; it was 28 ft high, 6 ft square, and on its two windows, illuminated at night, were the words 'Dangerous Hill, change to low gear'. The *Congleton Chronicle*[59] commented that the 'searching beam' of the 'majestic and efficient-looking lighthouse' seemed to reveal by night, more clearly than the hidden sun by day, the whole of this ambitious alteration'. Unfortunately there was a fault in its construction; it was useless by 1929 and demolished in 1939. The fountain was removed in 1936, and traffic signals were erected at Swan Bank and Duke Street, and at the dangerous crossroads at the bottom of Park Lane. Pedestrian crossings with 'Belisha beacons' were established in High Street, and in Park Lane opposite to Townsend Road. The by-pass scheme from Rood Hill across the Dane to West Road was first mooted in 1935, but there were many difficulties to be overcome. No sooner had it been commenced in 1939 than the outbreak of war brought it to an abrupt halt. A number of other streets, however, were made up.[60]

The Lloyd George coalition government of 1918–22 was committed to its campaign promises of 'homes fit for heroes', and Congleton corporation faced its responsibilities by appointing its first housing committee in June 1919. The first proposal was to build 250 houses, later reduced to 160. Under the Housing and Town Planning Act of 1919 the government subsidy took the form of a guarantee of payment for the annual loss incurred on municipal housing less the sum of a 1*d* rate. These first post-war houses were built on Marlfields (the Crescent and Crescent Road), Brunswick Street, High Lowe Avenue and Weathercock Lane. The rents were 10*s* per week for the 'parlour' type, and 6*s* 8*d* for the 'non-parlour' type. They had two, three and four bedrooms and a bathroom. They were costly to build, owing to an artificially stimulated over-demand on skilled labour, materials and transport during the brief post-war boom. This 'Addison Scheme' was abandoned, and under the 1923 Housing Act a subsidy of £6 per house for 20 years was substituted; the Ruskin Road houses were built under this Act. Between 1927 and 1933, under the Wheatley Housing Act of 1924, by which government subsidies were also available, the corporation built over 250 houses at Bromley Road, Norbury Drive, Tall Ash Avenue and Havannah Street. Under the Slum Clearance Act of 1930 which gave a government subsidy of 45*s* per person moved to new dwellings, the local authority having to provide 75*s* per house, 262 houses were built at Bromley Farm and Jubilee Road. Today it is difficult to recognize the locality of such old slum areas as Silver Street, Hollow Yard, Broad Entry and Gibralter (Gibraltar) Rocks.

The building of over 700 council houses, together with private development, accentuated two other problems, those of the water supply and sewerage. The consumption of water per head per day increased, and the waterworks at the Forge and Corda

Well found it difficult to supply it. Year by year, in times of drought, water was cut off during the night. A report on the water situation was commissioned in 1925, and in 1927 it was recommended that extensive alterations be undertaken at the Forge, and new water mains should be laid in various parts of the town. In 1929 the daily supply was 342,000 gallons, and the daily consumption 365,000 gallons, or 28 gallons per person per day. The scheme was implemented but did little to alleviate the situation, and a search was made for further sources of supply, such as at Rushton Spencer, Bosley, Biddulph, Hulme Walfield and Hug Bridge. The Hug Bridge scheme was adopted in 1939, but the onset of war prevented its completion.

The sewerage works was not capable of serving the increasing number of houses, and some parts of the borough were not sewered at all. In 1920 there were only 981 water closets within the borough; most houses still had the privy, or pail system, and a horse-drawn tank was used for the emptying of these, making its malodourous journey through the streets. The cost of peat for these pails was as much as £452 in 1924. The reconstruction of the sewerage works at a cost of £38,000 was undertaken in 1931, and sewers were laid in many areas, including Mossley; the whole scheme was completed by the end of 1933, and by 1940 2,111 pail conversions had been made. Negotiations were begun in 1936 with the Congleton Rural District Council for a joint scheme to sewer West Heath, Astbury Marsh, the village of Astbury and Black Firs, but the war once again prevented the work being put into operation.

The Baldwin administration of 1924–9 may not have had a remedy for unemployment, but its domestic legislation affected Congleton considerably. The Electricity (Supply) Act of 1926 transferred the wholesale distribution of electricity to a national body, the Central Electricity Board. The corporation appointed its first electricity committee in 1929; an electricity engineer was engaged, substations built and arrangements made for obtaining a supply, Congleton being a member of the N.W. Midlands Electricity Authority. At 6 p.m. on 20 February 1931 electricity was switched on in the town hall, and the *Congleton Chronicle* reported that electricity 'has ceased to be a luxury; it is a convenience which eases the drudgery of life, renders conditions healthier, and does all kinds of things for us that cannot be done by any other means'.[61]

The Rating and Valuation Act of 1925 made many sweeping changes. The council became the new rating authority, displacing the overseers of the poor; rates were to be consolidated into one general rate; provision was made for uniformity of valuation and for a five-yearly revision of valuation lists. So in 1927 Congleton corporation appointed its valuation committee and a rating and valuation officer. Undoubtedly the most extensive transfer of functions to the county councils (established in 1888—Congleton has one county councillor) came with the passing of the Local Government Act of 1929. The poor-law unions and boards of guardians were abolished and their powers and buildings transferred to the county councils to be managed through their public assistance committees. The final meeting of the Congleton and District Union took place in March 1930. The county received additional powers over roads, public health, maternity and child welfare, town and country planning, some of which could be shared with or delegated to the borough. Agricultural land and buildings were exempted from rates, and industrial property and railways were relieved of three-quarters of their rate burdens. To make up for this loss the treasury gave a 'block' grant. The county council precept became the greater part of Congleton's rate poundage.

Thus, slowly, and sometimes painfully, Congleton passed from the nineteenth to the twentieth century. During the 1930s there was much local controversy over a swimming pool, and eventually that in Park Road was opened in May 1936. Two years later a public library was opened in temporary premises in North Street. The corporation and townsfolk processed to St. Peter's on 6 May 1935, for a service of thanksgiving for George V's silver jubilee; parties were held in the streets, sports took place in the Park, and an ox was roasted whole on the fairground. Early the next year the king's death was as solemnly mourned. Congleton took special pride in George VI, who had opened the War Memorial Hospital, celebrating his coronation in 1937 by a civic procession and service, a pageant of kings and queens in the Park, and tea-parties in the streets. Two unusual council resolutions of these inter-war years included in 1924 a condemnation of 'pillion-riding' which sought to make it illegal; and in 1929 a vote in favour of a Channel tunnel.

Coming events, though, were already casting their foreboding shadows. In 1935 'Air-raid precautions' first appeared on the agenda of the general purposes committee; and in 1937 the Chief Constable was made responsible for organizing the air-raid warden system. On 30 July, 1939 a review was held in the Park of over 500 volunteers for the civil defence services. Congleton was 'tackling the problem of civil defence in a larger measure than perhaps many realized',[62] and was ready for hostilities when they came.

During the second World War the council concentrated on the war effort, and its development schemes were put into cold storage. Air-raid shelters were built in the streets, and by 1943 a personnel of 2,435 had been trained. The food control committee and the fuel and lighting control committee supervised the rationing of these important commodities. Children from Manchester were evacuated to Congleton,[63] and Dutch and U.S. troops were stationed in the town. The mayor organized comforts for these men and a prisoners-of-war fund; National Savings were encouraged by 'War Weapons', 'Warship' and 'Wings for Victory' weeks. The annual wakes holidays became 'holidays at home', with many entertainments in the Park. They were financially successful, too, and local charities benefited from the proceeds.[64] The only municipal event of note was the appointment, for the first time, of a full-time town clerk.

Congleton itself emerged unscathed from the war, but with a great deal of necessary reconstruction to be done. The success of the Labour party in the national political arena in 1945 was reflected when local politics were resumed. Fourteen councillors and four aldermen had to seek re-election. Labour won ten of the fourteen seats, and became the largest group on the council; it decided to claim all of the aldermanic seats, and won two of the three by-elections. Six years later, when the Conservatives regained the majority, these four Labour aldermen were themselves unseated. Fortunately, good sense then prevailed, and an agreement was drawn up between the two parties regarding aldermanic vacancies, and the sharing of committee chairmanships on the basis of proportional representation; this is still observed. The first lady mayor (Mrs. Jessie Burgess) was elected in 1945.

In 1945 the vote in local government elections was extended to all those entitled to vote at parliamentary elections, that is to all men and women over the age of 21. The electorate in the various wards was thus doubled: in 1967 there were 13,129. In

1948 the date of municipal elections and the annual council meeting were changed from November to May; the mayor and councillors who should have retired in November 1948 remained in office until May 1949. Throughout the fifties and sixties, except for a fitful Liberal revival and the election of an Independent, a curious political pattern has evolved. North Ward (6 seats) and Buglawton Ward (3 seats) have elected Labour councillors; South Ward (6 seats) and West Ward (6 seats) have elected Conservatives.

By 1945 the work of the council had proliferated as the following list of committees indicates: electricity, gas, general purposes, health, highway, housing, new streets and buildings, park, public lighting, sewerage, water (all of which were committees of the whole council), air-raid precautions, allotments, baths, children's road safety, education, finance, fuel and lighting control, library, markets and fairs, valuation, watch, and food (which were all standing committees).

The national policies of the Attlee government (1945-51) affected Congleton considerably. The implementing of the Education Act of 1944 involved the abolition of the education committee, which held its last meeting in March 1945. The Cheshire County Council assumed overall responsibility, local administration being delegated to the South-East Cheshire (No. 11) Divisional Executive, on which the council has five representatives. The National Health Service Act of 1946 transferred the administration of this portion of the welfare state to county and county borough councils. Cheshire County Council divided the county into divisions, and Congleton has five representatives on the South-East Cheshire Divisional Health Executive. The nationalization of gas and electricity caused the transfer to national undertakings of electricity in April 1948, and gas in May 1948. In 1947 the borough police force was merged with the Cheshire county constabulary. In 1946 the fire brigade became part of the National Fire Service, maintained by the county council; a new fire station was opened in 1967. Responsibility for the valuation and rate assessments of property was transferred to the Inland Revenue in 1950.

In 1953, in an attempt to reduce and streamline the council's work, several of the committees (such as the baths, parks and pleasure grounds, and sewerage committees) were made smaller. This proved successful and the policy of telescoping the work of committees was continued. In 1967 the following were committees of the whole council: development, establishment, finance, general purposes, general works, housing, planning and building; and there were the following standing committees: accident prevention, allotments, civil defence, health, parks and pleasure grounds, twinning.

Although thus denuded of many of its powers and responsibilities, the council found that it had much hard work to do, especially with regard to housing, slum clearance, water, sewerage and traffic control.

Housing proved to be a difficult problem immediately after the war; because of national demand for materials in the bombed cities and the unprecedented demand for new houses, the number each authority was permitted to build was fixed by the government. This did not meet local demand in Congleton, and a points scheme for the allocation of houses was devised by the housing committee which, if not perfect, at least insured a certain amount of rough justice. Government subsidies varied, as did the council's contribution from the general rate fund, until in 1966 the latter was frozen at £7,410 a year. The main estates were built at Bromley Farm, Rood Hill, West Heath, Waggs Road, Parson Street and Buglawton. As general need became satisfied slum clearance proceeded and old people's bungalows, some of them centrally heated and with warden supervision, were provided. Since the war the council has built 1,182 houses; 31 have been sold to occupiers, though this policy of sale has been abandoned. The council has also built a number of garages on its estates. To bring older houses up to date the council adopted the policy of giving improvement grants under an Act of 1949; and to help private developers made advances under various Acts. It seemed at one time probable that Congleton would re-house some of Manchester's overspill population under an Act of 1946. In 1947 Congleton was designated a 'New Town'. The council was anxious to press forward with plans for receiving Manchester overspill, but the director of Jodrell Bank, Professor Lovell, sought assurances that those parts of Congleton closest to the telescope would not be expanded. Consequently a reply to a question in the House of Commons in 1953 was 'construed as a guarantee that the claims of the telescope would be respected'.[65] The project was abandoned in 1952. Congleton, however, still had plenty to occupy its local government.

The demand for water in 1939 had risen to almost 700,000 gallons per day, but the yield from the various sources of supply did not reach this figure; owing to the outbreak of war the scheme then adopted was retarded but never allowed to lie in abeyance. Investigations continued, and in 1945 the site at Hug Bridge was acquired. Despite the great difficulties existing immediately after the war the scheme was proceeded with, and a supply was eventually turned on in 1952, and the completed works was officially opened in May 1953. In accordance with national policy it was transferred to the Macclesfield and District Water Board in 1961.

With the building of many new houses and the provision of an adequate water supply, sewerage improvement became not only urgent, but possible. The original West Heath sewerage scheme was delayed by the uncertainty of the New Town status and ultimately abandoned. A new scheme embracing Padgbury Lane, Astbury Marsh, Sandbach Road and Holmes Chapel Road was devised, and work on it was commenced in 1959 and completed in 1960, thus enabling the extensive housing development to take place on the western approaches to the town. To cope with this and the other housing schemes the sewerage works was extended at the same time, and finished in 1960.

The flow of traffic continued to build up as the number of motor vehicles on the roads increased. To alleviate this problem various measures were adopted. The junction of Mill Street, Duke Street and Swan Bank was improved in 1952. Swan Bank, West Street and Mill Street became a one-way traffic system in 1959. The county council in 1955 secured ministerial consent to complete the Rood Hill by-pass, which was opened and re-named the Clayton by-pass in October 1956; much heavy through traffic was thereby removed from the main streets. Free municipal car parks have been provided. The level-crossing gates at the railway station, a nuisance for generations, were removed by the construction of a fly-over in 1965. Electric street lighting has now been extended to most parts of the borough.

Other problems dealt with included the provision of playing fields, central development and the extension of sand quarrying. Hankinson's Field was bought in 1956, and has proved an excellent addition to the Park. A comprehensive scheme for the redevelopment of the central area of High Street proved to be both costly and controversial; it was even imagined that the town hall was to be pulled down. The question of sand-working has proved more difficult; the silica sand which surrounds Congleton is, it is claimed, a valuable national asset, and since 1944 it has been extensively worked. Whilst not willing to appear obstructive to industrial progress, the planning and buildings committee of the council has resolutely opposed quarrying extensions which it thought detrimental to the amenities of the town—though not always with success.

After the second World War many British towns entered into a close association with similar towns on the continent, especially in France. This became known as 'twinning', and in 1962 Congleton became the 'twin' of Trappes, a town not far from Paris and Versailles. At a special council meeting on 9 June the first ceremony took place, and the Trappes delegation was entertained to a luncheon in the town hall; it was also Carnival Day. Later in the year the mayor and a large delegation from the borough visited Trappes where a similar ceremony was held. Since then parties of young people from the two towns have exchanged visits.

This survey of the development of the borough would be incomplete without reference to finance. In 1900 two rates were levied in the borough; the poor rate by the overseers, and a general district rate; these were 2s 6d and 2s 2d in the pound. The rateable value of the town was £32,766, and the municipal expenditure was £15,591. The net loan debt stood at £20,007. The income from the Common Land Trustees of £600 went direct to aid the poor rate. In 1925, as detailed above, the council became the new rating authority; the two rates were consolidated and a fresh valuation made. In 1939 the rateable value had risen to £69,662, and the rate poundage to 13s 8d. Municipal expenditure was £104,619, and the net loan debt stood at £589,915, most of it for housing needs. The income from the Common Land Trustees, £1,227, was applied in reduction of the rate levy. By 1965 these figures had paled into insignificance, despite the removal of responsibility for financing education, police, fire brigade, gas, electricity and water. Costs have increased, and the value of money has fallen; the services provided by the county council have widened in their scope, and the county precept is higher. The rateable value in

1965 was £602, 221 with a rate poundage of 10*s* 4*d*. Municipal expenditure was £218,053 and the net loan debt had risen to £2,481,293. The contribution from the Common Land Trustees of £8,000 was included as income.[66]

Notes

[1] Much of this section is based without detailed references on council resolutions and accounts contained in: Court Book, 1705–26; Order Books, 1663–1714, 1655–1815, 1713–65, 1747–95, 1795–1833, 1846–61, 1881–1904 (all manuscript); printed minutes from 1905; Treasurer's accounts, 1713–47, 1789–1814 (manuscript); printed statements of accounts, 1836–66; abstracts of accounts from 1867; and volumes of miscellaneous papers: all in the town clerk's office, Congleton. For education see separate chapter.

[2] *Rep. Mun. Corps.*, 2652.

[3] Oaths are to be found in Borough Order Bk., 1655–1815.

[4] *Rep. Mun. Corps.*, 2653–4.

[5] Report to council in Borough Order Bk., 18 March 1814.

[6] Astbury Church, indenture.

[7] Warwickshire Record Office, Rate Books of St. Mary's Church, DR 126/12.

[8] Yates, 73–4.

[9] *Abstract of Returns relative to the Poor*, Parl. Paper (1803–4), xiii, 56–7.

[10] City Library, Stoke-upon-Trent, Mr. Johnson's MS. book.

[11] H. Wedgwood, *Romance of Staffordshire*, i, 103–10.

[12] *Abstract of Returns relative to the Poor*, Parl. Paper (1803–4), xiii, 56–7.

[13] Yates, 100.

[14] *Rep. Silk Trade*, (1831–2), 805.

[15] *Rep. R.C. on Market Rights and Tolls*, Parl. Paper (1888), liii, 145.

[16] Report to Council in Borough Order Bk., 1655–1815.

[17] *Rep. Mun. Corps.*, 2656.

[18] Yates, 47.

[19] Minutes Congleton and District Union, now in Arclid Hospital.

[20] *Poor (United Kingdom)*, Parl. Paper (1864), ii, 6.

[21] *Poor Law Relief*, Parl. Paper (1908), xcii, 54–5.

[22] *Creevey Papers* (3rd edn.), p. 650.

[23] Congleton, misc. papers, i.

[24] Head, 124–7.

[25] H.O. 45/242; H.O. 48/34/44; *Jnl. of Modern History*, xxv, 367.

[26] Head, 124.

[27] Congleton, misc. papers, i.

[28] *Ibid.*

[29] *Ibid.*

[30] Copy of letter printed in *Cong. Chron.*, 27 October 1917.

[31] *Macclesfield Courier and Herald*, 6 November 1852.

[32] *Ibid.*

[33] Congleton, misc. papers, i.

[34] *Public Health Act Return*, Parl. Paper (1850), xxxiii, 591.

[35] *Ibid.* (1852–3), xcvi, 3.

[36] *Macclesfield Courier and Herald*, 5 November 1881. It is thought that the poet was W. H. Krinks, the borough treasurer.

[37] M.O.H. Report for the year ending 31 December 1887: MS. copy in corporation minutes, 2 May 1888.

[38] *Rep. Boundary Commrs.*, 1837.

[39] *Valuation of Corporation Properties 1901*, produced for the corp. by R. Burslam, borough surveyor.

[40] Council memorandum to Lord Chancellor, 23 July 1881.

[41] Congleton, misc. papers, i.

[42] *Kelly's Dirs. Ches.*, various edns.

[43] Congleton Gas. Co., minute book 8 April 1833. The early history of this company is contributed by D. A. Iredale.

[44] 3 and 4 Will. IV, c. iii.

[45] Gas Co., minute books.

[46] *Congleton, Sandbach and Crewe Advertiser*, 16 June 1866.

[47] Congleton corp., *Abstract of Accounts, 1887*, 66.

[48] *Ibid.*, 70.

[49] R. W. James, *To the Best of our Skill and Knowledge* (Hist. Ches. Constabulary), 117. Local inhabitants allege that this practice was continued until well into the present century.

[50] *Cong. Chron.*, 2 March 1895.

[51] *Ibid.*, 5 May 1894. R. W. James (*op. cit.*) says of John Wilson: 'He domineered over all, not least the local council and magistrates. He was a regular guest of the local Licensed Victuallers Association at their annual banquets, at which he would rave against the police whom he described on one occasion as "officious and glib swearing and corroborating officers".'

[52] *Corporation Minutes, 1948*, 66–77.

[53] Medal now held by present high steward.

[54] Congleton, misc. papers, i.

[55] *Cong. Chron.*, 26 April 1913.

[56] *Ibid.*, 130.

[57] *Ibid.*, 1 September 1928.

[58] *Ibid.*, 14 June 1930.

[59] *Ibid.*, 9 February 1924.

[60] It is interesting to compare these figures of traffic movement at Swan Bank: 23 August 1919 in 14 hours, 616 vehicles (44 p.h.); 25 August 1928, during one week, 2,640 motor-cycles, 7,053 motor-cars, 560 vans, 728 buses, 1,746 lorries, 8,133 bicycles, 527 horse-drawn vehicles; 14 September 1935, in one day, 2,000 motor-cars, 2,000 bicycles, 32 horse-drawn vehicles; 16 July 1965, Bridge St., 7 a.m. to 7 p.m., 8,277 motor-cars, 1,548 lorries, 255 buses, 430 motor-cycles and scooters, 744 bicycles.

[61] *Cong. Chron.*, 21 February 1931.

[62] *Ibid.*, 4 August 1939. Present were the St. John Ambulance Brigade, British Red Cross, Fire Brigade, Auxiliary Fire Service, Women Ambulance Drivers, Decontamination, Rescue and Road Repair Squads, Special Constabulary, and Police.

[63] Ducie Avenue Boys and Girls Central Schools, and the Ardwick Municipal Mixed and Infant Schools.

[64] In 1942: £250 to the War Memorial Hospital; £100 to the Mayor's Comforts Fund; £50 to the Prisoners of War Fund.

[65] J. M. Lee, *Social Leaders and Public Persons: a study of County Government in Cheshire since 1888* (1963), 208–9.

[66] Inf. from borough treasurer.

V Industry, Trade and People since 1700[1]

by David Iredale

By the end of the seventeenth century Congleton had grown into a 'large and noted town'.[2] Not only the market and fairs but important leather and lace workshops attracted traders from far afield. Wattle-and-daub, timber-framed, thatch-roofed dwellings stretched along the High Street. At Swan Bank in the town centre, where roads converged from the Potteries, mid-Cheshire and Lancashire, stood the ancient inn, the *Black Lion and Swan* (often called the *Lion and Swan*). Neighbouring crowded alleys like Duck Street contained some dozens of wretched sixteenth-century hovels both timber and stone built. St. Peter's chapel, partly wood, partly stone, with the old grammar school stood on rising ground south of the Market Place and High Street. Houses climbed up Moody and Chapel Streets towards the chapel. The decayed Lower Chapel on Dane Bridge at the end of Mill Street lay in the centre of workers' dwellings not far from the equally decrepit King's Corn Mill.

All round the borough centre stretched acres of common pasture and moorland. West Heath, Mossley Moss, Congleton Moss and Congleton Edge with Buglawton common lands provided a useful source of timber and fuel for the people of the district and extensive grazing for animals. But these areas remained very lonely and desolate, places for highwaymen and vagabonds.

Much of Congleton's cultivated area and enclosed pasture lay within large farms like Mossley Moss or Puddle Bank. Enclosed fields surrounded neat farmhouses, often newly built. Most of the western land of Congleton, on the glacial deposits, was arable, while that to the east, on the older Carboniferous sandstones and shales, was pasture for dairy farming. Many farms belonged to proprietors who did not themselves work their estates.

Congleton took on a new look between 1700 and the end of the Napoleonic Wars in 1815. In 1771 it was described as 'extremely prosperous',[3] and by 1815 the traveller approaching from the hills looked at a town more extensive, less squat, smokier, but better-off than it had been in 1700. Brick houses with dark-slated roofs, large glass windows and handsome doors had replaced many of the tiny cottages of an earlier century. From the Market Place spread neat new streets overshadowed by tall mills, chapels and public buildings. About 1808–9 a visitor remarked on the flourishing silk industry, the fairs and market and the great increase in population.[4] Expansion of industry and trade had helped Congleton's growth. Much building took place in gardens and courtyards, filling in the old town. Yet outlying commons and arable remained to give the borough a still rural appearance. Nevertheless by the end of the Napoleonic Wars the silk industry had changed Congleton into a factory town, dominated by the Old Mill, 'the most elegant building' in the place.[5] Prosperity meant that several families could afford to live in fine old houses or new brick villas according to their tastes. The Reades, silk merchants, for example, found a home in Moody Hall.

Along the main roads between Dane Bridge and Lawton Street End and out westwards towards West Road stretched rows of houses and business premises, though many still looked directly on to fields and gardens.[6] In 1814 houses finished at Lawton Street End. By 1818 new buildings had appeared in Moor Street and Bromley Road, and at the other end of town people were building along West Road itself. Behind the main roads were many alleys and courts. Old streets round the chapel had long been completed. Many buildings stood in the lane adjoining the graveyard and grammar school. New structures were appearing in the Kinsey Street area, north of High Street, just opening up in 1818, and regular blocks of workers' dwellings were started about 1816 in the Astbury Street district south of West Road. So between 1790 and 1820, when Congleton reached the height of its prosperity, much of the town was rebuilt, and by 1830 the place had acquired many of the features it kept for another century or more.

Samuel Yates described how in 1819–20 the Market Place and High Street, for centuries the centre of town life, were always crowded despite their great width, sufficient to accommodate on market days two rows of stalls.[7] Many of the surrounding buildings had just been built though some mean timber hovels still remained. The appearance of High Street in general was 'not uniform, but extremely irregular'. Several tradesmen had erected commodious shops, and the *Roebuck* and *Golden Lion* were now among the town's inns. The ancient timber-framed town hall had been replaced in 1804–5 by a new brick and stone one. In 1823 Sir Edmund Antrobus added an assembly room with market hall underneath. In 1848 was built a county lock-up in the Market Place, and the fire station appeared in Tanner Street in 1858.

St. Peter's chapel, rebuilt in brick in 1740–2, overlooked the Market Place. Nearby on rising ground stood not only the new grammar school building but also the magnificent Wesleyan chapel 'newly erected nearly the size of the Church', typical of the 'chaste and elegant' palaces put up by prosperous Methodists which so took the eye of the editor of the *Chester Chronicle* when he visited Congleton in 1817.[8] The chapel was attended by many prosperous silk makers, such as William and Sarah Krinks of Daneinshaw, William and Sophia Bloor, and Thomas and Sarah Davenport.[9] Houses on this hillside all looked prosperous. In Chapel Street lay 'several good buildings, and the parsonage house'.

The main road followed Mill Street to Dane Bridge, rebuilt in stone in 1784. There the ancient Lower Chapel, turned into a workhouse during the eighteenth century, had been abandoned in 1810–11 with the opening of a new poor-house at Mossley. Dwellings for artisans and labourers, some with hand-loom weavers' garrets, had crowded Mill Street by 1790. There could be seen a rope works with its long walk. The new Stonehouse Green Mill, soon to be overshadowed by the gas works, rose above a dozen small shops and faced the Unitarian chapel. Several times a day coaches arrived at the busy *Bull's Head* inn and at its neighbour the *Coach and Horses*. In nearby Bridge Street stood the town well which through overuse always seemed to be in need of a new pump. Many houses there had been re-erected since 1800.

The main road southwards passed along Lawton Street, distinguished as we have seen by some fine mid-eighteenth- and early-nineteenth-century town houses. But the heights of Park Lane were not developed until the appearance of the canal and railway. Beyond, stretched wide pastures, plantations and mosses, largely enclosed as recently as 1798. Here and there rose farmhouses and residences like High Daneinshaw and Belle Vue.

Just across the Daneinshaw brook, however, industrial development was proceeding apace. Buglawton had 1,300 houses in 1830, one-third built during the previous decade. Mean dwellings crowded each other on the steep hillside between factories and workshops. 'Extensive mills for spinning and preparing lace thread for the Nottingham and Birmingham manufacturers' were in active operation there.

The west side of the borough also experienced a building boom. Beautiful residences dating from the eighteenth century still stood, though some of their gardens and meadowland were disappearing under bricks and mortar of new ways like Dane Street. Nearby was Nathaniel Pattison's West House, 'not surpassed by anything of the sort in the county', built of brick, with high rooms and with garden and rockery which drew admiring comments from passing travellers. John Johnson (1772–1847), banker and salt merchant, possessed Mortlake House near the town mansions of the Roe and Lowndes families. This fashionable quarter with wide views across the Dane valley was, however, soon to lose its charm when crowded settlements like Henrietta Street and factories like Taylor's Prospect Silk Mill appeared. The fine Georgian houses gradually became business premises as prosperous people moved away.

Visitors in 1828 thought Congleton highly 'clean and respectable', yet the old dwellings in the meaner eastern part of the town compared unfavourably with the 'numerous stately mansions and elegant villas' in the western part. When boundary commissioners came to Congleton in 1837 they found a community 'increasing rapidly in every direction'.[10] The main streets had long been filled up with dwellings and trading premises. Many single-storeyed hovels and even larger old buildings had been replaced with tightly packed terraces, back-to-back dwellings and long narrow mills. In 1837, along the main road from West Street to Lawton Street, there stood 358 houses. Short Moody Street indeed had 49 dwellings, tiny Lion Street 29. Gibralter (often spelt Gibraltar) at the east of Congleton contained in a few square yards 42 back-to-back hovels. In Silk Street and Elizabeth Street lay dozens of two-

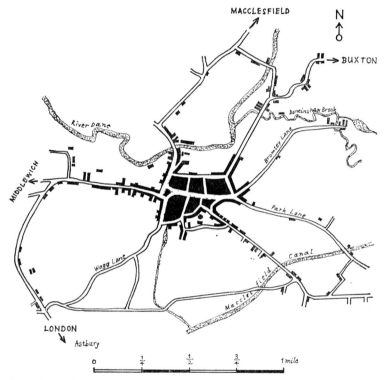

Congleton in 1837

storeyed houses with no gardens but only tiny backyards. This situation had arisen when owners of comparatively small plots of land decided to pack in as many dwellings as possible. Joseph Harwar, a solicitor, erected or rebuilt seventeen houses in Lawton Street with three dozen elsewhere before he died in 1808, leaving further property suitable for building purposes.[11]

The development of Buglawton lay mainly in the capable hands of millowners.[12] Henry Hogg of Lower Daneinshaw, silk merchant, put up nine cottages in King and Queen Streets. John Johnson (1772–1847), who owned the Havannah Street Mill at Lower Daneinshaw, possessed 50 houses in the vicinity. Thomas Johnson of Bank Mill and House erected Hardings Bank estate and Charles Vaudrey of Bath Mill possessed cottages at his mill gates. Such men, members of Congleton's most influential textile families, also led the way in opening shops, brewhouses and taverns.

Although men like Harwar built as a speculation pure and simple, others had further aims. Benjamin Johnson (1756–1826), a prosperous but not wealthy joiner, wanted a house for himself. He erected eight others in Bromley Lane and Moor Lane while building his own. When William Slate, a Congleton merchant, and his two sons in 1788 took land by the Dane for a silk mill they probably found workers would not be available unless homes were provided next door. Their houses they let out in 1798 on long lease, though the usual practice was renting by the week.[13] The Vaudreys, cotton manufacturers, built their estate at the junction of Moor Street and Bromley Street. The 1851 census reveals that this district, known as Gibralter Rocks, sheltered the last surviving cotton workers of Congleton.

The most renowned because most isolated housing estate lay at Havannah, north of Congleton. Development began in 1763 and continued through the nineteenth century as more houses became necessary for workers at the copper, corn, silk and tape works there. Each of the houses built about 1820 had two rooms up and two down with outside sanitation. By 1841 23 dwellings and a public house stood at Havannah. The estate belonged to the Antrobus family of Eaton Hall.[14]

After 1860 population growth slowed down but the face of the town altered considerably in the hundred years 1860–1960. In 1860 the visitor from central Cheshire came upon the first streets of the borough only three-quarters of a mile from the town hall.[15] At Rood Hill on his way north he could leave the town again. Rows of houses in Buglawton nestled at the foot of the hill near the Daneinshaw, and the remaining wide acres of the township sheltered scattered dwellings amid woodland, green pastures, and cornland. The Moor Street and Willow Street area, some 500 yards from the town hall, marked the eastward limit of expansion of the borough. Of course, settlements existed, lost in the countryside, at Daneinshaw and Mossley.

The visitor about 1900 still found a tightly packed town, towering mills and churches, terraced houses and cobbled streets, all clustered round the town hall,[16] with, beyond, Daisy Bank House on the hillside, Town Wood, Buglawton, and half a dozen mills in the countryside. Already, however, the villas of prosperous traders and craftsmen, of bank officials and foremen, tended to widen the area of dwellings considerably. Buildings like the Mount and West Villas began to open up West Heath. There was still plenty of land in the town centre for such people: Victoria Buildings was erected in 1897 in Park Road to be rented by professional men. But some families preferred to live further out, perhaps along Park Lane towards Hightown. Hightown Villas, built about 1905, were still not a mile from the town hall. Nurseries and allotments to the west and south of the town centre contrasted sharply with meadow land rising eastwards.

In many towns private residents moved out to the country in order that industry and shops might take over a town centre. But Congleton mills, though mainly in the central area, had themselves long since spread out into the country. Bath Mill and Primrose Vale Mill on the Daneinshaw, a third mill far away in the woods along Timbersbrook, Daneinshaw Mill, Forge and Dane Mills to the west of the town, and Cotton Shop Mill near the canal in Canal Street, encircled the town. Fortunately textile mills did not themselves occupy many acres. Contemporary drawings and photographs show that Congleton still appeared from the hills a tiny town set in delightful country.

New houses appeared after the first World War all round the town, on the west, to the north near Daisy Bank, southwards towards Astbury,[17] and between Park Lane and Buglawton eastwards. The corporation built several estates to supplement private enterprise. After the second World War and the end of severe building restrictions the corporation again began to build, partly to house slum dwellers from Buglawton or east Congleton, partly to house workers at the new light industrial factories. Private developers built at Hightown and near Sandbach Road.[18] Buglawton hilltop also became a popular residential area. Much open land therefore disappeared under bricks and mortar, though well-kept gardens, small trees or shrubs, and green road verges provided a reminder of the countryside. Wider roads, like the new by-pass to Manchester, took over open land and changed the look of the town. By 1940 few structures remained along the main thoroughfares of pre-nineteenth-century date save inns like the *King's Arms* and the old *White Lion* (both considerably altered). Yet behind the rebuilt areas and further out also, say in West Street and West Road and at Crossledge, dozens of older premises remained to add charm to the town. Nevertheless there was much slum clearance. In June 1937, for example, the eighteen houses of Gibralter Estate (the Rocks) disappeared. The bleak pre-1860 town had been brightened by stretches of playing field, and by the public park (1871) with its bandstand and boats. At the same time open spaces like Town Wood or beautiful Priesty Fields were preserved by decree of the borough council. And even in the 1960s the traveller from mid-Cheshire comes suddenly on the town.

Communications to 1848

Congleton's growth depended on the development of communications for it lay far from its best markets and its source of raw materials. For centuries traders had to rely on roads. Congleton stood on one of the great roads between London and Liverpool, though most traffic by 1700 used the highway through Lawton, south of the borough. Traffic between Manchester and the Potteries usually passed through Congleton, and the High Street followed the course of the old east–west route from mid-Cheshire into Derbyshire.[19] Packhorses, carts, coaches and travellers on foot had, therefore, always been a regular sight within the borough.

Regardless of width and the condition of surface, Congleton roads could be classified as either king's highways leading from town to town or else common and private ways which belonged to the community or individuals.[20] The Congleton Supervisor of the Highways, short of time and money, fought a losing battle against deteriorating road surfaces over much of the borough, though the main central streets had been paved in a fashion before 1700. Even these the boundary commissioners criticized in 1837.

In 1762, soon after Congleton's first silk mill opened, a

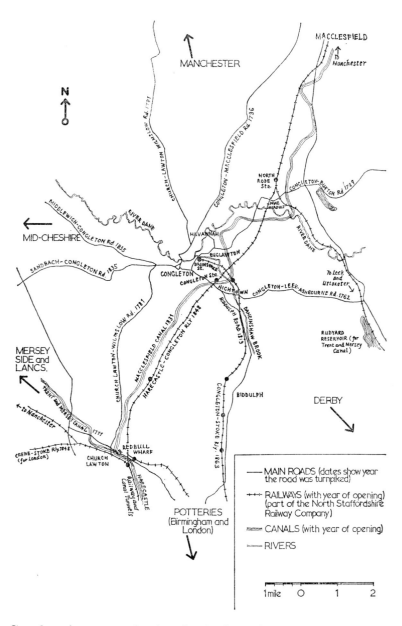

Congleton's communications in the late nineteenth century.

number of merchants and landowners formed a company which, securing an Act of Parliament, took over the upkeep of the main Congleton–Ashbourne highway leading to the silk centre of Derby.[21] The turnpike company erected toll bars and also obtained the right to take 'furze, heath, stones, gravel, sand' with other materials from 'any Commons or Waste Grounds ... without paying anything'. In return the company had to keep the highway in good repair. The upkeep of the road, however, probably cost very little.[22] A good foundation of gravel, sand, earth and large rounded stones might be overlaid with hard-packed earth or cinders.[23] The company did not make improvements overnight, and as late as 1804 certain conditions of an enlarging Act of 1782 had still not been fulfilled.[24]

The tolls in 1804 included 5*d* for a score of cattle and sheep, 4*s* for a wagon with wide wheels, and for 'Coach, Berlin, Landau, Chariot, Calash, Chaise, or Chair, upon Four Wheels, drawn by Six or more Horses or Beasts of Draught, Two Shillings'. Farmers, funeral parties, the post and Congleton people moving within the township paid nothing. Coal, lime, peat and turf passed freely under certain conditions, and one millowner secured free passage for his coal between Staffordshire and Congleton.[25] New vehicles appeared and became subject to toll: 'For every Carriage moved or propelled by steam or Machinery, or by any other Power than Animal Power, the Sum of One Shilling for every wheel thereof.'[26]

In 1781 the main road from Manchester to the Potteries was turnpiked as far as Church Lawton, followed by the Buxton road with a diversion to Havannah Mill (1789), the Macclesfield road (1796), the Biddulph New Road (1819) and highways to Sandbach and Middlewich as late as 1835. By the last date the eight main ways to Congleton had been taken into the hands of companies, though the town centre roads which all trusts used in common remained the responsibility of the corporation itself. The only new road, as opposed to improvements to old roads, was the two-mile length of the Biddulph turnpike through east Congleton.[27] Previously travellers had avoided the boggy land there by using the longer route through Overton.

Roadway improvements resulted in an increase in goods and passengers. Professional carriers with regular timetables emerged. In 1828 some seven firms plied, perhaps three times a week, between the borough and its markets in Manchester, Derby and Birmingham. One carried goods twice a week to the Trent and Mersey Canal wharf at nearby Lawton. John Johnson and Son, a Manchester firm, left the *Wolf's Head* in Swan Bank twice weekly for Manchester taking goods of all sizes, and Pickfords promised to deliver to all parts of the country.

The great age of passenger coaches between 1810 and 1835 turned Congleton into a busy tourist resort. Every day seven coaches journeyed southwards, the first leaving in the middle of the night from the *Bull's Head* for London. Four coaches went daily to Manchester and two to Liverpool. Congleton inns with their cobbled yards, large dining rooms and travellers' bed-rooms probably became busier than they had ever been.

Two gates on the Macclesfield to Congleton turnpike pro-duced a profit of £670 in 1838, a good sum, considering canal competition. The gates on the Congleton to Thatchmarsh Bottom road were leased in 1838 for over £360.[28] An inquiry of 1840 showed that of the six turnpikes converging on Congle-ton five were good enough for the traffic of the area though the Nantwich and Congleton road company had allowed its nine miles to degenerate into 'very bad repair'.[29] The trustees them-selves were responsible for repairing four roads while two com-panies relied on the help of townships along the route. The Macclesfield and Congleton trust undertook all repairs as far as the borough boundary before leaving town roads to Congle-ton corporation.

By 1840 the trusts were worried not only about the loss of statute labour services, abolished in 1835, but also, and more seriously, about railway competition. Two of the trusts, how-ever, were unaffected by the railways, their route lying away from them. Another expected competition and two others had already been materially affected. The Nantwich and Congleton trust claimed that its 'securities are almost unsaleable, indeed quite so, except at a great sacrifice'. Revenues from tolls fell by one-third. The solicitor of the Ashbourne–Congleton trust proposed that loans from the Exchequer should be cancelled since Parliament had allowed railways to be built in competi-tion with turnpikes. However, the companies survived, with difficulties, beyond 1860, the Buxton company continuing till 1881.[30]

It is difficult to know exactly the condition of the majority of

Congleton's minor routes during the years 1700 to 1860. These miles of unturnpiked lanes were important because they led to fields, quarries, moorland and farms, and the users no doubt objected if the township surveyors ignored them too much. Records, however, are lacking, though we know that bridges across the Dane and at Daneinshaw were rebuilt in the late eighteenth century.[31] Almost certainly it would be true to describe most Congleton lanes at any date between 1700 and 1860 as being, in the words of the 1835 Nantwich–Congleton Road Act, 'much out of repair and in need of Improvement'.[32]

Waterways rather than roads provided the best means of communication before 1830, but Congleton suffered on account of its lack of a navigable river. When the Bridgewater Canal proved the value of artificial waterways in the later eighteenth century merchants pressed for an east Cheshire canal to join up with Manchester and mid-Cheshire.[33] The influence of Staffordshire and Lancashire landowners, coal proprietors and merchants overruled purely Cheshire interests. The Bridgewater Canal was linked with the navigable Trent by a canal opened in 1777 which wound through Cheshire and passed half a dozen miles south of Congleton at Lawton. Of course this was not too far to transport goods, especially following the road improvements after 1781. A wharf was built near the *Red Bull* in Lawton, and Congleton carriers ran regular services to the wharf.[34] James Morris in the early nineteenth century journeyed from the *Wolf's Head* at Swan Bank twice a week, and more often on request. Pickfords left West Street daily to carry goods by road and waterway. Coal became immediately cheaper in the town after the opening of the Trent and Mersey Canal in 1777, and merchandise could reach ports like Liverpool swiftly. Yet the route to Manchester, for example, by way of Runcorn remained long and wandering.

Not till 1826, however, did Macclesfield and Congleton ease themselves directly into the canal system. A plan in 1811 for a Macclesfield canal from Marple into Staffordshire, by-passing Congleton,[35] collapsed. In 1826, however, an Act was obtained for a canal between the Peak Forest and Trent and Mersey canals winding down through east Cheshire via Macclesfield and Congleton.[36]

Thomas Telford planned the canal, completing it in 1831. He laid it on but two levels connected by a series of locks at

Bosley. In the engineer's own words the two levels comprised 'one, 10 miles, by which all traffic in and near Congleton has access to the Trent and Mersey Canal, without lockage; while on the upper level the numerous works in and near Macclesfield are supplied with coals from Marple, also without lockage'.[37] The canal, 26 miles in length, could take craft up to 70 ft long with a 3 ft draught. This standard size allowed the carriage of sufficiently large cargoes to make transportation pay handsomely. Indeed the low costs of canal transport proved very attractive to traders, a ton of sand, bricks or lime costing 1*d* a mile, a ton of coal or slate 1½*d* a mile, and bulkier goods like machinery 2*d* a mile.[38]

The canal's southern section had its headquarters on Congleton Wharf beside the old Dog Lane, later called Canal Street, some half mile from the town hall. Here the company built a large warehouse, store yard, quay and superintendent's house. The merchant family of Vaudrey set up a wharf with cranes near the place where the canal crossed the Daneinshaw.[39] The prospect seemed hopeful. At these wharfs all kinds of goods might be transhipped: cheese from Congleton farms, silk, cotton or paper from its mills, Mow Cop millstones, Adlington coal, Swithland slate, Burslem bricks and tiles, Worthington's Burton beer, Wedgwood's Etruria pottery, Kerridge stone, Cumberland red-ore, Birmingham knives, textile machinery, wines, sugar, gravel, sand, timber and tobacco.

But east Cheshire's canal came 30 years too late to be of great help to Congleton. Indeed the canal followed a contour through the district which by-passed main centres of population. Mills did not appear along its banks. Thus products like raw silk, coal or finished silken goods always had to be transhipped for a short but usually difficult road journey. Contemporaries thought Congleton's canal would 'materially facilitate its trade',[40] but in 1847 the canal fell into the hands of the North Staffordshire Railway Company[41] which soon sadly neglected it. The canal probably never really returned adequate profits to its builders.

Congleton people saw railed ways as early as 1806, possibly earlier, to bring coal to townsfolk and millowners. One way existed from that date between Mow Cop and Weld House near Congleton Moss so that coal might be brought to Congleton. John Farey, an observer of agriculture and industry of that time, described how at the south-east of Congleton, 'about 2 miles, at the N.W. corner of Congleton Moss, a Coal-yard was established about the year 1807, for the supply of this Town . . . and a railway was laid therefrom S. about 2 miles, to Stone Trough Colliery, in Woolstanton. It was laid with oval bars of iron, on the top of which the pulley-formed wheels of the trams ran . . . but when I saw this railway in July 1809, it seemed to be almost or quite disused, the reason of which I did not happen to learn.'[42] This way is, however, marked on Teesdale's Cheshire map of 1830 and on Bryant's of 1831, and ends at a 'Coal Wharf' on Peel Lane.[43]

From Stone Trough another railed way later led down the hill to Kent Green Wharf on the Macclesfield Canal. A third private railed road, marked on the Macclesfield Canal plan of 1825, led to a coal wharf on the Leek road at Daneinshaw. John Wright who ran the Biddulph Hall colliery constructed this railway in 1818 after taking a lease of land along the route. It followed the course of the brook Daneinshaw within Congleton, closely passing Whitemoor and the *Castle Inn*, and may well have survived at least until the partition in 1838 of the Wright estate.[44] The railed way is not marked on Bryant's map of 1831, but since he surveyed only Cheshire the short stretch in that county might have escaped the record.

Communications since 1848

The building of railways for steam locomotives became a practicable proposition from 1828. Plans to link Staffordshire, Crewe and Manchester were put forward in 1836-7, and the Manchester and Birmingham Railway Company began to build a line through Congleton and Stone in 1837. The company even started on the immense Dane viaduct.[45] A quarrel in 1839 over the Crewe portion of the line between the company and its powerful neighbour, the Grand Junction Railway, however, led to the abandonment of the plan. Only the short stretches between Manchester and Macclesfield and the Crewe to Potteries branch were opened. The bricks from the giant foundations of the viaduct were, according to legend, used to build houses in Antrobus and Astbury Streets.

In 1845 the North Staffordshire Railway Company was formed to take over the interests of the Manchester and Birmingham Railway. This company with a large capital attracted investments from many businessmen, and possibly Congleton people also joined in the railway 'mania' of the time. The new line was to link Macclesfield, Congleton, Harecastle, Stoke and Stone with Manchester, Crewe and London. Investors hired great engineers like Robert Stephenson and G. P. Bidder. They guaranteed the Trent and Mersey shareholders a fixed income in return for railway management of their canal and they purchased the Macclesfield Canal. The North Staffordshire had to fight with the Grand Junction until, after many threats, the former withdrew from all mid-Cheshire projects and the latter from the Crewe–Derby area.

The contract for building went to Thomas Brassey, the world's leading railway contractor. Brassey had to build the Dane viaduct at North Rode, 'one of the most stupendous works in this part of the country', and smaller viaducts in Buglawton over the Macclesfield Canal and Daneinshaw Brook. The Buglawton section was ready in 1848, though reconstruction proved necessary within a year on account of faulty piers. By July 1848 Brassey finished the Dane viaduct with its 20 arches of 50 ft span each. The viaduct was 1,300 ft long and 100 ft high, constructed in brick and stone.

The high level of the railway meant that Congleton station was built above the town near the canal, a mile from Dane Bridge. The town could count on rail connection with Crewe and the south from October 1848, and with Manchester a year later. James Worth, landlord of the old *Navigation Inn*, promptly renamed his house *Railway Inn*. In 1849 five trains passed through Congleton on their way southwards each day. The early morning passenger train provided connections at Stoke, Stone, Stafford and Birmingham for London, which could be reached in twelve hours. Between times ran goods trains. Neither canal nor roads could promise to move people and goods so swiftly and so far in safety and at such reasonable fares. By 1858 six trains left the town for Macclesfield each weekday (and three on Sundays) and six left for the Potteries.[46] The line was not, however, one of the main routes through Cheshire and never carried the traffic of the main Manchester–Crewe line which passed through nearby Sandbach.

The railway from Brunswick Wharf near the Dane and from the Upper Junction on the main line to Biddulph and Stoke did not open until 1863. Brunswick Street had been until 1859 an isolated settlement near the Buxton Road toll gate. Then the railway company brought a branch line downhill to the toll gate during the years 1859–63 and the development of the area proceeded apace. Passengers could board trains at the Mossley Halt for Macclesfield in the north or Biddulph and Stoke in the south.

Railways and canals seriously threatened carriers by road during the years after 1860. Carters, however, found themselves jobs taking passengers and goods to the railway station or canal wharf, and as late as 1930 a horse-drawn wagon transported passengers to Sandbach market. At this date, too, began a period of new road building which eventually led to the movement of traffic from the railway to road. The Manchester by-pass is typical of this work. Congleton got its first motor bus connections with outside places in 1914.[47] In that year Chris Dale and F. E. Goodwin began a regular service from Congleton to Biddulph. Soon afterwards the British Omnibus Company began to run to Sandbach and Biddulph. The great increase in travel after the first World War necessitated larger companies, frequent services and good organization. A decade after the end of the war the North Western and the Potteries Motor Traction companies took over all regular local routes, and both flourished until about 1955–60. Then the competition of the private family motor-car caused cuts in services.

The canal which wound through east Congleton, built too late to earn the rich dividends of eighteenth-century navigations, enjoyed, however, 20 years of useful life before the railway grew into a serious rival. It is clear from local directories of the late nineteenth century that by then the railways and even the road catered for much of Congleton's needs. Nearly everyone wishing to reach Manchester or to travel southwards went by train. Much local farm and market traffic used roads. The canal seemed to be decaying by the early decades of the twentieth century, and by about 1950 pleasure craft began to outnumber commercial boats.[48]

In contrast, Congleton railways were very busy until after the first World War. Reasonably cheap rates for passengers and goods turned Congleton station at Hightown and the Brunswick Street goods yard into important centres of business. Both stations soon attracted to their vicinity dwellings, shops and worksheds. Later, however, buses and private cars worked against the railways. Following the difficult war years when trains came into their own again the post-war period has seen train services deteriorating and fares rising. Even in 1960, however, 20 trains a day left Congleton station for the south.

It is difficult to assess the importance of transport improvements to Congleton's growth. Industrial development in the form of silk mills began before roads were turnpiked or canals and railways built. The improved facilities did not prevent periodical trade crises or the great depression between 1826 and 1848. On the other hand the cheapness and ease with which goods and passengers came to and left the borough in 1860 cannot but indicate the advantages of excellent communications. The journey to London in a day or the delivery to Congleton of large pieces of machinery, both possible after 1800, would have been unthinkable in 1700.

Although improved communications in the later nineteenth century did not rescue Congleton from economic depression they probably saved the town from complete stagnation and eventually encouraged the advent of new industries. On the other hand inhabitants were enabled to travel outside Congleton to their work, while products from the Potteries competed with Congleton goods.

The Textile Industry to the 1830s
Before the middle of the eighteenth century industry and trade in Congleton were organized much as they had been for centuries. Only freemen might trade in the town without paying heavy tolls, and freedom could be achieved by being the son of a freeman, apprenticeship or payment of an entry fee. Freemen claimed wide privileges when they went to trade outside Congleton, in certain towns entering and setting up stalls without restriction. Freemen's lists of the time show a town of small tradesmen with the leather and woollen cloth industries predominating.[49] As late as 1771 it was said that Congleton 'people carry on a great trade in making gloves'.[50] Industry organized on the domestic system enabled mercers and drapers like the Parnells, ancestors of Lord Congleton, to grow prosperous. People manufactured goods at home, sometimes in garrets, more often in living rooms. This applied to shoemaking as

much as to spinning and weaving of textiles. Some larger houses and workshops undoubtedly existed where there were paid employees. The third-storey garrets of houses in Mill Street near Dane Bridge may have housed half a dozen adults. Yet the domestic organization of industry had long been dominated by capitalists. Such men supplied families with raw materials, cloth already spun and tools. Their representatives or undertakers gave out work and collected the products later, paying according to the work done.

This sort of enterprise survived in Congleton well into the nineteenth century, but the most significant development in the 100 years between 1750 and 1850 was the transformation of the town into a textile factory town. The change from a domestic industry controlled by a commercial capitalist to a factory industry controlled by an industrial capitalist was an obvious step. Congleton, however, differed from many industrial towns of the north-west, because it grew famous for silk rather than cotton, although cotton, too, became part of the local scene.

English silk manufacture expanded considerably after the prohibition of French and Asian imports between 1698 and 1701.[51] In 1717 a silk factory had been set up in Derby by John Lombe, and in 1743-4 Charles Roe opened another in Macclesfield.[52] Growing unemployment in Congleton led the corporation in 1752 to sponsor the introduction of silk manufacture into the borough.[53] They leased a site long used as the poorhouse garden, called Byflete or Byeflatt, on the north bank of the Dane between Dane Bridge and the King's Corn Mill and south of this mill's stream, to the partners John Clayton, a Stockport silk spinner, and Nathaniel Pattison (1726-56), a young and ambitious London merchant.

Pattison and Clayton erected a new factory, long, high and narrow, later called the Old Mill.[54] Its narrowness was due to the necessity of having windows down both lengths so that no worker might complain of poor light. This was vital in processes where absolute accuracy of cutting had to be maintained all day long. The lower floors eventually held 75 winding engines, 21 cleaning engines and the doubling, spinning and throwing mills. The mill specialized in 'throwing', that is twisting fibres into thread, and all the related spinning processes. 'Manufacturing', the equivalent of weaving in other textile trades, was also undertaken. The factory's bright, severe appearance, its 390 windows, and its setting on the river bank before the green Town Wood usually greatly impressed visitors to Congleton. James Brindley designed the Old Mill's machinery and the wheel, 20 ft in diameter and some $5\frac{1}{2}$ ft broad. Five floors of moving machines certainly demanded the efficient use of water power.[55]

In 1754 the partners also rented the old King's Corn Mill for 120 years to prevent disputes over land and water supply. The next year the silk mill opened, during John Clayton's mayoralty. People found employment at reasonable rates and immigration followed.[56] The industrial revolution in the borough had begun. By 1771 the mill employed over 600[57] and by 1795 dominated employment in the town.[58]

Pattison survived only a year of the factory's working, dying in May 1756 at the age of 30. John Clayton himself, a much older man, died in June 1758.[59] So the new mill passed to the brother and nephew of Pattison and to the wife and children of Clayton. Only Nathaniel Pattison, nephew of Pattison the elder, wanted the works so he paid £2,500 to the other owners, the Claytons, and became sole director. Nathaniel, dying in 1784, left the property to his children, one of whom, Nathaniel Maxey Pattison (1760–1827), resided in Congleton as manager.

The making of thrown and spun silk encouraged experiment in other fields. About the same time the production of ribbons was introduced into Congleton. At first it was in the hands of handloom weavers. A 'ribbon weaver' is recorded in Congleton chapel register in 1754. A merchant of Coventry, the centre of the ribbon trade, claimed that in 1755 he had begun to put out work to small master ribbon manufacturers (undertakers) in Congleton and Leek.[60] Shortly afterwards small factories appeared in Lawton Street and at Swan Bank where firms manufactured ribbons to the order of Coventry merchants. By 1789 the borough had four ribbon-weaving firms, including the important concern of Elizabeth Jackson and Son of Lawton Street. Presumably other families worked in their own homes for Coventry firms on the outdoor system.

Cotton spinning came to Congleton a little later, about 1784. It was introduced by Richard Martin (1760–95), dealer in textiles, alderman of Congleton and mayor from 1788 to 1789. The Martins had lived in the town for generations and during the eighteenth century prospered in trade. Richard Martin the elder (1689–1769), father of the cotton merchant, seems to have been a grocer who invested in landed property and eventually became a borough alderman and mayor in 1758–9.[61] He died in 1769 leaving a young family who all did well. The son, Richard, probably went for some time to Manchester to learn the cotton business.

In 1787 there were two cotton firms, and gradually silk and cotton began to be manufactured in the same establishments. John Booth, a textile merchant, set up a cotton mill in Lawton Street near to the establishment of William Slate and Son, silk and cotton manufacturers. Slate seems to have come to the town about 1770 and described himself in Congleton registers as early as 1773 as a silkman. In 1788 the Slates took land in Whitakers meadow by the Dane for the erection of their new silk mill and housing project.[62] Jesse Drakeford of Dane Side in Mill Street, born in 1756, the son of Joseph Drakeford, a Congleton craftsman, set up a modest silk-spinning business during the late eighteenth century. He was one of the first men to install Boulton and Watt's steam engines. Possibly about 1805 he began to manufacture cotton goods. He and his son, Jesse, born 1786, combined silk and cotton till about 1835.[63] George Reade (1760–1838), a Congleton general merchant and thrice mayor, set up a cotton-spinning mill at Stone House Side off Mill Street possibly as early as 1788, turning also to silk throwing about 1821. Reade lived at Moody Hall, and his whole family engaged in textile manufacture. The businesses survived all trade depressions, though cotton was abandoned before 1850.[64]

John Vaudrey (1766–1828), son of William Vowdry (1737–1777), a Congleton trader, manufactured cotton in Lawton Street mill from 1788, but about 1810 moved to Bath Vale in Buglawton.[65] The new mill was powered by water which rushed down Timbersbrook to join the Daneinshaw. Vaudrey eventually extended his mill, building eleven cottages for workers nearby and a mansion for himself.[66] He owned houses and shops in High Street, Thomas Goodall's timber yard, the paper mill at Tenter Meadow, six houses at Kinseys Croft in Congleton, the large farmhouse called Belle Vue, much land in east Cheshire and estates in Staffordshire, all presumably purchased from the profits of his mill. By the time of his death in 1828 he had begun to manufacture silk, and a portion of his extensive premises at Bath Vale had been leased to John Wild, a waste silk spinner. Vaudrey had retired while still able to enjoy retirement and two of his sons, William (1794–1836) and Charles (1796–1858), took over his interests. In his will of 1827 he mentions 'Cotton and Silk Factories, Steam Engine, Engine House, Gas Works, Apparatus and Buildings used by my said Sons William and Charles in conducting the Cotton and Silk Businesses'. The sons expanded the business, perfecting the private gas works at Bath Vale.[67] They invested in farms and houses. They became proprietors, and Charles a director, of the Congleton gas works. The brothers sent their goods from 1831 by canal boat, renting an extensive wharf near Danein-shaw valley crossing. William (d. 1836) left £3,000 and much real property in Leek, Gibralter Rocks in Congleton, the residence in Buglawton and property elsewhere. This methodical man carefully divided his valuable goods, his brother Thomas (1801–50), for instance, getting 'one Dozen Table Spoons' and 'One Drinking Cup, being that without a handle'. His mistress and two children received £600 and his servant got shares in the gas works.

But it was silk rather than cotton that came to dominate Congleton and it was the fortunes of the silk industry that dictated the prosperity or otherwise of the town. Events outside local control had considerable influence. As far as silk was concerned the main factors were foreign competition and the effectiveness of British restrictions on foreign imports. The success of Pattison's mill gave other investors confidence. Additional silk mills opened in Congleton. By 1773, there were four or five silk mills in the town, although only one was working because of a trade depression.[68] By 1787, besides the Old Mill, there were the Slates' cotton and silk factory, a cotton factory and a ribbon establishment.

By 1800 the ribbon trade was depressed, and manufacturers helped their mills survive by branching out.[69] Richard Edwards of Booth Street, a ribbon weaver, had become also a silk and cotton spinner. Samuel Yates in 1820 mentions him as one of the only three ribbon makers left in the town. Peter Gent of Lawton Street and Vale Mill controlled two ribbon works in 1828, but he also was a silk throwster, and eventually by 1840 ceased to make ribbons.[70] The silk industry generally, however, prospered because the Napoleonic Wars prevented the import of French silk goods, and cotton, too, shared in the expansion. A minor boom around March 1815 was followed by a short depression in 1815–16. A contemporary described this post-war depression in hopeful terms: 'the industrial inhabitants have very patiently endured a few privations, and appear content with a diminution of wages, since the price of provisions has also been diminished'.[71]

In 1817 Congleton had seventeen silk mills and five cotton factories. There was a further expansion in 1817–18, by which time there were 32 silk throwsters. In 1820 possibly some 2,000 Congleton people found regular work in textiles, 400 of them at the Old Mill, and 200 at Hall and Johnson's.[72] Another boom followed in 1822–5. In 1823 there were almost 4,000 hands employed in the town.[73] Mills, many single-storeyed, hastily erected, stretched down Lawton, Wagg, Booth, West, Moody and Mill Streets. Cotton mills lay in Mill and Booth Streets, at Stonehouse Green and in Buglawton. Indeed by 1820 Buglawton had become the centre of the local cotton industry, and was still so in 1835.[74] The spinning of lace thread, too, introduced into Buglawton about 1800 was stimulated by the Napoleonic Wars and still important in 1831.

As well as being helped by the stoppage of French imports in the wars, the silk industry prospered in those years because of heavy duties on foreign imports. In 1824, however, the government drastically cut the duties on thrown and raw silk, and further reduced them between 1826 and 1829. At the same time the home industry was affected by the growing use of cotton garments.[75]

The consequent depression after 1826 caught Congleton in the midst of expansion which could not be halted easily. Some fourteen new mill premises were built in 1824–6. Half opened as silk factories, half remained empty, and few investors got any return on their capital. Even though no further building was undertaken anywhere from 1826, the town had in 1828 three cotton works, four ribbon manufacturers, nineteen silk manu-facturers and 59 silk spinners or throwers.[76] By 1832 Congleton and Buglawton had 45 factories housing 58 concerns and employing 2,219 people. But already 1,700 hands were unemployed. Soon eighteen mills stood idle and six were converted to other uses. In 1831 73 houses stood empty in the town; in

a High Street in the Eighteenth Century, *b* View of Congleton (eighteenth century)

a

b

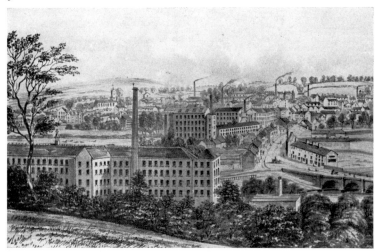

a The Old Mill (late 1920s), *b* Berisford's Mill, office building (built 1962)

a

b

1841 332, with only eight building. Between 1823 and 1832 the number of spindles working fell alarmingly, and some mills worked only three or four days a week. The workers rapidly sank into a pitiful state: 'their bellies go half full, their backs half clothed'.

Many owners felt as much distress as the employees, because they had known real prosperity and could not get used to straitened circumstances. Thomas Johnson, the Buglawton silk throwster, giving evidence in London in 1832, pointed out that he had virtually all his capital in real property, being otherwise penniless. 'I am keeping this mill in action in hopes of better and improved times . . . the mill is no more value to me than this piece of paper.' The factory, comparatively modern, 'beautifully situated as a mill', worked by waterpower and boasting as cheap a labour force as anywhere, suffered not from bad management but from foreign competition.

Worst hit by the depression, however, were the handloom weavers. Even before the general depression they were adversely affected by the output of power-driven looms. Boom years had attracted many immigrants, including Irish, who must have lowered wage levels.[77] They worked on piece rates as handloom weavers, in their own homes or garrets, as at Dane Bridge. As a result of competition and depression, however, piece rates dropped by four times between 1814 and 1833 and many handloom weavers disappeared from the town.

In 1829 the owners and mill overseers petitioned Parliament about unemployment and a relief committee was set up.[78] The town's industry survived, partly as a result of the introduction of steam power. Mills had, of course, been attracted to the town partly by the abundant supply of water for power. Dane Mill lay in a narrow bend of the river north of West Lane. Factories at Daneinshaw used the brook flowing from Congleton Edge. Burdett's map of 1777 shows small mill wheels at Timbersbrook and along the Daneinshaw to indicate water-driven establishments. Thomas Johnson's factory, newly erected in 1810 and considered most advanced, still ran by water power in 1831.[79]

Manufacturers were slow to adopt steam power, partly because they distrusted the ability of steam to drive large numbers of machines, partly because they refused to spend money on installing equipment. It was not easy, before the opening of the Macclesfield Canal in 1831, to bring coal to Congleton whereas water power remained always abundant. Yet as early as 1801 Thomas Slate, son of William Slate, installed a 32 h.p. rotative, beam crank steam engine from the Birmingham Soho foundry of James Watt and Matthew Boulton. Soon afterwards, Jesse Drakeford purchased a 6 h.p. rotative side-lever engine for his silk mill.[80] But in 1820 Samuel Yates still saw most mills being driven by water. The waterwheels at Havannah dating from about 1761 were refurbished and re-used when the mill building was rebuilt in 1840 by Gibbs Crauford Antrobus, M.P., of Eaton Hall, the local landowner. Congleton had some 34 mills in the central area, however, which could not rely on water. These mills needed hand or steam power. Three or four mills below Howey Pool near Chapel Street used the mill race from which water ran in a culvert through Stonehouse Green Mill and then alongside William Reade's Brookside Mill and so into the Dane. Park Street area had a small pool fed by a stream flowing towards Lawton Street.[81] So even in 1831, steam engines in Congleton totalled a mere 316 h.p.

The Textile Industry from the 1830s to 1900
The introduction of machinery, especially steam-powered, completed the destruction of the handloom weavers' living. Yet the continued improvement of machines speeded up the pace of work and the amount turned out.[82] By 1834 more people than ever got some kind of living from textiles in Congleton.[83] In 1835 Parliament heard that 'there has been a gradual improvement in the trade of late'. Congleton produced more thrown silk than its greater neighbour Macclesfield, even though no new mills had been erected since 1825.[84] A Parliamentary Report of 1884 described the period 1830–60 as Congleton's greatest trading decades.[85] Immensely difficult years these were, but masters and men survived. Mills produced ferrets, which were both coarse binding tapes and pretty ribbons, woven of floss silk, silk and cotton, and wool; broad silks; handkerchiefs; velvets; black satin and plain coloured ribbons made mainly on handlooms.[86] Men still invested money in factories. In 1830 Samuel Pearson of Buglawton Hall, landowner and textile merchant, purchased the Old Mill from James Pattison. Samuel's brother, James, took over Dane Mill

soon after 1830 and began to make silk sarsenets and ferrets to supplement the Old Mill's production.

By 1838 Congleton mills worked at throwing raw silk, spinning waste silk into schappe, and making thrown silk into plain ribbons by power looms.[87] There were only about 100 hand engine-looms in the town and power-driven mills dominated the ribbon-weaving industry. The broad-silk looms, worked by hand, and once numerous, had also declined in numbers, most of their operators having removed to Macclesfield. About 100, however, remained, employed largely by Reades, to weave bandanas, a kind of handkerchief, and twills for pocket kerchiefs. Two firms gave out work to undertakers employing domestic workers. But power-loom weaving was 'the staple weaving-trade of the town'. The chief manufacturers of plain ribbons were Pearsons (100 power looms), Johnsons (50), Charles Johnson (50) and Reades (30).

The town underwent another crisis in 1839–40 when mill-owners closed eighteen factories and dismissed workers. They refused to spend money in hard times, shortsightedly allowing skilled workers to leave Congleton. At the height of depression about 1840 only fifteen mills remained open in the town. The Old Mill employed 600 people, Halls of Marlfield Mill 400, Johnsons of Buglawton 300. Five other factories in the town centre gave work to 200. Altogether some 3,250 hands went to the textile mills more or less regularly, though more women than men found work there. Consolidation of firms and pruning of staff, especially presumably the higher-paid male labour force, further reduced employment opportunities. In 1842 Congleton workers rioted, trying to destroy machinery, driving plugs out of boilers, besieging factories, intimidating shop-keepers and foremen. The armed presence of the yeomanry alone prevented chaos, because the ill-organized borough police were terrified and powerless. In 1845 and again two years later workers attempted to take the law into their own hands.[88]

About 1848 the economic climate improved. By 1850 ten new concerns had started to throw silk or make ribbons, employing 1,300 people, so that the textile labour force topped 5,000, one-third of the district's total population. Pearsons made ribbons, Bracegirdles lawn and crape, Robinsons broadsilk and handkerchiefs, Havannah silk small ware. At this date modern enterprises like Wallworths of Wallworth Bank, Barrows of Canal Street and Hunts of Swan Bank were once again employing over 200 workers each. The 1851 census indicates, however, that most mills were smaller than this and employed two women to every one man. In 1859 the district had 40 throwing mills and over 5,000 textile workers.[89]

The importance of Congleton as a ribbon centre increased in these years. Before 1831 Congleton had been a satellite of Coventry in this respect, but in that year a riot at Coventry destroyed the first steam-driven ribbon factory there. As a result 'much of the plain ribbon trade, especially in black sarsenets, went from Coventry to Leek, Congleton, Derby and elsewhere'.[90] So Pearsons of the Old Mill and Reades began to make plain ribbons and the plain black sarsenets used to produce fine ribbons. By 1860 twelve firms in Congleton and Buglawton manufactured ribbons and sold these without the intervention of Coventry merchants.[91] Among the leading firms were George Kinsey of Lower Park Street, Lees and Leadbeater of Back High Street, and the new family business of Berisford Brothers of Victoria Mill.

Then in 1860 a heavy blow fell on the English silk and ribbon industries. The Cobden trade treaty with France in that year resulted in an enormous increase in the imports of French finished silk. At Congleton, as elsewhere in England, the mills could not compete with this. Moreover, on account of cost and fashion people were turning from Cheshire silk to cotton, wool, flannel and foreign-labelled garments. Parisian goods, because of their perfect finish and reputation, rivalled Congleton's produce. Foreigners put duties on English silk while England allowed foreign silk to enter freely. Congleton later reported to Parliamentary commissioners that the decline of the silk industry could be blamed on a 'falling off in the throwing branch caused by the importation of thrown silks, duty free, from the cheap labour districts on the Continent'.[92] The collapse of the silk industry cannot, however, be blamed entirely on the Cobden treaty. Lack of technical training, out-dated machinery, expensive raw materials and changes in fashion all contributed.

The situation during the years after 1860 demanded, firstly, constant changes of basic materials and finished products to satisfy the market and, secondly, continual introduction of new equipment and processes to keep abreast of rivals at home and abroad. Perhaps half of Congleton's textile firms never adapted themselves to the demands of a changing world, and the directories and trade catalogues tell the stories of businesses both old-established and new which failed to survive. The number of mills which in 1860 stood at 38 silk throwing, three silk spinning, ten silk manufacturing, and twelve ribbon manufacturing was reduced immediately to 30, and by 1883 to twelve with no more than 1,275 hands. There were empty mills all over the town.[93] One, behind Moody Street, was converted soon after 1860 into workshops and then demolished.[94] In 1883 only three-quarters of machinery might be profitably used, and some places closed down for long weekends. But Robert Head writing in 1886 noted a slight improvement. He found 22 mills in operation with over 2,000 workers.[95] There were still twelve active silk throwsters, including Pearsons of the Old Mill with 564 hands and Henry Hogg of Buglawton with 200. Three manufacturers used silk to some extent, and these firms included the forward-looking Berisfords of Victoria Mill who employed 110 workers. The silk spinners were three in number: Peter Wild of Forge Mill (with 70 hands), Reade and Company of Brook Mill (156) and Conder and Company of Bath Vale (130). There were but seven silk mills in 1910. By 1928 there remained no silk throwsters or weavers in Congleton, though three silk spinners survived: Peter Wild, Reades and George Davenport of Prospect Mill. Firms like Berisfords had concentrated on other textiles by this time, while other mills went over to entirely different work such as cardboard-box making. No silk manufacturer as such survived to 1960.

Of those firms existing before 1860 which experienced the crises from 1860 and weathered the storm, perhaps the most successful was Berisford Brothers of Victoria Mill. Originally from Longnor in Derbyshire, the farming family of Berisford moved to east Cheshire only in 1829.[96] The father, Isaac (1794–1854), worked in Congleton and Buglawton silk mills before returning to farming during years of depression. Presumably many hundreds of silk operatives must have done the same. At least six of Isaac's children entered mills, and Charles, the seventh child, born at Buglawton in 1830, began work at the age of nine. Possibly apprenticed in Macclesfield as a maker of ferrets and black ribbons, he worked hard, attending Sunday and night schools, until he became a journeyman and then a master. In 1858 Charles Berisford with his brothers William and Francis took the spacious Foundry Street mill in Congleton, with its powered looms, erected as a speculation on Hunts Eye by Robert Bradwell, brass and iron founder. The prospects, not unclouded in 1858, seemed fair even after the trade treaty of 1860 because Berisfords concentrated on the more popular ribbon trade. When French silks began to flood into England, Berisfords turned immediately and exclusively to the making of ferrets, Prussian bindings and galloons (that is bindings for hats and clothes). Thus the firm won through. Charles Berisford died in 1898, owning mills in Congleton and Prestwich.

Some of Berisfords' neighbours changed to cotton after 1860, and in 1867 Thomas and John Shepherd of Royton introduced fustian and velvet cutting to the town, opening a mill at Eaton's Bank. The consequent rush to imitate when people saw the Shepherds' prosperity turned silk mills and garrets over to fustian. But fashions changed, and some manufacturers were ruined. Robert Shepherd, however, brother of Thomas and John, managed to survive into the next century. Shepherd, born in 1837 at Royton, fourth son of John Shepherd, a fustian manufacturer, came to Congleton only in 1882. Despite American and German competition he invested money and prospered. His Liberalism and interest in education endeared him to his townspeople and he became mayor in 1893–4.

Thomas Taylor (1835–94) also belonged to Royton, where he began as a worker and manager in the mill of John Shepherd, father of Robert. Then he migrated to Congleton and worked for Thomas Shepherd from 1867 at the Meadows Mill. Finally he took over the old Primitive Methodist chapel at Eaton Bank and established his own fustian factory, which prospered. He became in addition an innkeeper and ended by owning Salford Mill in Rood Lane.[97] The firm sold out to the United Velvet Cutters' Association of Manchester in 1900.[98]

Textiles in the Twentieth Century
In 1912 Berisfords began to make shoe galloons for good quality shoes. In 1929 the firm started to use rayon and, in 1932, introduced bias bindings. After 1932 when the government restricted imports Berisfords immediately went back into ribbon making and added to this wrist-watch galloons and taffetas. Man-made fibres became a significant Congleton

trade about 1930. After the second World War nylon and terylene were popular, and Berisfords learned new processes to produce goods of these materials. By 1960 the firm specialized in making ribbons for facing hand-knitted garments, hair ribbons, blanket bindings and woven labels. Mill equipment, power supply and processes had continually to be improved. The increase in the number of pieces of ribbon or binding produced by each worker may be taken as an example of progress. By giving each man two facing looms to work and by introducing doubledecker battens some firms raised productivity four or five times. Berisfords not only purchased machines from America and Germany but also designed their own looms to meet the demands of the market after 1945. The firm knew that old-fashioned machines would not produce high-quality goods from these new man-made fibres. Robert H. Lowe of the Old Mill, successor of the Claytons and Pearsons, also kept abreast of the times by erecting a modern extension to the factory and refurnishing it with up-to-date equipment after the second World War.[99]

Berisfords had used steam power since 1858 and introduced electricity in 1928. Other mills lying on the river employed water power: indeed a Buglawton water-wheel was in operation in 1958. By 1930, however, electricity had so many advantages over water and coal that millowners ignored these at their peril. The complexity and fineness of work demanded bright lighting: both electric lamps above the looms and large windows in all rooms. Berisfords and the Old Mill saw the change from tallow candles, oil lamps and naked jets of gas to gas lamps, electric bulbs and fluorescent strip lights. Yet at the same time some mills lagged half a century behind, using a few dim gas lamps as late as 1940.

The character of managers and owners perhaps helped a number of Congleton firms to survive. The Berisford family were Methodists, hard workers, shrewd and thrifty. Charles (1830-98) and his son Harry (1864-1936) took care to know all their workers. Neither strikes nor needless dismissals figure in the firm's history. In 1954 a pension and life insurance scheme was started. Modern premises and machines made work easier and pleasanter and working hours were reduced from the eleven, normal in 1890, to eight or nine after 1945. Hours and wages were greatly standardized in all Congleton mills after 1900 partly under the influence of trade unions like the Amalgamated Society of Textile Workers and Kindred Trades, partly through government action. The extraordinary reliance on women workers especially after 1914 (when wartime and cheap materials necessitated the cheaper female labour) militated against improved factory conditions because some owners took advantage of women workers' lack of trade union organization.

Berisfords steadily expanded. In 1908, for example, a Derby mill was taken to supply cotton bindings which could be finished at Congleton, in 1913 R. Thorp and Sons of Macclesfield was purchased, and in 1920 Lower Park Street Mill replaced the Derby mill. The Thorp firm, begun in 1794 in Manchester, took over Congleton's Dane Mill in the late nineteenth century and produced small wares. Lower Park Street Mill (built in 1854 by George Acton, woodturner, purchased by Robert Shepherd, the fustian manufacturer, in 1894 and taken over by Berisfords in 1919) provided additional space for departments squeezed out of the Victoria Mill. In 1948 further extensions were designed by Berisfords' staff.

The second World War hit industry severely, and though this time there was little unemployment, portions of most mills were closed, machinery left idle, trained staff lost, and raw materials scarce. Government orders which had to be completed meant less time could be given to demands of old customers. In one way this proved a boon because loss of old machinery and abandoning of traditional processes allowed some firms to start from the beginning, looking forward to post-war competition, not yearning for the past.

Congleton's textile trade between 1945 and 1960 concentrated on synthetic fibres like nylon and terylene together with cotton and a little silk. Robert Lowe of Roldane Mill, the new extension to the Old Mill, produced knitted and woven garments. In the case of knitted goods Lowes undertook every process from thread to finished product. George Davenport Adams of Vale Mill, successor to the silk spinners of Prospect Mill, produced nylon hose, knitted outerware and jersey fabric. Stott and Smith of Empire Mill made cotton terry towels, bath mats and napkins. Thus many Congleton mills turned themselves into light clothing and small-ware producers rather than manufacturers of great rolls of silk and cotton.

Yet not every firm which clung obstinately to silk to the exclusion of other fibres went bankrupt. Careful management and expert craftsmanship enabled the spun-silk business of Peter Wild of Forge Mills to survive until 1952. The Wild family ran silk manufacturing in Buglawton and Rushton from about 1820. In 1865 Peter Wild (1838–78) took over the silk spinning mill at Crossledge occupied by James Holdforth, successors to Robert Thompson and Company, and about that time went into partnership with John Bradwell of Congleton.[100]

The Bradwells belonged to Bradwell in Derbyshire. Dennis Bradwell, founder of the family, born in Bradwell in 1801, settled in Congleton as a brickmaker and built up by 1851 a prospering business. His sons originally followed him in his trade before they moved into textiles.[101] By 1865 John and Dennis Bradwell already ran a throwing business in Dane Street, while Dennis in conjunction with Charles Ginders worked a small mill on Timbersbrook in Buglawton.[102] Dennis Bradwell (1828–97) of Higher Daisy Bank became a magistrate and mayor of Congleton in after years, and in 1888, as an investment, bought half of the Old Mill. He was followed in the business by his son Charles Dennis Bradwell (1861–1943), town councillor, magistrate and trustee of Congleton Common Lands.[103] He worked along with Peter Wild's widow, Ann (1840–1918) and son Peter Bradwell Wild (1866–1951).

The Wild–Bradwell business underwent difficulties during the years 1860–90, but Dennis Bradwell from his own pocket injected money into the business at crucial moments.[104] Peter Wild and Company never grew into a large firm but remained about the same size as the majority of Congleton businesses in the later nineteenth and early twentieth centuries. Its sales in 1913 were £34,000 and its trading profit £2,600. Despite the decline in money values Peter Wild's sales between 1918 and 1938 were rarely even one-quarter above the 1913 figure. Net profits in 1913 were £1,900, in 1924 £1,600. The trading profit of £4,000 in 1923 must be set against increased taxation and higher production costs. It was impossible at times to find buyers of ordinary shares, and the position deteriorated after the depression of 1929.

Fortunately government policy in restricting imports after 1932 saved the firm, though the directors' reports and minute books indicate deep suspicion that a reduction in import duties might occur at any time. Though this fear was not realized a worse disaster struck. From 1935 to 1945 it became increasingly difficult and costly to get raw material from the East on account of wars, and Wild's prices rose steeply. Once again the government saved the day by placing large orders with the company during the years 1940–5. Profits and dividends rose immediately. In 1944 scarcity of silk raw material alone led to the spinning of some long-staple rayon yarns for export. For a short time after the war the demand for spun silk encouraged production, but by 1948–9 raw material prices stood so high that costs had to rise. Devaluation of the pound made imports of silk waste prohibitively costly, and other fibres began to replace silk. Public demand for silk had almost disappeared by 1951, if the directors' reports are to be believed.

In 1952 came one of those fateful decisions which alter the course of business history and affect the economies of whole towns. Peter Wild might have changed from silk to other fibres, but the directors reported that the 'silk machinery is not productive enough to enable us to turn over to the synthetic fibres and produce them competitively'. Old engines were too big and consumed too much fuel, the machines ran too slowly. High-priced silk repaid production costs, but synthetic fibres, produced in the same quantity, could not be an economic proposition. It was just possible to make blends of silk and nylon, but few customers could be found for these goods. The firm decided to stay in silk, but to rent smaller premises with efficient engines. Some machinery from Forge Mill could be used. Modern equipment could also be acquired which would dress raw silk economically. The firm found the best premises in Leek, Staffordshire, and early in 1953 installed themselves there. Peter Wild therefore chose the opposite course to Berisfords, but both more or less successfully met the difficulties in textiles after 1860.

Congleton has been a textile town, therefore, for over two centuries. Products have varied to suit conditions at the time: in one period silk and cotton came from the mills, in another knitted and nylon garments. Ribbons, once produced for Coventry merchants, were later turned out by Congleton capitalists. Then the manufacture died out until re-introduced in 1932. The borough has remained a relatively prospering textile town only because its industry has been willing to make changes at appropriate times.

Other Trades in the Eighteenth and Nineteenth Centuries
Apart from the textile industry, Congleton had at various times other small industries.

Congleton ropery existed from about 1750. In 1789 James Morgan, a High Street grocer, ran the ropeworks near the new 'great bridge' over the Dane. Ropemaking demanded a long ropewalk and much skill. The fibre had to be spun outdoors on a walk 200 yards long. The spinner took the hemp and wound a length round his waist, crossing the ends behind his back. He then fastened a quantity to a large hook which lay near the rim of a wheel. This wheel's axle was connected, waist high, with the storehouse wall. An apprentice might thus turn the wheel giving the regular twist to the fibre as the spinner moved backwards. After three measures of yarn had been finished the ends were secured to three hooks on the wheel, and the lengths were twisted into a single strand. Strands could be twisted into ropes on a second walk.

By 1816 Congleton had two ropemaking establishments. The works grew more important when the canal opened because towropes always seemed to be needed. Joseph Goldstraw, one of the rope manufacturers during early Victorian days, specialized in producing engine yarn for factory use.[105]

William H. Burslam's ropewalk survived until the first World War. The Burslam family business in Congleton began about 1815. When William Burslam and his son Jesse (born 1805) came from Liverpool they worked not on ropes but in stone.[106] William appears in Pigot's *Directory* of 1828 as a stonemason and Jesse, who succeeded him, employed three men at the time of the 1851 census. Jesse's son, Jesse, also continued in the trade. But a stepson, John Burslam, born in 1830, was apprenticed as a ropemaker and he founded the Burslam's ropery in Mill Street. Then, about 1890, the demand for strong ropes by mill-owners dropped steadily. For over a century prior to this date machinery relied on rope as much as on leather thongs for the transmission of movement, but modern inventions made rope obsolete. In any case good cheap rope could be purchased in Stoke or Manchester. So Congleton's ropery closed down, though the shop at 66 Mill Street stayed open to sell manufactured products first under the Burslams, then under Thomas Gara.

The eighteenth century also saw the introduction of copper works. Charles Roe and partners who had introduced silk to Macclesfield also began copper smelting there in 1758.[107] The Macclesfield Copper Company depended for its ore on nearby copper mines at Alderley Edge and for its coal on Macclesfield's own seams. The proximity of raw materials thus gave the company a good start, though before long copper ore had to be brought from as far afield as Coniston and Anglesey.

Operations during the early years proved so successful that Roe and his partners looked for additional factory sites. In 1763 they therefore took a 99-years lease from Richard Ayton Lee, a substantial landowner in Eaton, north of Congleton, of land by the Dane in Eaton.[108] Lee's annual rent demand was moderate. The land lay near the Macclesfield–Congleton main road. The river could supply power. To commemorate the British capture of Havannah in 1762 the site was called 'The Havannah'. Soon a small community grew up, consisting of seven cottages and premises for producing brass wire and for rolling copper and brass sheets or bolts. Here also could be made copper sheets for ships, household utensils and brass nails. The Roe company later built a similar factory at Bosley, and both Havannah and Bosley copper works are clearly marked as 'forges' on Burdett's map of 1777 and Aikin's map of 1794.

After Charles Roe's death in 1781 the business fell under the capable control of Edward Hawkins of Congleton, brass and copper merchant, who in 1778 took out a patent for 'making shaven or bright latten'. The great James Watt visited the Roe works in 1785. His letter to Matthew Boulton still survives to indicate his satisfaction with what he saw. Watt then stayed in Congleton and dined with Robert Hodgson of Moody Street, merchant, brother-in-law of Hawkins, and a partner in Roe's business.[109]

The Macclesfield, Havannah and Bosley works were advertised for sale in 1801 and again in 1806.[110] By the latter year portions of the factories were used for cotton spinning and corn grinding. Havannah copper works, however, may well have survived until about 1808–10.[111]

About the end of the Napoleonic Wars corn and silk mills were established at Havannah, and these flourished for many years. Indeed their presence wiped from men's minds the memory of copper works so that mid-nineteenth-century directories assume that Havannah got its name 'from the circumstance of cigars having been manufactured here'. They admit that this trade 'has altogether ceased'.

With the gradual expansion of the borough the building industry, too, was of some importance. Congleton builders changed materials and methods during the eighteenth century when bricks, slate and large glass windows replaced timber frames, thatching and daubing. Higher, more solid buildings appeared, notably, of course, the church and the mills. Then Congleton from 1780 and Buglawton from 1810 experienced a building boom on an unprecedented scale. Carpenters, joiners, plumbers, painters, glaziers, decorators, plasterers, slaters as well as bricklayers and house planners or architects all worked in Congleton. Few craftsmen belonged to large establishments, though the Browns of Mill Street, builders of the 1804 town hall and a family with perhaps a century of experience in the timber trade in Congleton, seemed to possess a considerable organization. Despite their small-scale organization, local builders put up 769 houses during the decade 1821–31.

Bricks must have been made locally at least until the opening of the canal on account of the difficulty of transportation. The bricks in St. Peter's church of 1740 and in the Old Mill were excellently produced, strong, and well-burned. Many Congleton houses in the nineteenth century contained locally produced bricks perhaps the product of the Hill Fields yard.[112] The Browns probably baked their own bricks. The Bradwells, later silk spinners, began as brickmakers and Martin of Park Lane produced bricks at the end of the century. Facing bricks were generally bought as far afield as Ruabon and Accrington, even in 1860, and transported to the town by rail or canal. In 1906 Martin ceased operations and even common bricks thereafter had to be purchased outside Congleton, usually from Heath of Biddulph or Peake of Tunstall. Between the two world wars most common bricks came from Stoke-on-Trent firms like the Birchenwood Brick Company. After 1945 virtually all bricks of all qualities came from Stoke-on-Trent and Manchester.

Congleton men also found employment in stone quarries and coal mines. The production of stone from quarries high up on Congleton Edge for use in building or as millstones became profitable when canals rendered transportation easier and cheaper. Small quarries dotted the hills. In 1831 Buglawton had three important stone quarries. William Hancock owned two stone and gravel pits at Timbersbrook.[113] Coal was not mined within Congleton, so the town relied on supplies from the Mow Cop region, from Adlington or from Lancashire. Stone Trough colliery at Mow Cop was connected by railed way with Weld House coal yard from which Congleton drew some supplies. The remainder came by packhorse, by the Trent and Mersey Canal after 1777, and by Macclesfield Canal to the coal wharf on the Moss after 1831.[114] The census returns show that some Congleton men found employment as coal miners, carriers and merchants.

Congleton blacksmiths necessarily undertook almost every sort of metal work. At first employed mainly by farmers the smiths later served travellers and by 1780 branched out to become general ironmongers and metal founders. The Ford family were forgemen, presumably producers of iron ware, in 1750, and the Jacksons of Mill Street agricultural implement makers from 1773. The smithies stood in places convenient for travellers, farmers and business people. Burdett's map of 1777 and Aikin's map of 1795 plainly show an important forge at Havannah (though this specialized in copper work), but none on the main roads themselves, perhaps because the lack of water power along the roads allowed only small smithy establishments there, unworthy of a mention on a map. By 1828 the town had fourteen blacksmiths, among them the Bentleys in West Lane and Aaron Scragg at Buglawton. William Edwards of Park Street catered for the millowners, turning out precision tools and machines and undertaking machinery repairs; William Jackson of Mill Street and his son Charles served the local farmers and gardeners.

After the opening of the Trent and Mersey Canal in 1777 ironmongers could deal with midland merchants for the supply of goods like nails and files. In 1828 the town had a firm of iron and brass founders, two braziers and tinmen, and seven machine makers. William Madder of Spragg Street produced silk machines. Edward Drakelow specialized in a patent winding machine. Samuel Smallwood, landlord of the *Pack Horse*, also produced machines, as did George Wallworth of Flint Mill Lane, timber merchant.

Corn milling was an ancient occupation in Congleton. The King's Corn Mill on the Dane was owned by the corporation and continued to function during the eighteenth century, despite a lease in 1754 to the owners of the Old Mill. Indeed the lessees had to rebuild the premises and see that the new equipment remained as efficient as ever. Corn milling obviously produced excellent profits because the rent of £150 a year, with an increase to £187 in 1797, was very high. The Broadhursts worked as corn millers here in the eighteenth century, becoming also bakers and confectioners. In 1826 the Pattisons leased the mill to Roger Broadhurst, victualler, and George Cookson, corn dealer and miller.[115] Cookson already possessed a warehouse at Swan Bank for the sale of corn and flour, and other men naturally combined allied trades: Matthew Hand and Matthew Heath who took corn from the Bridge Mill or the Broadhursts were corn and flour dealers in Mill Street and in addition general grocers.

In 1828 Congleton district had five corn millers. Besides the King's Mill, Jonathan Broadhurst, a Buglawton farmer, ran Buglawton Old Mill on the Dane south of Havannah, soon to be abandoned on account of the failing supply of water; William Ford ran Havannah Mill on the Dane; Daniel Oakes, Daneinshaw Mill; and John Pointon North Rode Mill.[116] All mills survived into the later nineteenth century.

During the eighteenth and nineteenth centuries small craftsmen survived in Congleton as elsewhere. Thus carpenters, cabinet makers, joiners and wheelwrights found employment because timber remained a basic material in so many activities. William and Charles Garside ran a flourishing carpentry business in Lawton Street during the second half of the eighteenth century, producing furniture and undertaking household repairs. Charles's son, Thomas Garside of Swan Bank, born in 1767, ran a large timber yard from 1790 onwards. Lewis Porter, one of the town's three cabinet makers in 1828, built up also a grocery and tea business at Swan Bank and eventually owned a large landed estate in Buglawton. Four coopers worked in Congleton, including Edward Goodall of High Street, keeper of the *Red Lion*. John Oakes, cooper, ran a grocer's too, and engaged later in tanning, plumbing and glazing. Thomas Goodall, one of three timber merchants, possessed a yard off Market Place.

Congleton's tailors specialized in men's suits and leather breeches. Broster's guide to Congleton in 1782 mentioned but two tailors and one breeches maker. Pigot noticed six tailors round the Market Place in 1828, and 30 appeared in a directory 20 years later. Leather trades remained always important on account of the good quality and cheapness of hides in Cheshire. Skinners, tanners, saddlers, leather clothing tailors and shoemakers worked in Congleton. There were half a dozen shoemakers in the eighteenth century and 30 or more by 1848. Five boot-makers occupied shops in the main street. These men included in 1828 the town's postmaster. Three curriers, dressers and colourers of tanned leather, and leather cutters found employment though none any longer produced 'Congleton points'. Thomas Booth of West Street, like his fathers before him, made saddles. William Hind of Bridge Street sold harnesses.

Shops for the sale of foodstuffs and general ware multiplied in Congleton during the late eighteenth century, and a number appeared in the new suburb of Buglawton after 1830. Most shops could not compete with the town market in range of goods offered or in price but were conveniently situated at street corners and open at least six days each week.

The bakers and confectioners, two in 1782, sixteen in 1828, and seventeen in 1848 often possessed merely a bakehouse into which people went to make purchases of perhaps home-made barley bread or more expensive white wheaten loaves. Some bakers provided oven space for wives to bake their own bread. Men like Richard Goodwin of Market Place combined a grocery with bakery.

A dozen grocers and general shops stretched down High and Lawton Streets by 1790. Thomas Pedley of Lawton Street headed a family which later expanded into farming, auctioneering, silk spinning and liquor merchandizing. The Yearsleys of High Street combined grocery and mercery, and James Morgan possessed a ropeworks and grocery. Many of the grocers seem to have been prosperous: Thomas Lowndes, a grocer who died in 1769, left legacies totalling £500, a substantial sum at that date, but he was a poor man compared with later tradesmen.[117]

No special silk drapers appeared in the borough despite the town's great silk manufacture, presumably because linen and woollen drapers could also sell silk if ever people found the money to pay for these goods. Drapers seemed always to be prosperous.

a The White Lion, *b* the Lion and Swan

a

b

a

b

Men like Richard Duff and William Bull (1773–1852) became local councillors and, for example, proprietors and directors of the gas works. Bull set up in business next to the Post Office in West Street,[118] and was followed by his son, William (1807–66). Druggists, chemists, hatters, haberdashers, clothiers, milliners, clock makers all opened shops in Congleton. Increase in the number of skilled chemists tended to keep pace with the improvement of medical facilities. Congleton's apothecaries in the eighteenth century competed with old people's herbal remedies. During the next century men like Thomas Goode tried to keep a balance between modern medicine and traditional potions. Goode described himself on his bill heads about 1830 as a 'chemist, druggist and dealer in leeches': 'Physicians and Family Prescriptions carefully dispensed under the immediate inspection of the Principle with Medicine from Apothecaries Hall'.[119]

Several families combined trades. Thus in 1828 Ralph Ardern, a corn and flour dealer, possessed a Mill Street grocery. William Hadfield of Market Place ran a chemist's and druggist's with general ware. Enoch Hill was a butcher and grocer. Daniel Morris's grocery and tea shop in High Street adjoined his small silk spinning mill. As far as can be seen all shops were run by their owners. No outside interests controlled trade, and only a handful of partnerships existed.

The alehouse counted among the most important of Congleton's businesses.[120] The keeping of an alehouse had been made conditional on a magistrate's licence in 1552, though inns remained outside this law so long as they provided accommodation for passing travellers. The town's two inns, the *Lion and Swan* and the *Bull's Head* in Mill Street, provided staging posts for coaches where passengers, goods and mail might be unloaded. Some 30 or 40 common alehouses lay all round. In 1729 annual brewster sessions began. Magistrates could get rid of superfluous, disreputable taverns, though it appears that Congleton's alehouses remained noted for gambling, rowdiness, cockfighting and bearbaiting. In 1763 Alderman Joseph Hill, merchant and borough benefactor, trying to control the alehouses, ordered the number to be reduced to 34 or one for every 50 inhabitants. Congleton's eighteenth-century innkeepers seem to have been prosperous, as the probate records indicate. Thomas Martin who had an alehouse in Buglawton Street for many

M

years until his death in 1773 left an inventory[121] which tells that his house consisted of an extensive living room, parlour and dining room, with several chambers or bedrooms, a garret, brewhouse and outbuildings. The most valuable article in the place was the 'Clock and Case £4. 10s.' Five beds were worth £10 together. There was much pewter ware, several large tables, and no fewer than 24 chairs (not counting stools which would be used in the bar). Martin still brewed his own ale, possessing boiler, brewing pan, tubs, coolers, barrels and bottles in the brewhouse. Very significant, too, is the farming equipment. Like most tradesmen, until 1750 anyway, Martin farmed some acres, perhaps growing only vegetables; but he owned six hay rakes, nine pitch forks, two hay knives, milk pails and churns, and other articles which suggest he had pasture land for hay and cows. After all, meadowland stretched almost to his door. His goods were valued at over £154.

By 1828 Congleton's town centre had some 30 alehouses situated every few yards along the way. By this time a number of landlords had tried to become respectable, engaging in trades and handicrafts, becoming town councillors. Each year at this time these men had to swear before the justices that they would not 'knowingly suffer any gaming with Cards, Draughts, Dice, Bagatelle . . . by Journeymen, Labourers, Servants, or Apprentices, nor knowingly introduce, permit or suffer any Bull, Bear, or Badger-baiting, cockfighting, or other such Sport'. They were not to allow drinking during hours of divine service.

But while the keeping of alehouses grew respectable, the movement against government interference with the economy unleashed a widespread demand for free trade in beer. By an Act of 1830 any ratepayer might open a shop for the sale of beer. Beerhouses appeared in the Lawton Street area of the borough and in Buglawton. By 1848 Congleton possessed 52 named alehouses, with probably more than 100 beershops interspersed. Meanwhile the respectable burgesses stocked their cellars and drank at home. For these families wine and spirit shops opened. John Parsons of the *Horse and Jockey* in High Street owned a liquor establishment next door.

The turnpiking of the eight main roads to Congleton increased the volume of traffic especially between 1790 and 1849. Progress remained sufficiently slow and uncomfortable to ensure that travellers still halted the night in Congleton. By 1828 there was a third hostelry, the *Coach and Horses* in Mill Street. Fourteen express coaches stopped in Congleton to pick up or put down passengers, seven coaches choosing the *Bull's Head*, four the new inn and three the *Lion and Swan*. Of course many slower coaches, wagons and private vehicles also passed through Congleton.

Changing Business Activity since 1860

The century that has elapsed since the silk depression of the 1860s has seen profound changes in Congleton's economy. The town had to absorb a labour force made redundant by the decline of the staple industry, and shopkeepers had to meet the new conditions of mass-produced goods combined with better transport.

What were the main characteristics of Congleton businesses in the late nineteenth and early twentieth centuries? Units tended, firstly, still to be small, giving employment to perhaps one man, one family, to perhaps half a dozen people, but rarely to more. Pictures of shops and worksheds at the turn of the century quite often show the entire staff, some six or seven men and boys, lined up outside. Secondly, one person, usually the master craftsman, owned the business, though there are examples of partnerships. Finally, many goods, perhaps most goods, were produced on the premises, and this applied equally to boots, cakes and machinery.

A few examples of these units must suffice.[122] Joseph Birk's boot and shoe factory of High Street, established in 1849, employed three shoemakers and a couple of apprentices. Many of the shoes sold were made in the workshops in High Street. Salt and Stubbs of Compton House built up by 1900 a very large drapery business, selling much locally produced ware. But the shop retailed a large amount of linen and cotton, and the boot department contained Northampton products. The Pedley family's butchery business, established about 1845 in Bridge Street, grew to be perhaps the largest shop in its line, selling all kinds of meat, corned beef, pickled tongues and pork sausages by 1890. Soon after this date the family advertised their 'Fresh Meat kept . . . in Refrigerator'. A photograph of the outside of the building shows carcases hanging all along the two storeys of the house, presumably to catch the housewife's eye.

Changing tastes and fashions also had an effect on the types of businesses, as did rising living standards. After 1860 more and more women began to buy rather than bake at least a portion of their necessary supply of bread and cakes. The practice of preparing the dough at home for baking in large shop ovens, however, continued till after the first World War.

The Maskery family prospered by catering for the growing market for bread and confectionery. Samuel Maskery, born in Leek in 1808, founded his confectionery business in 1831. He married Elizabeth Booth, daughter of a baker, and survived the town's economic depressions. Both he and his son Samuel, born in 1852, did well. The old Swan Bank premises were several times enlarged, and included a cake and sweet shop, restaurant and large bakehouse. Here the Maskerys baked, among other things, Congleton gingerbread, with its distinctive flavour produced by a secret recipe, which in a yellow packing sold widely. Samuel Maskery the younger grew sufficiently prosperous to devote much time to public service, leaving the business to be run by his staff, large by Congleton standards, of a dozen men and women. He became an alderman, mayor and magistrate, a trustee of a local nursing society, of the Savings Bank and of Congleton Common Lands, and appeared almost alone among Cheshire shopkeepers in Robert Head's gallery of worthies, *Cheshire at the Opening of the Twentieth Century* (1904).

Even in 1860, however, most articles of clothing and much furniture which Congleton people purchased had been produced in large quantities outside the borough. Such articles tended to be as cheap and acceptable as anything manufactured in local workshops. Hence mass-produced goods began to pose problems for local traders even in the nineteenth century.

Such goods available in Congleton included bricks from about 1900, and bread and cakes before the second World War. The daily arrival of swift lorries from Stoke and Kidsgrove with bread and cakes seriously threatened local confectioners like Maskery and Hickson. Similarly, bags of flour from large national concerns undermined the businesses of Havannah and Buglawton corn mills.

Multiple shops arrived in Congleton just before the first World War when Boyce Adams, a Potteries firm, opened a Congleton branch. Then followed Home and Colonial (1922–1936), Woolworths, and similar establishments which soon attracted customers. The town's population was hardly rising after

1860 so one shop's gain tended to mean another's loss. Then after 1950 came supermarkets on the American model. Local craftsmen and shopkeepers such as tailors, bakers or brickmakers all felt the menace of large-scale production and distribution. The borough gave employment to some six to twelve craftsmen-tailors during the nineteenth century, people who made men's clothes on the premises, themselves or with the help of assistants. In addition dozens of men and women undertook some kind of tailoring work, as the 1851 and 1861 census returns show. Through competition from multiple shops and ready-to-wear clothes the number of tailors was reduced to four by 1930;[123] these included the old-established Pedley of Lawton Street and Bailey of West Street, who were the only ones who had survived in 1960. One of their rivals had been taken over by the multiple firm of Hepworth.

In the same way the two dozen bakers and confectioners who could all produce bread and cakes in the nineteenth century were reduced in number. Congleton's nineteen bakers named in Morris's 1874 directory included Samuel Maskery and the Co-operative Society. In 1960 eleven confectioner's shops survived, some of these branches of combines, most selling mass-produced wares. Some half-dozen firms still made their own bread.

One Victorian enterprise which has continued to the present is Congleton's Co-operative Society. Founded in the dark year of the borough's history, 1860, it tried to sell goods as near as possible at cost price 'by returning to each purchaser any surplus of profit which was left in hand after all expenses had been paid'.[124] The society also attempted social and educational work, becoming much more than a mere cheap shop for labouring families. It grew out of informal meetings of silk workers, craftsmen, tradesmen and others interested in political and social matters of the mid-nineteenth century. Admiration of the work of the Rochdale Pioneers led to the establishment of a shop in Astbury Street where wholesome foodstuffs could be had cheaply. Members subscribed the necessary capital and gave their part-time services free so that all profits would be returned in proportion to the purchasers. The original members were not poor men: the Shaws were linen drapers, the Jacksons smiths and implement makers. William Bloor, silk throwster, ran the Moor Street Mills, employing 62 men and 96 women at the time of the 1851 census. Bloor, a Congleton man and devout Wesleyan, born in the town in 1798, had known real prosperity, though he was about to fall on hard times. Other manufacturers included Henry Krinks and Noah Vernon. The latter, born in nearby Marton in 1816, began by establishing a provision business in Bridge Street before opening a silk throwing business at Rope Walk.[125] A number of silk workers also joined the society, so that membership soon represented the middle economic and social group in Congleton life. The first secretary worked as shoemaker.

The society, known as the Congleton Equitable and Industrial Co-operative Society, relied for finance on share capital of members. Dividends were declared annually. Only on one occasion apparently was share capital not sufficient: in 1880 after the building of the central premises in Mill Street. So much money usually awaited investment, however, that limitations were placed on the amount each member handed over. This limit was reduced to £60 in 1891.

Congleton Co-operative Society began to sell groceries in 1860, expanding into tobacco, colonial produce, meat, cheese and hosiery later. Certain traders in the town were, until 1871, asked to supply members with goods like footwear that the society did not stock. This proved unsatisfactory and the opening of the Swan Bank drapery and boot department (1871) marked the growing independence of the society. Already in 1865 the Mill Street shop had a bakehouse attached where housewives could bake their own bread. In 1877 the society began to supply coal.

Congleton's society expanded despite trade depression after 1860 and very serious opposition from influential shopkeepers. By 1910 20 shops about the town belonged to the group. Many of them remained small, dark and uninviting, but the opening of Buglawton branch in 1873 marked the beginning of larger, brighter and financially sounder establishments. Of course even the small corner shops made money and attracted customers. Sales, less than £3,000 in 1861, rose to £80,000 in 1908. Membership was 850 in 1877, over 1,500 by 1895 and over 2,500 by 1907.

There were, however, difficulties. The town was no longer expanding as it had been before 1860, and trade was often bad. The crisis of 1867 and 1886–8, for example, seriously hit members. The society overcame its problems partly by an enlightened policy of employing and paying for good staff. In 1867 the trustees invited James Mellor of the large and prosperous Macclesfield society to be shop manager at Mill Street. He introduced reforms, cut down the credit system, and economized wherever possible, and so put the society on its feet again. A permanent secretary was appointed in 1870. The society also began to train its own employees, taking as first apprentice in 1867 James Cooke, who rose to be secretary and general manager in later years.

It remained one of the aims of the society 'to convince members that they are not organized simply for making a "divi" '. Members never neglected educational work, limited though this had to be in the early years by small profits. Discussion groups for adults, grants to members' children attending technical schools, newspapers and books were all provided. The newsroom and library really got under way in 1892 when the society began to devote 1 per cent of net annual profits to education. The library, containing over 2,000 books by 1910, would, it was hoped, form the basis for an adequate municipal library available to all. Social work included grants to members in distress, even to non-members whose case seemed worthy. Entertainments and discussions took place in the large assembly room at the new Mill Street central shop (1879).

Members after 1860 desired to establish a factory, perhaps for boots or ribbons, to employ local men and to provide goods for the shops. The establishment of the Congleton Trimming Manufacturing Company in 1895 and its subsequent collapse showed that such plans could not succeed, because Congleton was not big enough to provide the capital or the market for such goods. However, during the years after 1890, the Congleton society purchased more and more goods from co-operative production societies. Thus shoes were generally mass-produced and sold to hundreds of local societies. In this way Congleton co-operators eased themselves into the national wholesale society (C.W.S.) which helped local groups to survive in the difficult years of the twentieth century.

The inns were affected by the change in travellers' needs after 1860. The railway carried mail, goods and passengers. People no longer wanted to halt at Congleton's coaching inns. Thus these establishments began to cater more for customers who called for drinks than for guests asking for beds. The town's hotels and inns remained modest and small, run by the proprietor and his wife in most cases with two or three maids. From 1860 more and more premises fell into the hands of breweries, but this made little difference to management for many years. A number of commercial hotels not connected with public houses were established after 1880. J. D. Stubb's 'Temperance, Family, Commercial Hotel and Dining Room' in High Street was run in conjunction with a confectionery shop. In 1960 as in 1828 three hotels (as distinct from 'boarding houses') took in overnight guests.[126]

Some business people carried on by changing their line of trade, sometimes a gradual process. Thus the Jacksons, smiths and agricultural implement manufacturers in Mill Street, survived throughout the century 1860–1960 by changing the emphasis of their business while remaining, in general, craftsmen in metal. By family tradition William and Elizabeth Jackson founded the business in Mill Street in 1773.[127] William, their son, born in 1762 continued as whitesmith and produced such wares as keys and small tools. William's son, Charles, born in 1803, described himself in the 1851 census simply as whitesmith though he probably also completed blacksmiths' jobs. Blacksmiths were sought not only by travellers and farmers but also by millowners. At some time in the nineteenth century the family became well known for producing virtually every kind of equipment needed by local farmers. Perhaps six men and boys found full-time work in producing ploughs, shares, milk churns, boilers, fire grates, even steam engines during the last half of the nineteenth century, and under the personal supervision of the head of the family the business flourished into the twentieth century. But Jacksons ceased to produce implements for farmers some time after the first World War and normally did not even carry out repairs after 1945. Farmers who provided the firm as late as 1920 with four-fifths of its trade were by 1925 tending to buy all their equipment from factories like that of Bamfords of Uttoxeter. The important point is that the Jackson family stayed in business by embarking on new lines. The proprietor, for example, gradually concentrated on bicycles which the firm had dealt with from about 1892.[128] The Jacksons' interest in motor-car engines lasted from 1919 to 1937 when increased specialization made business uneconomic.

The influence of new forces, however, caused not a few of Congleton's businesses to founder. The Goodalls, for more than a century coopers and timber merchants, went out of business before the second World War, partly because innkeepers, shops and private clients no longer purchased barrels locally.[129] The town's many skilled carpenters, craftsmen who would undertake on the premises almost any kind of woodwork including coffins, dwindled from the fourteen named in Morris's directory of 1874 to three or four by 1939, and had disappeared almost entirely by 1960.

The borough's iron and brass foundries in the nineteenth century relied heavily on selling machines to textile mills, on supplying spare parts, and on repairing damaged parts. The decline in the textile trade and the increasing complexity of machines employed by such firms as Robert Lowe meant less business for foundries. The Herbert Street foundry and Woolliscroft's Dane Foundry, founded in 1908, alone survived the second World War.

The 100 years following 1860 did, of course, produce new opportunities. Public health regulations, higher living standards and better education led to a demand after about 1848 for good plumbing and sanitation. As early as that Pedley and Massey, plumbers, glaziers and ornamental painters, were advertising their 'new self acting closet'. Joseph Thursfield began to instal water closets about the same time from his workshop in West Street.[130] F. W. Pass of Antrobus Street subsequently took over Thursfield's.[131] Later in the century R. Burgess and Company satisfied the Victorian need for family photographic portraits, setting up shop in High Street. At the end of the century the motor-car created a demand for petrol pumps, repair shops and spare parts. Watson and Wadeson of Park Street was probably the first service station, followed by Alan Dixon of Victoria Street. Then about 1900 Hiskins and Wooltorton set up their 'Mid-Cheshire Carriage and Motor Works' in Congleton: 'Motor bodies designed and built to customers' own requirements'.[132] The motor trade expanded and old family firms like the Jacksons of Mill Street (by origin blacksmiths) began to sell petrol and deal with motor repairs. The number of garages which sold petrol within Congleton increased to some ten or dozen by 1960. Although Hiskins' motor-car body factory did not survive long, the same trade returned to the borough

when Bowyer Brothers began production on the Greenfield
estate about 1960.

During the later nineteenth century Congleton got its cigar
factory.[133] Writers of local directories had long been saying
incorrectly that Havannah in Eaton took its name from a cigar
factory established there some time in the eighteenth century.
But a cigar firm wishing to use the name Havannah on its products did indeed establish itself there in parts of the old silk mill.
The enterprise failed at Havannah, though the Marsuma Company survived until the second World War by moving to the
Daneside New Mill in Congleton some time before 1914.

Paper and cardboard packaging grew increasingly important
after the first World War. The borough council's publicity and
its provision of industrial sites encouraged firms to set up in
Congleton to make cardboard products. The real expansion
came after 1945. A number of businesses were founded in empty
textile mills: Stonehouse Green Mill was taken by manufacturers of cardboard components and fittings for the shirt and
pyjama trades. Thomas Preston Cartons Limited of Sutherland
Mill produced all types of boards and wrappings for the packaging industry. The Congleton Board Company in new premises on Buxton Road made cartons and boxes, possessing a
wax laminating department where, for instance, moisture and
vapour-resistant boards could be obtained.

Among recent industries the artware producing firm of W.
H. Bossons of Brook Mill is noteworthy.[134] The business was
founded in 1945 by W. H. Bossons who had moved into Congleton during the war purely for domestic reasons. Only a handful of helpers was needed in the early days, and the firm acquired rooms in Brook Mill during 1947–8. The firm specialized
in the production of ornamental artware from pottery and plaster. 'Artware' covers such products as highly detailed, high
relief models in the form of wall plaques, wall masks and animal figures, and from the early days at least 75 per cent of production went overseas. Bossons expanded rapidly taking over
much of Brook Mill and employing just over 100 people by
1960.

Bookselling and Printing
One trade which has had a continuous existence in the town
from at least the eighteenth century is bookselling and printing.[135]

The small but prosperous community of teachers, clergy, attorneys and doctors demanded service, and one printing house attached to a bookshop was founded about 1750. Samuel Yates, wealthy stationer and businessman, raised this enterprise to some fame in the county and printed not only the usual notices of sale and handbills but books. Yates (1797–1833), a cultured and enterprising man, produced Congleton's first history just after the Napoleonic Wars, when he himself was in his early twenties, presumably writing most of the book himself. His connections with local families of standing like the Lowndes Mallabars provided useful information. The borough boasted no fewer than four bookshops in 1817. Such places not only provided novels for young ladies, law books for attorneys, and school books, but stationery and newspapers.[136] Among the booksellers at the time of the 1851 census was Peter Cotterill of Lawton Street, born in the town in 1807, a member of an old Congleton trading family. Probably as a result of the industrial climate after 1860, however, the number of booksellers did not increase during the rest of the nineteenth century. These establishments survived partly by expanding activity into binding, producing account books and ledgers, or serving local schoolchildren with pens, pencils, slates and exercise books.

Printing shops in the borough functioned on a very small scale, possibly employing no more than six men. Henry Hopwood of the Leipsic Printing Works, Bridge Street, specialized in printing pamphlets, notices of sales and amusements and general poster work in the years around 1850. More detailed printing projects seem always to have gone to the firm of Yates-Head. Thomas Gordon of Lawton Street Post Office, printer, stationer, bookbinder, and bookseller, also produced some good work in the last decade of the nineteenth century and the early part of the twentieth century. Gordon in addition ran a circulating library, a newsagent's, and a greeting card shop. He printed many of the calling cards of Congleton's genteel and business families.[137]

After Yates's death in 1833 his business fell into the hands of William Clarke, a man who seems to have been, to judge from his advertisements, most interested in his circulating library (started about 1839).[138] The printing side of the business languished also under his successor Andrew Cockayne. Then in 1869 Robert Head joined the firm.[139]

Born in 1857, Robert was the son of James Head, manager of the nearby Howey Hill silk mill. The elder Head had considerable responsibility in Congleton because the owner of the mill did not live in town and his manager found himself in 1851 in charge of 86 men and 37 women workers. Robert left school at the age of twelve to become errand boy for Cockayne. He was eventually apprenticed and on completion of his contract went to work in a Stafford bookshop. Here he saved hard against his return to Congleton. In 1880 came an opportunity. By borrowing money he was able to purchase the Cockayne business and he set up the County Publishing House at 11 High Street. Hard work and a flair for the business brought Head success. He soon acquired shops elsewhere. A 'journalist by instinct' if not by training he established a second Congleton newspaper, the *Chronicle*, in 1893 to rival the old *Mercury*.

Since the eighteenth century local people had been buying newspapers printed as far afield as Chester and London.[140] From 1825 short-lived attempts to issue a newspaper for Congleton and Macclesfield together bankrupted several men. Then in 1856 Edward Joyce, the Bridge Street bookseller and printer, began to publish the *Congleton Advertiser*. This survived until economic depression destroyed much of its local readership in 1861.[141] It then functioned until 1876 as the *Congleton, Sandbach and Crewe Advertiser*. In 1858 during the final years of Congleton's silk boom Robert Clarkson of Bridge Street began to issue the *Congleton and Macclesfield Mercury*. It was this journal which Robert Head set out to rival.

The new editor was a born writer. His intense interest in local history and affairs had already produced a greatly admired history of Congleton in 1887. A Liberal nationally, Head shunned politics in local affairs. His articles in the *Chronicle* fostered public confidence and civic pride during difficult years. Enterprising tradesmen, mill-owners, craftsmen and councillors were soundly praised. Robert (1857–1937) and his sons spread the influence of the *Chronicle* over south-east Cheshire and north Staffordshire. The Heads took over the *Mercury* in 1896 and one of Robert's sons continued to edit the united newspaper till 1963.[142] The Head firm, operating from High Street, managed to survive all difficulties and depressions. In 1960 printing and publishing jobs were still undertaken, but after that date Head's closed down their stationery and bookselling business.

Congleton's industries have been diverse: from 'points' in in 1700 to Bosson's artware in 1968. People have been able to make changes as circumstances demanded: the Jacksons are a good example. Small trades and industries have employed quite a large number of local men and, taken together, at times rivalled textiles as producers of the town's income.

Agriculture[143]

Agriculture remained during the eighteenth and the first half of the nineteenth century a most important activity in Congleton. Most of the borough and nearly all of Buglawton lay not beneath paved streets, terraced houses and factories, but within the bounds of farms or tracts of common land. The majority of inhabitants before 1755 and very many afterwards got at least a part of their living from agricultural pursuits, and when the situation in mill, workshop or garret deteriorated men returned to the land. New methods and tools, with much capital, however, alone got the best out of the district's rich boulder clay and sand. Knowledge and skill, when given free rein on the new, efficient, consolidated and enclosed farming estates, could produce wealth from the soil.

As elsewhere in Cheshire the main crop in the eighteenth century must have been barley, though farmers also grew oats and wheat. War years between 1793 and 1815 increased the profits from arable farming, so more land than ever came under the plough. At the same time farmers grew potatoes and green vegetables. Peas, beans, cabbages, carrots and fruits took up much of the available land. A map of 1818 marks unenclosed one-acre strips of open-field farming where possibly shopkeepers and craftsmen still grew crops. These strips disappeared when such ways as Astbury Street and Crescent Road were laid down. The extensive West Heath was three-quarters arable at the time of the tithe survey of 1844–5.

Pasture and water meadows, however, stretched over three-fifths of the areas of Congleton and Buglawton. Meadows bordering the Dane and other streams produced a rich hay while pastures fed hundreds of animals. Indeed this part of Cheshire had long been known for its dairy produce and especially for cheese.

Timber, though no longer plentiful even in 1700, supplied householders, builders and industrialists with fuel and building material. Willows gave sheep hurdles, fencing and wattles for house walls. Tanners took oak bark. The navy wanted oak, elm, beech and fir. An observer looking across Cheshire about 1810 noted: 'the number of trees in the hedgerows and coppices is so considerable, that from some points of view, the whole county has the appearance of an extensive forest'.[144] By then, however, not many actual woods remained beyond river valley areas, Town Wood and Forge Wood. Yet the soil yielded sand, gravel, clay, lime and stone for road and housebuilding.

Cows, goats, poultry and bees produced the staple foods needed by the town. Small households kept perhaps a pig, pigeons or rabbits. The leather workers demanded that farmers raise animals with hides. Horses were needed long after 1860 for transport work.

Congleton's area of 2,565 acres and Buglawton's 2,852 acres consisted of about 80 acres of urban land in 1795, 800 acres of open common, and 4,500 acres enclosed in one or other of the farms, comprising both arable and pasture.

No single farm dominated the district. Many consisted of one or two hundred acres. Puddle Bank, a typical dairy farm in south-east Congleton, had about 130 acres in 1840. The greatest landowner possessed at the same date no more than 460 acres. This estate belonged to Charles Peter Shakerley (1792–1857) of Somerford. This Lancashire family married into the Grosvenors and acquired Cheshire lands including the manor of Congleton. The family settled down at Somerford just beyond the borough to live as gentry and local politicians.[145]

Outside the enclosed farms lay large acres of heath where all those who possessed common rights might cut fuel and timber, graze beasts or collect sand, gravel and stone. Thus in 1818 wide areas of West Heath and Congleton Moss were still not enclosed by hedges or walls, the topography having changed little in the previous 50 years. Common rights could be obtained through possession or renting of certain lands and tenements in the district. Usually the farmer of an extensive acreage had the right to graze a large number of animals on the common. Officials of borough or township carefully regulated the commons. Certain areas might be closed, especially alongside streams, while hay was allowed to grow. But vast areas of upland could never have been adequately policed, and probably any man freely used this area. This may account for a number of tiny cottages which appear on this land, looking very like sixteenth- or early seventeenth-century squatters' hovels. Thus the common as a whole, including many acres of woodland, could be used for all purposes by many of the district's families.

At the same time, however, many landholders felt the common would be better employed if divided and added to the various farms, especially during wartime after 1793 when efficient farming yielded such good rewards. Every additional acre under plough or supporting a healthy cow produced excellent profits.

Of course some landowners did not want to disturb open common land, partly because such areas provided excellent hunting. The capital outlay for fencing, draining and ditching, the need for more plough-teams and labourers, and the trouble in securing an agreement all worked against change. Some of the poor did not want to lose fuel or grazing rights: it certainly would not pay them to fence or cultivate the tiny share of common they could expect to receive. On the other hand large efficient farms might provide jobs for labourers who would no longer be saddled with the responsibilities of proprietorship of a smallholding. And so the discussion continued.

Congleton common land lay all around the town centre. On the hillside north of the Dane just across from the town lay the Town Wood which was usually leased to yield an income for the poor and in part of which the Old Mill was erected. North of Town Wood stretched Lower Heath, while Mossley Moss lay to the town's south-east. Congleton Edge adjoined Biddulph, high barren land, good for sheep and yielding excellent stone. The largest portion of common stretched north of Sandbach road to the Somerford boundary and took in two large shallow ponds, Big and Little Black Lakes. Buglawton common lay along the tracks of most public roads, at Birch Moss south of the Hall, at Buglawton Green on Buxton road, at Rainow, and across the Cloud.

In 1795 certain Congleton persons possessing 'Rights of Common for their Cattle at all Times of the Year' pointed out to Parliament that the common lands had become valueless; but, 'if they were divided and inclosed, and leased, or let, and the Produce therefrom applied in Aid of the Poors Rate, and other Public Expenses of the said Borough and Township, it would be of very great Advantage to the Owners of Estates therein'.[146]

Portions of common had doubtless been enclosed previously by agreement among inhabitants. The wholesale destruction of the common, however, needed an Act of Parliament to force all landowners to co-operate. A majority of these people met, therefore, made contributions towards the necessary costs, and drafted a petition to the Commons and an enclosure bill. Since most local people with a voice seemed to desire enclosure, Parliament swiftly passed an Act in 1795.

The Act appointed commissioners to superintend all proceedings, and divide the commons. To the Shakerleys as lords of the manor went one-sixteenth of the area, including, for example, much land on West Heath and Mossley Moss. A certain amount had then to be set aside to pay for the costs of enclosure. The whole of Congleton Edge was sold for this purpose. Next each freeholder entitled to the common received his share in proportion to the acreage and value of his tenement. Finally land at Mossley, Lower and West Heaths was set aside to be leased at a rent of £600 for the use of Congleton poor. A portion of this estate on Park Lane provided a new site for the poor house.[147] In all, the commissioners dealt with nearly 370 acres of common, ignoring certain areas like Town Wood already producing a rent for the corporation.

Buglawton enclosure, allowed by Parliament in 1813, was completed only in 1831. Once again a small acreage went to the upkeep of the poor. The lord of the manor, Wilbraham Egerton of Tatton, received one-fifteenth. Most valuable of allotments were probably the stone quarries on the hillside.

The enclosures of 1795-1831 changed the district's life to some extent. Farms became larger. Cottagers lost common rights and their last means of survival save as labourers for farmers or millowners. It is impossible, however, to say whether people made the most of the change, or whether in fact Congleton gained very much as a community. Presumably the ratepayers gained when the poor rate received its annual subsidy from the enclosures. However there is no evidence of any opposition.

By about 1850 Congleton and Buglawton still retained their rural scenery. Some 200 holdings embraced the farmland in units generally below 100 acres. In fact only seven men in Buglawton and two men in Congleton owned more than this amount each. Samuel Pearson of Buglawton Hall, the owner of

Congleton Silk Mill, possessed over 300 acres. The Lowe farm on Buxton road of 220 acres was held by Charles Wallworth; and the Mote Homestead at Crossley, of over 160 acres, by George Wallworth. Only small farms like Thomas Stringer's 70-acre Crossley Hall, occupied by the Brown family, could boast of land consolidated in one block round the farmhouse. Most land lay in the possession of local men, people living in Congleton, Buglawton, Somerford, Biddulph and adjoining places, though it remained the exception always for the farmer who worked the land to be also its owner.[148] The district did not, however, suffer from irresponsible absentee landlords. Families like the Shakerleys had the money, interest and local knowledge to insist on improvements such as the laying of brick drains, even when the farmers were too busy to ask for improvements themselves.

Congleton's farming population remained small in the century following 1860. About 7 per cent of the male working population were occupied as farmers, labourers or gardeners, no more than three or four hundred men. During the industrial depression of 1929–39 more workers than previously tended to find jobs on farms while, in contrast, after 1945 improved methods and mechanization reduced the number of farm workers.

Buglawton's lowland acres rather than the unfruitful highlands of Congleton Edge provided homes and jobs for the majority of farmers. This is clear from the 1911 census return which surveyed in detail only Congleton borough. Without Buglawton farmers the proportion of agricultural workers in the population as a whole was 1 per cent.

Farming prosperity in modern times dates only from the time of the second World War. Wartime national emergency and peacetime subsidies after 1940 greatly helped landowners and their farmers. Despite farm crises Congleton remained an important market for agricultural products, perhaps more for animals than for grain. The loss of land for houses and industry was insignificant on account of the borough's very extensive acreage.

Population and Society to 1860
Analysis of church and chapel registers[149] shows but slow increase in the number of baptisms from the beginning of the eighteenth century until about 1746, but then the rate speeded

N

up till 1776. A similar trend is suggested by the fact that during the period 1700–50 there was a balance of burials and baptisms, but that after 1750 baptisms ran well ahead of burials. The relationship between baptisms and total population is, of course, not always constant. In 1831, for example, there were 421 baptisms when the population was 11,400; in 1841 for 12,000 people there were only 166 baptisms. Nevertheless if the relation between population and baptisms for the period 1801–1851 was the same in the period 1701–51, a population for Congleton and Buglawton in the earlier eighteenth century of some 2,000 is suggested. In 1752 there was already a large unemployed labouring population. Baptisms increased again from 1786 to 1796 and in 1789 there were said to be some 3,000 persons in the town. This estimate fits well with a report of 500 houses in the borough in 1778, and with the 3,861 noted in the first official census of 1801. Buglawton then had 517 people.[150] From 1801 to 1811 Congleton saw a 20 per cent growth. But the decade 1821–31 was even more remarkable because the borough had a 46 per cent increase and Buglawton 120 per cent. Expansion of the district's population continued until about 1833 when the number of people in Congleton was 9,500 and in Buglawton, over 2,000. Trade depression halted growth. Indeed between the census of 1831 and that of 1841 both places actually lost a few hundred people and, in once-crowded settlements by the Dane, over 300 dwellings stood empty. From 1842 trade revived and population increased. Between 1841 and 1851 1,300 people were added to Congleton's population, and a further 1,800 came during the following decade. But increase was always slower than before and in many ways the peak of population had been reached as early as 1831. Buglawton did not regain its 1831 population figures and Congleton lost people again in the later nineteenth century. The years 1831–3 marked the end of the borough's swift early expansion.

Congleton kept ahead of many Cheshire places in terms of population during the eighteenth century. The textile neighbours, Stockport and Macclesfield, remained larger than Congleton in the period 1700–1860 but the borough, even in years of trade depression like the thirties of the nineteenth century, retained its lead over most other Cheshire market towns. Buglawton's growth in the first half of the nineteenth century— 300 per cent—was almost the highest in the county.

Despite population increase, however, infant mortality remained high. Those up to one year in age formed the largest
single group of burials, indicating the insanitary housing, poor
food and lack of medical care common at the time. In the
decade 1813–23 infants accounted for 338 deaths out of 901.
Half the deaths occurred below the age of 20, and between 65
and 85 per cent were between the ages of one and five. In the
years 1823–33 only one-third of burials were of those over 30.
Nevertheless a reduction in the death rate was one cause of
population increase. In 1796–1806 it was 16 per cent, but it fell
steadily in every decade to 1851.

A more important cause of population growth was the increasing birth rate. Baptisms averaged 2·7 per cent in the period
1801–31 but in 1821–31 were 3 per cent. Only with depression did the picture change. From 1841 burials again out-
numbered baptisms as young people drifted away and births
fell off.

The population of Congleton increased partly because many
new families arrived, presumably farm labourers from nearby
places seeking employment in the textile mills. The 1851 census
showed that only about half the town's population had been
born in the borough, while one-quarter came from elsewhere in
Cheshire, and one-quarter from outside Cheshire. Indeed people
came from Ireland, Germany and even New South Wales.
Probably there were even more outsiders living in Congleton
about 1830, but many must have gone elsewhere when depression made Congleton less attractive. Some of these post-1840
immigrants came with the railways, some were Irish servants.
The majority of households, even quite modest households in
Congleton, usually managed to support one maid. Derbyshire
and Staffordshire were the homes of many girls. The servant of
farmer Ralph Washington of Park Lane belonged to Newcastle-
upon-Tyne. Other immigrants included William Thomas of
Gibralter Rocks, born in Birmingham in 1783, who had lived
for some time in the Potteries before arriving in Congleton to
find work as a cotton spinner. James Cooke, born in Newcastle-
under-Lyme in 1812, came to live in New Street only in 1850.
He found work in the reviving silk trade, and four of his young
children were silk piecers. John Ashley, a Northampton man,
born in 1802 lived in Moor Street from about 1840 and worked
as a bricklayer. Many men of course did not travel so far,

coming merely from the overpopulated Cheshire countryside. Thus John Capper, an agricultural labourer of Barthomley, born in 1812, moved to the borough about 1835 as a silk weaver.

Congleton and Buglawton possessed an agricultural population, tenant farmers, labourers and casual workers, which rarely knew disastrous long-term depression between 1700 and 1860. Bad harvests and low prices were experienced, sometimes for years on end, but the farming families remained on the land. Some 40 prosperous tenant farmers lived in the two places, and the 1837 Boundary Commissioners were probably about right when they numbered the farm labourers at some 400. Agricultural improvements and enclosure prevented any large increase in farm population. Indeed the 1831 census noted only 69 men over 20 years of age as farm workers within the borough, with a further hundred in Buglawton; others probably worked part-time, however, and found full-time employment during the period of industrial depression after 1831.

On the other hand the wealth, number and influence of the trading and industrial families considerably increased between 1700 and 1860. To craftsmen, shopkeepers, innholders and handloom weavers were added, after 1754, silk and cotton workers. Four hundred people laboured in the Old Mill alone in the late eighteenth century. By 1801 some 650 men out of a labour force of 830 in Congleton itself worked in trade and manufacturing. Ten years later 750 families found jobs in mills or shops, while 158 remained on farms. Buglawton of course stayed largely agricultural at this date with 79 families on farms, 35 in trade and mills. Yet at the end of the boom years in 1831 there were twenty times as many men in manufacturing and trade as in farming. Buglawton mill workers trebled in number in one decade 1821–31. Some 1,800 Congleton men were in industry with probably an equal number of women and children.[151] Indeed Congleton's population invariably contained more females than males, reflecting the opportunities for women in a textile town. Depression tended to encourage men, like Isaac Berisford, to move back to the land or to leave the town altogether.

On the whole the prosperity and standard of living of this large section of the population could not be denied. The humblest mill worker tended to have better prospects and pay than his brothers on the farm. Foremen, independent shopkeepers, diligent craftsmen and millowners might expect good living standards. John Bulkeley Johnson of Mortlake House, textile and tea merchant, possessed sufficient wealth to invest in farms, houses and quarries. William Vaudrey (1794–1836), cotton spinner in Buglawton, left £3,000 in personal goods alone when he died. Benjamin Johnson, son of Edward Johnson, joiner, a carpenter, owned nine cottages and £600 in money at his death in 1826. John Twemlow, a cabinet maker, left £800 in 1830.[152] The mass of industrial workers have left no such details, but the prosperous town described, for example, by Samuel Yates in 1820 must have gained at least some of its opulence from the good living of the majority of its people. Of course once people have tasted rising standards any setback, such as occurred between 1828 and 1848, would seem doubly disastrous. Complaints of these years, though very real, must not therefore be overemphasized.

Congleton gained as a community from the presence of a comparatively large professional population, economically and socially very lively and influential. Some of the Vaudreys, for example, were solicitors whose interests extended also to textiles and borough improvements.[153] The Harwars were attorneys-at-law—possibly as early as 1730. Clergy, surgeons, apothecaries, schoolmasters, attorneys and retired businessmen gave Congleton a standing and reputation in the county which equally bustling and growing new towns like Winsford and Crewe did not have. John (1708–56) and William Malbon (1709–63), the sons of Ralph Malbon (d. 1721), minister of Congleton, remained in the town as apothecaries.[154] In Broster's *Chester Guide* of 1782 Congleton possessed 58 named traders and industrialists and 25 professional men. The latter group comprised people like Philip Antrobus, gentleman, John Barratt, surgeon and apothecary, Thomas Harwar, attorney, and the Revd. Sandbach. This social group tended to live in West Lane area. The numbers grew continually partly because retired millowners or tradesmen like John Vaudrey (d. 1828) tended to become 'gentlemen' and to send their sons into the professions. By 1828 the borough had no less than five practising attorneys. There were at the same date six surgeons and one veterinary surgeon. John Mollart, a surgeon in 1851, had been educated at Glasgow University and was a member of the Royal College of Surgeons.

He was a Staffordshire man, born in 1802, and came to Congleton in 1837.

The presence of agricultural, industrial and professional groups, representing each step in the social and economic scale, together with the marked absence of any resident and powerful squire or noble lord, probably ensured that no one group should seize the reins of local government and seek entrenched privileges.[155]

Of course social divisions remained very evident. High status could be acquired by having a certain kind of job or house, possessing money or a gig, and such status conferred on a family a gracious mode of life: entry to the best homes, the best seats in chapel, the prime attention of doctor and lawyer. While economic or political power did not fall to any one group in Congleton, the borough and its suburbs in Buglawton did contain elements which from time to time threatened the peace. For instance 552[156] casual industrial labourers, if unemployed, would certainly not be restrained by their fellow skilled workers or by any other group. Presumably this group caused the terrible disturbances in the town between 1831 and 1847.

An Act of 1766 forbade 'unlawful Combinations of Workmen employed in the Silk Manufacture', allegedly to protect against harm both workshops and mechanics. Offenders might suffer death as felons. In days of boom when nearly everyone found work the absence of unions mattered little, and there is no doubt that unions to protect workpeople were both short-lived and ineffective until about 1831. On the other hand friendly societies and burial clubs flourished. For 2*d* or 3*d* a week a man might receive 5*s*–6*s* a week when ill, and funeral expenses would be met. During the last years of the Napoleonic Wars between 1813 and 1815 some 600 Congleton people had joined these societies, though Buglawton seems to have had no society of its own.[157] The 'Congleton Club' friendly society possessed between one and two thousand members in the distressed years 1830–40.[158] By then the Foresters and Odd Fellows had grown strong partly as insurance clubs, partly as social gatherings. In 1845 Congleton had three lodges of Odd Fellows belonging to the Manchester Unity. The 'Widow's Protection' Lodge, for example, met every other Tuesday at the *Old Black Boy* in the Market Place.[159]

When depression nearly ruined Congleton, people immediately sought in trade unions a means of protecting their livelihoods.

The employers also united themselves. The worst distressed labourers of all, handloom weavers, never managed to form a union partly because of their independence and poverty, partly because these men had no bargaining counters. John Newman, 'an intelligent master weaver' in the Congleton ribbon trade from 1825, dated the formation of the workers' union at 1831. Newman, giving evidence to the 1840 Handloom Weavers' Commission, pointed out that employers, having informal associations of their own, refused to sign on unionists if it could be avoided.[160] Nevertheless the power of unionists for a time closed some mills.

Apart from trade depression the introduction of new methods, machinery and steam power were also blamed for the growth of trade unions. They throve, too, on resentment against employers who seemed to possess economic and political power. Unionism tended to gain its bad name about 1840 through its connection with Chartism. This sought political reforms and in Congleton at least led to much rioting from 1839. Officials of the weavers' unions in the north of England began to organize Congleton labourers, demanding a weekly subscription to build up a strike and sickness fund. Every member agreed not to accept a job which did not return an agreed wage. No man should work for a master who disobeyed union rules. On few occasions could such conditions be carried out, though officials tried ruthlessly to impose their will on all members.[161] Such activity had led to strikes as early as 1834 which turned into riots. Soldiers had to be called out on this occasion, though acute depression of trade put unionists in a very weak bargaining position.[162]

Extreme suffering between 1834 and 1842 led to excesses. Workers who refused to obey the union rules might be punished severely: 'the obnoxious workmen, having little property, suffer in their persons, the punishments rising from simple assaults to blinding with vitriol and beating to death'. Employers speaking to a parliamentary committee in 1841 demanded the curbing of the unions' 'powers of intimidation' and the restoration of 'liberty to the working classes'.[163] By then union wrath had been turned on employers' property, so these men had grown desperate.

The distress of 1839–40, when mills fell idle and hundreds of families were leaving the town, led to great union activity. A committee of Congleton labourers began to supply 'subscriptions to a turn-out shop in Manchester', though people had so little money that the attempt was not successful. Employers in association had already drawn up a list of agreed wages and not one took on men at higher rates. Men preferred paid work to union benefits, and this feeling destroyed the union. In 1840 relations had so improved that a Parliamentary committee could be informed with regard to Congleton, 'that the feeling between masters and men is not generally bad'.[164]

In 1842, however, the worst riots in Congleton's history took place on account of the association of Chartist and trade union activity. People had the idea that to destroy boilers would destroy steam-powered machinery and this would bring back full employment.[165] The seizure of political power might put government in the hands of people favourable to labourers and craftsmen, to traders and shopkeepers. These riots are described in detail in the chapter on local government.[166]

Economic improvement soon brought peace and a decline of union activity. Though disturbances occurred in 1846 and 1847, the officials were able to say: 'We are happy to be able to report that this borough is perfectly quiet and that work which has been suspended for a week has generally re-commenced this morning. A company of the 34th foot arrived today from Newcastle.'[167]

Not until economic problems again became acute after 1860 did workers' agitation reappear. In the early 1880s it was reported that strikes began in 1863 and had broken out periodically three or four times since.[168] Unfortunately the unions were in no strong position and all strikes ended to the employers' advantage.

Many people did not, even in 1860, depend for a living on fixed regular wages. The shopkeeper settled his own hours and prices according to his own desires and the state of the market. The handloom weaver could work as long or as little as he wished. Craftsmen might produce food on their own strips of land. To work stipulated hours for agreed wages became common practice only with the opening of the Old Mill in 1755. The level of wages then became an important factor in consideration of standard and condition of living.

Factory owners called for regulation of wages. Parliament acted first in the case of the Spitalfields silk weavers in London. The system of regulating wages, seemingly to the satisfaction of both workers and employers, fell under the control of local magistrates and was later adopted unofficially elsewhere in England, including Congleton. According to London silk weavers in 1818, this had proved beneficial and guaranteed an adequate wage at all times.[169] A worker sacrificed increases during good years in exchange for security during depressions. Skilful and careful work brought rewards, and workers did not need periodically to resort to the poor-law officer for relief. The Spitalfields Acts were repealed in 1823, and factory workers sought what wages they could. This was unfortunate because the silk trade at this time began to experience crisis and unemployment. It is significant that economic depression and strike action coincided with the period of unregulated wages. However, it must not be thought that millowners reduced wages drastically. In 1835 it could be reported, admittedly not by workers themselves, that the 'manufacturing population are actively employed at fair wages; women and children as well as men'.[170]

The wages of a skilled craftsman, whether bricklayer or weaver, rose from some 8s or 9s a week in 1770 to 20s or 30s during the war of 1793–1815.[171] A bricklayer in Congleton in 1815 and 1839 could expect about 4s a day. Workers at the silk factories in 1823 got about half-a-crown a day, and skilled men might receive more. Though wages rose during the early days of Congleton's economic depression, from 1832 factory workers certainly faced reductions. Women's wages fell from 1826 onwards, and since child and female labour was so important in every mill the whole town felt the effect of this reduction. The wages of unskilled male and female workers might be about two-thirds that of skilled workers.

Spinners and weavers using their own machines at home earned good money until 1815. In 1793 a man might expect 15s a week, as much as any skilled workers could receive anywhere. Wages tended to increase and remain high until economic crisis about 1825 and competition of factories robbed the handloom worker of his livelihood. By 1838 some men could earn only 7s a week, less than their ancestors got a century before. Piece rates fell by four times between 1814 and 1833. Money earned could not support a family no matter how careful a housewife was. Commissioners in 1840 pointed out that the domestic worker labouring unduly long hours each day still could not earn as much as the factory worker.[172] He might receive 27*s* a fortnight out of which came cost of material, loom rent, heating and lighting at home. Of course, the garrets could be lit by windows in the roof and men might shiver rather than have a fire. Even so actual earnings rarely covered the weekly budget. Agricultural workers were from about 1795 falling behind their industrial brothers in their power to earn adequate wages. The situation was concealed during wartime farm prosperity, but was very evident between 1815 and 1850. On the other hand men with skills which employers eagerly sought could ask very high wages. Stokers at Congleton gas works in 1833 earned 18*s* a week.[173]

It would seem that working-class wages generally together with additional items like food and free board were just adequate between 1770 and 1805 to pay the weekly budget for rent, food, clothing and fuel. The worst years of war around 1810 tended to throw all but the most skilled workers at times on poor relief. Between 1813 and 1832 industrial labourers' position improved, though domestic and farm workers tended to become, at times, distressed. Economic depression between 1828 and 1848 reduced wages and prices: but the worst problem remained periodic unemployment. On paper, a worker ought to have had a surplus. In practice short-time working meant many labourers lived always near starvation level. In 1840 Congleton people often existed entirely on potatoes and porridge 'with seldom any butchers' meat'.

Neither the factory nor the domestic system provided ideal working conditions for Congleton people. Small houses full of infants could not contain the equipment needed by weavers if the men were to do their job expertly. Long hours in cramped ill-lit premises destroyed the health and patience of handloom workers, though such abuses were of course self-imposed by the independent weavers. On the other hand strict hours, factory discipline and boring routine jobs characterized mill-work, but mills themselves had to be light and airy before delicate silks could be produced. The surviving mill buildings certainly indicate careful planning. Most workers in the mills enjoyed reasonable conditions: many men were glad to escape from cellars and garrets, dark shops and sheds. Adults began work at six o'clock in the morning and finished at nine at night during the early nineteenth century. Two hours would be allowed for meals. Men worked six days a week in times of prosperity. One of the most tiring jobs demanded running up and down in order to finish the material by cutting off hairs, and the marks of feet on mill floors remained to be pointed out for a century. It can be no wonder that a reporter stated: 'the population are generally strong and healthy, though they have often a pale and haggard appearance'.[174]

Children in silk mills were not protected by laws even when cotton workers received protection. Inspectors in 1840 found children working ten hours a day, leaving no time for education or leisure. Children's labour even in 1860 was an important factor in most mills. At the time of the 1851 census the Danein-shaw mill, run by Richard Ginder, a Blackburn cotton man turned Congleton silk thrower, employed 20 men, 70 women and no fewer than 120 children. Some of these little labourers had not reached nine years of age and it was widely believed that children had to learn the trade before they were thirteen years old 'or they will never be valuable workers'. The worst abuses, for children as for adults, consisted of continuous running up and down for twelve hours a day. 'I have been struck in going through a silk-mill with not seeing them sit down,' said one inspector. 'I should think it hard to stand 12 hours in the course of a day.' Boys in the throwing department ran 20 miles a day: 'I mention this as a curious fact.' Playtime had to be taken during meal breaks, and dinner, the main meal of the day, usually consisted of bread and cheese eaten in ten minutes with 50 minutes set aside for recreation. But the children had plenty of exercise in working hours.[175]

Work in factories could not have been easy for people used to farming or unregulated domestic work, but life for those who clung to outmoded methods was worse. The hand spinners and weavers of textiles were impoverished when mills turned first to water, then to steam power, increasing productivity and cutting costs. Their sufferings were in 1834 said to be of 'an extent and intensity scarcely to be credited or conceived'. The families bore their troubles with 'patience unexampled', blaming their calamities on everything from corn laws and taxation to machinery and unbridled competition between millowners. They did not understand that the root of the problem was their own conservatism, chronic overpopulation and foreign competition. A later report stated precisely: 'the great cause of this distress is a disproportion between the supply of hand-loom labour and the demand for it; the demand being in many cases deficient, in some cases decreasing, and in still more, irregular, while the supply is, in many branches, excessive, in almost all has a tendency to increase, and does not appear in any to have a tendency to adapt itself to the irregularities of the demand'. Families did not realize that they had after 1815 but two hopeful choices: to enter factories as textile workers or to change their trade completely. Upheaval deterred some families. The change often caused as much distress, initially, as it was meant to alleviate. In any discussion of Congleton's condition, including the practice of child labour in factories, these people must be taken into account. 'There is positive suffering wherever there are families of young children of which none, or very few, are capable of working in the mill . . . The whole of the family of a weaver are now worse off than ever.'[176]

Part-time handloom weaving on the other hand seems to have survived until at least 1860 subsidized by other activities. The story of Joseph Delves, an innkeeper of Park Street, illustrates the possibilities of survival as late as 1845.[177] Delves and his wife were accused in 1845 of keeping a disorderly house and harbouring prostitutes. Charles Bracegirdle, silk manufacturer, of Royle Street Mill, however, swore to Delves's innocence. For years the innkeeper had worked for Bracegirdle, hiring looms from him which were kept in the attics of the inn and taking piece-work assignments. Bracegirdle had regularly tramped through the house to the garret to examine the looms and the condition of the work. He had never seen anything immoral going on. Despite this Delves and wife were found guilty and sentenced to twelve months' imprisonment.

What was the result of economic growth in Congleton between the beginning of the eighteenth and the middle of the nineteenth century? Some families certainly made money and knew considerable luxury. Mill owners, forward-looking shopkeepers, attorneys, skilled craftsmen prospered. The town paved streets and speculators erected dwellings. Public and church buildings appeared. Indeed much of the town—church, chapels, bridges, town hall, shops—dates from after 1700, one sure sign of prosperity during the industrial era. Samuel Yates in 1820 told of the 'progression of society from its rude origin, ignorance and indigence, to a flourishing population, enjoying all the benefits of intelligence, opulence and refinement'. Few could ignore the 'commercial wealth, and profuse luxury' of districts where industry affected people's lives.[178]

On the other hand industrial life, with its economic crises, had its disadvantages. Swift expansion encouraged the rapid building of a town in parts of which people could not live decent and full lives. Many turned to the borough authorities for occasional relief during bouts of illness and unemployment so that the poor rate increased by ten times between 1750 and 1814, a far swifter increase than the general rise in population.[179] According to reporters of one side of Congleton life the bulk of families survived during hard times 'some on the poor's rate, others by begging, others by thieving, and many of the females by prostitution'.[180] Men found it relatively easy to live by their wits, stealing from canal boats and factories. Silk goods had little bulk but great value, so a modest theft went unnoticed by inefficient local police. Reports of the time clearly show that despite the ferocity of the law crime was a popular means of getting a living. Commissioners of 1835 found that the 'only persons out of employ are represented to be young and able-bodied men, who subsist on these depredations' of valuable silk wares. However in other years the streets must have been full of starving families: 1,700 people were unemployed in 1831. The operatives were sinking fast into degradation because 'their bellies go half full, their backs half clothed'.

Even in busier times Congleton workers were not highly thought of. In 1839 it was reported that there 'are nearly 50 licensed public-houses and 52 beer-shops within the space of 300 yards; they are represented here as universally to have aggravated greatly the habits of intoxication of the lower orders. When turned out of the regular public-houses the people are said to resort thither, and very young boys to be found tippling at them in the outskirts of the town', and in 1838 it was said that 'little time as they have for dissipation, they are generally of dissolute habits'.[181] Many 'exceedingly improvident' people spent freely all they had merely to show their superior earnings.

For some years between 1843 and 1862 the prosperous Congleton which Yates described in 1820 seemed to be returning. The town grew and trade revived. Reasonably full employment at textile mills and in workshops provided capital not merely for necessities of life but for new homes and leisure activities. Shop-keepers, craftsmen and professional people benefited from the labourers' increased spending power. Industrial peace returned while unduly long working hours and wretched conditions at home and mill began to be dealt with. The disappearance both of handloom weaving and of much child labour removed from the town two groups of distressed people. In many ways the year 1860, which saw the signing of the disastrous Cobden agreement, marks the end of Congleton's first industrial revolution as truly as the year 1752 marked the end of Congleton's period as purely a country market town.

Population and Society since 1860
The year 1860, when some 12,500 people lived in Congleton, proved to be the high water mark of population growth in the town. From that time until after the second World War there was little expansion. After the collapse of the silk industry the population actually fell by one thousand in the decade 1861–71, and emigration of young people became a regular and necessary habit. Houses fell empty, some 300 being unoccupied at the time of the census returns of 1871 and 1901. Men could not find work. The years 1891–1905 seem to be the low water mark, so to speak, in the history of modern Congleton, when population had fallen to under 11,000. From 1905 onwards, however, opportunities of employment and new houses not only encouraged people to stay in the town but also brought to Congleton some immigrant families. Thus there began the slow recovery. Resettlement of some people from the Potteries, envisaged in economic plans of the early post-war years, began by 1960 to have its effects.[182]

Buglawton, a crowded riverside community of 2,000 people in 1860, experienced a drastic decline of population between 1861 and about 1895. Regularly, 100 houses lay empty, and many had to be demolished when damp and neglect took their toll. The population fell to under 1,400 in 1891. Despite economic development after this date the township and urban district did not regain the 1860 population figure. Buglawton faced the fact that its cotton and silk trade of pre-1860 days had disappeared, that it could no longer grow as a thriving and separate unit. Hence in 1936 Buglawton joined Congleton borough. Houses and small factories then appeared between the

wars, and the borough council erected a large housing estate
north of St. John's church after 1945.

Congleton and Buglawton had in fact formed since about
1810 one economic unit dependent on textiles. The two places
together had in 1861 some 14,000 people. The population fell
to 12,000 by 1891, and even in 1931 after years of careful encouragement of trade and industry the 1861 population figure
was only just surpassed. But efforts were not wasted for the town
began to grow again, the population being over 15,000 in 1951,
over 16,000 in 1961.

Population decline certainly was a disaster for the town which
lost skilled workers and young vigorous families. Industry and
trade contracted. Merchants refused to invest capital in housing
and factory projects. People no longer spent money freely and
shopkeepers ran into difficulties. But one benefit of this decline
is important: the overcrowding of dwellings, very serious before
1860, became less of a problem after that time. Congleton and
Buglawton possessed in 1861 over 3,000 inhabited houses. This
meant 4·8 persons per house, a high though not a seriously high
average for that time.[183] The fall in population meant people
could spread out. Houses became cheaper to buy. The worst
slums could fall or be knocked down. So public health benefited.
In 1901 there were 4·3 persons in each dwelling, in 1931 under
four persons, at the end of the second World War 3·3 persons.
Even at this date, however, some 4,700 people lived in unfit
dwellings.[184]

Congleton society transformed itself in the period from 1860.
Local newspapers give the impression that people recognized
only three social layers in the later nineteenth century. There
were the gentry who lived in the countryside about the town;
the 'respectable' citizens, lawyers, shopkeepers, councillors,
teachers, skilled craftsmen; and finally, the labouring population. The farming community, small and distressed though this
had become after 1870, remained in two sections: farmers and
their labourers. The division had grown more marked than ever
because labourers now tended no longer to live under the same
roof as their masters nor to eat at the same board. The owner,
partners, company, and managers of mills generally knew little
of the workers, though Berisfords proved an exception in
Congleton. The workers, too, were divided into skilled craftsmen,
foremen and clerks on the one hand and unskilled labouring

men and women on the other. To some extent men were divided from women workers by differences of hours, pay and type of work.

Congleton and Buglawton have remained since the beginning of the nineteenth century manufacturing and trading centres. Between three-quarters and four-fifths of employed males generally found work in factories, craft workshops or retail businesses. This industrial group has divided more or less equally into factory workers and retail or handicraft shopmen.

After the end of wartime farming prosperity about 1815, local agriculture employed only about 7 or 8 per cent of men. Similarly 7 to 10 per cent of males were professional or domestic or miscellaneous workers. It is significant of a town diversifying its economic pursuits that this group grew more important especially after 1931.

The 1831 census noted over 2,400 men workers over twenty years of age. Of these 779 were in manufactures, 753 in retail trade or handicrafts as masters or men, and 552 were industrial labourers. There were only 81 professional men, 57 farmers, 112 farm labourers and 101 domestic servants and others. Exactly one century later the male working population had almost doubled, to 4,700. There were in 1931 2,663 in manufacturing and handicrafts occupations and 494 in shops as owners or assistants. On account of economic depression the percentage in industrial jobs had fallen from 85 per cent in 1831 to 67 per cent in 1931. By 1931 agriculture had tended to increase its labour force partly to absorb men who lost factory jobs while professional and miscellaneous work accounted for 24 per cent of the labour force probably for the same reason. Even in 1961 there were not more than 1,100 professional and miscellaneous workers despite population increase so the 1931 figure must have been artificially increased by odd-job men.

In 1931 textiles still employed by far the largest number of men (768) and women (945). Shops in the case of men and domestic service for women accounted for the second largest group. Agriculture was the third largest employer of men aged fourteen upwards.

Twentieth-century census returns indicate the increasing number of old people in the population. In 1951 there were 660 retired men compared with 4,881 occupied. The 1961 census provides a socio-economic table partly to illustrate the per-

a Swan Bank, 1960s, *b* Duke Street and Bridge Street, 1960s

a

b

Lawton Street and High Street, 1960s

centage of men with good qualifications for their jobs compared with unskilled labourers. Congleton's largest group (37·8 per cent of the male working population) consisted of fully-skilled manual workers and the second largest group (15·9 per cent) of semi-skilled men. This high proportion indicates the preponderance of factory or workshop occupations demanding comparatively high degrees of skill. There were consequently very few unskilled men, capitalist employers, self-employed shopkeepers, and managers in the borough.

During the twentieth century Congleton society became much more harmonious. Firms like Berisfords led the way in industrial relations. Farmers found labour so difficult to hire that they were forced to introduce a new deal for the manual worker (involving better pay, hours of work and housing).

The varying fortunes of industry, crafts and shops have already been traced. But what about that important group of the 'respectable', the professional people? Many professional families were descended either from landowners or from rich industrialists and businessmen. They are important in Congleton history up to the second World War because the town relied on their services in several fields beyond those in which they were trained: government, militia, library, Bible societies, lectures. What kind of people were they? A few examples must suffice.

The Reades began as textile manufacturers in the eighteenth century. The family bought land, took part in politics and read law. George Reade (1796–1865), landowner, merchant and town councillor, developed an important law business. He left £16,000 in personal goods alone when he died.[185] His son, Henry Lister Reade (1835–1906), continued as solicitor, becoming clerk to turnpike trusts and to magistrates, interesting himself in school boards. He in turn was succeeded by his sons Henry (1872–1952) and William (1875–1940).

Richard Martin (1760–95), uncle of George Reade above, made his money partly by introducing cotton to Congleton. He settled a substantial dowry on his daughter Anne (1793–1861) so that she might marry a young surgeon John Hall. Hall (1785–1861) was son of the Revd. Samuel Hall of Manchester. By his ability and with his wife's money Hall built up an excellent practice, becoming in due course a magistrate and alderman of the borough. John's and Anne's grandson, Charles Russell Hall

o

of Homefield, born in 1861, was a land agent, surveyor and architect, known all over Cheshire. He served local landowners, was engineer to the Buglawton and Biddulph water under- takings, and served diligently on the town council, in the Primrose League, the Volunteers, the Savings Bank, and the British and Foreign Bible Society.

The Wilsons are typical of Congleton professional people. Two generations of the family before 1860 produced Congleton clergy and school-masters. Edward Wilson (1787–1858), school- master, and incumbent of Buglawton for eighteen years, sent his sons to university. Of these, William (1820–96) was ordained, becoming Fellow of St. John's College, Cambridge, and for 49 years rector of a Norfolk parish. Another son was a doctor, and a third a teacher. Yet another, John (1817–95), took a doctorate of laws, served as clerk to Congleton magistrates for 50 years and town clerk for 39.[186]

During the late nineteenth century the number of professional people in Congleton increased. New professions emerged: den- tists, public health inspectors, chartered accountants. The general practitioners, Davidson and Fildes of Damian House, described in Kelly's *Directory*, served as surgeons and were employed as medical officers of health by local poor-law unions and Buglawton council. Walter Eric Fildes served the nearby National Children's Home as doctor and his wife Marjorie, also a surgeon, was school medical officer of Congleton. Although people had long since accepted women teachers, Marjorie Fildes is an early example of a Congleton professional woman in a man's world. It must, of course, be recalled that the first World War, reducing manpower, opened up of necessity many jobs for women.

The standard of living of Congleton people rose between 1860 and the 1960s despite economic depression and war. New, larger houses, better-planned, with gardens, bathrooms, garages, central heating, indicate rising standards. The houses built in 1860–80 are worlds apart from hovels like Gibralter or Lower Daneinshaw. Excellent businessmen's and shopkeeper's dwel- lings appear in 1890–1910. Then after 1920 a maze of council houses shelter the working population. Furniture, too, im- proves. The table, mattress, chairs and few utensils over a small fire of the early nineteenth century are replaced by five or six rooms full of furniture. Ornaments, pictures, pianos (for long a sign of gentility), radio, television all litter many houses. Bicycles and cars crowd driveways and yards.

Not everybody benefited. Not all those who benefited, benefited equally. The labourers in the nineteenth century, especially after 1860, tended to increase their living standard at a much slower rate than, say, professional families. On the other hand, people on fixed incomes after 1914 could not compete with mill workers or young skilled artisans.

Professional people together with those living on fixed incomes from shares and securities lived in fine state from about 1870 to about 1920. The documents of Eleanor Lowe of Moody Terrace show what comfort such families might expect. A spinster, Eleanor Lowe inherited money from her father, a businessman. She invested this and lived on the income, giving much away every year to such organizations as the Cottage Hospital and the National Society for the Prevention of Cruelty to Children. But still she had enough left to purchase finely-bound books, cut glass and silverware. An inventory of her goods taken in 1904[187] after her death shows, for instance, a forty-piece early Minton pink and gold tea service and a forty-piece Old Staffordshire dessert service by Neale. She possessed, too, a valued set of a dozen antique dessert knives and forks.

Shopkeepers and craftsmen also lived in comfort, not on the same level as Eleanor Lowe but extremely well all the same. Inventories of stock which survive in solicitors' collections, inventories of goods at home and in the shop for probate purposes, and sale catalogues reveal the possessions of these people. The families which survived the onslaught of big business after about 1910 shared in the general rise of living standards of the twentieth century.

The labouring population both on farms and in the mills probably gained most in the century following 1860. Of course even in the 1960s most workers could not boast of the fine houses and possessions owned by Victorian inhabitants of Congleton like the Reades and Lowes. But twentieth-century demands and needs were not those of the Victorians.

The population of Congleton and Buglawton increased tenfold in the period 1700–1960. Not only more people but new people helped to change the character of the Tudor and Stuart country market town. There were in 1700 farmers, craftsmen and shopkeepers. During the next two centuries textile workers and professional men became important in the social and economic life of the town. Living standards of many, possibly most, families rose in the late eighteenth century and for many years in the nineteenth and twentieth centuries. Congleton's social problems have been less dangerous than those of many industrial districts, perhaps because businesses were never very big and impersonal. In general population growth and economic change have not overburdened the delicate balances on which society hangs.

Notes

[1] Much information in this chapter derives from the following, not normally cited further: Directories of Cheshire—Bagshaw (1850), Broster (1782), Cowdroy (1789), Kelly (1910, 1913, 1914, 1928, 1939), Morris (1874), Slater (1848), White (1860); and Tunnicliff, *Topographical Survey* (1787); *Commercial Directory* (1816–17; 1818–19–20); Pigot, *Commercial Directory* (1828–9); *Congleton Official Guide* (1961); and also Ormerod.

[2] See p. 48.

[3] N. Spencer, *Complete English Traveller* (1771), 419.

[4] D. and S. Lysons, *Magna Britannia* (1810), 488–91.

[5] J. H. Hanshall, *County Palatine of Chester* (1817–23), 580.

[6] Manchester Central Library, Plans of Congleton, 1814, 1818. These are probably drafts for J. Moorhouse, *Map of the Borough and Lordship of Congleton* (1818); copy at Messrs Charlton and Co., solicitors, Congleton.

[7] Yates, *passim*.

[8] Hanshall, *op. cit.*, 580.

[9] RG 4/535, Congleton Wesleyan chapel register, 1813–37.

[10] *Rep. Boundary Commrs.*, 207.

[11] C.R.O., Will of Joseph Harwar. Thomas Vaudrey, another solicitor, later owned 80 houses.

[12] C.R.O., Buglawton Tithe records, 1844.

[13] C.R.O., Will of Benjamin Johnson; Lincolnshire Record Office: White III Box 2/8 and 7/9.

[14] C.R.O., Tithe records of Eaton, 1840; and Buglawton, 1844.

[15] There are O.S. maps of 1858 and 1875–6.

[16] The following is based on: Head, frontispiece; O.S. map 25 in. to 1 mile, 1909; *Kelly's Dir. Ches.* (1914); *Cheshire by the Camera, the Pencil and the Pen* (c. 1906); inf. from old inhabitants; existing buildings.

[17] Private developers lagged behind the council because of building restrictions. Thus Coniston Avenue and Delamere Road appeared only in 1963. Solley Crescent (1947) was a council development, though Heath Crescent nearby was private and about the same date.

[18] Inf. from R. G. Whiston Esq., chief public health inspector, Congleton.

[19] *T.L.C.A.S.*, ix, 110, 122–3; Lysons, *Cheshire*, 488.

20 J. Paul, *Parish Officer* (1806), 178.

21 For turnpike roads in Cheshire, see *T.L.C.A.S.*, x.

22 Accounts of turnpike companies survive only from the nineteenth century. In 1816–20 the annual average expenditure for administration and repairs of the Macclesfield–Congleton road amounted to but £183. The Wilmslow road company spent £1,250 a year: C.R.O., Returns of Revenues and Expenses of Turnpike Road Trusts, 1820.

23 Sir Henry Brooke Parnell (1797–1842), later Lord Congleton, championed road improvements, writing a treatise on the subject in 1837.

24 44 Geo. III c. x.

25 *Ibid.*

26 5 and 6 Wm. IV c. xxviii (Nantwich–Congleton road).

27 C.R.O., Plan (Biddulph, 1819: Quarter Sessions Plans).

28 *Macclesfield Courier and Herald*, 3 November 1838.

29 *Rep. R.C. for inquiring into the State of the Roads*, Parl. Paper (1840), xxvii; five trusts are found under Cheshire, one under Staffordshire.

30 44 and 45 Vic. c. xxxi. See also C.R.O., Returns of Revenues of Turnpikes, for difficulties as early as 1820. *T.L.C.A.S.*, x, 237–8, shows when the various companies ceased operation.

31 Yates, 58.

32 5 and 6 Wm. IV c. xxviii.

33 A. Kippis, *Biographia Britannica* (1780), 597, 602; Anon., *Inland Navigations* (1779), *passim.*; *Journal of House of Commons*, xxx, *passim.*

34 British Waterways (Liverpool), Trent and Mersey Canal Surveys 1778, and 1816.

35 QDP 26, Plan and reference book.

36 QDP 68 and 76.

37 A. Gibbs, *Story of Telford* (1935), 221.

38 7 Geo. IV c. xxx.

39 C.R.O., Congleton and Buglawton Tithe records, 1843–6, 1844.

40 Lewis, *Topographical Dict.* (1831), i, 506.

41 9 and 10 Vic. c. lxxxix.

42 J. Farey, *General View of the Agriculture of Derbyshire* (1817), iii, 331.

43 Bryant is very accurate.

44 Messrs. Greenall, Whitley & Co., of Wilderspool, brewers: *Castle Inn* records.

45 For the history of railways in the Congleton district see Manifold, *North Staffordshire Railway* (1952).

46 *Congleton Advertiser*, 6 February 1858.

47 Inf. from R. G. Whiston Esq.

48 Between 1830 and 1850 directories and guide books foretold increased trade for the canal; but later works, e.g. *Kelly's Dir. Ches.* (1914), indicate how little economic value the canal then retained.

49 J. Corry, *Hist. of Macclesfield* (1817) prints lists of Congleton freemen; cf. Blome, *Britannia*, 57.

50 Spencer, *Complete English Traveller*, 419; cf. J. Aikin, *Countryside around Manchester* (1795), 433.

51 *V.C.H. Staffs.*, ii, 206.

52 *T.L.C.A.S.*, lxii, 135.

[53] It is possible that some east Cheshire families used waste silk in the late seventeenth century to make stockings, ribbons and other goods: Davies, *Macclesfield*, 124.

[54] Much of the following is based, without further reference, on the title deeds of R. H. Lowe Ltd., Old Mill, kindly made available by J. Robertshaw Esq., secretary of the company.

[55] Yates, 75, 92–8; S. Smiles, *Lives of the Engineers* (1862) i, 325.

[56] Astbury and Congleton parish registers: new names appear.

[57] Spencer, *op. cit.*, 419.

[58] Aikin, *op. cit.*, 433.

[59] C.R.O., Will of John Clayton.

[60] *Journal of the Proceedings of J. Hewitt, Alderman of Coventry* (2nd ed. 1790), 32.

[61] C.R.O., Will of Ric. Martin, senr.

[62] Tunnicliff, *Topographical Survey* (1787), 64; Lincolnshire Record Office, White III Box 7/9 Lease, 1 July 1788.

[63] *T.L.C.A.S.*, lxi, 135. Drakeford installed the engine *c.* 1808.

[64] St. Peter's, Congleton, monumental inscription of Reade, 1838; C.R.O., Will of George Reade.

[65] QDL, 1810–15.

[66] For a detailed survey of his estate see C.R.O., Will of John Vaudrey of Buglawton.

[67] The following information is based on Congleton Gas Light Company, Minutes; C.R.O., Buglawton Tithe records, 1844; Wills of William and Thomas Vaudrey.

[68] *Jnl. House of Commons*, xxxiv, 240.

[69] Lysons, *Magna Britannia*, ii, 489; C.R.O., Will of Samuel Johnson, proved 1813.

[70] Yates, 100; Head, 154.

[71] Lysons, *Magna Britannia*, ii, 490; Corry, *History of Macclesfield*, 197.

[72] Yates, 98; *Census*, 1821.

[73] *Rep. Silk Trade* (1831–2), 805.

[74] *Rep. Mun. Corps.*, 584.

[75] *Rep. Silk Trade* (1831–2), 807.

[76] *Ibid.*, 805–7; Pigot, *Directory* (1828–9).

[77] For a general discussion of this problem see *Explorations in Entrepreneurial History*, 2nd series, i, no. 2, 164–83.

[78] Head, 151.

[79] *Rep. Silk Trade* (1831–2), 806.

[80] *T.L.C.A.S.*, lxi, 133, 135.

[81] C.R.O., Congleton Tithe Map, 1843.

[82] *Rep. Silk Trade* (1831–2), 806; *Rep. Handloom Weavers* (1840), 337; Records of Charlton & Co., Congleton: catalogue of silk machinery of Charles Gent, 1840.

[83] *Rep. Handloom Weavers* (1834), 332.

[84] *Rep. Mun. Corps.*, 584.

[85] *Rep. Tech. Instr.* (1884), xxix, xxxii–ix.

[86] *Berisfords*, 13–14.

[87] For this paragraph see *Rep. Handloom Weavers* (1840), 336–7.

[88] Head, 152, 154; *Censuses*, 1841, 1851.

[89] *Rep. Tech. Instr.* (1884), xxxii, xxxiv.

[90] B. Poole, *History of Coventry* (1870), 361.

[91] *Rep. Handloom Weavers* (1840), 353; Head, 154; White, *Dir. Ches.* (1860).

[92] *Rep. Tech. Instr.* (1884), xcii, xxxii–ix.

[93] *Ibid.*, xxxii–ix; Head, 154–7; White, *Dir. Ches.* (1860): the numbers given for 1859 above cannot include the silk manufacturers. The 1860 number in the text does not include the 11 Buglawton mills of mixed throwsters and manufacturers.

[94] C.R.O., Accession 1167, uncatalogued.

[95] Head, 155–6.

[96] The following is based on *Berisfords, passim,* and on information kindly supplied by J. F. Sebire Esq.

[97] *Cong. Chron.*, 11 November 1893; 20 January 1894.

[98] R. Head, *Cheshire at the Opening of the Twentieth Century*, 399.

[99] Inf. from company secretary.

[100] Wild MSS. (held by Mrs. E. H. Gilmour of Congleton), Plan of Forge Mill, 1865.

[101] H.O. 107.

[102] C.R.O., Buglawton Tithe map, 1844.

[103] Records of R. H. Lowe Ltd.; Head, *Cheshire at the Opening of the Twentieth century*, 233.

[104] The following is based on Wild MSS.

[105] Charlton & Co., Congleton, accounts of Goldstraw.

[106] For Burslam family see Bagshaw, *Dir Ches.* (1850), White, *Dir. Ches.* (1860); H.O. 107; *Kelly's Dirs. Ches.* and *P.O. Dirs.* after 1860.

[107] For Charles Roe's enterprises see *T.L.C.A.S.*, lxii, 142–3; J. R. Harris, *The Copper King* (1964), *passim*; Davies, *Macclesfield*, 113–40.

[108] C.R.O., Buglawton and Eaton Tithe records, 1844, 1840.

[109] *T.L.C.A.S.*, lxiii, 67–8.

[110] *Manchester Mercury*, 20 October 1801, 1 April 1806.

[111] Lysons, *Magna Britannia*, ii, 427; Davies, *Macclesfield*, 120–1.

[112] Inf. on bricks collected by R. G. Whiston Esq.

[113] C.R.O., Buglawton Tithe records, 1844; Buglawton Enclosure Award, 1831; Congleton Land Taxes, 1820–25; Congleton Tithe records, 1843; Congleton Enclosure Award, 1798.

[114] Hanshall, *op. cit.*, 580; Farey, *op. cit.*, 288. Coal is said to have been brought to the town by donkey in *c.* 1828: *Cong. Chron.*, 4 November 1893.

[115] Records of R. H. Lowe, Ltd.

[116] C.R.O., Eaton Tithe records, 1840; Buglawton Tithe records, 1844. The Havannah corn mill had long served the township of Eaton, and at some time before 1753 the river had been diverted to supply a good mill race.

[117] C.R.O., Will of Thomas Lowndes.

[118] H.O. 107.

[119] Charlton & Co., settled bills.

[120] Head, 61; C.R.O., Alehouse recognizances about 1826.

[121] C.R.O., Will of Thomas Martin.

[122] The following is based on local newspaper files; *Cheshire by the Camera*; local inf.; H.O. 107; R.G. 9.

[123] The figures for 1930 and 1960 supplied by R. G. Whiston Esq.

[124] The following is based on A. & J. Cooke, *Jubilee Hist. of Congleton Equitable and Industrial Cooperative Soc., 1860–1910* (1910).

[125] H.O. 107.

[126] Inf. from R. G. Whiston Esq.; directories.

[127] Inf. from C. F. Jackson Esq.; directories, and parish registers.

[128] *Cong. Chron.*, 14 May 1937.

[129] *Ibid.*, 31 August 1916.

[130] Charlton & Co., Congleton, papers of George Reade.

[131] *Cheshire by the Camera* (1906), 180. His descendant in 1937 was building houses: e.g. 44 corporation dwellings in Lamberts Lane and York Rd.: *Cong. Chron.*, 14 May 1937.

[132] *Cheshire by the Camera*, 198.

[133] Inf. on the firm's motives for going to Havannah kindly provided by C. F. Jackson, Esq., of Mill Street, cycle dealer.

[134] Inf. on the firm kindly provided by W. R. Bossons Esq., son of the founder.

[135] For printers and booksellers see Yates, *passim*; C.R.O., Wills of S. Yates, S. Johnson.

[136] QDL, Congleton, 1780–90. About 1780 William Drakeford set up a paper factory in Congleton.

[137] *Cheshire by the Camera*.

[138] Charlton & Co., papers of W. Clarke.

[139] Head, *Cheshire at the Opening of the Twentieth Century*, 298.

[140] Examples survive in document accumulations preserved in local solicitors' offices; e.g. Charlton & Co., to whom thanks are due for making papers available.

[141] Charlton & Co., papers of Edw. Joyce, 1851–61.

[142] Inf. from A. J. Condliffe Esq., editor of *Cong. Chron.*, 1966.

[143] Few sources give any details of Congleton farming practice. The following is largely based on C.R.O., Tithe records for Congleton 1843–6, Buglawton 1844, Congleton Enclosure records, 1798, Buglawton Enclosure records, 1831, *Censuses*, 1861–1961, and Moorhouse, *Plan of Congleton* (1818); Burdett's Map, 1777. Other findings agree well with the conclusions on east Cheshire farming in C. S. Davies, 'Agricultural History of Cheshire', *Chetham Soc.*, 3rd ser. x.

[144] G. Cooke, *Chester* (1830), 38.

[145] The Shakerleys' male line had died out in 1781, but the heiress's husband's son changed his name to Shakerley. This man was involved in Congleton enclosure 1795–8 and became sheriff of Cheshire in 1791.

[146] *Journal of House of Commons*, l, p. 118.

[147] Yates, 73.

[148] QDL, Congleton, 1780–1831 detail the owners and occupiers. C.R.O., Will of John Sherratt jun. of Buglawton, yeoman, mentions the farm in Buglawton 'which I lately purchased' (1808). Such a purchase remains an exception.

[149] Much of what follows is based on analysis of the following registers: Astbury, 1702–40; Congleton section in Astbury register, 1712–40; Congleton, St. Peter, 1740–1851; Buglawton, St. John, 1840–8; Congleton Wesleyan, 1808–37; Congleton, Mill Street Presbyterian, 1820–35; Congleton, Mill Street Independent, 1788–1837; Congleton, Zion, 1823–37; and on certificates after June 1837. Grateful thanks are due to Miss M. Cinnamon and the sixth-form girls of Congleton Grammar School for undertaking search of some of these registers.

[150] EDV 7/1/70 and 7/2/63 for 1778, 1789; J. T. Danson and T. A. Welton, 'On the Population of Lancashire and Cheshire, 1801–51', *T.H.S.L.C.*, ix–xii.

[151] *Censuses*, 1801–1831.

[152] C.R.O., Wills.

[153] C.R.O., Will of Thomas Vaudrey of Congleton, gentleman, proved 1850. He left £12,000, a large estate including 'Gibralter Rocks near Lawton Street End', and railway and gas company shares.

[154] Inscriptions in graveyard.

[155] Pigot, *Directory* (1828–9) notices 19 professional men; 95 manufacturers; 108 prosperous traders; 94 smaller craftsmen.

[156] *Census*, 1831, Congleton and Buglawton.

[157] *Expense and Maintenance of the Poor*, Parl. Paper (1818), xix, 44–5, Congleton and Buglawton.

[158] *Rep. Handloom Weavers* (1840), 339.

[159] *List of the Lodges composing the Manchester Unity of Independent Odd Fellows, 1845–6* (Oldham, 1845).

[160] *Rep. Handloom Weavers* (1840), 337–8.

[161] *Rep. Handloom Weavers* (1841), 309.

[162] Head, 151.

[163] *Rep. Handloom Weavers* (1841), 309, 403.

[164] Head, 152; *Rep. Handloom Weavers* (1840), 338–9.

[165] See *T.L.C.A.S.*, lxvii; H.O. 45/242.

[166] See pp. 94–6.

[167] H.O. 45/242.

[168] *Rep. Tech. Instr.* (1884), xl.

[169] *Rep. Silk Manufacture* (1818), 200.

[170] *Rep. Mun. Corps.*, 584.

[171] Congleton wages may be discovered here and there in local records and in several of the Parliamentary Papers cited above.

[172] *Rep. Handloom Weavers* (1840), 338–9.

[173] Congleton Gas Co., Minutes 9 May 1833.

[174] *Rep. Handloom Weavers* (1840), 338–9.

[175] *Rep. Sel. Cttee on Mills and Factories* (1840), x, 126, 197, 758, 764.

[176] *Rep. Handloom Weavers* (1834), 3; *Rep. Handloom Weavers* (1841), 402; *Rep. Handloom Weavers* (1840), 339.

[177] C.R.O., Accession 1167.

[178] Yates, x, xii.

[179] *Ibid.*, 73.

[180] *Rep. Silk Trade* (1831–2), xix, 805, 807; *Rep. Mun. Corps.*, 584.

[181] *Rep. Handloom Weavers* (1840), 339.

[182] See, e.g., *A Plan for Cheshire* (*Country Life* for Cheshire County Council, 1948), 147 which saw a possible overspill of 10,000 people from the Potteries.

[183] Based on census returns.

[184] *Plan for Cheshire*, 55, 147.

[185] C.R.O., Will.

[186] St. Peter's churchyard inscriptions.

[187] C.R.O., Accession 1167.

VI *Religion in Congleton*

by W B Stephens, Robert W Dunning,
Joan P Alcock & M W Greenslade

INTRODUCTION

Nothing is known of religious differences in Congleton before
the later years of Elizabeth I's reign, by which time the breach
with Rome had long since taken place. The first part of this
section traces the history of the church in Congleton before the
Reformation and of the Established Church after that. Puritan
elements, probably in existence in the town by the late sixteenth
century came into the open in the seventeenth and for a short
time gained control of the Anglican church in Congleton as
elsewhere. The restoration of episcopacy in 1660 really marked
the end of any possibility of a comprehensive Anglican church
and the beginnings of some of the modern dissenting churches.
The history of these dissenting groups, together with that of the
Methodists and other Protestant sects of later origin, is covered
in the second part of the section.

The enthusiasm with which some leading Congleton townsmen embraced Puritanism and supported Parliament against
King in the Civil War forms a background to Congleton's later
emergence as a centre of religious dissent. At first the strongest
nonconformist group were the Presbyterians or Unitarians, the
distinction then not being as clear as it later became. By the
early nineteenth century these were overtaken in popularity by
the newer Methodist movement and to a lesser extent by a
revival of a Congregationalism with Calvinistic leanings. By
1811 Methodism was clearly the dominant dissenting sect in
the town, its establishment being coincident with Congleton's
emergence as a textile manufacturing centre.

In 1759 there were said to be only 23 Methodists in the town[1] but Richard Sandbach, the Anglican minister, in 1778 noted that there were then 30 Presbyterians (or Unitarians) and 90 Methodists 'which are in general the very lowest rank of persons'. He complained that although they had a place of worship they were allowed to preach in the streets and that 'the mayor and other magistrates, when desired, have refused to proceed against them'. By 1789, however, some of the 100 Methodists then reputedly resident in Congleton were still attending St. Peter's,[2] although the Congregationalists, also numbering about 100, never visited it. The Presbyterian–Unitarian congregation was said to be about equal in size to the Methodists and Congregationalists in 1789, but by 1804 had diminished very considerably,[3] and in the following year the Congregationalists were said to number only 44.[4] On the other hand in 1811 the minister of St. Peter's reported that the Methodist congregation was very large[5] and ten years later[6] stated that about 4,000 of Congleton's population of some 6,400 were dissenters. This, he said, compared with an average attendance at St. Peter's of some 400, plus a Sunday school of 200–300 children. There were then said to be no known Roman Catholic dissenters in the town, but by 1825 an influx of Irish weavers seems to have marked the beginning of a Roman Catholic congregation, and the history of Roman Catholicism in Congleton forms the last part of this section.

It is possible that the 1821 figures just given exaggerated the size of the nonconformist element at that time. Nevertheless in the 1830s the Methodists do appear to have multiplied, the numbers at Wagg Street chapel allegedly doubling between 1831 and 1835.[7]

In 1851 a religious census gives an overall picture of denominational allegiance in Congleton, and has here been summarized in a table.

The total number of attendances on the census day at all places of worship making the return was 7,180. This, however, would include many who went to two services in the day and some who went to three. If we take the largest number of adults and children at any one service in each place of worship we arrive at a total of 4,320—but this would be a minimum figure for it would exclude those who only attended one of the other services. Moreover, two important places of worship—Holy

Attendance at Public Worship, 30 March, 1851[a]

		Morning			Afternoon			Evening		
		General	Sunday School	Total	General	Sunday School	Total	General	Sunday School	Total
Church of England	St. Stephen's	100	261	361	—	—	—	300	—	300
	St. Peter's	343	226	569	183	226	409	410	—	410
	St. James's	131	173	304	—	—	—	204	80	284
	St. John's, Buglawton	50	130	180	80	130	210	—	—	—
Primitive Methodists	Lawton St.	—	—	—	210	208	418	270	—	270
	Mossley	—	—	—	40	40	80	50	—	50
	Key Green	—	—	—	75	95	170	102	—	102
Wesleyan Methodists	Brom (Bromley?) Lane	—	—	—	—	—	—	60	—	60
	Congleton Edge	—	—	—	38	—	38	64	—	64
	Brook Street, Buglawton	—	—	—	—	—	—	80	20	100
	Wagg Street	400	150	550	40	150	190	600	—	600
New Connexion Methodists	Queen Street	?	?	250	—	—	—	?	?	290
Independents (Congregationalists)	Mill Street	96	82	178	—	—	—	152	47	199
Presbyterians or Unitarians	Cross Street	20	—	20	—	30	30	50	—	50
Baptists	Zion Chapel	23	13	36	—	—	—	55	—	55
Roman Catholics	St. Mary's	160	60	220	—	—	—	100	40	140

[a] H.O. 129/457. No returns from Holy Trinity (C. of E.), Mossley, and Buglawton Primitive Methodist Chapel. No return traced for Cloud Primitive Methodist Chapel.

Trinity, Mossley (seating capacity 366), and Buglawton Primitive Methodist chapel (seating capacity 203)—failed to make returns. The actual number of persons who attended worship in Congleton on that day was thus probably somewhere between about 4,320 and 7,500. If this was typical, then it represents a church attendance of possibly between 35 and 60 per cent of Congleton and Buglawton's total population of 12,572. If we allow only for 'eligible population', that is total population less those for whom church attendance was impossible—the senile, the sick, infants, those necessarily at work, and so on—the effective percentage was no doubt higher.[8] We must take into account, too, that not everyone who absented himself on that Sunday, necessarily absented himself every or even most other Sundays.

Though by no means rendering exact statistics the census suggests[9] that by the standard of the day church attendance in Congleton was somewhat above the average for the whole country, but lower than that in many small towns and rural areas, and in some larger places.[10] Attendance in towns tended to be lower than elsewhere. The return also indicates the importance of protestant nonconformity in the borough, though the nature of the census may tend to exaggerate this.

A similar survey was undertaken on 31 March 1968, through the joint efforts of the Congleton History Society and the Congleton Council of Churches,[11] for the purposes of providing information for this volume. Its results are here tabulated.

Making use of these figures in the same way as those for 1851 we find that the number of churchgoers on the census day in 1968 was between 1,641 and 2,630, representing some 10 to 16 per cent of the total population, a very considerable decline since 1851. Roman Catholic attendance figures show an absolute rise, however, and on the whole a higher proportion of the total number of worshippers (though far fewer in actual numbers) may have attended the Established Church than in 1851.

The causes of the great fall-off in churchgoing since mid-Victorian times belongs to national rather than to purely local history. It is interesting, however, to note that in 1811 the minister of St. Peter's had reported that there were then in Congleton 'no known infidels'.[12] By 1851, as we have seen, perhaps up to half the town's population did not attend public worship. By the late nineteenth century there was a sufficient

Attendance at Public Worship, 31 March 1968[a]

		Morning			Afternoon			Evening		
		General	Sunday School	Total	General	Sunday School	Total	General	Sunday School	Total
Church of England	St. Stephen's	98	54	152	—	—	—	96[b]	—	96
	St. Peter's	55	27	82	—	—	—	83	—	83
	St. James's	72	44	116	—	—	—	54	—	54
	Holy Trinity, Mossley	109	28	137	—	24	24	53	—	53
	St. John's, Buglawton	99	47	146	—	—	—	41	—	41
Methodists	Central[c]	131	—	131	—	163	163	115	—	115
	Rood Lane	—	25	25	—	45	45	130[d]	—	130
	Key Green	—	18	18	—	—	—	15	—	15
	Daneinshaw	7	—	7	—	—	—	4	—	4
	Congleton Edge	—	—	—	5	10	15	—	—	—
	Kinsey Street	20	—	20	—	62	62	54	—	54
	Biddulph Road, Mossley	—	10	10	—	25	25	15	—	15
	Cloud	—	10	10	—	7	7	14	—	14
Congregationalists	Antrobus Street	122	160	282	—	—	—	112	—	112
Salvation Army	Cole Hill Bank	—	—	—	—	5	5	6	—	6
Roman Catholics	St. Mary's[e]	205	85	290	—	—	—	114	57	171

a No return from other bodies including Buglawton Primitive Methodists and small Apostolic, Baptist, Unitarian, Pentecostal and Jehovah's Witnesses congregations; but estimates of average Sunday attendance have been kindly provided by the Unitarian (evening 20), Pentecostal (morning 20, evening 30, Sunday school 30) and Apostolic (12 afternoon, 12 evening) officials.
b Said to be normally about 65.
c Temporary name for new chapel (now called Trinity) in which are combined the old Wagg Street, Brook Street and Queen Street congregations.
d Said to be normally about 35.
e Also at 8.30 a.m. 138 including 39 children.

number of sceptics in Congleton to form a local secularist society. A visit to the town by Charles Bradlaugh and Annie Besant in 1876, sponsored by this society, provided evidence that the population was as yet, however, far from apathetic about religious matters. The meetings took place on 25 and 26 September at Salford Mill (the town hall having been refused to the society). The first night Bradlaugh held forth 'the right to speak and the right to think' to the accompaniment of broken windows and shouting from a huge crowd outside.[13] Mrs. Besant, who was sitting on the platform with Mrs. Wolstenholme-Elmy, the suffragette, was cut on the back of the head by a stone hurled from the crowd. Afterwards they walked to the Wolstenholme-Elmy house at Buglawton accompanied by a huge crowd which alternately cursed and sang hymns on the way and remained outside the house until midnight. On the next evening the crowd gathered round the house waiting for the visitors to appear and the arrival of the cab to take them to the hall was the signal for a further outburst. Mrs. Besant found her audience a tamer one until a tradesman and local wrestler, named Burbery, stood up with the intention of causing a riot. Charles Bradlaugh said he must either keep quiet or go. Burbery said 'Put me out!' whereupon Bradlaugh, who had some skill at wrestling, grabbed him and propelled him to the door through the amazed stares of his friends. On leaving the hall, the party greeted by further stones.[14] In 1968, however, apathy rather than strong belief or disbelief appears to hold sway at Congleton as elsewhere.

THE CHURCH

The history of the Church in Congleton begins with the history of the parish of Astbury. There was certainly a priest at Astbury at the time of the Domesday survey of 1086, and carved stone in the present church at Astbury may have come from an earlier, late Saxon, structure on the site.[15] Astbury parish was very large, and included several villages and hamlets within its boundaries. At two of these, daughter churches were built at an early period and, acquiring independence, broke away from the mother church to form their own parishes. Brereton is said to have become independent at the time of Richard I, but continued to pay a pension to Astbury in recognition of its former subject status.[16] Church Lawton also broke away before

a St. Peter's Church, *b* St. John's Church, Buglawton, *c* Congregational
Chapel, Antrobus Street

a

b

c

a Methodist Chapel, Queen Street (closed 1969), *b* St. Mary's Roman
Catholic Church and Presbytery

a

b

the end of the twelfth century, and its original relationship with Astbury was recalled in a payment to the mother church of a pension for the right to have a burial ground, a payment established before 1280 and continued until 1700 at least.[17] The development of parochial organization in the thirteenth century made the creation of further parishes increasingly difficult and, ironically perhaps because of its growth from a dependent hamlet to a chartered town, Congleton failed to establish for itself a parish and an independent church. Very possibly it had its own chapel by the thirteenth century, but the rectors of Astbury were no doubt reluctant to lose an important part of their revenue.

Inevitably, some kind of working arrangement between the rectors of Astbury and the townsmen of Congleton was early arrived at, the terms of which we do not know. It is very probable that by the time Congleton had become important enough to have a charter, it had also acquired a chaplain serving a chapel in the town and supported by the inhabitants. The relationship of both with the rectors is not known and, except for the occurrence of men described as 'chaplains' in rolls of the borough court,[18] we have no direct evidence of church or clergy in the town until the end of the fourteenth century. Thus in 1358 Thomas Boydel and Hugh Pymmesone, chaplains, were recorded as paying for turf sold to them in the turbary at Congleton, though whether they served cures in the town is not known. But we can be more certain about Richard de Chelle, chaplain, whose servant was fined in 1357 for breaking the assize of ale.[19] Richard seems to have been a local man, possibly the brother of Alexander de Chelle, one of Congleton's leading burgesses. Richard was certainly town chaplain just over 20 years later.

In a full court at Congleton held on 7 November 1379, it was agreed by all the lord's tenants that Richard de Chelle, chaplain, should serve in the chapel of Congleton as long as he was able to do so, and gave satisfactory service. He was to have six marks (£4) as salary 'from the whole community of Congleton', payable in equal parts at the Annunciation and Midsummer. The court agreed that if the salary or any part of it was not paid 'by each man then being in Congleton', then the bailiff should collect from defaulters twice the sum they owed. Further, the chaplain was to have his tenement free, in addition

P

to his salary, and was to hold it with all profits and fees belonging to the chaplaincy.[20]

This formal enactment was obviously in some sense a new arrangement, but probably only in terms of finance. The chaplaincy itself seems already well established, the profits and fees attached to it well enough known not to require further definition. The rectors of Astbury had doubtless acquiesced in allowing some sort of ecclesiastical liberty to the townsmen of Congleton. The status of Astbury itself was in dispute at the end of the fourteenth century, and the rector in 1379 was an absentee.[21] The townsmen of Congleton would have been less than human not to take advantage of the situation to gain some measure of stability and independence for their chapel.

For the next two centuries the history of the church is obscure. The names of several chaplains have survived for this period, but there is no proof that all of these served a cure in the town.[22] The few surviving local wills, however, show that the town had two chapels: one, presumably on the site of the present St. Peter's Church, then known as the Upper, or Higher, Chapel; the other by the bridge, on the other side of the Dane, known as the Bridge, or Lower, Chapel.[23]

Very little is known about the Bridge Chapel. Bequests in surviving wills are often made for the upkeep of the bridge and the chapel together;[24] it apparently formed part of the structure of the bridge itself, perhaps bestriding the entrance, as it was said to be 'maintained for the defence of the said bridge'.[25] Its position suggests that, like other such chapels all over the country, it may have been intended for the use of travellers. In 1549 it was evidently still used and then possessed a chalice and a bell,[26] but by 1566 it was said to be 'converted to no use'.[27] Described as 'the Loar Chappell, situated at the end of a certain bridge called the Dane Bridge', it was granted by the Crown in 1574 to John and William Mershe of London.[28] The corporation evidently acquired it by 1589 and regularly cleaned and repaired it, while using it as a store for building materials.[29] It was extensively repaired with stone from Congleton Edge in 1623, the end wall was rebuilt, 'bastyng stones' laid under the sills, and the whole structure plastered.[30] Part of the building continued as a store throughout the seventeenth century, but part was let to a firm of bellfounders by 1631.[31] In 1730 the corporation decided to convert the old chapel into a workhouse.[32] It was so used until 1810, and demolished in 1814.[33]

The Upper Chapel was in existence by 1418,[34] and by the end of the sixteenth century it was the only church in the town, and thenceforth became the object of the corporation's care and attention. The small gifts of money bequeathed to it for repairs during the fifteenth century[35] and the annual collection of the chaplain's salary as settled in 1379 were replaced by the financial support of the mayor, aldermen and burgesses for salary, repairs and furnishings. In return, however, the minister was required to be their servant and to follow their directives. The ancient connection with the mother church at Astbury was still retained in theory: the mayor of Congleton was *ex officio* one of the posts or *prepositi* of Astbury, having a pew there for which the corporation paid each year.[36] Similarly the three proctors or sidesmen of Congleton[37] were assistants of the churchwardens of Astbury, and one was noted as absent in 1703 when the churchwardens made their presentments.[38] By 1687 the Congleton sidesmen had become known as chapel wardens.[39] This, however, did not imply independence from Astbury; no baptisms, marriages or burials could legally be performed at Congleton, and the minister, William Redman, was presented by Astbury churchwardens in 1637 for celebrating what they called 'unlawful clandestine marriages'.[40] A 'christening basin' was acquired in 1659 for the chapel, but perhaps only for use in emergencies.[41]

To all intents and purposes, however, it was the corporation which, having paid the piper, called the tune. In 1584, for example, it ordered all householders to send young people to church seven times a year 'upon warnynge geven by the curatte, to be instructed in the chathachisme and other articles of the Christian faythe' on pain of a fine of 2*d* a day.[42] In 1589 this order was modified to four attendances.[43] The minister was, in the phrase of the corporation accounts, 'hired', and was removable at will; this point was later to strengthen their case for right of patronage. William Redman, already in trouble for performing illegal marriages, apparently complained of his wages, and in 1637 was peremptorily told to be content or face dismissal.[44] He left in the same year. Mr. Barbour (minister 1663–9) was removed summarily for 'neglecting' and 'sliting' the town.[45]

Little is known in detail of the ministers themselves during this period. In general it will be seen that several held degrees and others, such as John Pemberton, Thomas Brook and Daniel Bayley attended a university, though apparently they did not proceed to degrees.[46] Few held the benefice for more than a few years; by far the longest holder was William Redman, minister 1621–37. No generalizations can be made about their backgrounds. Only two were certainly local men: Ralph Malbon was a native of the town,[47] and John Whitaker went to the grammar school there. Francis Ford's father was a farmer at Kingsly, Staffs.; John Smith came from Audley, Staffs.; Richard Jackson was a native of Hough End, Withington, Lancs.; John Pemberton was born at High Ongar, Essex; Thomas Meakins came from Rutland. Some, like Pemberton and Meakins, came to Congleton as their first benefice, but when they left, they did not move far, Pemberton to Chester, Meakins to Leek. Others held cures in the area before coming to the town: Brook was minister at Gawsworth, Bayley at Stafford, Jackson probably at Nantwich.

We know more than these meagre details about two of the town's ministers. John Smith, minister 1643–6, came to Congleton after being expelled from Bowdon for 'grand offences'. He left Congleton without notice, 'being invited to better preferment at Audley'. He left there to become rector of Barthomley in 1649. Articles drawn up against him in 1646 described him as 'covetous, exacting treble damages for any failure to pay tithes, lying, envious and a vilifier of other ministers'. He was said to have deserted the public cause at Worcester, although he had been employed as an army chaplain. Smith signed the Staffordshire *Testimony* in 1648, but at the Restoration he was temporarily imprisoned in Chester castle. He died at Odd Rode in 1660–1.[48] Like Smith, one of his successors, Thomas Brook, was a Presbyterian. His career probably began as a curate at Great Budworth in 1627, whence he removed to Gawsworth, where he signed the Covenant. He settled at Congleton in 1651. His career is detailed below.[49]

Brook's period at Congleton probably marks the height of the town's Puritan and Presbyterian fervour. At the end of the sixteenth century two preaching services were held each Sunday, and under an order of 1597 morning prayers were to be read each day at 6 o'clock.[50] At this time, however, the minister was aided by a reader who seems to have been responsible for the weekday services. James Broster, minister 1594–7, received a further 10s in his last year at Congleton 'for his paynes in saying morenynge preeyer this quarter' when no reader was available.[51] The readers, particularly Richard and Daniel Grene and Mr. Price the schoolmaster,[52] bore much of the burden of the services in the chapel during the long vacancy after Broster left in 1597. During this period, but also frequently on other occasions, preachers came from elsewhere to occupy the pulpit in the chapel. Feast days of the church, Gunpowder Plot Day,[53] 'the Wednesday in the great Cock Fight Week'[54] or 'Wakeday Week'[55] were occasions when the corporation invited visitors to the town. Some, like Mr. Palmer of Macclesfield[56] or Mr. Gerrard of Stockport[57] might receive a fee for their pains; others might be regaled with a meal or a drink. After Mr. Plante preached in the autumn of 1637 he and Mr. Bradshaw, who probably invited him, consumed between them a gallon of wine and a quantity of sugar, costing the corporation 3s 4d.[58]

Preachers figure largely in the accounts of the corporation relating to the church, a fact which has a bearing on the religious complexion of the town. It seems clear that even before the time of Thomas Brook, indeed, from the later years of the sixteenth century, the chapel at Congleton was an active preaching centre. Further, from 1624 at the latest, the corporation actively supported preaching exercises held in the town, gatherings of puritan clergy to be found also in other parts of Cheshire. Thus in 1632 Alderman Rode of the *Swan* was paid 10s 4d for dinners and wine 'bestowed on ministers that have preached here on Exercise Days'.[59] References to these exercise days occur irregularly; this may be accounted for either as a failure in accounting, an indication that the meetings themselves were not regular, or that Congleton was not the usual place for meetings. There are indications that there were more meetings in the 1640s: in 1642, for example, three meetings seem to have been held there each quarter. The size of these meetings and the number of clergy involved is not known; the sum spent varies, though in the late 1650s the cost was usually more than one pound. In June 1647 John Smith, innkeeper, was paid £1 2s 4d for exercise dinners, and a further shilling was given to a messenger 'to fetch a minister the same time'.[60] These exercises at Congleton continued certainly until January 1657, and most probably until the end of 1659.

It is clear that a town which made Bradshaw its High Steward, a town which had Thomas Brook as its preacher, was a town with Puritan sympathies. But the accounts of the corporation also indicate that this attitude did not go hand in hand with iconoclasm, for money was lavished on maintaining and beautifying the chapel and its surroundings. In 1613, for example, there were extensive building operations at the chapel. John Dale[61] added two timber-framed aisles and a porch, and for this 'and other work done at the chapel and for the town's good will towards him in doing it well' he was given £3. At the same time John Glasyer put in glass in iron-barred windows, and new seats were made from board brought from Rushton.[62] In 1634 it was the turn of the interior. A new green pulpit cloth and cushion were made by William Rathbone, and Thomas Lathum wound the silk and wove the fringe for both. Material left over was used for the cushion at the reading desk. Hemp cloth was bought at the same time to be painted with the Royal Arms and the Ten Commandments. The sum of 12*s* was spent on a new chest to store the church books, and a surplice was also provided. Later in the same year the interior of the church was whitewashed, and was painted with 'divers sentences and texts of scriptures'. Nicholas Thornelaye, painter, was paid 'for painting and laying in several colours the vault or Rood Loft and the pulpit with other places in the church'.[63] These were, of course, unusual cases, but the recurrent items of expenditure reveal the general concern of the town for the chapel: the bells, the clock and the chimes were regularly maintained, running repairs constantly undertaken in church and churchyard, prayer books and books of homilies renewed. Occasional items reveal more personal details: the 'Lawton folks' who brought rushes and flowers to the chapel in 1621 and 1622; payments to Margery Rode, chapel cleaner from 1681 until at least 1688; or similar entries concerning Mary Hamond who washed the ministers' surplice from 1674 until 1690, and her successor Mary Parnell, from 1698 until 1715.[64]

The religious crisis of the seventeenth century[65] as it affected Congleton has left ambiguous traces. The ejection of Thomas Brook at the Restoration was to be expected: his continued activity not far from Congleton may well be a measure of the lack of extremism which seems to have characterized the town. The restoration of episcopacy might be signalized by the provision of a new surplice of fine holland, trimmed with lace and sewn with silk, which the corporation provided in 1664;[66] it was left until later in the century for blood to run high. The subservient status of the chapel *vis-à-vis* Astbury was probably always a bone of contention, and as the town grew the likelihood of trouble became more probable. The corporation might be able to choose its own minister and dismiss him at will, but they still had to pay much more than lip service to the rector of Astbury. For baptisms, marriages and burials Congleton people had to travel up Wagg Street and down over Fol Hollow to the parish church; their own chapel could only be used for ordinary services, their own chaplain could perform only part of that duty for which his orders made him capable. In 1686, perhaps taking advantage of a vacancy in the see of Chester, a licence was obtained from the Dean of York permitting baptisms and burials at Congleton.[67] This evidently caused some trouble, but in the following year Bishop Cartwright, the new bishop of Chester, after a summary hearing in his study, allowed burials to be made at the chapel provided fees were still paid to the rector of Astbury. The bishop thought that each party 'seemed well satisfied' with the settlement[68] and this specific matter was not raised again, ministers at Congleton being quite prepared to submit copies of their registers to the rector when transcripts were made each year for the bishop.[69] There was, however, a more important point as to who had the patronage of the chapel. Technically, a dependent chapel like Congleton was in the patronage of the rector of the parish in which it lay. The corporation of Congleton, however, regarded it as a 'chapel domestick', and during the previous century if not for longer had established a prescriptive right to ownership and control. The disputed appointment of a minister in 1698 gave the rector of Astbury an opportunity to assert his claim.

On the death of Thomas Lowndes, the corporation met on 2 February 1698 and elected in his stead Ralph Malbon.[70] On 23 February a letter was sent to the bishop, signed by some of the aldermen and capital burgesses, complaining that in several full meetings of the council they had 'desired a fair election of a minister' but that the mayor had 'trick't . . . (them) with an undue election of a young man' who was 'voted for by several who have forsaken the church'.[71] They asked the bishop not to grant Malbon a licence, but to accept 'one who is supported by the earl of Macclesfield and Sir Thomas Bellot'. This candidate was a Mr. Hammond, who evidently was also supported by the rector of Astbury, John Hutchinson.[72] A whispering campaign was mounted against Malbon: 'how he crept into Deacon's orders while . . . at Cambridge, or before, seems a little odd', wrote one opponent; 'the youth mine eyes have seen, and if I am not mistaken, his temper is ambitious and aspiring, which is unbecoming him, whose parents are but low in the world and live in the same town...'. And, furthermore, he had the support of a magistrate said to be a Dissenter.[73] But Malbon's strength was just this local support: he was, said the mayor, 'very firm in the affections of the whole town except of one or two unruly persons', and aspersions cast by his enemies 'as to the marriage' were a 'malicious fiction to hinder his ordination'.[74]

The corporation soon realized, however, that its own quarrels were strengthening the claims of the rector of Astbury,[75] and by April it had taken its case to the bishop. There is a draft plan, perhaps drawn up by the bishop at this time, which was to give the chapel two wardens and the right to have baptisms, marriages and burials there, dues and registers still being submitted to Astbury.[76] This was evidently not enough; the corporation wanted a definition of its right of patronage, and called upon witnesses to rehearse the town's undoubted historical claims. William Hackney remembered the summary dismissal of William Redman in 1637 when the rector was not consulted; Thomas Malbon, Ralph Malbon's father, who had lived 52 years in the town, could recite correctly the names of all the ministers 'from Oliver's time', but knew of no interference by the rector.

Before the bishop gave judgment the parties seem to have come to some agreement, for the first election of Malbon was quashed and another held, on 10 June, at which Malbon received 14 votes and Mr. Hammond 5.[77] Malbon was there upon duly nominated by the corporation, and on 5 September presented by the rector of Astbury.[78] Later in the same month the bishop finally gave judgment on the case which he had submitted not only to his own chancellor, but also to the chancellors of London and York. He agreed that right lay with the corporation 'but do withal think it fit that the minister so elected or nominated by the corporation should make application to the rector of Astbury for his recommendation to the bishop for a licence to serve the cure, which if the said rector shall refuse without any legal exception against the said minister the bishop then to grant his licence . . .'.[79]

All this must have been very expensive, but only one item has survived: the mayor, parson Malbon, Alderman Shorne and Thomas Brook spent 14s 8d at Chester, and the mayor gave the bishop's secretary a guinea, ten shillings and three bottles of wine on different occasions.[80] They celebrated back in Congleton by having a new green pulpit cloth and cushion of silk and broadcloth.[81]

This was not the end of the dispute with Astbury. After Malbon's death in 1721 the corporation chose William Watwood, curate of Astbury, as their minister. The rector, Dr. Philip Egerton, entered a caveat in the bishop's court against the corporation's right; in reply the mayor wrote that he was prepared to accept the rector's position if Egerton was only trying to preserve his right of recommendation.[82] The matter was settled by the bishop who collated Mr. Watwood by lapse.[83] There was a difficulty, again, at the next vacancy in 1768. Even before Mr. Watwood died, the rector of Astbury, Dr. Joseph Crewe, announced that he would challenge the patronage right of the corporation, and the corporation in its turn, decided to enter a caveat on the next vacancy.[84] On Watwood's death the corporation nominated Richard Sandbach[85] in face of opposition from Crewe.[86] The case was heard at Chester Assizes, the judges finding in favour of the corporation, and its right was not further challenged until the Municipal Corporations Act of 1835.[87]

The history of the church at Congleton in the eighteenth century is not all dispute and litigation. The century saw an important consolidation of the stipend of the minister, the expanding work of Ralph Malbon and, above all, the rebuilding of the church itself, creating the Georgian gem of today. Successive ministers during the sixteenth and seventeenth centuries had been paid a stipend of only £25 a year, though some had also acted as schoolmaster and thus supplemented their salary.[88] The minister also received small surplice fees, £2 for an annual sermon from 1675, and £14 from houses and land.[89] Early in 1720 Dr. William Stanley, Dean of St. Asaph, gave £200, and obtained a like sum from Queen Anne's Bounty. The second sum was invested in land worth £36 a year. Thereupon, the corporation guaranteed the old stipend as a rent-charge on the town's corn mills.[90] In 1702 James Hall of Stockport bequeathed a house at the head of Moody Street, which was rebuilt in 1726 as a residence for the minister.[91] By the end of the century the church had houses in West Street which were sold in 1791.[92] By 1809 the income of the benefice was said to be £126 6s 10d, and in 1834 it was £140.[93]

Much of this improved situation came during the incumbency of Ralph Malbon (1698–1721). The confidence of the corporation in the young man was evidently not misplaced: combining his charge from 1709 with the headmastership of the grammar school,[94] he seems to have been both active and popular. In 1704 he erected galleries in the nave of the church at his own cost, and in 1711 was given leave to erect more in the chancel, this time by private subscription.[95] In giving its consent, the corporation reserved the right of its members to first choice of seats, and all who owned pews were to be responsible for repairs to the windows and roofs of the galleries. These additions, perhaps a measure of the popularity of Malbon's preaching, and certainly a reflection of Congleton's growing population, must have put a considerable strain on the fabric, and by 1740 the corporation decided to rebuild.

Over the years the church had been so frequently repaired and patched that its description as 'an irregular piece of timber building'[96] must have been something of a euphemism. Originally, perhaps, a simple timber-framed nave, with stone chancel and tower, it had two aisles and a porch added in 1614. The cost of a new building was estimated as £2,120, and briefs were issued throughout the country to collect the money.[97] Not enough was forthcoming from this source, so the corporation found itself having to borrow and in order to recoup sold surplus seats.[98] This explains the detailed seating plans submitted to the bishop in 1742 and 1765.[99] It also explains the care with which the corporation watched over expenditure, appointing a committee to oversee the work, and demanding of the minister an account of his own spending in the matter.[100] The present building, incorporating part of the tower of the old church, was substantially finished in one build in 1740–2, but the last stage of the tower was not completed until 1786.[101]

The history of the church in Congleton, as elsewhere in the second half of the eighteenth century, reflects the relative loss of ground in growing industrial communities, particularly to the Methodists. Richard Sandbach, the minister at this crucial stage, was unpopular in the town, and this must have affected the position of the church. In 1772 he clashed with the corporation when he attempted to charge high burial fees.[102] Four years later the corporation complained to the bishop because he refused to visit the sick and to baptize privately.[103] The church bells rang all night at the news that the minister had lost his case.[104] Sandbach was evidently not at all in sympathy with the Methodists in the town, and complained that the mayor and magistrates openly encouraged them.[105] In answer to a visitation enquiry in 1778, he said that he had been absent from Congleton for several weeks, staying with his mother at Sproston 'to keep her company and be out of a place where I have been very ill used, and which I have an utter dislike to'. But he seems to have been a busy priest: with the help of the schoolmaster, who held two other cures, he officiated twice each Sunday in the chapel, preaching once. Prayers were said on Wednesdays, Fridays and Holy Days, and Sacrament was celebrated once each month. There were said to be about 80 communicants, though about 150 were present on the previous Easter Sunday. And, given the opportunity, Sandbach confided to the bishop that tippling was rife in the town, and that shops were opened during divine service. 'I have', he added, 'complained often of the dirtiness of this chapel, and the want of a carpet to cover the altar. At present it has more the appearance of a side board than a communion table.'[106] Sandbach's removal to the rectory of Stepney in 1785 probably came as no surprise.[107]

His successor, Samuel Williamson, was an American by birth, and during his long tenure of the benefice (1785–1831) was twice mayor of the borough.[108] At first he was more successful than Sandbach: by 1789 the number of communicants had risen to about 200, and 200 children attended the Sunday schools.[109] By 1804 his flock had fallen to about 140 communicants,[110] and their numbers had 'not increased or diminished' by 1811.[111] Williamson reported in that year, however, that the children were 'carefully instructed in religious subjects'.[112] There were then said to be 700 children in three schools, but a decade later there were only 200–300.[113] Only about 400 people attended services, which were held every Sunday morning and afternoon.

Prayers were said in Lent on Wednesdays and Fridays, and every day during Passion Week. Sacrament was celebrated monthly to about 80 communicants.[114] Williamson estimated that in comparison there were about 4,000 dissenters in a total population of nearly 6,500. By 1825, however, with the help of Charles Bishope Hodges,[115] his curate, and Edward Wilson, master of the grammar school,[116] the average congregation had risen to about 800–900, and 450 children attended the Sunday schools. 'I believe I may say', Williamson reported, 'without arrogating too much to myself, that the congregation *is increasing.*'[117]

But if the congregation had doubled during the 1820s, the church had done little more than keep pace with the growth of population in the area. Much more accommodation was needed for worshippers, and more clergy were an urgent necessity. The Municipal Corporations Act of 1835 prevented the corporation from taking steps in this direction and, indeed, required it to sell its hard-won right of patronage, which it did with the greatest reluctance.[118] Yet until 1840 the old church, seating 1,424 people, remained the only Anglican place of worship in a town which at that date had a population of over 9,000, with a further 2,000 at Buglawton. This was a situation paralleled in many towns affected by the Industrial Revolution, and Congleton was fortunate in being in Chester diocese, the first to establish a diocesan building fund.[119] Only by means of outside grants could the situation be remedied. Thus between 1840 and 1851, although the population increased still further, great advances were made by the church authorities: three new churches —St. John's, Buglawton, St. James's, and Holy Trinity, Mossley —were built in the area, and a fourth congregation had been formed, later to become St. Stephen's. By 1861, when this had been built, there were seats in the town for 3,316 worshippers, 2,679 of which were free. Money for this work came from a variety of sources: a private gift was largely responsible for Holy Trinity; public subscriptions helped to build St. James's and St. John's; and grants from the Diocesan Church Building Society, the Incorporated Society, and the Church Building Commissioners ensured the large number of free sittings. To each of these churches a parish was assigned, either out of Congleton chapelry or Astbury parish, and it is curious that the last parish to be formed was that of St. Peter's, the town's original church.

The Protestant tradition of the former town chapel has, in all but one case, been followed by the more recent foundations, a tradition which the ministers of seventeenth-century Congleton would probably have applauded.

The church of ST. JOHN THE EVANGELIST, Buglawton, was the first of the new churches in the borough. Originally a 'district church' in the parish of Astbury, it was consecrated on 13 October 1840.[120] The site was the gift of Mr. Thomas Chapman of the Lowe, though the originator of the whole project seems to have been the Revd. Edward Wilson, the first vicar of the parish.[121] The church, which cost just over £2,286, was paid for by voluntary subscriptions and a grant from the Diocesan Church Building Society.[122] At its consecration, the procession of the corporation and the bishop was preceded by Chartists and Socialists bearing a black flag and the Death's Head and cross bones.[123]

The sum of £120 was settled on the incumbent in 1840, augmented later when the rector of Astbury settled the tithes of the township on the benefice.[124] The value was £189 in 1851,[125] £374 in 1882,[126] and £717 in 1961–2.[127] The patronage is in the hands of the rector of Astbury.

In 1851 services were held twice each Sunday. The morning congregation was said to average 80, and the evening 120, though the actual figures for the census day were 50 and 80 respectively, the incumbent explaining that numbers were small 'chiefly on the score of a very stormy day'. The average, however, was only 'given from conjecture, no actual account having been taken'. Sunday schools in both morning and afternoon were attended by 130 pupils, though 160 was said to be the usual number.[128]

The church, in pseudo-Norman style, consists of a wide nave and chancel under a single roof, with central and side passage aisles, a small sanctuary and a pretentious western tower, forming the main entrance. There are small vestries to the north of the sanctuary and to the north of the tower. An outside stair from the tower leads to the choir and organ gallery, projecting on cast-iron pillars into the west end of the church. This gallery was erected in 1860.[129] A wooden screen was erected at the east end of the nave to form a choir in 1924.[130]

Incumbents of St. John the Evangelist, Buglawton[131]

1840 Edward Wilson
1858 Henry Rowland Bramwell, M.A.
1868 William Besant, B.A.
1908 Herbert Gardner, B.A.
1918 Edward Norman Dodd, M.A.
1928 Lancelot Wilson Foster, M.A.
1934 Herbert William Meakin, M.A.
1944 Maurice Woolley
1959 Ronald Spencer Moore, B.A.
1963 Ernest Burrell Charnock, Dip. Th., A.C.I.S., A.A.C.C.A.
1969 Colin Crumpton, A.K.C.

The parish of ST. JAMES THE GREAT was constituted a new district out of St. Peter's chapelry in 1844.[132] Services were held in a schoolroom in Astbury Street until the church was consecrated in 1848.[133] The church was designed by James Trubshaw of Newcastle-under-Lyme, and was built by Samuel Faram of Odd Rode and Edward Massey of Lawton.[134] It was paid for by public subscription and grants from the Chester Diocesan Society, the Incorporated Society and the Church Commissioners, and cost £3,760.[135] All 650 pews were free.[136] The benefice was originally endowed with £150, and was augmented in 1862 and 1868.[137] Its net value was said to be £240 in 1905[138] and £711 in 1961-2.[139] The patronage was at first in the hands of the Crown and the bishop alternately, but since 1869 has been exercised by the bishop alone.[140]

In 1851 the population of the parish was 3,363, and attendances at church on 30 March in that year were 131 in the morning and 204 in the evening. There were 173 morning Sunday-school pupils and 80 in the evening. The incumbent stated that the congregation had been increasing gradually since the church had been built two and a quarter years earlier. They were chiefly poor people 'who did not until that time go to any place of worship'.[141] It is not clear when the Catholic tradition of St. James's was first developed: in this it is unique among the churches of the borough.

The church, designed in the Transitional Early English style, consists of a nave and aisles, a chancel with a clergy vestry on the south and a north porch. The exterior, including the bell turret at the west end, is of Cloud-side grit; the high-pitched roof is of Westmorland slate. The interior arcading is of Hollington stone. The furnishings include a pulpit, probably of Belgian origin, of about 1600,[142] and several examples of modern woodwork. The organ, at the west end, was built by R. Hope-Jones in 1901, and was restored and enlarged by W. F. Rogers of Stoke on Trent in 1940. Faculties for furnishings include one for a new Holy Table, candlesticks, and fitting out Holy Cross Chapel in 1926, the installation of electric light in 1939, and the purchase of an aumbry in 1940.[143] A church hall and new vicarage are projected.

Incumbents of St. James the Great, Congleton[144]

1844	Thomas Green
1844	Gustavus Barton
1846	John Wilson, B.A.
1869	Frank Edward Hopwood, M.A.
1879	George Arthur Edwin Kempson, M.A.
1887	Roger Kerrison Preston, M.A.
1893	James Stapleton Cotton
1895	Charles Steward Stubbs, M.A.
1896	Walter Taylor Warburton, M.A.
1904	Ambrose Heygate, M.A.
1905	Harold Herbert Tweedy, M.A.
1918	David Harrop Boyle, M.A.
1919	John Henry Barr, M.A.
1925	Thomas Vickers, B.A.
1930	Thomas William Barker, M.A.
1943	Philip Seymour, L.Th.
1952	James Stanley Leather
1966	Peter David Bradbrook

The parish of ST. STEPHEN was originally constituted an ecclesiastical district in August 1845.[145] The area had apparently been assigned to a curate at least as early as 1842, when Robert Houghton was appointed to work there by the minister of St. Peter's. In the following year Houghton became a stipendiary curate.[146] John Scott was nominated first minister of the district in 1845, and services were held in the National School in Spragg Street.[147]

The original endowment of the living was £130,[148] but was increased in 1864.[149] By 1892 it was valued at £219, by 1926 it had increased to £400, and by 1961–2 was said to be £845.[150]

In 1851, when the population of the parish was just under 3,000, and before the church was built, the average morning congregation was 350, and the evening congregation 250. On 30 March, when the census was taken, however, the figures were 100 and 300 respectively. The morning Sunday school had 261 pupils on that day.[151] There were said to be about 50 communicants in 1858.[152] With a population of 4,425 in 1961, the average number of communicants for April 1967 was over 75.[153]

The church, on a site overlooking the river Dane costing £575,[154] was designed by Joseph Clarke, F.S.A., and built by Samuel Faram of Odd Rode. It was consecrated on 5 September, 1860, and all 400 sittings were free.[155] 'Executed in the stateliest character of ecclesiology and architectural taste', the beauty of its interior was said to be widely recognized.[156] The church consists of a nave and chancel under one roof, with a small sanctuary, aisles and a south porch. The sanctuary was built and decorated in memory of the Revd. Edward Wilson (d. 1858), first minister of Buglawton. The Lady Chapel in the north aisle, originally a vestry, was formed and furnished in 1929, the choir and clergy vestries having been moved to the west end of the nave in the previous year.[157] The baptistry in the south-west corner of the nave was created by the Revd. Charles Tansley in 1940 to commemorate the twenty-fifth anniversary of his work in the parish, the money having been given to him by parishioners.[158] Faculties for other furnishings include those for the organ (1907), the iron chancel screen (1918) and the pulpit (1930–1).[159]

Incumbents of St. Stephen's, Congleton[160]

1845   John Scott, B.A.
1852   Joseph Oakden, L.Th.
1872   George Edward Hignett, M.A.
1873   James Macleod Bannerman, M.A.
1914   Charles Tansley, L.Th.
1943   John Russell Edwards, M.A.
1948   Charles George Mead
1960   Harry Chamberlain Sutton, B.A.
1964   John Michael Pennington, M.A.
1969   Geoffrey Fairbanks Parsons, M.A.

The church of HOLY TRINITY, Mossley, was built after a

perpetual curacy had been carved out of the parish of Astbury. The rector of Astbury is the present patron. The benefice was originally endowed with £80 a year,[161] had increased to £174 in the 1880s, and in 1961–2 was £745.[162] In 1860 there were 366 sittings, 276 of which were free, the result of contributions from the Incorporated Society.[163]

The church is built on land given by the Revd. James Brierley of Mossley Moss Hall.[164] The foundation stone of the building was laid in 1844 and the church was consecrated on 23 October 1845.[165] Designed by James Trubshaw,[166] and built by John Brown, the church consists of a stone-built nave and chancel, the nave having a gallery at its west end. The west porch was added in 1859 and vestries in 1914.[167] James Brierley, who gave the site, also gave £500 for the fabric, and later £100 for the porch. He was the first incumbent.[168]

Incumbents of Holy Trinity, Mossley[169]

1845   James Brierley, M.A.
1871   William Edge Elijah Mason Bull, M.A.
1893   James Duncan Ozanne, M.A.
1896   James David Griffiths, B.A.
1897   Charles Faulkner Chorley, M.A.
1903   Maurice John Ransome, M.A.
1908   Ernest Mostyn Ellis, M.A.
1919   Edward Philip Comber
1924   Herbert Russell Sherwen, M.A.
1943   John Sellors, M.A.
1953   George Cyril Green, M.A., Hon. Canon of Chester, 1964.

The 'chapel domestick' of Congleton, the church of St Peter (ad Vincula)[170] was the last in the town to be assigned a parish, when it became a district chapelry in 1867 and a parish in the following year.[171] Tithes were transferred to the new vicar by the rector of Astbury,[172] and by 1915 the net income of the benefice was £255.[173] In 1961–2 it was said to be £872.[174]

Attendance at St. Peter's on 30 March 1851 was given as 343 in the morning, 183 in the afternoon and 410 in the evening. There were 226 Sunday-school pupils both morning and afternoon. The six-monthly average required by the census authorities was not given; the incumbent explained that the morning congregation was normally more than 400, but that the

Q

day chosen for the census was Sacrament Sunday 'when there is not a good attendance'.[175] The average number of communicants in February 1967 was 23.[176]

The church of St. Peter[177] is, with the exception of the stone tower, of plain brickwork. It consists of a galleried nave with central and side passage aisles and a chancel, with flanking chapels (the north now a vestry), all under one roof in 'Basilican' form. The small north porch was added in 1842. The building is lit on either side by two rows of six cast-iron framed windows, replacing leaded ones about 1837. The east end has a Palladian window, flanked by external niches. The whole building, begun in 1740, is thought to have been substantially completed by 1742, though furnishings were not finished until 1748. The lower portion of the present tower is of medieval date, and contains a pointed arch not now visible.[178] During the rebuilding of the body of the church, the tower was evidently partially demolished, and then the upper parts rebuilt, being completed in 1786.

The galleried classical interior contains most of its original eighteenth-century fittings including box pews, carved oak wainscotting and a brass chandelier (1748). Murals at the east end, by Edward Penney (1714–91) and dated 1748, are of St. Peter and St. Paul. Beneath is a carved oak reredos. The Jacobean pulpit, set in the centre of the church, was originally used at Astbury as a reading desk,[179] and replaced a three-decker pulpit in 1877. The font was formerly placed in front of the pulpit. The whole effect is of an untouched Georgian interior of the greatest charm.

The Ministers, Clergy and Readers of Congleton[a]

Richard de Chelle	occurs 1357, 1379–80	Roger Williams, curate	1589
		Humphrey Phithion	1590–91
Thomas Boydel	occurs 1358	Edward Danner	1592–93
Hugh Pymmessone	occurs 1358	James Broster	1594–97
Robert	occurs 1398	Richard Grene, reader	1597–1607
Thomas Hassall	occurs 1398	Daniel Grene, reader	1607–9
Hugh	occurs 1403–4	—Price, curate	1608–11
Hugh Leche	occurs 1508	— Cappes	1612–18
James Rathebon	occurs 1533	John Wardle, reader	1612–13
Ralph Roode	occurs 1533	— Griffin, reader	1615–17
Hugh Hulse	occurs 1533	— Thorley, reader	1620–24
Ralph Lokett	occurs 1533	— Loddington	1621
Thomas Davenport, reader	1588	William Redman	1621–37
		Andrew Bowrey	1638–43

Robert Newcome,		Thomas Barker Ingham,	
reader	1642	M.A.	1838–42
Francis Ford, M.A.	1643	John Hughes, B.A.	1842–72
John Smith, B.A.	1643–46	Richard Garland, LL.B.	1872–81
John Pemberton	1648–50	Hubert Hunter Phelps,	
Thomas Brook	1651–61	M.A.	1882–90
Daniel Bayley	1661–62	Thomas Henry Watson,	
— Barbour	1663–69	D.D.	1890
— Armstrong	1669–70	Thomas Twistington	
Thomas Meakins, B.A.	1670–74	Higgins, B.A.	1891–1918
Michael Harrison	1674–75	James Neale	1918–29
Richard Jackson, M.A.	1675–83	Thomas William Castle,	
John Hancock	1683–84	F.R.A.I.	1929–33
John Whittaker	1684–89	William Robert John-	
Thomas Lowndes, M.A.	1689–98	son, M.A.	1934–53
Ralph Malbon, B.A.	1698–1721	Clement Thomas Walker,	
William Watwood, M.A.	1722–68	M.A.	1954–59
Richard Sandbach,		John Pringle Martin,	
M.A.	1768–85	B.A.	1959
Samuel Williamson	1785–1831		
Charles Bishope Hodges,			
M.A.	1831–38		

[a] Where not otherwise stated, the names of ministers and readers are taken from borough accounts, *passim*, until 1675, and subsequently from EDP 89/1, 7. For those before 1588 the sources are DL30/1/21, m.5; 2/29, m.9 (Chelle); *Ibid.*, 1/21, m. 5d (Boydel, Pymmessone); *Ibid.*, 3/40 (Robert, Hassale); Borough charters, iii (Hugh); DL30/6/85 (Leche); B.M. Harl. MS 594, f. 152v (for those in 1533. With the exception of de Chelle in 1379–80, the clergy before 1533 were simply described as 'chaplains', and were not necessarily incumbents of either chapel in Congleton. They were, however, almost certainly resident in the town. The chaplains named in 1533 were descibed as of Astbury and Congleton, taxed in that year, and listed after John Lawton, rector of Astbury, and John Crosby, his curate). For Smith (1643–6) the source is *Calamy Revised*, 446–7.

PROTESTANT NONCONFORMITY

English nonconformity had its origins in the sixteenth century when the Puritans objected to the replacement of a uniform Catholic orthodoxy by a type of uniform Anglican orthodoxy still insufficiently radical for their liking. Puritanism spread from the religious to the political sphere resulting in the vehement opposition to the Stuarts in the seventeenth century. The existence of Puritan inclinations in Congleton in the sixteenth and early seventeenth centuries has been described elsewhere:[180] by the mid-seventeenth century, when the struggle between King and Parliament was at its height, there seems to have been considerable sympathy towards Puritan views in the town.[181]

Presbyterians, Congregationalists and Unitarians
The Book of Common Prayer was suppressed in 1645 and the
incumbent of Congleton, John Smith, resigned in 1646.[182] For
two years the curacy remained vacant until, in 1648, the
corporation secured the services of John Pemberton, a Presbyterian. His name, together with that of John Ley, 'present
preacher of Astbury', appears on the Cheshire Attestation,[183]
drawn up by Ley himself, against those Puritan sects whom the
Presbyterians believed to be in error. Pemberton removed to
Chester in 1650 and was replaced in 1651 by Thomas Brook,
also a Presbyterian, who came from Gawsworth and whom his
enemies called 'Bawling Brook', no doubt on account of his
enthusiasm; he 'read the communion prayer till he read the
people out of church'.[184] He appears to have been conscientious,
carrying out his duties faithfully, and preaching at least three
times on Sunday and also in the week. Following the Restoration he was turned out of Congleton in 1661 and given shelter
at Moreton Hall by William Moreton. The corporation appears
to have been remiss about paying his salary. On one occasion
he left 'the 10*s*' in the town's hands to be given for the maintenance of ministers in New England.[185] This suggests either
that he may not have been dependent on his salary or that he
wished to show the corporation he was not subservient to them.
In 1662 the corporation tardily paid what was owing to him.[186]
Brook died in 1664 but he had preached what was to be his last
public sermon in 1662, in Astbury church, by the generosity of
the rector, Thomas Hutcheson.[187]
    A similar change of ministers took place at Astbury. In 1646
Thomas Dod, who had held the living probably since 1626, was
ejected and replaced by John Ley, vicar of Great Budworth
and once sub-dean of Chester, a zealous Puritan and later a
noted Puritan thinker.[188] Dod's ejection[189] resulted from his
contribution towards the Royalist forces in Cheshire. Since he
was over eighty and said not to have left his room for three
years,[190] the Puritans may anyway have felt that the parish was
ready for conversion.
    It has been suggested that the living of Astbury was seques-
trated from Thomas Hutcheson in 1643.[191] Hutcheson's (or
Hutchinson's) name, however, does not appear in the minutes
of the Committee for the Relief of Plundered Ministers until
June 1654 when it is noted that 'the rectory of Astbury is

sequestrated from Thomas Hutcheson and George Moxon is nominated as public preacher'.[192] If we accept the evidence of the minutes it would seem that in 1646 Ley replaced Dod who returned to Malpas where he died the next year, and possibly Hutcheson was presented to the living in 1649 only to have it taken away from him in 1654.[193]

Ley was instituted as rector of Ashfield and Astbury but did not stay long, returning to Budworth in 1649.[194] He had some difficulty during his tenure of Astbury. Just after his appointment, the mayor, aldermen and burgesses of Congleton petitioned against paying tithes for a year so that they could divert them to the uses of the Higher Chapel[195] but they were compelled to pay up. The next year Ley was opposed by 'some malignant and ill advised persons of the parish', who had been inspired by a proclamation issued by the King against the ministers put in by Parliament, and 'those ill minded persons have taken courage to hope for some alteracion and presume to deteyne from the Minister his rights'. The parishioners were ordered to pay the tithes to Ley just as they would have done to the former rector.[196]

Ley was helped, firstly by John Murcot, whom he ordained at Astbury in 1647,[197] and who left the same year to be minister of West Kirby, and later by Henry Newcome, who was also the master of Congleton Free Grammar School. Soon after his arrival in Congleton Newcome 'fell to preaching, sometimes at Congleton and sometimes at Astbury'. Ley encouraged him, appointed him reader, and in August 1648, after Newcome had moved to Goostrey, ordained him at Sandbach. Newcome seems to have had an unorthodox attitude to Puritan authority at first. Preaching before ordination was sometimes allowed as a person was regarded as being on trial. Newcome preached at Astbury, and presumably in the Higher Chapel at Congleton and was seemingly satisfied that he could do this without reference to a higher authority. Possibly the corporation was glad to make use of him in the vacancy between 1644 and 1648. He submitted his preaching notes to Ley 'who told me that I took too much pains (which was but his prudent insinuation and dulcifying of his counsel to me), put too much history into my sermons, the people came with bibles, and expected quotation of scripture; and also told me that I must not use notes so much, adding *Fortuna audaces juvat*, and I know not what memory would do until I tried it'. After this Newcome used few notes until one day he had to preach at a baptism at short notice. He had not time to reduce his sermon to note form and preached without. After that he did not use notes again.[198]

Ordination seems to have been far from his mind for he apparently asked Ley whether 'there would be an ordination or no', a few hours before the ceremony.[199] After ordination, however, he became devoted to the Presbyterian cause. Through his wife's influence, he went to Gawsworth in 1649 to replace Brook who had had little success there. Later Newcome moved to Manchester and was a highly respected member of the Presbyterian community.[200]

At Astbury William Cuxworth probably replaced Newcome, for it was he who was succeeded in June 1654 by George Moxon.[201] It is just possible that Cuxworth may have succeeded Hutcheson if Hutcheson was ejected in 1652, but the lack of accurate dating evidence makes for some confusion. Moxon had been chaplain to Sir William Brereton and had recently returned from the American colonies, where he had gone to escape from a citation put out for him in 1637 for his Puritan views.[202] Three months previously John Machin had been made public preacher at Astbury[203] and the two men and their families shared the rectory at Astbury between them and preached 'one the Lord's Day and the other t'other' alternately at Astbury and Rushton.[204] At his own expense of £8 12s a year, Machin also lectured ('a double lecture') in twelve Staffordshire towns on the last Friday in every month from 1653 to 1660.[205] When Hutcheson returned Machin went to Whitley and Moxon to Rushton where he preached until 1667, probably in farmhouses and on the surrounding moorland. Under the 'Clarendon Code', dissenters were not permitted to preach within five miles of any corporate town or address a meeting of more than five people, but Moxon may have avoided trouble since Rushton was over five miles from Macclesfield, Congleton and Leek.

After the declaration of indulgence of 1672 which gave some brief protection to dissenters, Moxon took advantage of this protection for himself and his house.[206] He applied on 30 April through his friend, Richard Steele, a native of Barthomley but then living in London, for a licence as a general teacher. This, dated 2 May, was collected by Matthew Leadbeater of Nether Whitacre, whose brother Thomas, ejected from Hinkley, was living near Sandbach and seemingly was a friend of Moxon's. Steele also applied on the same date for a licence for the house of Moxon and this, 'for the howse of George Moxon in the parish of Astbury to be a Congregational Meeting Place', was also granted.[207] Steele seems to have applied for licences for a large number of friends. Amongst them was Andrew Barnet (or Barnett) of Astbury parish for whom he applied on 6 May both for a general teaching licence and a licence for his house as a Presbyterian meeting place.[208] This was possibly the same Andrew Barnet who had been ejected from Holmes Chapel in 1650 for refusing to sign the engagement to be faithful to the new republic. Many Cheshire Puritan ministers refused to do this on the grounds that they had taken an oath in 1648 and now refused to take a second one. Barnet went to Roddington, Shropshire, and was ejected from there at the Restoration. If, as seems likely, he did return to Cheshire, he would have been a welcome member of the community 'for his skill in physick made him the more valued by the neighbouring gentry'.[209] Another licence was granted for the house, either at Astbury or Congleton, of John Burgess, a congregationalist.[210] There is no further mention of either Andrew Barnet or John Burgess but the J.P.'s returns of Dissenters to the Bishops Court at Chester record the house of 'John Barnet' in Congleton in 1710.[211] Moxon's house was situated in Congleton near to Dane Bridge.[212]

These licences confirmed an existing situation. A survey of dissent in 1669 recorded that in Astbury parish there were several meetings of unlawful conventicles including one of twenty persons.[213] This was, perhaps, Moxon's.

By 1687, Moxon's preaching had been so successful that a small chapel was built under the protection of James II's declaration of indulgence, but the first sermon preached in it was at Moxon's funeral by Eliezer Birch, who probably helped Moxon in his ministry after the latter had had a stroke in 1678.[214] The next minister was Thomas Irlam who in 1691 signed the Heads of Agreement (the union between Presbyterian and Congregational ministers) as 'Minister for Congleton'.[215] He seems to have fallen on bad times because he 'cannot subsist on his present allowance, the people can give noe more than they doe, the meeting like to fall if hee remove, has met with more opposition than usuall'.[216] He was granted sums of £5, £6 and £10 but in 1714 an even greater blow fell on the small congregation when the mob rioted at the accession of George I, broke into the meeting house, tore out the seating and burnt it on Dane Bridge. It would seem that the dissenters gave provocation if the story is true that, overjoyed by the death of Anne, after ringing the bells of St. Peter's and being turned out by the curate, they had started a fight in the churchyard. Feeling between the Established Church and the dissenters ran high at times. The same curate refused burial to them on the grounds that if they would not come to church when they were alive, they should not come when they were dead.[217]

The congregation petitioned the Cheshire classis for help towards rebuilding the chapel and received £10 but the chapel was not rebuilt until 1733. It was sited where the present Unitarian chapel stands today just off Mill Street.[218] In 1715 the congregation had been as large as 200,[219] though it is possible that some of these belonged to the 40 families of Astbury parish recorded in a return sent to the bishop of Chester in 1718 as dissenting families.[220] After Irlam's death in 1748 the fortunes of the society diminished. In 50 years the society had eleven ministers, very few of whom stayed more than two or three years and often the pulpit was vacant.[221] In 1773 it was noted that the dissenters in Cheshire were in a 'languishing state, and some congregations are likely to drop very soon. Congleton and Wheelock are at this time without ministers, and are likely to be so, as there are very few to minister to'.[222] This may have been due partly to dislike of the beliefs of the ministers, most of whom after Irlam followed Unitarian beliefs, and those of the congregation who disapproved met in other places. The Congregational Board recognized them until 1754, then discontinued the grant. The Unitarians bought the meeting house which remained on the site until 1883 when it was pulled down and replaced by the present Unitarian chapel. In 1851 there was a morning congregation of 20 and an evening one of 50. In 1968 there was an average Unitarian congregation on Sunday evenings of 20.[223]

Financial help was given towards the building of the Unitarian chapel by the Revd. James Brierley, who had been the vicar of Holy Trinity, Mossley, and had been extremely generous to that parish. During the 1860s he attended evangelical meetings in the town hall and became moved towards

Unitarianism. He resigned the living of Mossley in 1871 and eventually became a Unitarian minister.[224]

The Unitarian chapel, seating 300, was built in Cross Street in the Gothic style by James Brown. It is a stone building separated from a brick school room by a small courtyard. An extension to the school room was built in 1909 and the buildings occupy almost the whole of the north side of Cross Street. The south side of the chapel lies directly on the street; there are two corner buttresses and two inner ones. Between each centre buttress and the inner one is a small circular window with ogee moulding resting on leaf-carved corbels above it. In the centre, between the two inner buttresses, are two pointed windows placed within a square moulding outlined by small pillars. The upper part of the south wall has a large pointed window of five lights with tracery at the top beneath the moulded arch resting on leaf carved corbels. The top of the wall is crowned by a small gable. The side walls consist of four bays divided by buttresses; there are plain leaded-light glass windows in the bays in stone frames with stone mullions. The door in the bay nearest the street is set within a heavily moulded pointed frame. The interior has an unusual type of wagon vault roof with iron ties and a gallery at the south end. The pews are of pitch pine. The stones were quarried from Tegnose quarry near Macclesfield.

The revival of the Independents (or Congregationalists) came in 1782 when Captain Jonathan Scott visited the town.[225] Scott, one of the most colourful characters of eighteenth-century dissent and previously an officer in the 7th Queen's Own Dragoons, was converted in the 1760s and was active in founding congregations in Shropshire and Cheshire. Some of the dissatisfied members went to Hanley to hear him preach and afterwards invited him to preach at Congleton. He came in 1782 and preached in an inn yard after the Methodist minister had refused him permission to preach in the Methodist chapel. He fitted up a small room and then, in 1790, built a chapel for the Independents at his own expense (now the Masonic Hall).[226] Some of the Methodists, either angry at their minister's refusal or being of a Calvinistic turn of mind, joined the Congregationalists, much to Wesley's disapproval. The Revd. J. Reese, the first minister of the new Independent chapel, mentioned in a note dated 1790 'number of hearers about 50, afternoon 100, night 60'.[227]

Even so the society was not yet out of trouble. In 1806 Congleton was a founder member of the Cheshire Union of Congregational Churches (later the Cheshire Congregational Union) which aimed to spread 'the Gospel in the unevangelized parts of the County by means of Itinerant Preaching'.[228] The Congleton minister was a Mr. Bennett, who, in the same year, opened a house at Lawton salt works for preaching, but lack of money seems to have ended this activity. There were also doctrinal troubles. A new set of rules drawn up in 1806 was Calvinistic in flavour and visitors were appointed to visit members who did not attend the monthly communion and expel them if no satisfactory explanation for their absence was forthcoming. A trust deed of 1812 also explicitly stated that the church was to be for the use of Congregationalists and Independents.[229] Thus when the Revd. George Marris informed the deacons in 1822 that he supported the Countess of Huntingdon's Connexion he was asked to resign. He did so and built a chapel at the end of Park Street where he was joined by some of his congregation.[230] The next minister, John Johnson, was also not of Independent views for, after some difficulties with the trustees, he left in 1830 to be ordained in the Established Church. Money difficulties beset the society and complaints occur of declining seat rents and a general shortage of money. The congregation at that time was mainly working class— ribbon weavers, silk spinners, cloggers and tailors, with an occasional bookseller and coachbuilder.[231] In 1845 James Bruce was offered the post of minister but was warned that 'as you are aware we have no wealthy members in our church'.[232] There were 44 members of the society in 1805 and in 1846 the number was still only 49.[233] In 1848, however, the society made a most fortunate choice in offering the pulpit to Joseph Moore. His ministry lasted 40 years and he was held in affection and respect. The society flourished, new members were brought in and the finances improved. One of Moore's friends was David Livingstone and the latter visited the town several times, on one occasion giving a lecture on his travels. The affection in which Moore was held was shown by the presentation to him, not only by the congregation but also by the townspeople, of a purse of gold and his portrait on his retirement in 1888.[234]

As the chapel prospered so did the Sunday school which

dated from about 1810. Moore raised the numbers in the Sunday school to 250 and it was not surprising that with the increase in chapel and school membership the deacons should think about building new premises.[235]

The frontage of the chapel had been repaired in 1850 and new pews were put in eight years later. In that year a new Sunday school was built at the back of the old chapel replacing the building of 1812, but space was limited and the trustees were precluded from building on the whole site because of the adjoining burial ground (closed in 1853).

This chapel was later sold to the Freemasons. The land it was built on had been leased by Captain Scott to the trustees and after his death in 1807 the lease was conveyed to them by the executors. At the present time the building is of red brick with a tiled roof. At the front there are three upper windows, slightly arched; the lower storey had two square-headed doors and a central window. Only the left-hand door remains; the other door and window have been blocked up. The single-storeyed school room with five sets of double-arched windows still stands at the back. There are no windows in either chapel or school room on the north side. The flagged front still remains, but the railings and gates were removed in the second World War.

A seating plan (undated) in the deeds shows the chapel with two entrances and two aisles. The lower storey had side pews and box pews at the four corners. The central pews had doors to them. The plan might have been made when the new pews were put in in 1858. At the same time the floor was lowered and the ceiling raised five feet. There was a gallery round three sides, and a fourth side was added by the Freemasons. The burial ground has been grassed over but a few gravestones have been placed upright along the enclosing wall.

In 1851 there was an evening congregation of 152, and 82 children at morning Sunday school.[236] In 1872 a new site was bought in Antrobus Street and building began in 1875.[237] Moore raised £1,000 by written appeals and the congregation £5,000. The chapel, the present one, was opened in 1877. Of the £5,000, £1,000 was given by Benjamin Radley, who had served the chapel as deacon, Sunday-school teacher and treasurer since the 1840s, and £500 by Samuel Maskery, who was deacon and treasurer from 1840 to 1879 and who was succeeded by his son, Alderman Samuel Maskery, in both offices until his death in 1932.[238]

The Congregational chapel,[239] architect a Mr. Sugden of Leek, is an oblong building of hard grey local stone with Hollington stone dressings. The land dips at the choir end so that the school room, which is under the chapel, is at ground level at this point. The chapel stands back from the road and the space between it and the wall lining the footpath has recently been made into a garden of remembrance. The front has two circular side projections which contain the stairs leading to the gallery. Along the front are buttresses which rise above the roof to form pinnacles. The chapel is entered by two doorways at the head of a flight of steps. Above the doorways is a large, six-light traceried window. On either side of the doorways are trefoil lights whose outer moulded arches spring from detached columns. Over these are traceried rose windows. The side elevations have seven bays divided by buttresses. Each bay has two-light windows. The choir is 20 ft long and 15 ft deep and the sides project slightly, forming slight transepts. The choir apse has a traceried rose window of five feet diameter which is visible in the chapel above the organ. The interior, which seats 600 people, has a wooden vaulted roof resting on stone corbels. The walls are wood-panelled to window height and plastered above. The gallery at one end of the chapel, above the entrance doors, rests on large projecting corbels; the front is pierced and moulded. The rostrum, also of pierced and moulded oak, stands at the entrance to the choir; behind it is the organ and in front of it the communion table. There is some stained glass in the tracery windows at the front and in the round windows.

The two world wars receive little mention in the chapel minutes. In 1916 evening services were put into the afternoon 'in consequence of zeppelin raids'[240] and additional insurance was taken out because of such risks. During the second World War the school room was first used as a reception centre for refugees. From 70 to 100 mothers with young children slept there until billets were found. In 1941 a canteen was opened for the numerous allied forces stationed in the town, catering especially for the Dutch soldiers who were also allowed the use of the chapel for a weekly service held in Dutch. Prince Bernhardt of the Netherlands visited it during his review of the

Dutch troops stationed in the town during the war and a plaque in the chapel records the thanks of the Dutch Protestant churches.

The twentieth century has seen the innovation of the appointment of women deacons. Among the first to be elected was Miss G. Finger, a later mayor.

The Society of Friends

Quakers seem to have established themselves in the district very soon after George Fox's preaching tour of England in the 1640s. In 1676 he remarked that 'the Truth sprang up' in Leicestershire in 1644, Warwickshire in 1645, Nottinghamshire in 1646, Derbyshire in 1647, and in the adjacent counties between 1648 and 1650.[241] In Cheshire the seeds were well sown; communities sprang up throughout the county. Quakers refused to accept the authority of the Anglican priest, and, as this included the ministrations of the burial service, one of the first necessities was to ensure their own burial grounds. There are known to have been at least nine early burial grounds in Cheshire, one of them at Eaton, two miles from Congleton. In 1658 land was conveyed by John Oakes to Joseph Endon 'of Bossley', John Clewes of Gawsworth, William Hall of Congleton, shoemaker, Thomas Hall of Congleton, grocer, and Richard Smith of Swettenham, surgeon, on condition that it was used solely for the purposes of Quaker burial.[242] In 1757 it was purchased by the Society which then already had a meeting house there.[243] The house is said to have been built on it in the 1680s;[244] if so, it was one of the first such meeting houses in the country for most were built after the Toleration Act of 1689. Some authorities have stated that Quakers met for their meetings in the burial grounds, others that this is not so and that they met in each other's houses. A study of the digest of the marriage register for the area indicates that Quaker marriages took place in an important house in each district, in Congleton at William Hall's house, in Bosley at Joseph Endon's house, near Siddington at John Walker's house; and it is very probable that meetings were held in these houses until a meeting house could be established at Eaton. This was certainly in use in the 1780s—the last mention of a General Meeting held there is in 1781—but the Quarterly Meeting reported in 1801 that it was 'so much out of repair as to be dangerous' and recom-

mended that 'it should be taken down and the land let'. Either
that year or the next it was demolished.[245] It would seem from
a plan of the area made in 1848 that the building had been
seven yards square.

The burial ground still exists, surrounded by a stone wall,
set back some yards from a side road leading from Eaton to
Marton. The wall was built in 1879 when the site was restored
on the orders of the Cheshire Monthly Meeting; it was again
restored in 1919.[246] Burials took place there from 1672[247] (or
before) to 1766.[248] At least 185 burials are recorded and the
ground served the Friends living in the area stretching from
Biddulph to Macclesfield, and from Bosley to Siddington.
Early Quakers did not consider it necessary to have tombstones,
and only two survive. Some may have been destroyed in the
eighteenth century.[249] The Hall family, which is recorded in
these two stones, was one of three prominent Quaker families
in Congleton in the late seventeenth and early eighteenth
century. The others were the Welch (or Welsh) and the
Stretch families. There were other Quakers in the town but
no other large family group and the total number of Quakers
at any one time does not appear to have been more than
30. The Eaton Meeting house also served Quaker families
from Bosley, Withington, Siddington, Marton and, until 1705,
Macclesfield.

The earliest mention of the Friends in Congleton would
appear to be in 1653 when the preacher, Richard Hubberthorne, visited Malpas and 'a separate community in Congleton', where he was received 'by many'. He wrote in 1654, six
months after this visit, that 'about Congleton and Leek there
is a people drawing in, where we have had some meetings, and
many high separates and strong oaks that ways are convinced
by the power of Truth. Send some friends this ways as shortly
as may be—but some are not fit for the work of the Lord in
these parts, for they are a wise people and must be compre-
hended and kept out, for in their subtlety many would be
approved of.'[250] The 'separate community' may have been a
protestant community separated from either the Independents
or Presbyterians, or, more likely, it was a group which had
accepted Quaker ways but wanted to know more about them
before committing itself. Hubberthorne was asking for someone
to come and advise these people, not particularly a learned man

but one of their own status who could speak to them and be understood. Early in 1654, Thomas Holme, Elizabeth Fletcher and Elizabeth Leavens came to Cheshire from the Kendal area where there was a strong community of Quakers, and it is possible that they came to Congleton.[251] William Caton, one of the Quaker community at Cartmel, certainly came to the town; he preached there and for his pains was put into prison for a few days in 1655.[252]

Meanwhile Richard Hubberthorne had been imprisoned in the North Gate at Chester where he was visited by Richard Lightfoot, Thomas Welch and Ralph Stener, all of Congleton, who 'owned him and were convinced. And when he was released he went to Congleton where William Hall and Ester, his wife, owned him and received him into their house, where he had a meeting and several were convinced by him'.[253]

The Commonwealth was hostile to the Quakers especially in the Chester area.[254] After the Restoration they fared equally badly because of the passing of the Quaker Act of 1662 and the Conventicle Acts of 1664 and 1670. Once the Friends had established themselves in Congleton it was not long before the hostility of the authorities was aroused, partly because of the aggressiveness of early Quakerism and partly because Quakers wished to contract out of society especially in the payment of tithe. When they did this the church authorities distrained their goods, which were then sold to pay tithe, and they relied on the co-operation of the secular authorities to help them. The Quakers were often taken to Chester assizes. In 1660, for example, three journeys from Congleton are recorded.[255] At Chester they might be imprisoned in Little-Ease or the Hole-in-the-Rock situated under the North Gate prison. A contemporary account of 1657 says this is 'a hole hewed in Rock, the bredth and cross from side to side, is 17 inches from the back to the inside of the great door, at the top 7 inches; at the shoulders 8 inches; at the brest 9 inches and a half; from the top to the bottom, one yeard and half; now to take in the height of that as their malice puts them on, they have draw-boards which shoot over crosse into the two sides, to a yeard height, or thereabout'.[256]

In 1667 William Hall, Thomas Welch and Edward Sutton were presented at Chester quarter sessions for not attending church.[257] In 1669 Quaker meetings were reported in Astbury parish and at Gawsworth.[258] In July of that year a meeting at Congleton was broken up by Sir Jeffrey Shakerley and Quakers' goods were distrained.[259] These events may be connected with a report which Shakerley made to London in the same year that 'at Congleton, where one hundred people assembled . . . their chief speaker, one Boden, a pitiful broken butter merchant, has been committed to prison for refusing to give security to answer for his unlawful practices . . . There is one Ambrose Price, a notorious and dangerous fellow, who made his essay both at Bosley and at Congleton where he resides; as the mayor and his brethran are very remiss in their apprehension I shall be forced to issue a warrent, as deputy-lieutenant, to some officers of the militia.'[260] Both Price and Bowden were freemen of Congleton.[261]

Congleton corporation took sterner action in the 1670s and 1680s. In 1675 William Hall, one of the first trustees of the burial ground, was fined £20 because a meeting was held at his house, and goods worth £40 and his horse were distrained. When the horse escaped and returned to Hall, the magistrate indicted him for stealing it. He was imprisoned and tried for felony but was acquitted, 'this malicious attempt to commit murder by law being too barefaced to prevail on any judge or jury to bring him in guilty'.[262] He was fined in 1682 but afterwards left in peace until his death in 1684.[263]

From 1682 Quakers in Congleton and the surrounding area were fined continually either for absence from church or for non-payment of tithe. Very often goods were seized and sold to pay the fine, and it is significant that the value of goods taken was well in excess, often by three or four times, of the fine demanded. In 1682 these included food, pewter dishes, brass pots, a pair of shoes, an axe and clothing. The next year a calf was taken from Henry Booth and a cow from John Amery of Withington although a cryptic note records that the latter's son 'paid up and got it back'.

One family which suffered severely, but kept firmly to their faith, was the Welch family. The first Thomas Welch was convinced by Hubberthorne and was later summoned to Chester assizes to answer for his faith. He died in 1672 leaving two sons, Thomas and Shadrach. Thomas married Ann Smith of Leek in 1664 at William Hall's house where the Friends celebrated quite a number of marriages. He was admitted as a freeman of the town in 1672 even though he refused to take the oath. Shadrach was admitted, but not sworn, as a freeman in 1690 on payment of £5; other Quakers admitted were Edmund Sutton and Joseph Hall.[264] It would seem that the corporation had no objection to their being admitted as freemen or to their refusal to take the oath and that Quakers, for their part, did not object to taking a share in the life of the town. Shadrach is described as a 'furrer' on his marriage to Dorothy Ingham in 1687 but as a farrier in his will proved at Chester after his death in 1726. Both the brothers were heavily fined in the 1690s. In 1694 Thomas was imprisoned for his refusal to pay tithe until the next year when he was 'discharged upon the King's Act of Indemnity'. He died in 1699 and his widow continued to pay fines. Shadrach was fined and suffered such petty persecutions until 1672.

Thomas left two sons also called Shadrach and Thomas. The elder, apprenticed as a mercer and grocer in 1682 to his father,[265] died in 1690. The second son, Thomas, seemingly took over the business and handed it on to his children. He kept the 'book of sufferings' for the society as his father had done, sending the records to London, whilst his uncle Shadrach kept the marriage register.[266] Thomas paid fines until at least 1713. The family lived in the district until the 1750s when John Welch, mercer, a grandson of the third Thomas, died. Nothing more has been discovered of the family after that date. By then the Hall family had also disappeared. William and Ester seem to have had four daughters (and perhaps a son).[267] Mary died without issue in 1671 but the other three were married at the Hall house. Rebecca married a Leek man, Henry Bowman, and moved with him to Leek, where they and their descendants attended the Staffordshire meetings. Sarah married Elihu Hall, a grocer, of Longnor and they left the district. Hester married Hugh Crossby, a grocer from Warrington, in 1681, and they stayed in Congleton until their deaths (Hugh in 1709 and Hester in 1720), but as they left no issue this branch of the family died out. They were both staunch attenders of the Eaton meetings; Hester was sometimes the representative at the Women's Monthly Meeting and Hugh took his turn in keeping the 'book of sufferings' and attending to the travelling preachers. In 1679 Hester, a mercer, became free of the borough.[268]

R

The third large family was the Stretch family which seems to have scattered by 1740, some moving to the North Rode area, some to Stafford and some to the Nantwich–Mobberly–Peover area. Two more moved to Leek and their descendants attended the meetings there. The remaining Quakers, who resided in the town, were either members of another branch of the Hall family or individuals who have left no mention except in the 'book of sufferings' or in the digest registers. From close examination of these it is evident that Quakerism in the town was lacking support after 1730 because the families had moved away, or died out, or because there were no new recruits since the Quakers did not proselytize. They may also have 'married out' of the Society, in which case the Society disowned them. This in fact led to a general decline in the Friends in the late eighteenth and early nineteenth century. Indeed, meetings in the Macclesfield area were discontinued for this reason even later, in 1877, and did not start again until 1938.[269]

The meetings continued at Eaton until 1781 but were attended more by Quakers from Bosley, Marton and Siddington. Bishop Gastrell in 1718 commented that there was a Quaker meeting with about fifteen members in Astbury parish, that Marton and Siddington had each one Quaker family, and that a Quaker meeting was held at Bosley.[270] The fines, which the Quakers paid in this part of Cheshire, continued until the 1730s but by then the Eaton meeting house was serving a smaller area because the Macclesfield meeting house had opened in 1705. 'Workday' meetings were held at Congleton in 1700 but in 1715 it was noted that the meetings 'are attended well of Macclesfield friends but Congleton friends upon the work days have not been so well observed as could be desired, but tis hoped for the future will be better'.[271] Astbury churchwardens' presentments record Quaker meetings in the parish in 1725, 1728 and 1729 but do not specify where.[272] In 1738 it was reported that 'the meetings at Macclesfield are well attended but those at Eaton not so much'.[273] At Congleton Yearly Meetings were held in 1753, 1762 and 1764 and a Yearly Meeting for the northern counties in 1764;[274] but the meeting house decayed and was pulled down in 1801–2 leaving the meeting houses at Macclesfield and Wilmslow for the few remaining Quakers, if any, in the Congleton area.

There is no other mention of Quaker meetings in the town

until meetings were held at the houses of Friends in Congleton in the second World War.[275]

Methodists

John Wesley began the first of his preaching tours in 1738 but did not visit the north of England until four years later. There is no evidence that he visited Cheshire then but already Methodism was being preached in the Macclesfield area. Services were held at Mary Aldersley's house, Shrigley Fold, Higher Hurdsfield, and in 1743 this attracted the attention of a certain Thomas Buckley of Astbury. Buckley was already familiar with Methodist views. His friend, a Mr. Pedley, a silkweaver from Congleton, had heard George Whitfield preach in London.[276] Pedley sent one of the printed sermons to his father. It came into the hands of Buckley, who must then have made enquiries and, on hearing about the Hurdsfield meeting, went there on several occasions with his friends. Here he met John Bennet, one of the first Methodist preachers, who soon became a frequent visitor to Buckley's house.

Buckley wanted to hear Wesley and in 1745 received news that he would preach at the house of Roger Moss near Rode Hall.[277] Wesley's journal states merely that on Friday and Saturday, 26 and 27 April, 'at John Bennet's request, I preached at several places in Lancashire and Cheshire',[278] but Dyson adds that Buckley and his friends sat by the fire all night so as to hear Wesley preach at 5 a.m.[279] Buckley was so moved that, helped by Bennet, he formed a society which met at his house with himself as class leader. His employers disapproved and he was forced to leave that house and move to another nearer Congleton. In 1746 at Buckley's request Bennet added Astbury to his round. Bennet also visited George Pearson who owned Buglawton Hall and preached there. Later Pearson was to entertain Wesley.

The events in Astbury and Bennet's visits must have raised interest in Congleton and a society was probably founded in the town before the first visit of John Wesley. Charles Wesley recorded in his journal for 16 October 1746: 'I rode to Congleton and preached in a yard, and prayed with the little Society, who seem on the brink of a pool.'[280] The next day he preached to a larger congregation at the Market Cross, which at that time stood in the High Street. He said that he preached to the

poor people who 'heard me gladly' and also noted that 'two
ministers were of my audience'. These, no doubt, heard him
with very mixed feelings. John Wesley came the next year,
preaching on 10 May at Astbury at 5 a.m. and at Congleton at
7 a.m.[281] This was the first of 24 visits and it would appear that
both Congleton and Astbury were incorporated into John
Bennet's round, which was soon merged into the vast area of
the York circuit covering six counties. It was too large and as
more preachers became available it was split up, although the
districts were not formally settled for a long time. In 1752 the
Manchester circuit was formed and Astbury was one of the
original members. In 1753 the name Astbury alone appears in
a list of contributors to the circuit, but in 1763 Congleton
features in the circuit account with a quarterage of one
guinea.[282] Congleton and Astbury had divided by 1759 when
Congleton had 23 members—5 men and 18 women.[283] The
society included wireworkers, farmers, shopkeepers and silk and
ribbon workers. The most important member was Samuel
Troutbeck, an apothecary. He allowed the Methodists to meet
in 'a room' at the back of his house which was entered by a
narrow passage from Mill Street.[284] This was probably a large
room because it was partitioned into four cottages when it was
given up. In 1787 Wesley preached Troutbeck's funeral sermon
in a new chapel in Wagg Street.

The society was soon organized into classes for Wesley had
made meeting in class a condition of membership. A class
ticket of 1757 is mentioned and one belonging to Thomas
Garside, dated 1762, had a decoration of an anchor under a
crown and stars with the motto 'such hope we have for an
anchor of the soul'.[285] The Methodist Conference felt that they
were becoming too elaborate and after 1787 metal tokens were
issued. They were essential for admission to the 'love feast': the
handbill for the opening of the 1808 chapel stated that admission to the love feast would only be allowed on production
of the class ticket. Early Methodist services were very simple:
hymn singing, extempore prayer and short sermon. The services
were taken by the circuit minister, or, if he was absent, by a
local preacher. In 1772 Joshua Staton preached at Congleton
on over half the Sundays in the year as the minister was elsewhere. On quarter days he would walk to Manchester and back
to pay in the class and ticket money—usually about 10*s.*[286]

The early Methodists soon found themselves under attack. Although Wesley asserted his communion with the Church of England, his society was considered as one of the dissenting sects which came under the Toleration Act of 1689. This made no provision for those who insisted they were still members of the Church of England even if they would not worship in the Established Church, so that the Methodists were placed under the shadow of the Conventicle Act and were thus without protection. Troutbeck had registered as a dissenter in the bishop's court at Chester in 1758 and 1759 but this obviously did not protect the meeting house.[287]

Hostility to the Methodists took the form of abuse and physical violence, often incited by the clergy and ignored by the magistrates. The Anglican clergy thought Wesley was too enthusiastic and resented his departure from normal procedure. The magistrates were also worried about the enthusiasm and it did not help when Methodists wept for joy, shouted and struck each other in their emotion. Mobs were easily aroused in England in the eighteenth century, not troubling about issues or causes, merely looking for trouble.[288] At Congleton they had had their sport with the Independents in 1714—now the new sport was Methodist baiting.

On 20 July 1764 Wesley wrote in his journal, 'At noon we made the same shift at Congleton as when I was here last. I stood in the window, having put as many women as it would contain into the house. The rest, with the men, stood below in the meadow and many of the townsmen, wild enough. I have scarce found such enlargement of heart since I came from Newcastle. The brutes resisted long, but were at length overcome, not above five or six excepted. Surely man shall not long have the upper hand; God will get unto Himself the victory. It rained all the day till seven in the evening when I began preaching at Burslem. Even the poor potters here are a more civilized people than the better sort (so called) at Congleton.'[289] The setting would be the chapel at the back of Troutbeck's shop which stood on the top of what was the old river bank; the 'meadow' probably sloped down to the area now occupied by Victoria Street.[290] In a collection of notes in Wagg Street chapel there is a reference to Wesley being smuggled away from the mob and being laid on a dining table in a house to recuperate with a bible for a pillow. The 'better sort (so called)' may have been encouraged by the clergy, for the curate of St. Peter's was hostile; Wesley wrote on 6 March 1768, 'It seems that the behaviour of the society in this town has convinced all people in it, but the curate, who still refuses to give the sacrament to any that will not promise to hear these preachers no more.'[291] It may not only have been the behaviour of the society which convinced people that it was better to leave it alone. Dyson recorded that on one occasion a group of young men, becoming tired of the rowdiness, hid themselves until the mob started their noise then attacked the unsuspecting mob and 'so effectual was this lesson thus taught that they never could be rallied again'.[292]

The curate in 1768 was Richard Sandbach who seems to have been a contentious character, alienating not only the nonconformists but also his own parishioners. Wesley noted in 1772 that 'none except Mr. Sambach' was speaking against the Methodists[293] and in 1774 implied that the gentry of the town were attending the Methodist chapel rather than go to the parish church because the minister had 'disobliged his parishioners'.[294]

By the end of the century hostility against the society had died down. Sandbach left the town in 1785, the magistrates gave more protection and the Methodists themselves were held in greater respect. Unfortunately Congleton Methodism in the last two decades of the eighteenth century was troubled within the society itself. When some of the members joined Scott in 1782, Wesley was alarmed for he was opposed to the doctrine of predestination subscribed to by the Calvinistic Methodists. He wrote resentfully that 'the Calvinists were just breaking in and striving to make havoc of the flock'.[295] Trouble intensified during the next year when the circuit was divided and Wesley had to ride from Stafford to hear complaints against the minister, James Rogers. On Sunday 30 August 1783 he wrote, 'I heard all the parties face to face, and encouraged them all to speak their whole mind. I was surprised; so much prejudice, anger and bitterness, on so slight occasions, I never saw. However, after they had had it out, they were much softened, if not quite reconciled.'[296] James Rogers, whose first wife died during this appointment, later married Hester Anne Roe, a daughter of a prominent Macclesfield family.[297] He was a hard worker but seems to have had differences of opinion with some of the society. The circuit had been divided with Wesley's approval but Thomas Garside and some others quibbled about who should pay for the furnishing of the minister's house and questioned the changing of the stewards. The matter was not settled until the 1790s.

Wesley usually came from Burslem and went on to Macclesfield. The remarkable stamina of the man is shown by an incident which happened on a visit to the town in 1774. He had arrived from Newcastle on 30 April to find a letter waiting for him asking him to go to Bristol. 'So about one, I took chaise, and reached Bristol about half an hour after one the next day. Having done my business in about two hours, on Friday in the afternoon I reached Congleton again, no more tired (blessed be God!) than when I left it.'[298] He preached in the evening of that Good Friday, on Saturday and on Sunday morning, leaving later that day for Macclesfield. On his last visit in 1790 he was honoured by the presence of the curate of St. Peter's, the mayor, and all the 'heads of the town'. He left the chapel leaning on the arm of his host, Thomas Garside, a prominent Methodist and later mayor of the town, and called at the doors of John Ball, James Clark and Joshua Staton who all lived in Wagg Street.[299] In 1856, when Dyson was collecting material for his history, he noted that Hannah Dale said that she heard Wesley say in his last sermon in the town, which he preached at five o'clock the next morning, that 'he dreamed he was walking down a street in Bristol when he met a man he knew well, and went across to accost him; but on trying to shake hands he found his own were gone'. He took this to mean that his work on earth was done.[300]

By then the work of the society had expanded. The chapel behind Troutbeck's shop was no doubt inconvenient and so, either in 1766 or 1767,[301] the society bought a plot of land in Wagg Street. The new chapel, a plain brick building, had a gallery on three sides and held about 400 people. Wesley preached in it in 1768 and found it 'better contrived and better finished' than the new chapel in which he had been preaching at Burslem.[302] The society was still in the Manchester circuit at that time, which stretched from Congleton to Bolton, far too large and inconvenient, so that in 1770 the southern part was rearranged to form a new circuit taking in Congleton, Burslem, Leek and Buxton.[303] In winter preachers rode with shovels strapped to their saddles to cut their way through the deep drifts. There were chapels in these towns and the Congleton area included classes held at Astbury, Limekiln and Congleton Edge. The trouble in 1782 had come when Burslem was given a separate circuit, being replaced by Sandbach, and new societies were formed at Withington, Smallwood, Davenport and Bradley Green. This activity gave some importance to Congleton and the Methodist Conference in 1803 recommended that Congleton should be made head of a circuit. At the same time Nantwich was taken from the Chester circuit and attached to Congleton.[304]

This important step and the fact that there were 300 members in the society gave an opportunity to build a larger chapel. The chapel and three cottages in front of it were pulled down in 1807 when a contract was made between Timothy Lockett and Thomas Collins of Burslem to build a chapel, dwelling house and stable.[305] The surveyor, Thomas Sherwin of Burslem, rode over several times to inspect the work. The chapel was completed in 1808. It was 48 feet long, 42 feet wide and 24 feet high and it remained substantially unaltered until the front was taken down in 1949. An old drawing of the chapel shows that the minister's house was attached to the chapel on the south side, the two buildings forming an L-shape. The upper story of the chapel had five round-headed windows in the front and six oblong windows on each side. The lower story had a porch with two doorways separated by a central window. The minister's house was of the same height, but divided into three stories which had oblong sash windows.

The interior of the chapel was plastered and limewashed but the lower parts of the walls were oak-panelled. Oak benches were used until they were replaced by pews in 1893. At the front of the chapel was an oak pulpit standing on a single column; this was replaced also in 1893 by a mahogany rostrum. The gallery, round three sides, was supported on iron columns. The front of it was left in its original oak staining and was 'drawn and tongued' at the edge. Later, moulded iron flowers were let into the front panels. The ceiling had a design of moulded squares some with a diamond shape and some with a trefoil shape in the centre. Four large chandeliers were replaced by gas fittings in 1836. The interior of the chapel remained basically unchanged apart from the alteration of 1893 until it was pulled down.

When it was built, however, there was no chapel of comparable size for many miles and it was large enough to hold 900 people. It might have seemed that it was too large for, immediately the chapel had been built, Nantwich was given its own circuit and 200 people were transferred. Siddington also left the circuit but was replaced by Bosley and new societies were added at Daneinshaw and Buglawton—in the latter place probably because the opening of the silk mills there provided a new congregation. A room was hired but then two cottages were bought and fitted out as a school and chapel serving until new premises were built in 1835;[306] this congregation was later known as the Brook Street Society.

By 1831 there were said to be 680 people in the society and 1,130 in 1835.[307] This seems a large increase for the circuit even though new chapels had been built at Key Green (1821 and rebuilt 1835), Daneinshaw (1824), Congleton Edge (1833) and Gillowshaw Brook (1833), and a Methodist New Connexion (an offshoot of the Methodists founded by Alexander Kilham in 1797) had opened a branch in New Street in 1823, later moving to larger premises in Elizabeth Street.[308] It might have been partly due to the increase of political consciousness in the working classes which made them eager to join societies which they thought would further their cause. There was a trade depression in the town at that time, and the Methodist Society may have gained converts attracted to it by political and economic, rather than religious, hope. Most of the mills in the town were closed and when trade did revive it was disrupted by a series of strikes which led to a further depression in the 1840s. The increase in numbers may have been partly due to this and partly due to the desire to join any society which would provide the underprivileged classes with a smattering of education and this the Methodists were prepared to do. Whatever else might be said about the early Methodists it is obvious that some of the local preachers were not afraid to speak their minds. In 1831 James Hulme preached his trial sermon before the trustees of Wagg Street on the text Proverbs 34, 10. 'Harken unto me ye wise men, give ear ye men of understanding.' It consisted of a scathing denunciation of the ways of the Congleton corporation emphasizing especially their liking for food and drink at the expense of spiritual things. The trustees did not pass him and on his second trial sermon his text was appropriately 'Ye have despised me because I have told ye the truth.'[309] The records of the 1851 religious census show that on that particular Sunday 400 adults attended Wagg Street in the morning and 600 in the evening and 150 persons were present at Sunday school. Queen Street congregation (founded in 1836 by the Methodist New Connexion congregation from Elizabeth Street —and joined in 1837 by dissidents from Wagg Street who had seceded over Sunday-school policy) numbered 250 in the morning and 290 in the evening. Brook Street, Buglawton, had 40 and 80 respectively but the Sunday school numbered 150. At Havannah a Wesleyan congregation meeting in a room at a factory had an evening congregation of 74.[310] The number of worshippers was clearly quite high and compared favourably with the rest of the county. Even Congleton Edge had 64 for the evening service. The figures bear out the high estimate for the 1830s. By 1870, however, the number in the circuit was estimated at 600. This may have been the result of the removal of Sandbach to its own circuit,[311] in the 1850s.

The circuit, which includes Congleton, Bosley, Buglawton, Key Green, Withington, Siddington, Davenport and Biddulph, thus achieved its present size. There were then two ministers, both residing in Congleton. A third minister was added in the 1870s but, because of the trade depression, the circuit could not afford to pay the stipends and in 1882 it reverted to having two ministers. In 1893 the old minister's residence was pulled down and the present Westwood House built as a separate block, not attached to the chapel. The old house had had a stable block attached and the circuit accounts show that a horse was kept for the minister's use or, if he preferred it, one was hired. The new house had no stable for the minister hired a chaise. In 1911 the horse-hire fund became a car-hire fund.[312]

During the nineteenth and twentieth centuries several improvements were made to the circuit chapels. Wagg Street installed an organ in 1845, replacing on most occasions the string instruments which had accompanied the hymns. James Albison, the chapel keeper, had played the double bass from 1829 to 1850 on a salary of £5 a year. After the double bass was sold with the rest of the instruments in 1850 he resigned his post 'possibly for grief at the loss of Betty'. The organ, with its splendid case of deal and painted oak with Gothic tracery and a castellated top, gave good service until it was replaced in

1939 by a modern instrument built by Jardine and Co. of Old Trafford. When the old minister's house was pulled down in 1893, new vestries, classrooms and a lecture room were built at the back of the chapel. A mahogany rostrum with splendidly carved console brackets and approached by two flights of steps replaced the oak pulpit. The old porch was replaced by a larger one of two entrances, crowned by an acute-angled pediment. It was more impressive but the original simplicity had been lost. Railings had been added to the front of the chapel in 1876; these were re-used but the shrubs were cleared away and the entrance paved. Apart from alteration to the lighting in 1931, when electricity was put in, nothing further was done to the chapel until dry rot was discovered in the porch in 1949. The whole front was taken down, and a new one of Accrington red brick with a door frame of white Holland stone added. There was one entrance and above it was placed a huge stone cross set in a stone surround.[313]

Rood Lane trustees pulled down their old chapel in 1885 and built a new school and chapel on the site, adding extra classrooms in 1902. Withington chapel, built 1808, was renovated in 1893 and a new school room added in 1908. A fire in the school room the next year resulted in further improvements being carried out. Station Road chapel, Biddulph, was renovated about the same time, while the trustees of Brookhouse Green, who had been using the old Baptist chapel and had failed to buy it, decided to build a new chapel in 1907. Congleton Edge, rebuilt in 1890, had a new vestry added in 1931. The 1833 chapel had cost £90; the new vestry cost £250 and at that time the congregation was described in the minutes as 'mostly miners who are affected by the industrial depression'. To attempt such expenditure was no small undertaking at such a time.

The Congleton Edge chapel is a good example of a building fitting admirably into its site, its ruggedness merging with the forcefulness of the Edge above. It stands on a slope overlooking the Cheshire plain with a small graveyard to the north, the whole site lying along the road leading to the top of the Edge. The chapel is of regular stone blocks with a tiled roof. The side walls have each three round-headed windows.

Daneinshaw chapel was rebuilt in 1898 and an extension added in 1918. The congregation at Hulme Walfield had met in the old Hall since 1820 but in 1890 they bought the Primitive Methodist chapel and by 1892 services were in progress. This last chapel was closed in 1966 because the congregation had dwindled to a very small number.[314]

The Queen Street chapel is still basically the original brick building—small, plain, square—of the 1830s with a pitched roof. It was renovated in 1883.[315] The building is only a few feet from the road and the railings in front of it reach to the edge of the footpath. There are two small entrances which are placed in between three round-headed windows. The upper storey has five similar windows and the division between upper and lower stories is marked by a strong string course. On the left side is a small single-storeyed school room added in 1856. The interior had a gallery on three sides supported by iron columns. The rostrum at the front, of light oak, had a flight of steps on each side. Below the rostrum was the communion table placed within oak railings. The pews were also of light oak. Behind the rostrum was a small choir gallery with an organ at the back. The flat plastered ceiling is plain with a moulded panel in the centre. The building was closed in 1969.

The circuit had been administered entirely from Congleton but the 1908 centenary celebration of the Wagg Street chapel gave an opportunity for suggesting the moving of the second minister's residence to Biddulph, and this was achieved in 1911. Since that time the circuit has been administered in two parts, based respectively on Congleton and Biddulph.[316] In 1965 woodworm was discovered in the galleries on Wagg Street chapel. Further examination revealed that the high unsupported walls were bulging and the galleries were leaning into the bulge. The decision was taken to pull down the chapel and amalgamate Wagg Street, Brook Street and Queen Street under the title of the Central Methodist church. The latter two sites have now (1969) been sold. A new chapel of modern design and materials was built on the Wagg Street site, called Trinity Methodist church, and opened in November 1968. The Biddulph part also made changes. High Street (Wesley Hall) closed down and amalgamated with Station Road to form a new society, St. Andrews.

Successful societies in the twentieth century have included the Wesley Guild in the early 1900s which ran a very successful social group and attracted many good speakers to lecture to it, the Young People's Association, a Wives' Club and a growing Youth Group. Many members of the circuit sang in the J. L. Riley choir of Macclesfield, whose founder had a long connection with the circuit as organist at Rood Lane and Wagg Street. The choir gave many performances of *Messiah* and *Elijah* in the chapel and were successful in winning the Festival of Britain competition for mixed choirs in 1951.

Primitive Methodists
The Wesleyan and Primitive Methodist Societies have grown up entirely separately in the town. The formation of the Methodist Church in 1932 resulted in an exchange of pulpits and a mingling of congregations for special services but the administration remained long distinct under the respective ministers. During the second World War a joint circuit plan was issued but after 1945 it was discontinued.[317] In the Congleton area Primitive Methodism has strong support because of close connections with Hugh Bourne and Mow Cop. Bourne was born on the lonely slopes of Biddulph Moor. Whilst a young man he was converted from Anglicanism to Methodism but wanted to return to the early Methodist practice of field preaching. Wesley had done this but Bourne wanted to take matters further and hold camp meetings on the American model with preaching and praying for a whole day. In some ways Bourne was acting contrary to Methodist practice, for the Methodists by then had chapels and did little, if any, field preaching. Indeed many Methodists viewed the departure with horror because England was at this time engaged in the struggle of the Napoleonic Wars and they feared that any apparent eccentricity would draw upon them the wrath of the authorities. On the other hand Bourne may have been right in thinking that the time was ripe for a religious revival and that field preaching was a novel way in which to do it. The accent was not on formal preaching but on conversion by praying and talking.

In September 1804 James Clark brought a group of revivalists from Stockport to Congleton to attend a love feast. Bourne joined them and returned again to their second meeting on Christmas day; previously he had heard a sermon by the eminent Methodist, Dr. Coke, and was greatly impressed by the power of preaching and prayer. Next year Lorenzo Dow, an American evangelist, held a camp meeting at Macclesfield and Bourne took this opportunity to invite Dow to help him organize a similar meeting at Mow Cop.[318] Dow also preached during 1807 at Burslem, Tunstall and Congleton. Bourne heard him in all three places. At Congleton Dow preached on an open space in Lawton Street, the site of the present chapel. The Mow Cop meeting lasted from 6 a.m. until the evening and the huge congregation included many from Congleton. The Conventicle Act and the Five Mile Act were not repealed until 1812 so Bourne walked to Lichfield to get the ground licensed. On being told he could not be given permission unless there was a building on it he promptly built a wooden chapel at his own expense.[319] Other camp meetings followed including one at Buglawton in 1808, said to have been on the site of the present Primitive Methodist chapel.

The Methodist Church, however, was becoming alarmed, fearing that the camp meetings were dangerous opportunities for agitation. Bourne was therefore expelled from the Burslem circuit and started his own society to which in 1812 he gave the name Primitive Methodist, but which local people called Ranters. The first plan, dated 1811, shows seventeen preaching places including the Cloud and Roggin Row, Buglawton.[320] Cloud is now the oldest surviving Primitive Methodist chapel in use in England. Hugh Bourne preached twice at the Cloud in 1811 in the open air but in 1815 William Clowes (not Bourne's friend) gave a piece of land on which a chapel could be built. Tradition says that Thomas Bayley begged the money for it in three days, that it was erected within a month and cost £26.[321] The building, sturdy and stoutly built of local sandstone, stands on a platform cut out of the east side of the Cloud. The interior contains oak pews and the pulpit, into which two brass candlesticks are set, is said to be the one from which Bourne preached. The building remained unaltered until 1958 when a small extension in yellow brick was added, and a movable partition put in to divide it from the chapel.

Buglawton chapel was converted in 1823 from a small drying kiln and is a small building lighted by two windows on the north side. The trustees of the chapel included stonemasons and silkmen; as with the other branches of protestant nonconformity the appeal was to the working class.[322]

A reference in 1809 in Bourne's manuscript autobiography[323] suggests that a society had been established in Congleton by that date and, if this is so, it would have been part of the Cheshire group organized in that year. Later a house was taken in Canal Street but by 1822 land had been acquired off Lawton Street.[324] A chapel was built there in 1822 and registered.[325]

The society was very active in the town in the 1820s and 1830s. A group called the Religious Tract Visiting Society divided the town into six districts in order to visit families and distribute religious tracts. Many open-air meetings were held, some being camp meetings on the outskirts of the town, others held in the streets. Most of these were preceded by processions singing hymns through the streets. Thus in 1832 John Morton recorded in his journal that an open air meeting was held at 7 a.m. conducted by Hugh Bourne. 'We then sung round the streets and held another open air meeting', this time at Buglawton. The Primitive Methodist Conference approved of the early hours of the services although, if it was a weekday service, it had to be held early before the mills opened. The conference also praised the fact that, before any regular service in the chapel, the congregation met outside for an hour of singing and prayer and at length sang its way into the building.

Constant visiting was done by the local preachers, who were not deterred by distance or sickness. After the Buglawton meeting, Morton visited many families in the area who had typhus. John Hallam, in 1834, led camp meetings in June at Daneinshaw, Wornish Nook and Bradwell. In July he prayed with numerous families including 40 on 9 July. August saw him conducting a camp meeting at Swettenham and leading prayer meetings when 'we sung through the streets from the chapel to the Dog Lane'. On 4 September he wrote in his journal, 'In the afternoon went to Congleton Moss and prayed with 19 families. I then hastened to Daneinshaw and having a hour to spare before preaching time I improved it praying with 25 families making in all 44 families.' Hallam's work helped the Society to open a new chapel in the Mossley area. Land opposite the toll bar was leased from Lord Camoys and the chapel was built in two months beginning October 1840. In December Hallam preached the opening sermon.[326] The building was 30 feet long, 20 feet wide and about 16 feet high. It was extensively altered in 1890 and again in 1951.

Bourne says that the 'Congleton chapel was opened by the exertions of our Macclesfield friends'.[327] The Congleton and

Macclesfield Union recorded 747 members in 1838 but in 1839 Congleton became a separate circuit in the Tunstall Synodal District with 535 members.[328] One of the earliest ministers was Richard Jukes, the so-called 'Bard of the Poor' who wrote many poems and hymns, some of which are in the *New Methodist Hymn Book*. He is reported to have gained 99 new members in one year.[329] An obituary of him, written in 1868, implies that, though his preaching did attract large numbers, adherents to the society were more likely attracted by bad trade conditions and the fear of cholera.[330] Descriptions of the Primitive Methodist meetings emphasize lay participation in the service, the active seeking out of people, and the welcoming of 'believers'—all 'conversions', in fact, are faithfully recorded.

In the 1851 religious census the minister recorded that an average congregation of 400 adults attended Lawton Street and an actual congregation of 210 adults were present in the afternoon and 270 in the evening of 30 March. The Sunday school, which had opened in 1823, recorded 208 children in the afternoon. This compares with a figure given in the *Primitive Methodist Magazine* of 266 children and 44 teachers in the Sunday school in 1840. At Mossley in 1851 40 adults attended in the afternoon and 50 in the evening. There are no figures available for Cloud and Buglawton.[331]

On the night of the census of population taken in the same year, Hugh Bourne, is recorded as staying in Congleton at the house of James Broad in Park Street. He had visited Congleton in 1842 when he was seventy and had walked 21 miles that day between Macclesfield and Bemersley visiting the chapels. On his death in 1852 he was a member of Mow Cop chapel and thus was in the Congleton circuit.[332] When James Broad died in 1888 he left the Society some land in Kinsey Street so that the chapel could be extended.[333] The trustees bought more land, pulled down the old chapel and erected the present building in red brick in 1891 at a cost of £2,200. The builder was John Worrall and the architect, A. Tomkinson of Tunstall.[334] The chapel seats 300 and has a school room at the rear with an entrance on Lawton Street. This is used for the activities of the society and in the second World War was used both by the Civil Defence, and as a canteen for the many nationalities stationed in the town. The woodwork in the chapel is very pleasing, especially the rostrum and the pitch-pine organ case with its Gothic-style decoration on the top. The organ dates from the restoration of 1904, being partly paid for by the Carnegie Trust.[335]

At the society's 50th anniversary in 1857, its 100th in 1907 and its 150th in 1957, services were held in the circuit, and a procession walked from Congleton and Mow Cop and Congleton ministers took part in the services held on the original camp site at Mow Cop. In 1957 the memorial to Hugh Bourne, placed on his grave at Englesea Brook, was restored and rededicated.[336]

The present circuit consists of the four chapels mentioned in this account together with Newtown, Timbersbrook, Mow Cop and Kent Green. In 1923 the society numbered 242; at the present time (1968) it is 320.

Other Nonconformist Denominations

The record of other denominations in Congleton is a rather chequered one. Most flourished for a time and then ran into difficulties. As already stated, the Revd. George Marris left the Congregational Church in 1822; together with some of the congregation he opened a branch of the Countess of Huntingdon's Connexion. Selina, Countess of Huntingdon, had assisted George Whitfield in establishing Calvinistic Methodism which leaned towards the doctrine of predestination. It was this doctrine which Captain Scott had been preaching in 1782 in Congleton, thus arousing the wrath of Wesley. Marris seems to have thought he was returning to the purer thought of Congregationalism and so, for his followers, he built Zion Chapel, seating 400, at the end of Park Street. The society, however, declined and in 1842, his successor, the Revd. Newman, sold the chapel to the Baptists. The Baptists had met previously from 1811 at a farmhouse at Woodhouse Green, also used by the Primitive Methodists.[337] In 1851 the religious census recorded a General Baptist congregation of 55 adults and 13 children in the morning.[338] The Sunday school dates from about that year.[339] The Revd. William Goacher came to Congleton in 1885 but retired the next year although he seems to have continued to take the services as a new minister was not appointed. When he left for Thaxted in 1888 the congregation, which had fallen to 29 adults, must have decided to close the chapel.[340] It was sold to the Salvation Army which

s

was using it in 1892 and 1906 but soon afterwards it became an auction room.[341] In 1965 the Baptist Church was revived in Congleton and opened a new meeting place in Astbury Street. The only mention previously of any form of Baptists in the district before the nineteenth century is a record of some Anabaptist children whose date of birth is recorded for Buglawton in 1702 and Congleton in 1703.[342] There may have been others later but no Anabaptists are mentioned as being in the area in an inquiry of 1718.[343]

St. Stephen's school was bought by the parish about 1837 from the Aikenites who had probably built it 20 years previously. These were the followers of the evangelistic Revd. Robert Aiken.[344]

The Salvation Army has held meetings in various parts of the town. Unfortunately its records were destroyed in the second World War so that information on its activities is lacking. The Army had 'opened fire' in Congleton by 1892 and had started a mission soon after. General Booth visited the town three times—in 1901, 1907 and 1909—each time speaking to large and reportedly sympathetic crowds.[345]

The Latter Day Saints erected a meeting-house in Buglawton in 1830.[346] A 'Hall of Science' was registered in 1840 by William Booth, who described himself as a 'Rational Religionist'.[347] The 1840s also saw the founding of a branch of the Society for the Propagation of Christian Knowledge and also of a British and Foreign Bible Society depository. Both these were in High Street and both presumably acted as reading-rooms and lending libraries.[348] None of these organizations seems to have lasted very long. In the twentieth century were established branches of the Christadelphians (1934), the Christian Spiritualists (1936), who later built a chapel in Park Road, the Apostolic Church (c. 1956), and the Jehovah's Witnesses.[349] In 1968 these organizations were still in existence. The Apostolic congregation first worshipped at Spouthouse Farm, Buglawton, later moving to Chapel Street.[350] A Bethel Pentecostal Mission was established in 1936, but has since ceased to exist. The present Pentecostal church held its first meeting in Congleton in 1959 and met regularly in the Masonic Hall until its new church in Nursery Lane, off Bromley Road, was built in Congleton in 1968. The building is a timber one, holding about 150 people, and was constructed by members of the congregation. The present congregation numbers about 30.[351]

In 1966 a branch of the World Council of Churches, representing most Christian denominations, was established in Congleton.

ROMAN CATHOLICISM

If Congleton[352] is ever associated with the history of Roman Catholicism in England, it is as the birthplace of Margaret Ward, one of the Elizabethan martyrs; she was executed at Tyburn in 1588.[353] Evidence of recusancy in and around the town in penal times is, however, fragmentary. A report made to Sir Francis Walsingham, possibly in 1584, stated that 'the Lady Warberton at Congleton doth keep an old priest who calls himself Walkenes, but his name is William Worthyngton; he is her butler when he is there. At some times he goeth abroad for a month or six weeks, and he hath been twice at Rome'.[354] The chapel at Big Fenton Farm in Peover Lane, Buglawton, may possibly have been used for Catholic worship; a small room beneath the part of the house containing the chapel is traditionally known as the priest's hiding-place.[355] Catholics from the Congleton area may well have been among those who were stated in 1642 to be meeting regularly on Mow Cop for mass 'and other common prayers in Latin'. Eleven people and two Jesuits were said to have been sent to Stafford gaol after being caught at mass there.[356] Mary Bailey, a widow, had had lands in Congleton sequestrated because of recusancy by 1649.[357]

In 1667 Ralph Bann of Congleton and Maud Brookes and Alice Jodrill of Smallwood were presented as recusants although it is not stated that they were papists.[358] In 1686 the curate of Congleton reported Ann, the wife of Richard Smith, keeper of the *Swan and Sun*, and Mrs. Baughtry, a poor widow, as papists; 'besides whom', added the curate, 'we have neither papist nor reputed papist in our chapelry'.[359] Ann Smith and Mary Baughtry were presented in 1706 as reputed papists along with four more from other parts of Astbury parish.[360] For the rest of the eighteenth century, however, such returns of papists as are made at all for Congleton are nil returns.[361] Indeed as late as 1821 a nil return was made.[362] In 1825, however, some 200 Catholics were reported, mainly Irish weavers.[363]

By this time the town had a regular place of Catholic worship.[364] In December 1821 John Hall, the newly ordained priest at Macclesfield, began to say mass at Congleton in the house of a weaver named Tracey in Moody Street. The congregation numbered 24. A few months later the clubroom of the *Angel Inn*, also in Moody Street, was hired instead, presumably to accommodate the growing numbers. This continued to be used until 1826 when St. Mary's was built in West Road.

The new church, opened on 12 July, provided accommodation for some 280 people.[365] Of red brick, with pedimented gable and round-headed porch and windows, it is a simple Classical building in the 'nonconformist' style of many Catholic chapels of the period.[366] Inside, the church is unaisled, with the sanctuary at the south end recessed behind three arches. The organ gallery at the north end was added by Frederick Waterhouse (priest, 1873–80).[367] This part of the building is raised above street level, and the cellar-like room below, now used as the church hall, was originally the school. The present school, opened in the 1850s,[368] stands on a site to the west of the church previously used as the burial ground.[369] The church is now the oldest still in use in the Roman Catholic diocese of Shrewsbury.[370] The priest's house, which adjoins the church on the east, was built probably some five to ten years later.[371]

It took some years to secure a resident priest. John Hall continued to serve Congleton from Macclesfield until 1827 when Philip Orrell came as the first resident priest. He soon found the poor financial state of the mission too much for him, however, and left in 1828.[372] Hall took over again until 1830 when Charles Bigham was appointed.[373]

For a time the area served from Congleton was very extensive. By 1838 the priest there was responsible for both Nantwich and Northwich,[374] and Middlewich too appears in the baptismal register from 1840. In the course of the next few years, however, responsibility for these outlying places was transferred to other centres.[375] In the meantime the number of Roman Catholics in Congleton itself was increasing. There were some 300 by 1834.[376] In 1839 James Anderton (priest there, 1835–40, 1853–5) reported to his bishop that 'converts are numerous and continually increasing'.[377] The number of baptisms rose sharply in the late 1840s,[378] an indication no doubt of new Irish immigration. When the religious census was taken on Sunday 30 March 1851 the congregation at mass was estimated at 220 (including 60 Sunday-school children), with 140 at the evening service (including 40 children).[379]

Money remained a serious problem.[380] A debt of £600 was incurred in the founding of the mission, and since the building of a house would have raised this by another £200 or £300, one had to be rented. The income from a mission consisting mainly of weavers and labourers amounted to £50 p.a., and this figure included a £20 subsidy from the clergy fund for Cheshire. The increase in population evidently raised the income a little, and in 1839 James Anderton expressed cautious optimism. By 1842, however, the subsidy had been withdrawn, leaving an income of only £54, and Anderton's successor, James Fisher, issued an appeal for help in the *Catholic Directory* of that year. The position was complicated by the need to rent cottages as mass-centres in Northwich and Nantwich and by the cost of travelling there. The income from these two places was just under £40 in 1839, with rents and travelling expenses totalling nearly £38.

Congleton like most other places experienced outbursts of anti-Catholic feeling in 1829 and 1850. The first was occasioned by the Catholic Emancipation Bill. In March 1829 a meeting was held in the town at which an address to the king and a petition to the House of Lords against emancipation were passed unanimously.[381]

A much more violent wave of feeling swept the country in 1850 with the Pope's restoration of the Roman Catholic hierarchy. Early in November John Hill, the priest at St. Mary's, wrote to the *Macclesfield Courier* presenting the historical arguments for the Roman Catholic claims. The several replies included a challenge from John Scott, the incumbent of St. Stephen's; its tone was typical of the feeling aroused:[382]

I have been in Congleton seven years and during that period we have had no priest of a controversial character. You assume it today by your letter which I have read in the *Macclesfield Courier*. I cannot think you skilful with that weapon; but in these times when what we consider the matchless impudence of the Pope has brought his and our Protestant Church into apparent collision, if you have no objection to meet a clergyman of the Church of England in any public room in Congleton before a general meeting of the inhabitants, you shall have a full opportunity afforded you of defending and setting forth the tenets of your Church. This letter with your reply (if any) shall appear in the *Macclesfield Courier* of next Saturday. The bearer will wait for some reply.

John Hill declined to be called out:

It will not appear strange if I beg to be excused coming to a public room to hear a repetition of vague objections that have been abundantly refuted by Catholic writers.

In November the borough council sent addresses to the queen and the prime minister pledging loyalty to the Crown and the principles of the Reformation and expressing indignation at the papal bull restoring the hierarchy.[383] In December a public meeting was held in the school room of St. Peter's with the mayor in the chair; 800 people attended and more waited outside unable to get in. Resolutions were passed against 'the recent usurpation of power by the Bishop of Rome' and addresses to the queen and prime minister were adopted.[384]

The Roman Catholic mission has continued to develop quietly but steadily. New influxes of people have included Belgian refugees during the first World War and evacuees from Manchester and allied troops during the second; the church hall was used by these troops as a canteen and social centre.[385] By 1967 St. Mary's parish, covering a large country area as well as the town itself, had a Roman Catholic population approaching 1,000 and an average attendance at Sunday mass of about 500.[386]

Notes

[1] See below.
[2] EDV 7/1/70; 7/2/63.
[3] *Ibid.*, 7/3/132; cf. *ibid.*, 7/4/65.
[4] See below.
[5] EDV 7/4/65.
[6] *Ibid.*, 7/6/401.
[7] See below.
[8] *Jnl. of the London Statistical Soc.*, xviii. Cf. J. F. C. Harrison, *Learning and Living, 1780–1960* (1961), 156.
[9] For the question of the return's reliability and its defects, see *British Jnl. of Sociology*, xviii, 382.
[10] The total attendances at all places of worship expressed as a percentage of total population was 60 (not taking into account Holy Trinity and Buglawton Wesleyan chapel). In the country as a whole it was 61— though in rural areas and small towns generally it was 71: *Jnl. of Ecclesiastical History*, xi. 79–80.

[11] The co-operation of ministers of religion and other officials, and the assistance of the Congleton and District Council of Churches, in particular the secretary, Mr. A. Gilmour, are gratefully acknowledged.

[12] EDV 7/4/65.

[13] See *Cong. Chron.*, 8 June 1907 for a photograph. This paragraph was contributed by Miss Joan P. Alcock.

[14] A. H. Nethercote, *The First Fives Lives of Annie Besant* (1961), 109–10; A. Besant, *Autobiographical Sketches* (1884), 103; H. B. Bonner, *Charles Bradlaugh* (1894), ii, 54–5.

[15] Ormerod, iii. 21, 25; see p. 15.

[16] *Ibid.*, 92.

[17] *Ibid.*, 18; *Chartulary or Register of the Abbey of St. Werburgh, Chester*, ed. J. Tait (Chetham Soc., lxxix, lxxxii), 309; F. Gastrell, *Notitia Cestriensis*, ed. F. R. Raines, pt. i (Chetham Soc., viii), 245.

[18] E.g. DL 30/1/21, m. 5d.

[19] *Ibid.*, m. 5.

[20] *Ibid.*, 2/29, m. 9.

[21] Lichfield Diocesan Registry, Register Scrope (VI), ff. 97v–98, 99v; *Black Prince's Register*, iii, 161, 203; *Calendar of Papal Letters*, iv, 532; *Cal. Pat. R. 1396–9*, 8–9, 11, 136. The rector was John Grey, who was evidently employed by the monks in some official capacity: *(Second) Register of Bishop Robert de Stretton*, ed. R. A. Wilson (William Salt Arch. Soc. N.S. viii), 46, 52, 81, 86, 138, 169, 185–6.

[22] See list on p. 224.

[23] Borough charters, iii.

[24] *Ibid.*, wills of 1413, 1423, 1424. Borough charters, i, has a grant to the same effect dated 1407. See above p. 18.

[25] E 134/8 Eliz., Easter 1.

[26] E 117/1/46.

[27] E 134/8 Eliz., Easter 1.

[28] C 66/1119.

[29] Borough accounts, 1589.

[30] *Ibid.*, 1623.

[31] *Ibid.*, 1631; cf. p. 55.

[32] Borough Miscellaneous Book, ii, under 'schedule of deeds and evidences'.

[33] Head, 169.

[34] See p. 19.

[35] Borough charters, iii, wills of 1418, 1422(2), 1436, 1442, 1446, 1452, 1453(2).

[36] *Notitia Cestriensis*, i, 235–6; Borough accounts, *passim*.

[37] *Notitia Cestriensis*, i, 239. Only one proctor was mentioned in 1436: Borough charters, iii, will of 1436.

[38] C.R.O., Astbury Churchwardens' Presentments, 1703.

[39] Borough accounts, ?1687.

[40] C.R.O., Astbury Churchwardens' Presentments, 1637.

[41] Borough accounts, 1659.

[42] Borough Order Bk., 1544–1699, 77.

[43] *Ibid.*, 108.

[44] *Ibid.*, 249.

45 Yates, 42.
46 Inf. from J. & J. A. Venn, *Alumni Cantabrigienses*, and J. Foster, *Alumni Oxonienses* unless otherwise stated.
47 See below.
48 *Calamy Revised*, ed. A. G. Matthews (1934), 446–7.
49 See p. 226.
50 Borough Order Bk., 1544–1699, 162.
51 Borough accounts, 1597.
52 For the Readers see p. 224. Richard Grene the elder was also town clerk, from 1586 at least until 1605: Borough Order Bk. 1544–1699, 90, 251.
53 E.g. Borough accounts, 1606, 1616.
54 E.g. *ibid.*, 1624.
55 E.g. *ibid.*, 1623.
56 *Ibid.*, 1597.
57 *Ibid.*
58 *Ibid.*, 1637.
59 *Ibid.*, 1632.
60 *Ibid.*, 1647.
61 Perhaps a relative of Richard Dale who was responsible for the oriels at Little Moreton Hall: Head, 176.
62 Borough accounts, 1613.
63 *Ibid.*, 1634.
64 *Ibid., passim.*
65 For details of the Puritan incumbents of Astbury and Congleton see below pp. 226–8.
66 Borough accounts, 1664.
67 The dean was guardian of the spiritualities of the northern province during a vacancy at York. The petition to him is printed in Head, 202–3. The dean's licence is in Borough Miscellaneous Book, ii, under date 17 September 1686.
68 *Notitia Cestriensis*, i, 239n.
69 The practice was continued at least until 1778: EDV 7/1/70.
70 Borough Order Bk., 1663–1714, 89. For Lowndes see Venn, *Alumni Cantabrigienses* and *Chester Clergy List, 1691* in *Chetham Miscellanies iii* (Chatham Soc., N.S., lxxiii), 35.
71 EDP 89/1.
72 *Ibid.*
73 *Ibid.*, 89/7.
74 *Ibid.*, 89/1.
75 Borough Order Bk., 1663–1714, 89.
76 EDP 89/7.
77 *Ibid.*, 89/1; Borough Miscellaneous Book, ii.
78 EDP 89/1; Borough Miscellaneous Book, ii.
79 Borough Order Bk., 1663–1714, 92. The item is entered under date 25 August 1698, but includes a note that the entry was not made until 2 August 1720, when the corporation was preparing for another dispute (see below). See also EDP 89/7 and Borough Miscellaneous Book, ii. The former includes the deposition of Richard Jackson, minister 1675–81,

who said that he had a signed testimonial from the rector when he was licensed by the bishop, and that the rector had allowed him the Easter Roll.

80 Borough accounts, 1698.
81 *Ibid.*, 1698–9.
82 EDP 89/1.
83 Borough Miscellaneous Book, ii.
84 Borough Order Bk., 1747–95, 101.
85 *Ibid.*, 107.
86 *Ibid.*, 109; Borough Miscellaneous Book, ii; EDP 89/1, 7.
87 EDP 89/1; see below.
88 Borough accounts, *passim.*
89 Borough Miscellaneous Book, ii; *Notitia Cestriensis*, i, 237.
90 EDV 7/1/70; Borough Order and Sessions Book, 1713–65, 31; Borough accounts 1713–47, 70.
91 Borough Order Bk., 1663–1714, 110; Borough Miscellaneous Book, ii.
92 Borough Order Bk., 1747–95, 248; EDP 89/6.
93 Head, 189; *Rep. Mun. Corps.*, 2656.
94 Borough Order Bk., 1663–1714, 137.
95 *Ibid.*, 122, 146. Christopher Rode had erected a gallery at the lower end of the nave, probably along the west wall, in 1703: *ibid.*, 116.
96 W. Camden, *Britannia* (2nd. edn., ed. R. Gough), iii, 43.
97 Ormerod, iii, 39.
98 Borough accounts 1713–47, 30, 32; Borough Order and Sessions Book, 1713–65, 125.
99 EDP 89/2, 4; an earlier seating plan is printed in Head, 173–5.
100 Borough Order and Sessions Book, 1713–65, 119, 123.
101 Borough Order Bk., 1747–95, 214 is a payment to the contractor, George Burslam. See below for architectural description.
102 Borough Order Bk., 1747–95, 139–40; Head, 190; *Manchester School Register*, ii (Chetham Soc. lxxiii), 272–3.
103 Borough Order Bk., 1747–95, 162.
104 Head, 190.
105 EDV 7/1/70.
106 *Ibid.*
107 G. Hennessy, *Novum Repertorium Ecclesiasticum Parochiale Londinense*, 410.
108 Head, 190–1.
109 EDV 7/2/63.
110 *Ibid.*, 7/3/132.
111 *Ibid.*, 7/4/65.
112 *Ibid.*
113 *Ibid.*, 7/6/401.
114 *Ibid.*; in 1814 Williamson admitted that he had 'lately grown very infirm' and was 'scarcely able to walk to the church': EDP 89/1.
115 Curate from 1825, minister 1831–8: EDP 89/1.
116 Assistant curate 1814, master of the grammar school 1810–44: EDP 89/1; plaque in sanctuary of St. Stephen's Church.
117 EDV 7/7/141.

[118] The advowson was sold in 1860 to Mr. Thomas Rowley, and descended to his daughter, Mrs. Hugh Williamson. Her executors transferred it to Simeon's Trustees, the present patrons: Head, 190; *Crockford.*

[119] W. R. Ward, 'Some reflections on Church Building in Manchester', in *Studies in Church History, iii,* 278.

[120] H.O. 129/457/2/5/4. Head, 211, says 10 October.

[121] Head, 209, 211; plaque in sanctuary of St. Stephen's Church.

[122] H.O. 129/457/2/5/4; Head, 211.

[123] Head, 211.

[124] *Ibid.,* 212.

[125] H.O. 129/457/2/5/4.

[126] Ormerod, iii, 42.

[127] *Crockford.*

[128] H.O. 129/457/2/5/4.

[129] Head, 211.

[130] Plaque in church.

[131] EDP 52/1.

[132] *London Gazette,* 10 July 1844.

[133] H.O. 129/457/2/6/12; plaque in church. See M. H. Port, *Six Hundred New Churches* (1961), 140–1.

[134] Plaque in church.

[135] *Ibid.*; H.O. 129/457/2/6/12.

[136] H.O. 129/457/2/6/12. Port, *op. cit.,* says 610 pews.

[137] H.O. 129/457/2/6/12; *London Gazette,* 22 July 1862, 5 June 1868.

[138] *Clergy List.*

[139] *Crockford.*

[140] EDP 88/1.

[141] *Census;* H.O. 129/457/2/6/12.

[142] Head, 214–15.

[143] EDP 88/2.

[144] *Ibid.,* 88/1.

[145] *London Gazette,* 1 August 1845; H.O. 129/457/2/6/9.

[146] EDP 90/1.

[147] H.O. 129/457/2/6/9.

[148] *Ibid.*

[149] *London Gazette,* 12 July 1864.

[150] *Clergy List; Crockford.*

[151] H.O. 129/457/2/6/9.

[152] Head, 218.

[153] TS Parish Newsletter, Ascensiontide 1967. The figure does not include Easter Day (26 March) when there were 183 communicants.

[154] Head, 218.

[155] Plaque in church.

[156] Head, 219.

[157] EDP 90/2.

[158] Plaque in church. A plan to move the font to this position in 1928 was opposed by the Diocesan authorities: EDP 90/2.

[159] EDP 90/2.

[160] *Ibid.,* 90/1.

161 White, *Dir. of Ches.* (1860).
162 Head, 224; *Crockford.*
163 White, *Dir. of Ches.* (1860)
164 *Ibid.*; Head, 223.
165 Head, 223; plaque in church.
166 Head, 223, says J. and C. Trubshaw.
167 Head, 224; date on rainwater-head.
168 White, *Dir. of Ches.* (1860).
169 List in church.
170 For the possible origin of the dedication see W. T. F. Castle, *History and Description of Saint Peter's, Congleton,* 13.
171 *London Gazette,* 21 May 1867, 17 November 1868.
172 Head, 164.
173 *Clergy List.*
174 *Crockford.*
175 H.O. 129/457/2/6/11.
176 *Parish Magazine,* March 1967.
177 The architectural description is based on Castle, *History and Description of St. Peter's, Congleton.*
178 See Castle, *op. cit.,* opposite 17.
179 There is a print in Astbury church showing the desk in use, dated 1847.
180 See pp. 210–13.
181 Thanks are due to the Revd. R. Delbridge, the Revd. H. Swindells and the late Revd. E. Goodisson for allowing me to see the documents belonging to their respective chapels, to the Revd. J. C. Bowmer and Miss J. Gilbert of the Methodist Archives and Research Centre, London, to the librarians of Dr. Williams' Library, London, and of the Friends' Library, Friends' House, and to Mrs. M. Noble of the Friends' Meeting House, Wilmslow.
182 Head, 185–6.
183 W. Urwick (ed.), *Noncomformity in Cheshire* (1864), 152.
184 E. Calamy, *Ejected Ministers* (1713), ii, 133.
185 Borough accounts, 1655.
186 *Ibid.,* 1662.
187 Calamy, *op. cit ,* 133; Urwick, *op. cit.,* 153.
188 *Cal. S.P. Dom. 1625–6,* 512.
189 *Minutes of the Committee for the Relief of Plundered Ministers, 1643–54* (Rec. Soc. L. & C., xxviii), 163; B.M., Add. MS. 15670, 194.
190 A. G. Matthews, *Walker Revised* (1948), 90.
191 Quoted Urwick *op. cit.,* xxii–xxiii supposedly based on Walker, but Walker in fact merely states that John Machin was presented to the living in 1654.
192 *Minutes of the Committee for the Relief of Plundered Ministers, 1654–60* (Rec. Soc. L & C., xxxiv), 44.
193 He may have lost it earlier. Matthews (*op. cit.,* 91) says that Machin and Moxon were presented to Astbury in 1652. He refers to his own *Calamy Revised* (1934) but dates these as 1654 (Machin) and 1652 (Moxon). The *Minutes* seem to give the most accurate dating although

266   *History of Congleton*

in a petition of 1660, Hutcheson stated he was ejected in 1652. He died in 1675 and was buried in Astbury churchyard where his grave cannot now be identified.

194 *D.N.B.*
195 *Minutes of the Committee for the Relief of Plundered Ministers, 1643–54,* 167–8.
196 *Ibid.,* 185–6.
197 Urwick, *op. cit.,* 152.
198 *Autobiog. of Henry Newcome,* ed. R. Parkinson (1852), i (Chetham Soc., xxvi), 10–12.
199 Urwick, *op. cit.,* 152–3.
200 *Autobiog. Henry Newcome,* i, 16.
201 *Minutes of the Committee for the Relief of Plundered Ministers, 1654–60,* 44.
202 *D.N.B.* Calamy (*op. cit.,* 128) says Moxon 'became pastor to a congregational church at Astbury'.
203 *Minutes of the Committee for the Relief of Plundered Ministers, 1654–60,* 61. He was appointed lecturer at Astbury and came there in 1653: *D.N.B.*
204 Calamy, *op. cit.,* 128.
205 *D.N.B.*
206 The declaration was withdrawn on demand of the Commons but there was general reluctance to enforce the penal laws and dissenters were comparatively unmolested.
207 G. Lyon Turner, *Original Records of Early Nonconformity* (1911), i, 292; ii, 290, 695; iii, 287, 366, 370.
208 *Ibid.,* 370. Steele seems to have returned to Barthomley shortly afterwards.
209 Matthews, *Calamy Revised,* 29.
210 Lyon Turner, *op. cit.,* i, 522; ii, 698.
211 Somerset House, Returns relating to Dissenters' places of Worship recorded in the Bishop's Court at Chester, 1852.
212 Urwick, *op. cit.,* 156. He says 'on' Dane Bridge which may mean it was very near to the river.
213 Lambeth Palace Library, Tenison MS. 639, fol. 279.
214 Urwick, *op. cit.,* 158; A. Gordon (ed.), *Minutes of the Cheshire Classes, 1691–1745* (1919), 80.
215 *Ibid.* The name Jones appears in some lists between Moxon and Irlam. A. Gordon, *Freedom from Ejection* (1917) quotes in the returns of Dissenting Ministers 1690–2, 'Mr. Jones att Congleton' but in the index (294) suggests that it is possible that Congleton is a mistake for Chadkirk chapel which is not mentioned.
216 Gordon, *Minutes of the Cheshire Classes,* 183. His position appears to have improved. In his will, proved 1748, he left considerable landed estate— 2 cottages and land in Cross St. and property in Buglawton.
217 Urwick, *op. cit.,* 158; G. Pickford, *History of Congleton Unitarian Chapel* (1883), 5. E. Gilmour, *Short History of Congregationalism in Congleton* (1962), 6, gives 1712. A deed in the chapel, dated 1712, records a lease of a house for 21 years for 'use as a chapel', whence the impression that the chapel was burnt in that year. It is more likely that the riot was one of the many throughout England in 1714. The house was leased from

John Jolley who had already registered his house as a dissenter's dwelling house in 1700 according to J.P.s returns to Chester.

[218] The classis had originally been founded in 1653 as the Cheshire Association to bring some order amongst churches following the Presbyterian, Congregational and Independent views. It lapsed after 1660 but was revived in south-east Cheshire and held its meetings at Knutsford. It became little more than an association for licensing ministers although it does appear to have tried to help congregations, as in the case of Congleton.

[219] Dr. Williams' Library, Evans MS.: A Statistical Survey of the state of Dissenting Churches in England and Wales in 1715.

[220] F. Gastrell, *Notitia Cestriensis*, ed. F. R. Raines, pt. i (Chetham Soc. viii), 235.

[221] Lists of Ministers are in Urwick, *op. cit.* 159–61; Dr. Williams' Library, Wilson MS.: Biogs. of Dissenting Ministers; B.M., Add. MS. 24484.

[222] Dr. Williams' Library, Thompson MS.: List of Dissenting Congregations in each county of England and Wales, 1773.

[223] Inf. from the Revd. T. H. Davenport.

[224] Inf. from late Vicar of Mossley; *Cong. Chron.* 26 May 1967. The following description is based on the *Inquirer*, 9 June 1883.

[225] The term Independent was used by Scott to indicate those congregations of a more Calvinistic turn of mind.

[226] W. G. Robinson, *Jonathan Scott* (1961), 8–12.

[227] Document in chapel.

[228] Robinson, *op. cit.*, 12; F. S. Powicke, *Centenary History of the Cheshire Union of Congregational Churches* (1907), 292.

[229] Documents in chapel.

[230] Urwick, *op. cit.*, 160–1; Gilmour, *op. cit.*, 12.

[231] Congleton Congregational Chapel, Minutes of Deacons' meetings; Births, Marriages and Deaths register in church; Gilmour, *op. cit.*, 10.

[232] Letter in chapel.

[233] Minutes of Deacons' meetings.

[234] *Ibid.*; undated cutting from *Congleton Mercury* amongst chapel documents.

[235] Congleton Congregational Chapel, Minutes of the Sunday School.

[236] H.O. 129/20/459.

[237] *Congleton Mercury*, 3 June 1877.

[238] Tablets in church.

[239] Cf. *Congleton Mercury*, 3 June 1877.

[240] Gilmour, *op. cit.*, 20.

[241] W. C. Braithwaite, *Beginnings of Quakerism* (1955), 42.

[242] *Trust Property of Friends within Cheshire*, Monthly Meeting 1855 (copy at Friends' House); C.R.O., Abstract of Trust deeds of Eaton Meeting House, 1737.

[243] Abstract of Trust deeds of Eaton Meeting House.

[244] *Trust Property*, *op. cit.*; Head, 258.

[245] C.R.O., Minutes Cheshire Monthly Meeting, 3 December 1801.

[246] *Trust Property*, *op. cit.*, 1919.

[247] Friends' House, Digest registers.

[248] Head, 258.
[249] Inf. from Librarian, Friends' House.
[250] N. Penny (ed.), *First Publishers of Truth* (1907), 18; Braithwaite, *op. cit.*, 124.
[251] Braithwaite, *op. cit.*, 125.
[252] *Journal of William Caton, 1655,* 9 (1845) (copy at Friends' House), 448.
[253] Friends' House, Yearly return of Sufferings, i, 1654.
[254] *Chester Arch. Jnl.*, NS. xiv, 29–84.
[255] Borough accounts.
[256] *Chester Arch. Jnl.*, NS. xiv, 70.
[257] Quarter Sessions Records, 1559–1760; Rec. Soc. L. & C., xciv, 178.
[258] Lyon Turner, *op. cit.*, i, 170–1.
[259] Borough accounts.
[260] *Cal. S.P. Dom. 1669,* 373.
[261] Borough Order Bk.
[262] J. Besse, *Collection of the Sufferings of the People called Quakers* (1753), i, 106; J. Gough, *History of the People called Quakers* (1789), ii, 406. Head's date, 1690, is inaccurate.
[263] Inf. on individual Quakers is from Digest Registers; inf. on fines and imprisonments is from the vols. of the 'Sufferings' which contain the reports returned annually to London (all at Friends' House).
[264] Borough Order Bk.
[265] *Ibid.*
[266] C.R.O., Minutes Congleton and Eaton Preparatory Meeting, 1694–1737.
[267] C.R.O., Minutes of the Congleton and Eaton Preparatory Meetings.
[268] Borough Order Bk.; RG. 6/1256.
[269] Davies, *Macclesfield*, 325.
[270] Gastrell, *Notitia Cestriensis*, 234, 237, 286, 292, 297.
[271] C.R.O., Congleton and Eaton Meeting.
[272] In C.R.O.
[273] C.R.O., Congleton and Eaton Meeting.
[274] C.R.O., Minutes Quarterly Meeting in Cheshire; *John Churchman's Journal* (1780), 205.
[275] C.R.O., Lancashire and Cheshire Quarterly Meeting, 1938–45.
[276] J. B. Dyson, *History of Wesleyan Methodism in the Congleton Circuit* (1856), 18. For further information on Methodism see Joan P. Alcock, *Methodism in Congleton* (1968).
[277] Dyson, *op. cit.*, 19.
[278] *Journal of John Wesley* (ed. N. Curnock, 1938), iii, 175.
[279] Dyson, *op. cit.*, 19.
[280] *Journal of Charles Wesley* (ed. J. Jackson, 1846), i, 431.
[281] *Journal of John Wesley*, iii, 299.
[282] *Methodist Recorder*, 8 April 1908; inf. from secretary Lancs. and Ches. Wesley Historical Soc.
[283] Dyson, *op. cit.*, 49–50.
[284] *Wesley Historical Soc.*, iii, 116. This was at 27, Mill Street on a site later occupied by the *Admiral Vernon* (now demolished). Head records that in his time it still existed although decayed.

[285] *Methodist Recorder*, 8 April 1908.

[286] Dyson, *op. cit.*, 74.

[287] Somerset House, Returns relating to Dissenting Places of Worship, 1852.

[288] R. F. Wearmouth, *Methodism and the Common People* (1945), 19–77.

[289] *Journal of John Wesley*, v, 86. An earlier note in 1760 refers to 'rough treatment' and a 'scaffold' fixed in the window of the preaching house: *ibid.*, iv, 371.

[290] See also *Proceedings Wesley Historical Society*, iv, 30.

[291] *Journal of John Wesley*, v, 252.

[292] Head, 261.

[293] *Journal of John Wesley*, v, 450.

[294] *Ibid.*, vi, 99.

[295] *Ibid.*, 345.

[296] *Journal of John Wesley*, vi, 443.

[297] H. Bett, *Early Methodist Preachers* (1935), vii, 315.

[298] *Journal of John Wesley*, vi, 14.

[299] Dyson, *op. cit.*, 106; *Proceedings Wesley Historical Society*, iv, 33; *Journal of John Wesley*, viii, 55.

[300] Dyson, *op. cit.*, 105.

[301] Head, 261: 1767; *Methodist Recorder*, 8 April 1908: 1766. *Minutes Methodist Conference* (1766) records an appeal for help (perhaps for building) by the society.

[302] *Journal of John Wesley*, v, 252.

[303] Dyson, *op. cit.*, 73.

[304] *Ibid.*, 89–92.

[305] Accounts for the building are at Wagg Street.

[306] Dyson, *op. cit.*, 130–2.

[307] *Ibid.*, 149.

[308] John Young, *After a Hundred Years* (1903), 131.

[309] Collection of notes at Wagg Street.

[310] H.O. 129/20/457.

[311] Wagg Street Chapel, Minutes of the Circuit Quarterly Meetings. For a projected reorg. of circuits in 1969, see n. 317 below.

[312] Circuit Accounts, 1860–1920.

[313] Quarterly Meeting, Minutes, 1870–1903; Circuit Accounts, 1808–60.

[314] The minute books of the respective chapels are at Wagg St.

[315] J. Young, *After a Hundred Years* (1903), 34.

[316] Minutes of the Local Preachers' Meetings, 1896–1918.

[317] Since this book went to press a union of the Wesleyan and Primitive Methodist circuits has been arranged for Sept. 1969. The Biddulph chapels will join a new circuit.

[318] J. T. Wilkinson, *Hugh Bourne* (1953) (the best biog. of Bourne), 45; A. Wilkes, *Mow Cop and the Camp Meeting Movement* (1942), 11–12.

[319] H. B. Kendall, *The Origin and History of the Primitive Methodist Church* (n.d.), 530.

[320] J. Howe (ed.), *The Mow Cop Story* (souvenir handbook) (1957). This work also has a photograph of the Cloud chapel before the alteration of 1958.

[321] *Primitive Methodist Church Cloud* (souvenir programme) (1957).
[322] Trustee Indenture, *penes* Minister, Kinsey Street Chapel.
[323] Wilkinson, *op. cit.*, 67.
[324] Kendall, *op. cit.*, 540.
[325] Somerset House, Returns of Dissenter Meeting houses, 1852.
[326] *Primitive Methodist Magazine* (1822), 155; (1832), 235; (1833), 195; (1834), 65–7; (1841), 285.
[327] Kendall, *op cit.*, 538.
[328] *Primitive Methodist Magazine* (1838), 266; (1839), 436.
[329] Wilkes, *op. cit.*, 87–8.
[330] *Primitive Methodist Magazine* (1868), 102.
[331] H.O. 129/457.
[332] *Cong. Chron.*, 25 May 1905; Wilkinson, *op. cit.*, 137, 156.
[333] Documents in Kinsey Street Chapel.
[334] *Cong. Chron.*, 25 May 1907.
[335] Minutes of the Circuit Meeting.
[336] *Cong. Chron.*, 18, 25 May, 1 June 1907; 31 May 1957; Howe, *op. cit.*
[337] Local inf.
[338] H.O. 129/457.
[339] Minutes of Baptist Sunday School, 1858–77 (in private hands).
[340] *Baptist Handbook*, 1885, 1886, 1887, 1888, 1889. Congleton is not mentioned after 1889.
[341] *Kelly's Dir. Ches.* (1892); local inf.
[342] J. E. G. Cartlidge, *Newbold Astbury and its History* (1915), 106, quoting Astbury parish registers.
[343] *Notitia Cestriensis, op. cit.*
[344] *Congleton Advertiser*, 8 September 1860.
[345] Local inf.
[346] H.O. 129/457.
[347] Somerset House, Returns relating to Dissenters' Places of Worship, 1852.
[348] Bagshaw, *Dir. Ches.* (1850).
[349] Somerset House, Register of non-parochial Meeting Houses, 1961.
[350] Inf. from G. Shenton Esq.
[351] Inf. from the pastor.
[352] Thanks for help in the compilation of this section are due to Fr. K. Molloy, St. Mary's, Congleton, Fr. E. M. Abbott, Acton Burnell, Shrewsbury, Fr. G. T. Bradley, St. Patrick's, Bradford, Dr. R. W. Dunning, W. H. Semper, Esq., and M. Proudlove, Esq., of Congleton.
[353] R. Challoner, *Memoirs of Missionary Priests* (1924 edn.), 142–5.
[354] *Catholic Record Society*, liii, 189.
[355] *T.H.S.L.C.*, cvi, 105–8. Painted lettering in the chapel is dated 1629. See pp. 311–12.
[356] The incident is recorded in a pamphlet entitled *Strange News from Staffordshire* (London, 1642). See *Staffordshire Catholic History*, i, 20–3.
[357] Head, 25.
[358] *Quarter Sessions Records for the County Palatine of Chester, 1559–1760* (Rec. Soc. L. & C., xciv), 178.
[359] EDA 6.

[360] C.R.O., Astbury Churchwardens' Presentments, 1706.

[361] *Ibid.*, 1728, 1729; EDV 7/1/70 (1778); 2/63 (1789); House of Lords, Main Papers, Returns of Papists 1767 and 1780. There was one at Sandbach in 1780.

[362] EDV 7/6/401.

[363] *Ibid.*, 7/141.

[364] For this paragraph see Head, 247; *Diocese of Shrewsbury, 1851–1951: Centenary Record*, 60, 72–3. For the opening of St. Mary's see *Macclesfield Courier*, 29 July 1826. The registers at St. Mary's date from 1822.

[365] In 1851 there were 142 free sittings, 100 other, and free space or standing room for 40: H.O. 129/457/2/6.

[366] See B. Little, *Catholic Churches since 1623* (1966), 51. For a view of the church in the 1880s see Head, 248.

[367] *Dioc. of Shrewsbury, 1851–1951*, 60; Head, 249.

[368] See below, p. 279.

[369] Head, 247; inf. from M. Proudlove Esq., of Congleton (1967).

[370] *Dioc. of Shrewsbury, 1851–1951*, 60.

[371] There was no house in 1828: see below.

[372] Head, 247; Roman Catholic Diocesan Archives, Curial Offices, Leeds, Orrell to Bp. Smith, 17 February 1828. He had a small private income, but he claimed that this made things worse since people imagined him to be richer than he was.

[373] See list of priests to 1887 in Head, 247–9.

[374] Roman Catholic Diocesan Archives, Council House, Shrewsbury, Jas. Anderton to Bp. Briggs, 22 October 1839. This states: 'it is rather more than a year since you entrusted Nantwich in addition to Northwich to my care'.

[375] Middlewich was served from Runcorn by 1842, Nantwich from Chester by 1843, and Northwich from Runcorn by 1847: *Dioc. of Shrewsbury, 1851–1951*, 74, 77, 81. None appears in the Congleton Bapt. Reg. after 1842.

[376] *Rep. Mun. Corps.*, 2657.

[377] Shrewsbury Dioc. Archives, Anderton to Briggs, 22 October 1839.

[378] 1846, 20; 1847, 27; 1848, 39; 1849, 43; 1855, 49: St. Mary's Bapt. Reg. 1822–55.

[379] H.O. 129/457/2/6.

[380] For this paragraph see Leeds Dioc. Archives, Orrell to Smith, 17 February 1828; Shrewsbury Dioc. Archives, Anderton to Briggs, 22 October 1839; *Catholic Dir.* 1842, 30.

[381] *Staffordshire Advertiser*, 14 March 1829.

[382] *Macclesfield Courier*, 9 November 1850.

[383] Congleton Corporation minutes, 27 November 1850.

[384] *Macclesfield Courier*, 21 December 1850.

[385] Inf. from M. Proudlove, Esq. (1967).

[386] Inf. from Father K. Molloy, St. Mary's, Congleton (1967).

T

VII *Education in Congleton*

by E A G Clark

Before the Nineteenth Century

Until the nineteenth century the story of education in Congleton is virtually that of the ancient grammar school. There were parish and charity schools in the neighbourhood, for example at Astbury[1] and Odd Rode, but there are no references to similar schools at Congleton. It is surprising that a town with over 4,000 inhabitants in 1801 should have been without any facilities for non-classical education, and possibly the townsfolk used the Astbury parish school. In a will of 1792 money was left to help pay for 'the schooling (and books if necessary) of boys living in the township of Congleton who were thought too lame to be put apprentices to the common handicraft trades, and who showed a disposition and capacity for learning, in order to give them such an education as might fit them for country schoolmasters, or clerks in a counting house'. The free charity school at Odd Rode was established in 1681. A later deed defined its objects: 'for the educating and instructing of poor children belonging to the said township or to some of the adjacent townships, in the principles of the Church of England . . . and to read, write, and cast accounts, and other proper and useful learning for poor children'. At the beginning of the nineteenth century the school was rebuilt by Mr. Randle Wilbraham of Rode Hall. His wife and daughters managed the girls' side of the school, said to be 'the best conducted girls' school in the country'.[2]

The early history of the grammar school is obscure, and all documents relating to its foundation have disappeared. The earliest town accounts in 1584 show that the corporation was then already responsible for maintenance, and from the seventeenth century regular quarterly payments to the master are recorded. In the nineteenth century the borough was involved in a law suit about the school, and an extensive search was made in the records to try to establish its title. Lawyers drew attention to references in the town accounts of 1588 to 'the old schole' and to the carrying of 'small tymbers of the olde Scholehouse into the other schole' referred to in 1600.[3] These extracts prove that a new grammar school was erected near the old one in the 1580s, and therefore the origin of the school must be looked for much earlier in the century, if not before. When the grammar school finally closed in 1901, A. F. Leach, pioneer historian of the English grammar schools, searched the national records to see if something more definite could be found about the borough's title to the school, once again the subject of controversy. He discovered one new document of interest, a decree of 1583 in a suit by the duchy of Lancaster for the town lands. This mentioned as one of the purposes of the town lands, 'the maintenance of the free school of the town and the payment of the school master'.[4]

The names of the schoolmasters since 1584 are listed in the borough accounts and have been printed by Head and others. Nearly all were in holy orders, and the office was usually combined with a local curacy or living. A frequent entry is 'paid … for saying service and teaching scholars'. The early masters were young men, straight from Oxford, who held office for two to four years only. In 1612, for example, payment was made to Robert Shawe for 'bringinge downe Mr Cappes from Oxford'. Three years later there was another payment 'for goinge to Oxford for the Scholemaster'. Robert Newcome was appointed master in 1640 at the age of twenty, and seven years later his brother, Henry, at the same age. Henry left the headship to be reader to the rector of Astbury, and then became incumbent of Goostrey. A local scholar who became master was John Newton, son of a local shoemaker, who was recommended to the corporation by two ministers as having 'sufficient abilitye for a Schoolmaster'.[5] After the Restoration the school was rebuilt,[6] but it continued to provide free schooling for the children of burgesses.[7]

Little is known of the character of education in the seventeenth century apart from several references to the production of a play on Shrove Tuesdays. We must suppose that, like other small grammar schools, elementary work in Latin was most important. The succession of fledgeling schoolmasters ended in 1709 with the appointment of Ralph Malbon, who had left Oxford more than a decade before and had been working as usher at Macclesfield Grammar School. He held the headship until 1721. For the first time there was an assistant master or usher, and Malbon was permitted to supplement his salary by 'what he could make of country scholars and perquisites'.[8] Malbon wrote a detailed account of how he ran the school. He took boarders into his own house, and on Sundays met them to read the Bible in Greek, Latin and English. 'We begin our school every morning with Latin prayers . . . the six Head classes speak Latin while they are in the school or playground, and give an account of all lessons and exercises in Latin. I give out a ferrule every morning and noon to a custos. Whoever speaks English, receives it with a blow. And I punish him myself in whose hands I find it att noone or night.' Sunday sermons received much attention. All boys wrote out the text in English, Greek or Latin, while older boys presented a plan of the sermon, 'as near as they can remember in the preacher's very words'. Absentees from the church service had to 'gett by heart . . . some part of a chapter in the Bible. This makes them less fond of loytering at home'.[9]

Malbon was succeeded by his son and former pupil, Thomas, who ran the school for 56 years, in Head's words, 'leaving it as small in numbers and scholarship as it was great under his energetic father'.[10] His successor, Jonathan Wilson, was also vicar of Biddulph and wrote a successful grammar book.[11] He had about 60 pupils.[12] Meanwhile the school's endowments had been increased by gifts of land.[13]

An early nineteenth-century description of the grammar school shows the changes which had taken place since the days of Ralph Malbon and his obsession with spoken Latin. The curriculum was now much broader, including writing, arithmetic, merchants' accounts, French and geography, if required. The school was now open to the neighbourhood with fees of 15*s* a quarter, but the sons of freemen were still in theory permitted to learn Latin and Greek without charge. There were now twelve boarders who paid 40 guineas a year.[14]

In the eighteenth century Congleton had one or two small

dissenting academies and schools, though these failed to outlive their founders. Dr. Edward Harwood, a Unitarian minister and associate of Joseph Priestley of the famous Warrington Academy, kept an academy at Congleton between 1754 and 1765, and one of his pupils, John Palmer, went on to Warrington to study divinity.[15] John Ball, at whose house in Wagg Street John Wesley is reputed to have stayed, had a boys' school there.[16] Another Congleton schoolmaster of the second half of the eighteenth century was Samuel Pattison, who is listed in the *Universal British Directory* of 1791.

The Nineteenth Century
In the early nineteenth century Sunday schools were the chief medium of education for the children of the poor. A parliamentary return of 1819 stated of Congleton that 'the children of the poor are very generally employed in the mills or cotton manufactories but they avail themselves of the Sunday Schools, being their only means of obtaining instruction'.[17] At least two public day schools had been established by 1840, but the Sunday schools were still said to be 'the principal schools . . . for the silk factories, upon which the Factory Acts enforce no limitation as to the age of children employed, detain them from resort to day schools'. Wages were so low that it was essential for children to contribute to the family budget.[18]

There were Sunday schools in Astbury parish as early as 1789, when 200 children attended,[19] but there is no mention of a school at St. Peter's church until 1828, and the Wesleyans seem to have founded the first school in the borough in 1799. Dyson, writing half a century later, details the numerous moves of this school, from Moody Street to Wagg Street and then to High Street, before premises were built near Wagg Street chapel in 1818. But a valedictory address given when Wagg Street chapel was rebuilt in 1869 told a rather different story. The school began in a day school in Wagg Street, belonging to John Ball, a friend of John Wesley, moved to a garret in the same street, to a mill near the town pump ('town pump school'), to a building in Hare and Dog Yard ('the floor of which fell in one Sunday while the scholars were in school'), and finally to Wagg Street.[20] With three large classrooms the school could accommodate 800 children. It cost £665 to build. One of the thirteen trustees attended the site daily during the building, and an old minute book in the chapel records the fines levied when members failed in this duty.[21]

Rules published in 1818 provide an insight into the activities of this school. There were five managers, who kept order, divided the children into classes, allocated the teachers and checked the bibles, spelling books and writing equipment. Visitors were appointed to keep in touch with the homes and check on the reasons for any absence. The 'writing room' was the apex of the school. Here were grouped the best pupils, and when a place became vacant it was filled on reading ability. The children attended from 10 to 12 a.m. and from 1.30 to 4 p.m. Attendance on five successive Sundays earned 'Cards of Honour'. Three of these could be exchanged for a certificate, and three certificates won a religious text. The rules reveal a suspicion that the children were already contaminated by sin. Swearing, lying, quarrelling and calling nicknames were stipulated as offences warranting expulsion if repeated. No talking or reading aloud was permitted.[22]

The school played an important part in the history of 'the then vexed question of writing on the Sabbath'. The committee pledged themselves to abide by the majority decision, but when the vote went against Sabbath observance the defeated party threatened to resign. The majority, however, refused to go back on their decision, and in 1837 the dissidents went over to the Methodist New Connexion, taking their pupils with them.[23]

Most other denominations and churches built Sunday schools in the early nineteenth century—the Independents in 1810, for example, the Primitive Methodists in 1823, and St. Peter's in 1828.[24] In the 1830s Wagg Street had 629 pupils, St. Peter's 380, the Independent chapel in Mill Street 300, the Countess of Huntingdon's Connexion (on the corner of Moor Street and Park Street) 210 and the Primitive Methodists 200. There were three Wesleyan schools at Buglawton with 393 pupils.[25] There was, too, a Sunday school attached to St. Mary's Roman Catholic church.[26] With more than 2,000 children attending Sunday school, most of the children in the borough must have been receiving some rudimentary education, for even following compulsory school attendance later in the century it was 1879 before the number of children on the books of the borough's day schools exceeded 2,000.[27]

When public day schools were established, the Sunday schools lost their importance for secular education. Alterations in the Wagg Street Sunday school rules show the change in emphasis. The great end was 'to train children and young persons in the doctrines, privileges and duties of the Christian religion'. The children were taken to divine service, and the teachers urged 'to seek by all means in their power to lead their scholars to a saving knowledge of Christ Jesus'.[28] By 1851 the children were no longer attending Sunday school for the whole day but came for the morning or afternoon or evening sessions. With 790 pupils the Church Sunday schools (St. Peter's, St. James's, St. Stephen's, St. John's, Buglawton) were rivalling the nonconformists. Wagg Street Wesleyan Sunday school had 150 pupils, and there were Wesleyan Sunday schools at Brook Street, Buglawton (150 pupils), Key Green (95), and in a factory at Havannah (44). The Primitive Methodists had Sunday schools in Lawton Street (208 pupils), and Mossley (40), the Methodist New Connexion in Queen Street, the Independents (82) and the Unitarians (30) in Mill Street, the Baptists at Zion Chapel (13), and the Roman Catholics at St. Mary's (60).[29]

More Sunday schools were opened in the second half of the nineteenth century. The Primitive Methodists had premises in Kinsey Street and Butt Lane, the Methodists in Rood Lane, and the Congregationalists in Antrobus Street.[30] The Unitarians opened a large new school in 1865, and this was so well attended that another classroom was added four years later.[31] Congleton had its own Sunday School Union,[32] and the schools played an important part in official processions and celebrations.

Public elementary day schools had a late start in Congleton, but once the churches had founded day schools in the decade following 1838, they bore the burden of popular education until well into the twentieth century. The *Congleton Advertiser* boasted in 1861 that 'Congleton has reason to be proud of her National [i.e. Church] Schools; not only because they furnish a safe and cheap daily receptacle for the children of the operative classes . . . but . . . because they offer a sound English education, at quite a nominal cost'.[33] It was not the fault of the churches that the schools they contributed so much to build and run eventually became inadequate for the needs of the borough.

A day school opened in St. Peter's Sunday-school building in 1837, with a grant from the National Society.[34] Boys were taught in a large upstairs room, and the girls and infants downstairs were divided by a partition—'consequently they overhear each other most inconveniently'. The school was supported by voluntary contributions, weekly fees of 2*d* or 3*d* and, after 1846, it entered the new pupil-teacher scheme and received a substantial annual grant from the government. In 1851 a government inspector found the master teaching 'his first class very fairly, but . . . quite unskilled in the art of governing and organizing a school'. He was pleased with the mistress, 'who appeared to have a conscientous desire to do her work well'. The following year, however, he discovered that she was not 'sufficiently in advance of her pupils'.[35] The connection with the Sunday school was not as close as might have been expected. In 1849 less than half the children attended both schools, and over 200 went to Sunday school only.[36]

When three new Anglican parishes were established in the 1840s a day school was set up in each case. The parish of St. James was constituted in 1844 and the National Society gave £300 towards the erection of a school room in Booth Street (alternatively referred to as the school in Astbury Street).[37] A government inspector was impressed; he reported that 'the boys' school under Mr. Wood and his two pupil teachers, is in an efficient condition', while the girls' school was 'very fair', though handicapped by the admixture of infants. His advice was taken, and a separate room for infants was added in 1853. Most of the children at St. James's were half-timers from the silk mills.[38] In 1861 a new boys' school was opened in North Street, the girls' and infants' departments continuing in the Astbury Street premises.[39]

St. Stephen's National School opened in 1859 in Spragg Street. It had been a nonconformist place of worship and was purchased by the Established Church in 1840. The conversion to a school cost £1,361, towards which the National Society gave £100 and the government £367.[40] The two school rooms were fitted with galleries, permitting collective teaching to the whole room, and on its first government inspection there were 'some loose desks, ill arranged'. Standards of instruction were moderate: 'This school has suffered from neglect consequent on the change of incumbent and frequent change of masters.' The teacher was well qualified, 'but has yet to learn the necessity of patience and gentleness in the treatment of children'. The

a Big Fenton Farm, Buglawton, *b* Big Fenton Farm, chapel

a

b

Crossley Hall Farm, Buglawton

a Georgian houses, Moody Street, *b* classical façade, Bridge Street

a

b

a

b

inspector refused to recommend the school for the training of pupil teachers.[41]

Mossley National School was built opposite Holy Trinity Church in 1845, at a cost of £910, towards which the government contributed £250 and the National Society £265. The Revd. James Brierley, the first incumbent, was a major benefactor.[42] The school did not enter into the pupil-teacher scheme at first, and was maintained by school pence and voluntary contributions. Fees ranged from 2*d* to 6*d* per week according to subjects studied, and some children were admitted free (in effect probably paid for by the vicar or parishioners).[43] Because of the school's peripheral position in the borough, it catered for children from Biddulph, Whitemoor and Congleton Edge also.[44]

In 1838 a day school was opened in the large Wesleyan Sunday-school building in Wagg Street.[45] It entered the pupil-teacher scheme in 1853. In 1877, for example, £168 out of a total income of £387 came from government grants, while school pence brought in £110. The children paid 2*d*, 3*d*, 4*d* or 6*d* a week.[46] A new school was built in 1869, with four classrooms and a large room of 78 feet by 30 feet divided by a partition. The cost was £950, but the Wesleyans sacrificed help from the government so that they could have a school of their own design, with more space for Sunday-school activities. Such was the local support that the debt was almost cleared in a year.[47] Pupils came mainly from such streets as Astbury Street, Lawton Street, Wagg Street, Canal Street and Mill Street.[48]

In 1848 the Catholic Poor School Committee granted £15 to St. Mary's, to adapt the Sunday school as a day school.[49] A new school was opened in West Road in the 1850s with accommodation for 150 children. Fees were 2*d* a week. The school was not restricted to Catholics, and operated a conscience clause for religious instruction.[50] Protestants were in the majority. When religious teaching was in progress they sat in the same room, 'and read secular books but received no religious instruction of any kind'.[51] St. Mary's was enlarged in the 1870s and became grant aided.[52]

The six voluntary schools mentioned so far were the foundation of elementary education in the borough for 80 years. Other sects had schools for shorter periods. A day school opened at the Independent chapel, Mill Street, in 1861. Fees were 2*d* to

4*d* a week, or 2*d* half-time, and the curriculum included geography, history and natural history as well as the three Rs.
The school was not grant aided. When £29 was collected for
the school at a service the *Congleton Advertiser* commented that
the amount proved 'the power of the voluntary principle, and
the determination of the friends to be free from government aid
or control'.[53] In 1850 there were small day schools attached to
the Wesleyan chapels at Key Green and Daneinshaw.[54]
Another Wesleyan Sunday school which developed as a day
school was Brook Street. Erected by Joseph Steele and others in
1866, it opened in 1869. There were two classrooms downstairs for infants, and a large room upstairs for older pupils.
Steele's daughter was the first teacher and the promoters
declared their intention of fulfilling the government conditions
for grant aid. Brook Street continued as a day school until
1927.[55]

An elementary school of a special type was the Parochial
Union School for pauper children. This was in the workhouse
at Arclid. A government inspector was impressed with the
standard of the boys in 1850, when he reported that 'the school
master must . . . have a greater aptitude for teaching than many
who have gained higher Certificates'. A decade later, however, a similar inspection found the children 'in a low state . . .
they appear to be unusually dull'. But the inspector was being
rather severe on these neglected little children. As the chaplain
of the workhouse explained, 'it should be kept in mind that the
inmates of workhouses are generally people of the very lowest
class . . . the constant change . . . in workhouse schools is
another great drawback . . . of the 20 boys, only 13 were above
the age of six years . . . 14 had been admitted within the previous six months . . . of these only four had previously been in
any school for a period exceeding six months'.[56]

The elementary schools had many features in common, as a
comparison of their log books shows. The clergyman was usually the schoolmaster's mentor and most faithful unpaid
teacher, giving lessons in the three Rs as well as scripture, and
helping to give the children a trial examination before the
annual visit of the government inspector. In one week in February 1879, for example, the Revd. J. M. Bannerman examined
the upper standards of St. Stephen's school in geography on
Tuesday afternoon and Wednesday morning, and Standard II

on Thursday afternoon. He regularly called at the school three or four times a week at this period.[57]

Schooldays were brief for most youngsters. In 1860 it was reported that 'in this town and neighbourhood, the great majority of children leave the day school when they are eight years old, to work as half timers [i.e. in the mills]. They continue at school for half a day, until they are eleven, when they leave entirely and go to full work'.[58] In 1857 there were only five girls over eleven at St James's.[59] An inspector regarded as a major factor in the relatively low standard of education in Congleton in the 1870s, 'the imperfection of the law which allows children to work in the factories as half-timers at eight . . . as full timers at eleven'.[60]

Fees ranged from 1½d to 6d per week, according to subjects taken, and payment was a distinct hardship for the very poor. The log books record children absent for a while because parents were out of work or on short time. In 1872 one boy was forced to withdraw from St. Stephen's because he lost his pence in school. Lack of suitable clothing and footwear in bad weather affected attendance. On rare occasions children were admitted free or their fees paid by the vicar or the guardians of the poor. Other reasons for fluctuations in attendance were many—heavy rain, snow, floods, the demands of harvesting or potato picking, a waxworks or circus passing through town, an outbreak of scarlet fever.

Head teachers were certificated. In the mid-century they were receiving about £50 per annum and a house.[61] The larger schools had assistants, also certificated. In addition there were pupil teachers, who were apprenticed for five years and paid a salary rising from £10 to £20 per annum. Those who were successful in the Queen's Scholarship examination went on to training college. Pupil teachers were supposed to receive instruction. At St. Stephen's they did two subjects for homework on five nights a week, and were taught by the headmaster daily between 6.30 and 8 a.m. Sometimes the strain of doing an adult's job while still adolescent told on the pupil teachers. A girl at St. John's National school, Buglawton, was warned by the vicar for administering corporal punishment. In the same month she was hauled before the managers for absence, failure to do homework, and 'for the sullen and defiant behaviour she has lately shown'. Schools also employed stipendiary monitors, some of whom became pupil teachers when they reached thirteen.

The log books provide many insights into syllabuses and methods. Heads recorded their worries and successes. At St. Stephen's in 1890, for example, it is recorded, 'some of the children in the 3rd and 4th Standards seem to have gone backwards even in the week. Had to go over old ground, before advancing'; and in 1892, 'keeping a keen eye on the younger teachers: they are inclined to push past the earliest stages of Arithmetic and to get on to the Reading Books'. The log books record despair for writing that sloped backwards, puzzlement about difficulties in decimal multiplication, pleasure in the introduction of new textbooks. They also contain lists of the poems that were learnt by heart by each standard, the songs that were sung, and the objects employed in the object lessons —earthenware, beds, matches, candles, hardware and soap at Buglawton in 1885. The St. Stephen's log books show the gradual supercession of slates by exercise books, with the older pupils purchasing their own books to expedite their home lessons in 1867.

Punishments included caning, detention and written work. The cane was much used at St. Stephen's, the head noting with satisfaction in 1869, 'cane not used in school for eight days past'. Expulsion was the ultimate sanction. In 1874 the head of St. Stephen's expelled a boy for insolence and a girl for showing to her classmates an impertinent note about the teacher written by her father on her slate. Public shaming was used with effect. In 1868 'one little girl was found guilty of taking a knitting needle from another, and taking it home. Occasion was taken . . . to set before the children the great sin of stealing.' Small wonder that a parent wrote to St. John's, Buglawton, in 1907: 'I should esteem it a favour if you would be lenient with Stanley when he fails to do his lessons, as he seems afraid to come to school as we have been disturbed with him at nights screaming.'[62] Rewards figure less frequently in the log books, but St. Stephen's experimented with the issue of tickets for good work, twenty entitling the holder to a half holiday.

Funds were constantly short at the voluntary schools, and the government grants, which made up a third or more of the income,[63] were vital for the continued existence of the school. The various government grants depended on the inspector's report, and in the era of payment by results the log books record an obsession with overall standards in the three Rs, working up to a climax as the teachers and the clergyman tested and coached the children in the days before the inspection. In March 1885 the head of St. Stephen's recorded 'children excited and fidgetty: asked them . . . to try to forget the Examination until Monday morning'. For their part, inspectors kept up standards and tensions by threats and warnings—'the lowest merit grant is recommended with much hesitation' (1886); 'Better results will be looked for in the Elementary subjects next year' (1892).

Educational standards clearly varied from school to school and from year to year, and it would be possible to select inspectors' reports to bear out a thesis of excellence or its reverse. But on the whole the schools had good reports in the years before the 1870 Education Act. St. James's National School in particular had a long run of good reports. An inspector commented in 1856 that 'the children have passed an excellent examination' and in 1857 stated that 'I was very much struck with the thoughtfulness and interest in their work displayed by the boys'. In 1861 he found that 'the spirit and tone of all the schools are admirable', and in 1869 that 'this is an excellent school; the instruction and general efficiency afford . . . proof of the great pains and labour on the part of Mr. Wood towards his scholars . . . the elementary subjects are taught in this school with great care and success . . . the failures which are very few, are pretty equally distributed among the standards, as to indicate no particular defects'.[64]

The 1870 Education Act had fewer repercussions in Congleton than in most towns. Though a school board was set up, Congleton was one of the few boroughs in the country that did not establish its own board schools.[65] The voluntary schools continued to educate the children of the poor.

The town council welcomed the 1870 Act and resolved to seek powers to set up a board. Compulsory attendance was felt to be very desirable, and one councillor instanced a family in Silk Street where the children were sent out to steal instead of going to school. But there was some opposition to the Act in the town, and a public meeting nearly reversed the council's decision, on the grounds that there was sufficient accommodation already.[66] The first school board election took place in

1870. There were 21 candidates for the seven places. The religious bodies were careful to use the multiple vote wisely, and the successful candidates were three churchmen, and representatives of the Wesleyans, the Unitarians, the Primitive Methodists and the Independents. One disappointed candidate complained to the *Congleton Mercury* that the Church party employed 90 paid canvassers, and on the election day used a public house as headquarters, as well as 'the mill screw applied in a rather more disgraceful manner than usual'. The Wesleyans had three candidates in the field, but panicked two hours from the closure of the poll and packed for one only.[67]

The first school board was provided with statistics of school accommodation and attendance. In the seven elementary schools there was room for 2,266 children and with 1,359 on the rolls and an average attendance of 972, there was apparently some justification for the conclusion that 'there was more than sufficient accommodation for all the children of the town, without the establishment of additional schools'. A government inspector, however, was more sceptical and insisted that there was a lamentable shortage of separate accommodation for infants.[68]

Thus with no urgent need to build schools, the main concern of the school board was with attendance. The principle of compulsion was adopted in 1871, when it was alleged that 270 children in the borough were brought up in ignorance. Another estimate was that one-third of the children were educationally destitute. A by-law made attendance compulsory from 5 to 13, but children over 10 who had passed Standard IV could attend half-time.[69] Half-timers numbered 204 in 1892, and included domestic half-timers as well as mill workers. A government inspector commented wryly, 'to help at home or mind the baby is an easy cry to touch the heart of an attendance committee'.[70] The board appointed an attendance officer, and 31 parents were prosecuted up to 1876.[71] By 1879 the average attendance had increased from 972 to 1,499, all at the cost of £725, or less than a rate of $\frac{3}{4}d$ in the pound.[72] As we have seen, inability to pay fees led to some absenteeism but though the board had powers to remit fees they did not do so. In 1876 these powers were transferred to the guardians of the poor, who paid for several children when trade was bad.[73] Fees were virtually abolished in 1891, and the board warned parents that in future attendance would be strictly enforced.[74] In 1894 it was 76 per cent.[75]

After the excitement of the first election most of the triennial elections were not contested. In one year an informal meeting of candidates, summoned by the mayor, led to the withdrawal of the required number, so that the burden on the rates of contested elections could be avoided.[76] The Church party usually had three representatives.[77] In 1876 there were two Wesleyans, and the board was completed with a Roman Catholic and a Unitarian. Religious prejudice was rife, and when the Catholic died, only the Unitarian favoured electing another Catholic to take his place.[78] A wag remarked that only one member of the first board was a father,[79] but a more serious criticism was that the board was packed with the friends of the voluntary schools. As a 'Working Man' put it in an election broadside, 'they are all Denominationalists. They will represent their own Sectarian Schools . . . the only seven schools in the borough. They will have power to fill their own schools and keep them up at the expense of the Ratepayers . . . a Tory Mayor and a Tory Town Clerk fixed the time of polling to prevent working men voting. Tories are no good.'[80]

In 1879 there was a movement to abolish the school board and hand its functions to the town council, on the grounds that elections were costly and made bad blood. Presumably a desire to keep down the rates won the scheme support in the council. But the friends of the board hastened to its support. A petition referred to 'the secret and hurried way in which the matter had been dealt with in council, with only 10 out of 24 present'. The *School Board Chronicle* put the blame on the town clerk, 'who appears to speak for the Town Council and to be allowed to do very much as he likes with that corporation'. Wilson revealed his motives at a meeting. The council, he claimed, 'wanted to be lenient with the people, instead of erecting costly offices; for the people to be fed, rather than starving them for education'. From the chair the mayor diplomatically admitted that 'the opinions of the meeting were so nearly divided that he could not distinguish on which side the majority lay'. He supported the status quo, and the motion was withdrawn.[81]

After 20 years of existence the school board made a real effort to improve facilities as well as attendance. It suggested

that the council should raise a rate under the Technical Instruction Act to support evening continuation schools.[82] The
board opened classes at Wagg Street (for men) and Astbury
Street (for women), and an additional centre was opened in
Cross Street in 1894. Apart from the three Rs, the curriculum
included history, music, geometry, drawing and needlework.
About 70 men and 25 women attended, mainly of the 14–21
age group. The examinations of the Union of Lancashire and
Cheshire Institutes were taken.[83]

What were the achievements of the school board? On the
credit side, attendance improved considerably, though in 1876
an inspector poured cold water on the board's claim that attendance had increased by 468 in five years. He proved that if
achievement and not attendance were the test, the number presented for examination at the four largest schools in the borough
was the same in 1876 as it was in 1870, while the number of
passes had fallen.[84]

The truth of the matter was that with their obsession with
keeping down the rates the school board had little zest for improving standards or making innovations. Its boast in 1888 was
that only in one year had the education rate exceeded $\frac{3}{4}d$ in
the pound.[85] There was no board school to compete with the
voluntary schools. Improvements depended largely on more and
better qualified staff, which the voluntary bodies were unable
to afford. The board was under pressure from the beginning. An
inspector reported that 'much as he had been prepared by the
low standards . . . in other places, he was scarcely prepared for
what he witnessed at Congleton'. Out of 2,000 children, only
379 were presented for examination, and only 61 of these were
above Standard III.[86] He reported in 1880 that 'Only half the
children in the borough were presented for examination . . .
until the by-laws are more rigorously enforced, it will be in vain
to look for improvement'. The pass rate was falling—from 74
per cent in 1876 to 65 per cent in 1880. Congleton had the
lowest pass rate of nine Cheshire towns in 1894 (89 per cent in
reading, 63 per cent in writing and 59 per cent in arithmetic,
compared with 95, 85 and 87 per cent at Middlewich).[87]

The log books of St. Stephen's National School show how
the local schools were falling behind the standards achieved in
the areas of the large school boards. They begin on a happy
note in 1869: 'this school is in an efficient and satisfactory state

. . . in charge of a painstaking master'. The following year the inspector was concerned because so few of the children were presented for examination in the higher standards. He returned to this charge in 1873. In 1878 he commented that the school was 'in fair order considering the crowded state . . . but there is a marked and general weakness in the elementary work'. Year after year he was critical of the work with the older children, until finally he wrote in 1885: 'Of the rest I cannot speak at all favourably. The papers are excessively wanting in style and neatness, and the failures in Arithmetic are excessively numerous. Writing is poor and spelling uniformly bad. Much better results will be looked for in another year as a condition of an unreduced grant.' Things improved for a couple of years, but in 1889 the threats began again: 'Geography is too poor for any grant to be recommended . . . My Lords will look for a more favourable Report on spelling and arithmetic next year.' It must have been so dispiriting for the headmaster (who had a first-class certificate) and the vicar, struggling to run a school of 150–200 children with one female assistant and two pupil teachers. And another note was beginning to appear in the inspector's reports. Like the other voluntary schools of the borough, St. Stephen's was suffering from overcrowding and inadequate premises. A government report remarked of the senior school in 1910 that 'the building is a very poor one on the whole, and does not admit of permanent improvement . . . it would be better to abandon the hope of preserving it'.[88]

At the grammar school the Revd. E. Wilson succeeded his uncle as master in 1810, holding the mastership in conjunction with the living of Odd Rode for most of his 34 years of office. In 1814 the corporation built a new grammar school for £400, on a site donated by Sir Edmund Antrobus. In consideration for this and for the help given by the corporation for the enlargement of the headmaster's house, Wilson agreed to give up the ancient stipend of £17 per annum. The new school could accommodate 80 boys, and numbers rose from 30 in 1810 to 70 in 1818. In the 1830s there were 68 pupils. Sons of burgesses were paying 15*s* a quarter, and the charge for non-burgesses was a guinea. There were some 12 to 18 boarders, paying 40 guineas a year. The burgesses' sons were learning Latin, and four were said to be studying Greek. The rest of the curriculum included the three Rs, elementary mathematics and merchants' accounts,

French and geography. Wilson was assisted by his two sons at one period, and other under masters included several who went on to benefices.[89]

Wilson left the school when he succeeded to the living of Buglawton in 1844. The right to nominate a new master was claimed by the charity trustees who denied the right of the recently reformed corporation. A lengthy lawsuit began, and the school closed for a while. The decree in Chancery upheld the right of the charity trustees, but the corporation was permitted to nominate a candidate, and was held responsible for maintaining the school house.[90] In 1848 the Wilbraham Foundation was established for the education of three boys at the grammar school, as a memorial to Mr. Wilbraham of Rode Hall, to commemorate the 50th anniversary of his tenure of the high stewardship of Congleton.[91]

When the grammar school was inspected in 1867 by the Schools Inquiry Commission there were no boarders, because of the position of the house between a churchyard and a cemetery. Most of the 47 day boys entered the school between the ages of six and ten, and seldom remained for more than two years. The curriculum was described as 'semi-classical', but only the rudiments of Latin were taught, and there were only three boys learning Greek. Reading and writing were well taught, but history, geography and arithmetic 'imperfectly'. Fees were four guineas a year, while Drill was an extra at 24s a year. Only eight pupils learnt French, for which they paid four guineas a year. There was only one teacher, the Revd. W. B. Grix. The commissioner attributed the rather low standards of the school to lack of staff. 'Without some assistance it is hardly possible for the master to teach subjects so various to so many boys, themselves of many varieties of age and progress.' The punishments used resembled those used at the elementary schools— lines, impositions, learning by heart and corporal punishment (administered in public). There was two hours preparation per night. About a third of the boys were of what the commissioners called 'Social Class A' (independent, professional, mercantile), and two-thirds of 'Class B' (farmers, shopkeepers). Of the parents listed, five were millowners, and the others included surgeons, solicitors, shopkeepers, a head gardener, a wood turner and a silk throwster.[92]

Grix was headmaster for 46 years. He was an enthusiastic

oarsman and cricketer in his youth, and closely connected with the Volunteers, rising to major in the 5th Cheshires. His favourite riposte to his pupils was *mens sana in corpore sano*. Generations of his pupils paid respects to his memory and tried to keep the school in being after his death in his 73rd year in 1901, but half a century later an old pupil painted a more realistic picture of him as a martinet: 'I have feeling memories of Mr. Grix's signet gold ring which before he cuffed one he turned round so that the knob came in contact with our heads . . . the language is unprintable what we used to say about the pupils who subscribed for his solid gold ring to be given on his birthday . . . he was a strict disciplinarian especially with regard to cleanliness and punctuality. We country lads always felt we had a raw deal, we had no washing facilities at school, and had to go down the Cockshutts to Old Grannie Foxes . . . if by any chance we were a minute late we were well cuffed . . . the less said about the teaching the better.'[93] After Grix's death in 1901 the school closed.[94]

A number of private schools catered for the range of social classes above the labouring poor. Early in the nineteenth century there were 'Ladies Academies' in Wagg Street, Chapel Street and Moody Street.[95] The vicar of Biddulph ran a private grammar and commercial school. In 1815 he advertised for 'a young man who writes a good hand, and is capable of teaching Geography . . . he will have an opportunity of being instructed in the Latin, French and Greek languages'.[96] There was another school with a commercial bias at Eaton, where reading and writing was taught for 7s 6d a quarter, accounts for 5s, and book-keeping for 15s.[97] In 1852 there were fourteen dames' schools in the Congleton district, charging fees of 2d to 8d a week. A directory of this period lists two in Moody Street, and others in West Street, Kinsey Street and Lawton Street.[98] Later in the century there were genteel schools at High Town (Ladies' Seminary), Moody Terrace (Mrs. White's Young Ladies) and number 13 Wagg Street.[99] After the closing of the grammar school its place was taken to some extent by Victoria College, Congleton. This school had been founded in 1884,[100] and its history is detailed in the following section.

Night schools for young workers were held in several of the elementary schools in the nineteenth century. St. James's National School had an evening department from 1846. The curriculum resembled that of the day school, 'but by their own choice, the chief portion of their time is given to arithmetic'. There was a cultural side also. The Revd. J. Wilson related that 'some of them are really good singers . . . a relation of mine (an attorney) has taken great pains with them, and none of the musicians have gone wrong in moral conduct. The old piano . . . jingles away, and it is wonderful how soon and how much they learn on it. The young men's musical class has lately developed into a brass band.' Wilson found these lads a good recruiting ground for Sunday-school teachers, and some of them went on to fill 'respectable places as clerks, upper servants in factories, etc.' The teacher, an out-of-work silk weaver, was paid £10 a year plus school pence. Wilson found it difficult to replace him for 'the teacher *must* be a clever, energetic fellow, and a really superior man, or he will never do for a town like this'.[101] Under Mr. and Mrs. West the reputation of the night school flourished, and in 1865 it was described by a government inspector as the best in Cheshire. The pupils competed for the examinations of the Union of Lancashire and Cheshire Institutes, and had a drawing class which received a grant from the government Science and Art Department. Two-thirds of the youths were old boys of the day school.[102] Evening classes were also held at St. Peter's, Wagg Street, Buglawton and Rood Lane schools.[103]

The mechanics' institute movement reached a peak in the mid-nineteenth century, when there were almost 700 in the country, a quarter of these being in Lancashire and the West Riding.[104] An institute opened at Swan Bank, Congleton, in 1848. There were 171 members paying the subscription of 2s 6d a quarter in 1851. The aims of the new society, like those of its contemporaries, were grandiose: to instruct the members in literature and the arts and sciences; to establish a museum, a library, a collection of scientific implements; and to start classes in elementary subjects. Its patrons included the Marquis of Westminster and Mr. Randle Wilbraham of Rode Hall.[105] But political dissension ruined the institute, which was dissolved in 1857. Its president admitted that numbers were decreasing and debts increasing, because 'party is the madness of the many for the pain of the few'.[106] A new committee, which pointedly referred to themselves as 'working men', re-opened the institute in 1858 on a revised tariff and without aristocratic patrons. It was now 'entirely under the control and management of working men'. The subscription was now 1*s* 6*d* a quarter for working men, and 10*s* for tradesmen. There was a reading room taking seven daily and thirteen weekly papers. The library had 900 books and boasted an annual circulation of three times that number.[107] Lectures were sponsored, and local clerics came to inform members on the catacombs of Rome, and the morality of Socrates.[108] The institute was the most lively cultural centre of the borough. There were regular winter readings of poetry and prose both instructive and humorous, and interspersed with songs. Large audiences 'testified their approbation by repeated cheering and laughter'. The institute was getting too small for these free meetings. In December 1865, 'the room was crammed to suffocation, many being not only unable to get into the room, but within a reasonable distance of it'. The instructional side of the institute was not neglected.[109] Contacts developed with the Union of Lancashire and Cheshire Institutes, and students competed for its examinations.[110]

In spite of the popularity of the free meetings, formal membership of the institute remained small, and it was wound up in 1871.[111]

A number of more ephemeral classes catered for the varied cultural and instructional interests of the citizens. Music teachers and language teachers advertised for custom in the local newspapers in most years. In 1865, for example, a Dr. Muller gave French and German classes at Priesty Cottage, Priesty Fields.[112] A Dr. Orges from Manchester sought custom for German classes, travelling to many towns in Cheshire.[113] A music teacher taught tonic sol-fa choral singing in the Queen Street school room at a charge of 1*d* a week for class membership.[114] In 1869 the Congleton Ladies Education Association engaged a Professor Nichol to give a series of lectures on English literature. Forty enrolled, including several 'gentlemen'.[115] In the 1890s there were the evening classes of the school board, already described, and a number of technical instruction classes, including advanced art, tonic sol-fa, and tool-using at Joseph Worrall's workshop in Park Street.[116]

Public lectures were a regular occurrence in the winter months. Subjects included: the health education of England, panoramic views of Switzerland, the Indian mutiny, Old English signs and sayings, popular education in Holland, and 'the

world a great school'.[117] A lecture on the life and labours of
John Holworth delivered at the Baptist chapel, continued for
an hour and a half, when the lecturer 'found that he had
enough unread material for another lecture, which the chairman
suggested should be given on another occasion'.[118] In the 1860s
'Penny Readings', 'calculated to suit every taste, intellectual,
serious and humorous', were given before crowded audiences.
At the end of one season the *Congleton Advertiser* commented
that 'these entertainments were designed to develop the intel-
lect of the working man . . . whether its character was grave or
gay, humorous or sentimental, the behaviour of the working
class of Congleton . . . was always commendable'.[119]

The Twentieth Century
Under the 1902 Education Act the school boards were replaced
by Local Education Authorities (L.E.A.s). Counties and county
boroughs were now responsible for elementary and higher
education, while borough and urban districts with over 10,000
and over 20,000 inhabitants respectively were eligible for
recognition as the Authority for elementary education, dealt
with under Part III of the Act. Congleton was only just large
enough to qualify as a 'Part III' authority, and many citizens
preferred to hand over the responsibility to the county, an
arrangement calculated to save half the education rate, as well
as bringing all education in the borough under one large
authority. But negotiations began for Part III status without a
formal debate in the council. Details of the proposed Education
Scheme were published by the *Congleton Chronicle*, and a lively
debate ensued. Alderman Solly, leader of the High Church
Tory group, objected because the church schools, which
catered for most of Congleton's children, would be under the
control of a committee on which Free Churchmen and Liberals
would be in a majority. Nevertheless control over local schools
and the spending of the education rate had an undeniable
appeal, and the council voted by 12 to 6 to become a Part III
authority. Powers were delegated to an education committee,
made up of ten councillors and seven co-opted members experienced in local educational matters and including representatives of the Church (two) and nonconformist (one) schools
and an elementary-school teacher.[120]
    The new L.E.A.s had greater powers than the old school

boards. Apart from maintaining the board schools (where they existed), now known as council schools, they were responsible for the maintenance of the voluntary (Church and Chapel) schools, although the provision and repair of buildings remained the responsibility of the denomination. Thus for the first time rate aid was available for the hard-pressed Church and Wesleyan schools of Congleton. Yet though some members of the education committee were eager to help their own denominational schools, economy was the main concern of the town council, which had the final say on all money matters. It was well known in Whitehall that 'the L.E.A. has consistently aimed at saving the rates'. Rate aid was kept down to little more than 30 per cent of the income of the authority, well below the national average, and expenditure per head was half the Cheshire average.[121]

The legacy of the school-board era was not a happy one. School buildings were overcrowded and in want of repair. There were no board schools and the authority had to start from scratch in the provision of council schools. This it was loath to do. A long drawn-out war of attrition began between the L.E.A. and the Board of Education, which kept up a remorseless pressure on the borough to conform to national standards. In 1925 an interdepartmental memorandum observed that 'for many years . . . we have been endeavouring by moral pressure and occasional suspension of grant to induce Congleton to deal with the very serious arrears in the provision of accommodation and equipment, and in staffing'.[122] For their part, the L.E.A. had little time for the gentlemen of Whitehall, who seemed to care little for the financial difficulties of the small Cheshire industrial town, and who appeared insatiable in their demands for improvements. The constant harping on sanitary conditions irritated many, and led one councillor to ask, 'what qualification do they have in sanitary matters?'[123] Negotiations were complicated by the fact that the schools belonged to the voluntary bodies and not to the council. The education committee usually passed on the problem to the school managers, warning them that if matters were not improved, the committee would 'cease to recognize the premises as a public elementary school'. Mutual recrimination added to the delay. At one school, it was reported that 'the relations of the managers and the L.E.A. are particularly bad . . . both sides behave with great stupidity and neither has much consideration for the Head Master who is steadily losing his grip on the school'.[124]

The Board of Education concerned itself with tangible deficiencies in accommodation and premises rather than the less easily assessed question of educational standards. A general inspection of premises was ordered in 1908. A government inspector reported that, St. Mary's School apart, 'nothing has been done to remove the more serious structural and sanitary defects in the school buildings'. St. Peter's School had no playground, and the lavatories were reached through the street. At St. Stephen's the lavatories and cloakrooms were without ventilation, and there was no playground, 'a clayey site being used that is some short distance from the school . . . the building in which the elder scholars are taught is a very poor one . . . it would be better to abandon the hope of preserving it'. Mossley school was condemned, and the managers considered restricting it to senior pupils only. The Wesleyan schools were likewise in a bad state. Wagg Street was grossly overcrowded, with 296 children in a school with room for 180. The new chapel lecture room was used as a temporary classroom. As for Brook Street, 'the managers cannot be recommended to spend money on this school'.[125]

The Board insisted that the L.E.A. should prepare a comprehensive scheme for improvement.[126] A conference of managers was summoned. The voluntary system was warmly espoused, but some thought that it was time to give up senior schools to the L.E.A., leaving the church schools as junior schools. The Wesleyans were prepared to surrender Wagg Street, or make it a junior school. As for Brook Street, 'the action of the Board of Education for the past few years has been such that there appears no hope of permanently retaining the school'. But they were persuaded to make minor alterations to keep Brook Street open, and it lingered on, alternately condemned and reprieved, until 1927.[127] The L.E.A. was granted some respite in 1912, when a new council school opened at Buglawton. Until then, over 100 Buglawton children had attended Brook Street.[128]

The church schools were less resigned to handing over to the L.E.A. They formed a Joint Schools Committee which drew up a plan to save the three central church schools at a cost of £4,000. St. Peter's and St. James's were modernized by 1916, and work on St. Stephen's was completed in 1920. The committee could with reason boast that through their efforts they had saved the council the expense of building new elementary schools at a cost of £20,000.[129]

Meanwhile the Board of Education kept up pressure on the L.E.A., though its hands were tied somewhat by the wartime emergency. In exasperation one inspector recorded that 'Congleton had allowed its schools to be disgracefully understaffed . . . they are so deliberately negligent, and have been . . . for so long that they no longer believe . . . that the Board will bring Part III Authorities to book'.[130] The education committee had a shrewd idea of what was being said behind their backs, and a member commented that 'it would be better if some of these officials were employed doing work of national importance instead of dictating to the Education Committee'.[131] Both sides of the dispute were victims of a mistake by parliament in thinking that a small borough could be a viable education authority, especially one whose staple trades were going through difficult times, with hundreds unemployed or on short time.

The parsimonious approach of the education committee had a bad effect on the recruitment of teachers. 'The scale of salaries is not attractive; teachers are therefore either born or bred in the borough, or introduced from the Potteries. The latter come in daily by train, and resign as soon as a better post can be obtained.' On the whole the schools were staffed at the minimum level permitted by the Education Code. The cost of teachers per pupil was among the seven lowest for authorities in the country.[132] Forty-six out of 57 teachers were women in 1916. Only two of the schools had more than one certificated teacher in 1909, and when the managers tried to appoint another they met with resistance from the L.E.A.[133] Pupil teachers were still used because their salary was one-fifth of that paid to certificated teachers, but the headmaster of Buglawton school wrote to the press: 'Parents, I ask you how you like the prospect of your children still remaining in the hands of these well meaning though often most helpless child teachers?'[134] After the war there was an improvement. Pupil teachers were no longer engaged and 29 out of 54 teachers were certificated in 1921.[135]

In 1920 the surrender of Part III authority status was again considered. The L.E.A. was anxious to co-operate with the county in building a central school to serve Astbury, Hulme Walfield, North Rode and other country schools as well as

Congleton, where it was thought that there would be 150 pupils who would benefit from a more advanced course. The L.E.A.'s post-war scheme also included the building of a council school for 580 children. The merger with Cheshire fell through when it was realized that the borough's schools would have to be brought up to scratch first, and the central-school scheme was shelved.[136]

In this period the L.E.A.'s problems were complicated by the establishment in 1920 of a branch of the National Children's Homes at West House (which formerly housed Victoria College: see below). The managers of the Home wanted to use Congleton schools. This meant that more than a hundred extra places would have to be found at an additional cost to the ratepayer. Understandably, there was strong support for Alderman Solly's view that 'this orphanage should educate its own children or it should be a charge on the state. It was a most extraordinary thing to dump down other people's charity on Congleton and expect the town to bear the expense.' The L.E.A. excluded the West House children from its schools, but the Board of Education ruled that their action was illegal and unreasonable. Eventually the L.E.A. was accommodated by an agreement whereby a claim was made by its officers to the child's home district.[137]

Meanwhile a deputation from the borough went to London. For the Board Sir Edward Phipps took the opportunity to discuss the general question of education in the town. 'The Board's statistics showed that Congleton was in a most unfortunate position. They were almost at the bottom of the list judged by the amount they spent on education per child. The level of elementary education was so low as to be hardly compatible with the Board's requirements. Three of their school buildings had for years been in a most unsatisfactory condition.' The L.E.A. employed more uncertificated teachers than the average authority, and its classes were larger. 'It is the deliberate opinion of the Board based on the reports of several inspectors for some years past that Congleton had one of the lowest standards of educational efficiency in the country.' It was imperative that the L.E.A. prepare a scheme and give an earnest of their good intentions.[138] Criticism was not confined to Whitehall. One of the Wesleyan managers wrote to the *Congleton Chronicle*, complaining that by not replacing Wagg Street in 1905 the committee 'had made a fetish of economy and neglected efficiency . . . they like the proverbial ostrich buried their heads in the sand and brought extra expense to the town'.[139]

The council agreed to build a new school at a cost of £27,000, to take the children from Wagg Street and Brook Street, both long condemned. The new school was opened officially in April 1927 by Lord Eustace Percy, President of the Board of Education. He made good humoured references to the fact that Congleton was well known at Whitehall. Some Congletonians were a little disturbed because there had been no official reception for Lord Percy, and wondered whether it would have been more hospitable if more councillors had shaken him by the hand.[140] Nevertheless the occasion marked the beginning of more cordial relations with Whitehall, and the town now had a custom-built school, the first built for more than half a century.

The Board of Education continued to press for more places. In 1930 the council put forward a scheme for the construction of another senior school and the reorganization of the non-provided schools as junior schools. The churches were loath to give up their senior departments but after protracted negotiations they agreed. A new Boys' Senior School opened in Waggs Road in 1937, and the New Street Council School became the Senior School for Girls.[141]

It is difficult to generalize about educational standards in the elementary schools in the early twentieth century. Clearly until the 1930s, at least, the teachers were handicapped by antiquated premises, overcrowded classrooms and a shortage of equipment. An inspector reported in 1908 that the L.E.A. was not providing domestic and manual subjects, 'nor will it be possible until the L.E.A. is prepared to equip the schools better'. Twenty years later the borough was the only district in the north of England where these subjects were not taught.[142] At St. James's school the senior assistant taught the three top standards, some 70 children, in one room, while three of his colleagues taught 129 children in a narrow room 66 feet by 18 feet.[143] Small wonder that children lingered in the lower standards. Yet some schools did well in spite of the drawbacks. After the final inspection at Wagg Street the managers called the head teachers in to congratulate them on the excellent report received.[144] His Majesty's Inspector wrote of St. Stephen's in 1938 that: 'both rooms lack the lightness and airiness of the modern school premises, but the teachers are to be congratulated on the way in which by flowers and pictures so much is done to make them as attractive as possible. There is a very friendly tone in the school. Progress in the essential subjects is distinctly satisfactory . . . the results are neat but formal.'[145] In contrast another school had no records or syllabus, 'the children . . . apparently spend a great deal of time copying from the blackboard and from books. Some of the matter . . . is quite outside the . . . interest and comprehension of the children.' An inspector observed the head in action: 'the third lesson was a rambling discourse in which he supplied the information, asked questions and as a rule supplied the answers in part or in whole.'[146]

Some of the teachers' names were household words to generations of Congletonians, serving for all their career in one or two of the local schools. Mrs. Mary Bayley was connected with St. Stephen's for 60 years as a pupil and then as a teacher. Her headmaster, A. W. Charlesworth, taught at the school for 40 years, and previously had been a pupil teacher and an assistant master at St. James's. E. H. Davis was headmaster at St. Peter's for 35 years. In 1944 a self-styled 'old timer' looked back on his experiences at St. Stephen's in the days of 'payment by results': 'then there were those awe inspiring days when the government sent a Mr. Glendenning to inspect us. Those were the days when no compulsion was needed to make us wash our necks and be properly deloused, and to go to school in our Sunday best . . . I remember nothing directly but I suppose some of the three Rs must have seeped in under the constant pressure of the urge of Billie's cane, which often followed his flashing blue eyes.' Poor Mr. William Williams, First Class Certificate, a most concientious headmaster, who confided to his journal his unrelenting attempts to improve standards in the three Rs, wrote in 1886, 'Standard I progressing a little: the number of apparently immovable ones is dispiriting.'[147]

Details of other schools in the twentieth century are more difficult to find. After the headmaster's death in 1901 a conference between the town council and the Charity Commissioners was convened to discuss the future of the grammar school. Though there were many regrets on the part of the townsfolk, the general feeling was that 'for want of funds the school has become completely obsolete and out of date, not at all suitable for present day education', and that the building could no

longer be used as a school. There was a local movement to
re-open the school temporarily, but the Charity Commissioners
were adamant. The issue was complicated by attempts to link
the old grammar-school and the Wilbraham Foundation with
schemes for secondary and technical education in the town.
The Charity Commissioners favoured a mixed secondary school,
with provision for technical classes in the evenings. At a later
conference the directors of Victoria College entered the lists,
offering to develop their boarding school as a secondary school
aided by public funds and to award scholarships to local elementary schools. But the college fees were too high for local
shopkeepers' sons, the college itself was too peripheral, and its
managers were unwilling to yield to the town council a controlling interest in management. Once again it became clear
that the grammar school was doomed. In vain H. L. Reade,
former chairman of Congleton School Board, asked 'Why
should they let this little school fall out of use, and the corporation evade their responsibilities?' The mayor argued that to
re-open the school temporarily might complicate the issue of the
technical school, and would certainly cost the council £150 to
put the old building into repair. Meanwhile more than half the
grammar-school pupils had transferred to Macclesfield Grammar School.[148]

Attention now switched from the old grammar school to the
various proposals for a secondary or technical school. A site in
Market Street, originally selected for a technical school, was
adapted for the erection of a handsome new grammar and
technical school, that is to say, technical classes would use the
building at night. Plans were approved by the county council
and by the Board of Education, and articles of government
were drawn up, regulating the appointment of governors and
staff. Among the papers of the Board of Education the scheme
can be followed through to the drawing boards and the detailed
consultations as to architectural arrangements. It was a tragedy
for Congleton that the scheme got no further. Powerful persons
at Whitehall were opposed to the scheme, as a minute of 1908
shows. It refers to the 'intricate confusion of the Technical
School and Grammar School proposals. This confusion enabled
the local people to press for an unnecessary Grammar School
by urging the needs of a Technical School, and an unnecessary
Technical School by urging the needs of a Grammar School.

The proposals of either school would not stand a moment's investigation on the financial side.' Earlier an official had commented on a Cheshire County Council scheme for building a secondary school at Congleton: 'there can be no secondary school at Congleton—there are not sufficient suitable children to make one. Perhaps 30 or 40 might be obtained who really want secondary education. But they can easily go to Macclesfield for it.'[149] Congletonians continued to travel to Macclesfield for a grammar-school education for more than half a century. In 1921, for example, 55 children travelled daily from the town to attend the King's School and the Girls' High School there.[150]

Some private schools tried to develop secondary work. The largest of these was Victoria College. This had been founded in 1884 as one of the schools of the Cheshire and North Staffordshire Wesleyan Middle Class Schools Association. It occupied West House and stood in extensive grounds of more than 20 acres to the west of the town, and had large playing fields. In 1901 there were 35 boarders and 12 day boys, and a preparatory department for boys of 7 to 11 years. Wesleyans predominated, but members of other denominations were welcomed. Most of the boarders came from Manchester, Leek, the Potteries and elsewhere in the north-west midlands. The staff comprised three graduates, including the headmaster, L. M. Penn, a certificated teacher, two music teachers, and an ex-army colonel for physical training. The pupils were prepared for the Cambridge Locals and the Universities, but few boys stayed after the age of fifteen. Fees were three guineas a term for day boys, and twelve for boarders.[151] As we have seen, when the grammar school closed Victoria College made an unsuccessful bid to become the public secondary school for the Congleton district. The school was evidently in financial difficulties and closed soon afterwards. The headmaster, L. M. Penn, became head of another private school in the district, at Mossley Hall, and this was regarded as the descendant of Victoria College.[152]

Another private school with ambitions for secondary status was Halcyon College, the successor of Miss Broadhurst's long-established school in Wagg Street. About 1909 it moved to a large three-storied house standing in its own grounds. Boarders were taken at thirteen guineas a term, special arrangements being made for 'the entire care of Indian and colonial children, orphans and wards'. The children hailed from as far afield as Haverfordwest, Cork, Glasgow and Germany. There were 51 pupils, including 17 boarders. In 1909 the proprietor applied to the Board of Education for recognition of Halcyon College as a secondary school. But a government inspector was not impressed by the standards. Apart from the French mistress and one teacher with matriculation, the staff of five was completely unqualified, and the standard of the top class was 'working towards the Oxford Junior Certificate'. No recognition was granted. Two years later another application was made. The new principal, daughter of a Welsh vicar, submitted as support for her claim an imposing brochure, headed by the names of aristocratic patrons. Two of the staff had now passed the Intermediate examination but the Board was still adamant.[153]

Another girls' school of this period with a less academic approach was Congleton Ladies College, a boarding and day school 'for the daughters of gentlemen'. A well-qualified staff taught art, dancing, music, elocution and modern languages.[154]

After the first World War there were four private girls' schools in Congleton. Halcyon College had become the Mount School, Newcastle Road, and had 50 to 60 pupils. The premises at 13 Wagg Street were maintained by Miss Ward. Miss Kennersley had a school in Albert Chambers, while Miss Jackson was head of Meadows House School.[155]

When the school board was replaced by the Part III Authority in 1905 its evening schools came under the county council. A 'higher education' committee for the borough was set up. Art and science classes continued at 7 Swan Bank, and there were dressmaking, book-keeping, shorthand and continuation classes in the elementary schools. Local teachers made up more than one-third of the pupils at the science classes. The evening classes served a useful function. In a decade 1,806 pupils passed through the schools.[156] There were complaints, however, of low standards, and a Board of Education report in 1908 showed that these were well grounded. 'A determined effort is needed if the Congleton Evening schools are to be improved, more especially as the present method of conducting them is sanctified by the tradition of years of ineffectiveness . . . the Evening schools present a spectacle of badly organized classes, with badly adapted curriculums, badly attended.' At St. James's, for example, 37 enrolled, but attendance fell to two or three in

January. Likewise at St. Peter's, 'the most striking feature of the schools was the waste. Students came for a week or two and after sampling the classes left.' The inspector was convinced that the organizers failed to grasp the nature of the local demand for further education, which was essentially vocational and technical.[157] It is clear that the town lost much by the failure of the technical school scheme at the beginning of the twentieth century.

Evening classes with a technical and commercial bias continued in the inter-war years.[158] The old grammar-school building was pressed into service once more. Opportunities for adult education became wider when a branch of the W.E.A. was established in 1917. Classes were non-vocational, literature, philosophy, psychology and economics being popular.

Under the 1944 Education Act the Part III Authorities were abolished. Congleton's schools became the responsibility of the county, which in 1945 delegated powers to a Divisional Executive for south-east Cheshire. There was a lot of leeway to make up. The borough had two recently constructed secondary schools, but the primary schools dated from mid-Victorian times. It was decided to build new secondary schools and to convert the old buildings for use as primary schools. In 1949 a plan was put forward for building twin secondary schools, a grammar school and a county college on a campus on the Holmes Chapel Road. It was hoped to begin the girls' secondary modern school in 1953, but more than a decade passed before the twin schools were opened, the boys' in 1964 and the girls' in 1965. Waggs Road school was modernized, re-opening as Marlfields Primary School in 1968, and the Quinta Primary School opened in the West Heath district in the same year. It is intended that one by one the antiquated church schools will be replaced. St. Peter's closed in 1967, and St. Stephen's is under sentence. As elsewhere in Britain, the reorganization of primary education seemed too slow for many parents and teachers. In 1949 the old grammar school and Brook Street Sunday School were pressed into service to take overflow classes from St. Peter's and St. Stephen's. In 1967 a member of the Divisional Executive complained that 'it was farcical that a school built in 1845 was still the only one providing educational facilities in the Mossley area'.

Meanwhile in the secondary field the institution of the '11

a Mossley Church of England Primary School, *b* Quinta Primary School, Ullswater Road

a

b

Plus' examination brought concern about the lack of grammar-school facilities. About 8 per cent of the age group was receiving a grammar-school education in 1947, compared with 20 per cent in other Cheshire towns. The council put forward a scheme to purchase Buglawton Hall and convert it into a grammar school, but the county felt that this would prove too costly. The success rate remained much lower than the county average. The *Congleton Chronicle* commented: 'the fault does not lie with the children and is entirely due to the inadequacy of local grammar-school accommodation'. A fine Girls' Grammar School was, however, opened in 1957, serving a wide catchment area in south-east Cheshire. The boys also ended the long connection with Macclesfield, and henceforward those selected through the '11 Plus' examination attended Sandbach School.

We have now surveyed some 400 years of education in Congleton. The principal actors have been the clergy who founded and supervised most of the schools, leavening the pabulum of elementary Latin or the three Rs with Biblical stories and precepts, and the teachers themselves, some of whom stand out clearly over the centuries. Ralph Malbon, for example, who on the eve of the Industrial Revolution insisted that his pupils used Latin in the playground, and ingeniously delegated powers of corporal punishment to prefects who struck out when they heard their mother tongue; Grix, with his Latin tags, turning his gold signet ring to the fore before cuffing pupils for untidiness or unpunctuality; Mr. and Mrs. West whose night school for lads from the silk mills was reputed to be the best in Cheshire; William Williams at St. Stephen's, a martinet with flashing blue eyes and following cane who drilled classes of 60 in the three Rs, but whose log book revealed the intelligent concern with methods and the nagging dissatisfaction with results that mark the dedicated teacher.

After 1870 educational provision in Congleton fell below that of larger or more fortunate towns. The grammar school dragged on, a 'one teacher school' incapable of providing a proper secondary education, and when it closed in 1901 the town had to wait for half a century for a worthy successor. The Mechanics' Institute was wound up in 1871, and the technical evening classes started by the school board in the 1890s were a poor substitute for the technical school which did not get beyond the

drawing boards. Congleton's mid-Victorian elementary schools
had no board-school rivals, and in 1901 the Part III Authority
inherited the results of 30 years of neglect by local government
in this field. The Local Education Authority was pressed and
cajoled over the years by the Board of Education, but its limited
financial resources were a brake on progress, and though two
council secondary schools were built in the inter-war years, the
greatest improvement came when the Part III Authority handed
over to the county. For the long period of educational doldrums
it is more charitable to blame historical forces, notably the
trade recession and the imperfections of the Part III Authority
scheme, rather than the council and its ratepayers. One thing
seems likely; the provision of education in the borough in recent
years may well be better in all fields than at any other period
in its history. Local government, Whitehall and the local
churches and chapels have made their distinctive contributions
to this achievement.

Notes

[1] D. Robson, *Some Aspects of Education in Cheshire in the Eighteenth Century,* (Chetham Society, 3rd series, xiii), 191.
[2] *31st Rep. Charity Commissioners,* Parl. Paper (1837–8), xxiv, 693, 695–6.
[3] Head, 236; Ed. 35/212, 18, 19.
[4] *Cong. Chron.,* 14 December 1901.
[5] Head, 236–41; town accounts.
[6] *Ibid., c.* 1670; Head, 236.
[7] *Notitia Cestrensis* (Chetham Society, viii), i, 239.
[8] J. Corry, *History of Macclesfield* (1817), 200.
[9] Head, 242–3.
[10] *Ibid.,* 244.
[11] Robson, *op. cit.,* 183.
[12] EDV 7/1/70.
[13] Robson, *op. cit.,* 49.
[14] N. Carlisle, *Endowed Grammar Schools in England and Wales* (1818), i, 107.
[15] Robson, *op. cit.,* 73, 74.
[16] Head, 262.
[17] *Digest of Parochial Returns to select Committee on the Education of the Poor,* Parl. Paper (1819), ix, 73. Additional information on nonconformist Sunday schools is in the section on Protestant nonconformity, above.
[18] *Rep. Handloom Weavers* (1840), 339.
[19] EDV 7/2/63.
[20] J. B. Dyson, *History of Wesleyan Methodism in the Congleton Circuit* (1856), 114; *Congleton Mercury,* 26 June 1869.

21 Dyson, *op. cit.*, 138: Minute Book of Trustees during Erection of Wagg Street School, 1818 (Wagg Street chapel records).
22 *Address of the Committee of the Methodist Sunday School, Congleton* (Congleton, 1821) (pamphlet among Wagg Street chapel records). Thanks are due to the minister of Wagg Street chapel for making available books and documents.
23 Dyson, *op. cit.*, 159–60; H. F. Matthews, *Methodism and the Education of the People, 1791–1851* (1949), 67.
24 Bagshaw, *Dir. Ches.* (1850); S. Lewis, *Topographical Dictionary of England* (1851).
25 *Rep. Mun. Corps.*, 2657; *Education Enquiry Abstract*, Parl. Paper (1835), xli, 67. See also *ibid.*, p. 59.
26 *Pigot's National Commercial Dir.* (1834).
27 *Congleton School Board* (1888) (pamphlet in Wagg Street chapel records).
28 *Rules of the Wesleyan Methodist Sunday School, Congleton* (n.d.) (pamphlet in the Wagg Street chapel records).
29 H.O. 129/457.
30 *Congleton Mercury*, 2 October 1869; *Congleton Advertiser*, 21 April 1894; *Congleton Mercury*, 28 August 1869; Head, 257.
31 *Congleton Mercury*, 25 September 1865; 6 March 1869.
32 *Congleton Advertiser*, 29 July 1865.
33 *Congleton Advertiser*, 26 October 1861.
34 White, *Dir. Ches.* (1860); *30th Annual Report of the National Society* (1841), 35.
35 *Min. P.C.* (1851–2), 456; (1852–3), 864; Ed. 7/8 Preliminary Statement, St. Peter's National School.
36 National Society, *Results of the Return to the General Inquiry into the State and Progress of Schools for the Education of the Poor* (1849), County of Chester section, 3.
37 *34th Annual Report of the National Society* (1845), 27; Bagshaw, *Dir. Ches.* (1850).
38 *Min. P.C.* (1851–2), 436; (1852–3), 864.
39 *Congleton Advertiser*, 6 July 1861.
40 Bagshaw, *Dir. Ches.* (1850); *38th Annual Report of the National Society, Extra Paper* (1849), 26; *Min. P.C.* (1850–1), 284.
41 *Min. P.C.* (1851–2), 437; (1852–3), 864.
42 Bagshaw, *Dir. Ches.* (1850); Head, 223; *Result of the Return to the General Inquiry, op. cit.*, 3; Ed. 21/2085.
43 Ed. 7/8, Mossley National School.
44 Ed. 16/16, Supply File, item dated 4 December 1913.
45 Ed. 7/8, Wagg Street.
46 Summary of Attendance, Income etc., Wagg Street Day Schools, from 1867 (Wagg Street chapel records).
47 *Congleton Mercury*, 2 October 1869; 13 August 1870.
48 Attendance Book, 1854–61 (Wagg Street chapel records).
49 *1st Report of the Catholic Poor Law Committee* (1848), 59.
50 White, *Dir. Ches.* (1860); Ed. 7/8, St. Mary's Church School. The first source says the building took place in 1851, the second in 1858, and this latter date is confirmed by Head, 248.

51 Ed. 21/2088.
52 Head, 241; *Min. P.C., passim.*
53 *Congleton Advertiser,* 27 April and 16 November 1861.
54 Bagshaw, *Dir. Ches.* (1850).
55 Ed. 21/2085; Ed. 7/8, Brook Street; *Cong. Chron.* 5 February 1927.
56 *Reports relating to the Education of Pauper Children,* Parl. Papers (1850), xliii, 50, 188, 273; (1852–3), lxxix, 662; (1862), xlix, 572, 578, 591.
57 The log books of the public elementary schools of Congleton are in the custody of the headmasters. Unless otherwise stated, references to log books in succeeding paragraphs are to those of St. Stephen's, Congleton, and St. John's, Buglawton. I am indebted to the headmasters of both these schools for the loan of the volumes.
58 *Congleton Advertiser,* 1 December 1860.
59 *Ibid.,* 23 January 1858.
60 *Min. P.C.* (1872–3), 132.
61 Salaries given in Ed. 7/8, Preliminary Statements for the various schools. It is difficult to estimate some salaries, as at St. James's School, 'the pence paid by the scholars is received by the teachers towards their salaries, who take the risk whether it is less or more'; *Congleton Advertiser,* 29 April 1865. By the end of the century the head of the large Wagg Street School was earning £150 p.a., and the assistants between £22 10s and £40 p.a.: Wagg Street School Account Ledger, 1890–1903.
62 Letter enclosed in log book of St. John's, Buglawton.
63 Wesleyan Day School Account Book, 1867–96 (Wagg Street chapel records).
64 *Congleton Advertiser,* 18 October 1856; 23 January 1858; 26 October 1861; *Congleton Mercury,* 1 May 1861.
65 *School Board Chronicle,* 22 August 1884, 538.
66 *Congleton Mercury,* 10 September and 12 November 1870.
67 *Ibid.,* 26 November and 24 December 1870.
68 *Ibid.,* 31 December 1870; *Min. P.C.* (1872–3), 131.
69 *Congleton Mercury,* 5 April and 10 June 1871.
70 *Ibid.,* 3 February 1894; *Min. P.C.* (1898–9), 229.
71 *School Board Chronicle,* April 1875, 355.
72 *Ibid.,* 11 June 1879, 566; 23 August 1879, 178.
73 *Ibid.,* 23 August 1879, 178; *Congleton School Board* (1888) (pamphlet in Wagg Street chapel records).
74 *School Board Chronicle,* 3 October 1891, 356.
75 *Congleton Mercury,* 20 January 1894.
76 *Ibid.,* 17 November 1894.
77 Lists are published in the *School Board Chronicle* (indexed).
78 *Ibid.,* 17 September 1880, 57.
79 *Congleton Mercury,* 10 December 1870.
80 Broadside headed 'School Board Election' (in vol. of miscellaneous papers, town hall).
81 *School Board Chronicle,* 31 May 1879, 524; 7 June 1879, 541; 14 June 1879, 573; 21 June 1879, 596–7.
82 *Ibid.,* 21 March 1891, 300.
83 *Congleton Mercury,* 12 May and 8 September 1894.

[84] *Min. P.C.* (1876–7), 570–1.
[85] *Congleton School Board* (pamphlet in Wagg Street chapel records).
[86] *Min. P.C.* (1872–3), 131–2.
[87] *Ibid.* (1879–80), 243; (1883–4), 298.
[88] Ed. 16/16, Supply File, general report on premises, 1910.
[89] Head, 236, 244–5; *Rep. Mun. Corps.*, 2656; 31st *Rep. Charity Commissioners*, Parl. Paper (1837–8), xxiv, 687; Carlisle, *op. cit.*, 107.
[90] Head, 237, 245; *Rep. Schools Inquiry Commission*, Parl. Paper (1867–8), xxxviii, 35.
[91] Head, 245–6.
[92] *Schools Inquiry Commission, op. cit.*, 34–7, 112.
[93] *Cong. Chron.* 16 March 1901, 27 January 1956.
[94] *Cheshire by the Camera, the Pencil and the Pen* (*c.* 1906), 193.
[95] *Pigot's National Commercial Dir.* (1828–9).
[96] *Macclesfield Courier*, 11 February 1815.
[97] *Ibid.*, 28 December 1811.
[98] *Min. P.C.* (1851–2), 381; Bagshaw, *Dir. Ches.* (1850).
[99] *Congleton Advertiser*, 3 January 1863, 7 January 1865.
[100] *Congleton Mercury*, 14 July 1894; *Cong. Chron.*, 2 January 1904.
[101] *Min. P.C.* (1857–8), 427–8; *Congleton Advertiser*, 20 February 1858.
[102] *Congleton Advertiser*, 22 March and 15 July 1865, 1 November 1862; *Congleton Mercury*, 24 June 1871.
[103] *Result of the Returns to the General Inquiry, op. cit.*; Bagshaw, *Dir. Ches.* (1850); *Congleton Advertiser*, 19 August 1865.
[104] T. Kelly, *History of Adult Education in Great Britain* (1962), 125.
[105] White, *Dir. Ches.* (1860); Bagshaw, *Dir. Ches.* (1850).
[106] White, *Dir. Ches.* (1860); *Congleton Advertiser*, 22 November 1856.
[107] *Ibid.*, 27 March 1858; 2 March 1861.
[108] *Ibid.*, 31 October 1858; 27 October 1860.
[109] *Ibid.*, 25 November 1865; *Congleton Mercury*, 9 December 1865.
[110] *Ibid.*, 12 December 1863; *Congleton Advertiser*, 15 July 1865.
[111] *Congleton Mercury*, 30 December 1871.
[112] *Ibid.*, 7 January 1865.
[113] *Congleton Advertiser*, 25 May 1857.
[114] *Ibid.*, 26 January 1861.
[115] *Congleton Mercury*, 25 September 1869.
[116] *Ibid.*, 6 October 1894.
[117] *Congleton Advertiser*, 12 September 1863; 11 March 1865; 13 March 1858; 1 June 1861.
[118] *Ibid.*, 8 April 1876.
[119] *Ibid.*, 29 April 1865.
[120] *Cong. Chron.*, 21 March, 11, 18 April, 27 June, 13 July 1903.
[121] Ed. 19/19, L.E.A. Code File, 11 February 1916.
[122] Ed. 99/9, memo 27 August 1925.
[123] *Cong. Chron.*, 3 April 1920.
[124] Ed. 19/19.
[125] Ed. 16/16.
[126] *Ibid.*, 29 November 1913.
[127] Education Committee Minutes, 1910 (town clerk's department).

[128] *Cong. Chron.*, 21 August 1909.
[129] *Ibid.*, 24 January and 18 September 1920.
[130] Ed. 19/19, 11 February and 14 August 1916.
[131] *Cong. Chron.* 20 January 1917.
[132] Ed. 19/19, 11 February 1916.
[133] Education Committee Minutes, 1909, 177, 247.
[134] *Cong. Chron.*, 13 November 1903.
[135] Education Committee Minutes, 1921.
[136] *Ibid.*, 1920; *Cong. Chron.*, 28 February and 22 May 1920.
[137] *Ibid.*, 3 July 1920; 21 January 1938; Ed. 16/16, correspondence and minutes of 1920.
[138] *Ibid.*, 1921.
[139] *Cong. Chron.*, 13 November 1920.
[140] *Ibid.*, 2 and 30 April 1927.
[141] *Ibid.*, 3 May and 4 October 1930, 5 November 1937.
[142] *Ibid.*, 2 July 1925; Ed. 16/16, L.E.A. Supply File.
[143] Ed. 16/16, L.E.A. Supply File.
[144] Wagg Street School Minute Book, 1903–27.
[145] *Cong. Chron.*, 13 May 1938.
[146] Education Committee Minutes, 1909; Ed. 21/2088.
[147] *Cong. Chron.*, 15 December 1944, 3 and 24 January 1947, 10 February 1950; St. Stephen's log book, 1881–97.
[148] *Ibid.*, 16 March, 11, 18 May, 31 July, 2, 30 November and 14 December 1901; Ed. 35/214.
[149] Ed. 35/212, 213, 214, 216, Exhibition Fund.
[150] *Cong. Chron.*, 2 April 1921.
[151] Ed. 35/212; *Cong. Chron.*, 18 July and 14 December 1901; 18 July 1903.
[152] *Ibid.*, 23 January and 27 March 1909.
[153] *Ibid.*, 23 January 1909; Ed. 35/215.
[154] *Cong. Chron.*, 23 January 1909.
[155] Ed. 15/5.
[156] *Cong. Chron.*, 26 October, 16 November and 14 December 1901, 6 August and 26 September 1903.
[157] *Ibid.*, 6 August, 19, 26 September 1903; Ed. 35/214.
[158] The remainder of this chapter is largely based on reports in *Cong. Chron.*, and information kindly supplied by H. L. Morris Esq., Divisional Education Officer.

VIII *Congleton's Secular Buildings*

by P Timmis Smith

We have no record of what Congleton's buildings were like in Saxon times or the early Middle Ages. Probably the tiny population recorded at the time of the Domesday survey in 1086 lived in single-storey huts with clay walls, but, of course, these have left no trace. Indeed there is no original medieval structure in the town still extant—except perhaps part of the lower portion of the stonework of St. Peter's church, and possibly part of the structure of No. 1 the Vale, known as Yarwood's Farm, which may date from the later fifteenth century, and is thus one of the town's oldest dwelling houses. It has an external rendering of stucco and the slate roof and chimney are also of later date.

From Tudor times, however, a great deal is known about Congleton's buildings.[1] In the sixteenth and seventeenth centuries High Street was flanked on both sides by black-and-white timber-framed erections, two or three storeys high and either thatched or with thin natural stone roofs. In the crowded alleys that adjoined the main street were huddled wretched hovels of stone and timber. Many of the buildings of this period have, of course, disappeared, among them the house of John Bradshaw, the regicide, which was pulled down in 1820. A drawing of the High Street in the early eighteenth century shows others.

Buildings of the sixteenth and seventeenth centuries still standing at the time of writing include the *White Lion* inn, the *Lion and Swan*, No. 43 Lawton Street and buildings in Little Street. The internal construction of many buildings in High

Street, too, with their large oak beam frames, indicates their origin in this period. The *White Lion* inn stands in the High Street, a fine old black-and-white timber-framed building of the sixteenth–seventeenth century period, somewhat restored. It is double-storeyed with two gables and a restored slate roof and facsimile door. The building is said to have housed the attorney's office where Bradshaw served his articles. In West Street the *Lion and Swan*, another old inn, probably dates originally from the seventeenth century or before, though much of it has been restored and rebuilt. The frontage, largely if not wholly restored, is of timber-frame and plaster; the rest of the building is nineteenth century and of brick. It is two-storeyed with gabled dormer windows and two gables. The ground floor is older than the upper storey. Two stone Roman Doric columns of eighteenth-century date carry the first floor out on a projecting porch.

The *King's Arms* in High Street is also probably seventeenth-century in date, but restored. No. 43 Lawton Street is a small dwelling-house of the same period, bearing the date 1671 on the door lintel. It is of black-and-white timber-frame and plaster largely in its original state but with a restored slate roof. Stone steps lead up to the front door from the street.

No. 20 High Street is a seventeenth-century building which has been refronted in stucco. Timber framing in the passage and side elevation remains. Now a shop, it is reputed to have been an inn. Probably of about the same date is No. 7 High Street, a heavily restored black-and-white building of three-storeys with gable and slight overhangs, and with a modern shop front.

Congleton grammar school dated from at least the sixteenth century, and its history is discussed in the chapter on education. The school building, near the south side of St. Peter's church in Chapel Street abutting the Cockshoot footpath, was demolished in the early nineteenth century and a new school was built on the same site in brick in 1814. This is now (1969) used as a hall by St. Peter's church. A small part of a grammar-school house in the Cockshoot, perhaps of seventeenth-century date, remained until 1955. It was of two storeys with a cemented brick front, three gabled dormers, an old flag roof at the front, and slate at the rear. No. 50A West Street, a narrow one-gabled brick house, of three storeys, with a stone plinth and stone quoins abutting on the footpath. Much of the internal structure is of the large oak-beam system of the seventeenth century.

Two interesting buildings exist close together towards the north of Buglawton, tucked away in seclusion off the road leading from Buglawton to Bosley. These are Big Fenton Farm and Crossley Hall Farm.

Big Fenton Farm, in 1860 called Fenton Farm, was long part of the Antrobus estate, and is a black-and-white timbered building on a stone plinth, probably of sixteenth-century date. The ancient layout of the house was destroyed in nineteenth-century alterations, but a private chapel, occupying the first-floor of the gable-end wing of the house, remains largely intact.

The oak front door of the house is probably original. It hangs on its old iron strap hinges and has its original bolt. The living room of the house is constructed of oak beams with moulds similar to the beams in the nearby Crossley Hall and also to those in Moreton Old Hall. The walls are a mixture of plaster and beams, and wattle and daub. The rear of the premises has been rebuilt in the nineteenth century in brick. A number of doors date from the seventeenth century.

One such door at the end of the living room leads into the hall of the chapel. From this oak stairs lead down to a cellar which has window openings, and small recesses in its stone walls which may have been used as aumbries or shrines for the departed or to house the pyx. Similar old stairs lead to a small room possibly used for confessions. At one end of this room is a small raised gallery fenced with moulded oak spindles in grill providing ventilation and a limited amount of light. Another staircase of a similar kind which leads to the chapel room has in its adjoining windows a few of the original diamond-shaped oak mullions, but there is at the time of writing no glass to protect the structure.

The chapel room, measuring some 18 feet by 12 feet, contains much ancient timber. The ceilings are of timber and the walls of timber and wattle and daub. A few simple painted designs are still visible on the walls together with inscriptions of seventeenth-century date in black lettering. Some words were by 1965 illegible, and all were fading fast. The inscriptions were, however, recently recorded as follows:

So live as thy end Bee not ferefull,
Love thy neightbor as thyselfe alway,

Doe to all men as Thou would be du:un.
In my beginge, God by my good spide: Grace and
vertue long to proceede me. Hericy Smith, alias
Gilder, 1629.
Do nothing but to good advise: take counsell of the wise,
So tht the cloudes of ignorance shall banish fro thine eyes.
The compiny of him that's wyse, although hee bee but poore,
Is better than the foole that's riche who layes up croft in store.
Spar not to spend the golde and wealth for meat, for drink, for
    cloth,
For wisdom, lerneing, and for health, or else to spende by loth.
Before thou slepe, call to my mind what thou hast done that day,
And if thy conscience by opprest, to God for mercy pray:
Leade such a life that still thy soul may stand in state of joy,
Although the world a thousand waies thy conscience doe anoy.

These texts are protestant in flavour, though the 'confession room' and the partially hidden little room off it, popularly known as a priest's hole, might suggest that the house was a centre of the Roman Catholic faith in the period of religious persecution. It has been suggested that the texts may have been deliberately intended to deceive. There is, however, no evidence one way or the other.[2]

Crossley Hall Farm is also a timber-framed construction with a stone plinth. Of the late sixteenth or early seventeenth century, its timbers resemble those of Big Fenton Farm. At either end are two massive original stone chimney stacks which are most impressive (though the top brick parts of the stacks are not original), and two black and white gables. Some of the timber work is filled in with wattle and daub, but some has been repaired with brickwork filling. The front rooms contain the original oak moulded beams. The front door, of studded oak with long cast iron strap hinges, is set back a little towards the middle. The windows are eighteenth- and nineteenth-century. It was probably once the hall of a subordinate manor to Buglawton manor, and in 1819 was said to be 'ruinous.'[3]

The eighteenth and early nineteenth centuries saw the addition of many fine dwelling houses to Congleton. The picturesque row of later Georgian and Regency houses in Moody Street, for instance, is as fine as any to be found in the north. Further examples of the late Georgian style are the pair of houses comprising Nos. 2 and 3 the Vale, built in brick with a large central gable, and other houses in Moody Street. These include Moody Hall, a larger detached house, once the home of the Reades, silk merchants,[4] and later of Mrs. Wolstenholme-Elmy, a leading suffragette.[5] The original Moody Hall, perhaps on the same site, was a black-and-white timber structure.[6] Also very pleasing is the classic facade of the plastered upper portion of premises in Bridge Street which dates from about the end of the eighteenth century.

This period provided the town, too, with a number of well-designed brick houses standing in their own grounds. Some were erected in West Street, generally with their frontages facing south. Overton House is a splendid example of the larger town house.[7] The house is nicely set back from the street, with a walled garden, majestic entrance gates of eighteenth-century wrought iron, and stone gate piers with urns set centrally in front. The three-storeyed building stands out as a charming and dignified residence; the proportions of the windows to the brickwork are particularly pleasing, and the front elevation as a whole is artistically treated. Other such buildings are No. 29 West Street and in West Road two houses at the time of writing forming part of Danesford School, one of which was formerly known as Mortlake House, once owned by the banker, John Johnson. No. 3 West Street is a good mid-eighteenth-century house marred by the addition of a third storey probably in the later nineteenth century. Whitfield House was pulled down in 1966.

Eighteenth- and early nineteenth-century houses are to be found also in Chapel Street (Nos. 3, 6, 8, 17), Lawton Street (Nos. 21, 33, and 'Bradshaw's House'), and Rood Lane, Swan Bank (Nos. 10, 12, 14). Other detached houses of this period are Vale House (Priesty Fields), Throstle's Nest House and the Vicarage in Buxton Road, and Mossley Hall in Biddulph Road. Buglawton Hall, originally the seat of the manor of Buglawton, is a late-eighteenth-century house set in a small park. Added to in the nineteenth century and considerably enlarged, it is of brick covered with stucco.[8] Somewhat earlier are Nos. 5 and 7 Chapel Street, a pair (possibly once one building) of small brick houses, and No. 31 Lawton Street, which are of late-seven-teenth- or early-eighteenth-century date.

Bank House, Buxton Road, demolished in the first quarter of the twentieth century,[9] was a large irregular late Georgian House in its own grounds. Also recently demolished are late eighteenth-century houses at the corner of Mill Street and Bridge Street where many houses were built about that period.[10]

In 1804 the ancient black-and-white timber-framed town hall, on the same site as the present town hall, was pulled down and replaced by a new one completed in 1805. This was described soon after as 'a handsome modern structure of brick adorned with a colonnade in front, comprised of four columns of stone which support a piazza'.[11] Entrances were between the columns. The building contained, as well as a large chamber for public corporation business, a jury room, dungeons for the temporary imprisonment of criminals, and a room for the confinement of debtors.[12] At the rear were butchers' shambles.[13] An assembly room and a market hall were added at the expense of Sir Edmund Antrobus.[14] All, however, were removed on the building of the present town hall later in the century.

Another public building of this period was the workhouse erected in 1810 on Congleton Moss about half a mile from the town. It contained 19 rooms and was said to be 108 feet by 30 feet by 24 feet high,[15] and was replaced by a new workhouse at Arclid in 1844.

A perhaps less attractive result of industrialization at this period was the erection of mills and dwellings for their workers. After the introduction of silk in the mid-eighteenth century mills sprang up quickly in Congleton and Buglawton. Yet the largest of these, the Old Mill, was much admired. It was a five-storey brick structure 240 feet long, 24 feet wide and 48 feet high, having 390 windows, and built by Dane Bridge.[16] The poor condition of the upper portion led to the building being reduced to two storeys in 1940. The nearby old corn mill, demolished in 1966, was a mid-eighteenth-century building on the site of the medieval corn mill.[17]

Dwellings for artisans and labourers were a natural corollary of the factories. By 1790 workers' houses crowded Mill Street. By the time the Boundary Commissioners visited the town in 1837 many other streets had been filled with tiny dwellings and shops, often built back-to-back, where previously had stood larger buildings, or single-storey houses.[18]

Hand-loom weaving as well as factory production was also a feature of Congleton life in the eighteenth and nineteenth centuries, so that houses with built-in workshops for domestic textile manufacture were erected then in Congleton as elsewhere in the midlands and north. These were brick-built terrace houses with third-floor weaving garrets with long windows.[19] Nos. 21, 23 and 25 Wagg Road are examples of this type of building. No. 21 is now the *Royal Oak*.

The middle decades of the nineteenth century saw the building of several public buildings. Three new large stone churches were erected—at Mossley, Buglawton and St. Stephen's in Brook Street—and these are described elsewhere.[20] In 1864 the town hall in High Street was demolished, and a new town hall erected on the same site. The architect was E. W. Godwin (1833–86), one of the foremost practitioners of high Victorian Gothic, who had just completed the town hall at Northampton.[21] Congleton's new hall was built between 1864 and 1867 at a cost of some £8,000. Constructed of stone it has a square tower, and clock-tower turret. Small dormer windows peep out from the sharp sloping slate roof of hammer-beam design. Five large arched entrances at the front give access to the precepts, and above them, set in niches, stand the stone sculptured statues of Queen Victoria, Henry de Lacy and Edward I. A large assembly room, built to accommodate a thousand people, is set back at the rear. It is of single storey from ground floor to roof with a gallery round three sides. The front of the building contains a ground floor from which leads a stone staircase to a first floor with a court room and mayor's parlour. Above these rooms is a second floor lit by dormer windows. It may be considered the town's finest building, although the narrowness of the High Street does not at present permit a viewpoint from which the majesty of the facade may be appreciated.

The present Divisional Medical Office, originally the Cottage Hospital established in 1866, is in Park Street, occupying a corner site with Bank Street. The premises are brick built, having a well-proportioned Georgian front elevation. The Masonic Hall, in Mill Street, was formerly a Congregational chapel, built originally in brick in the late eighteenth century and added to in 1857. In 1878 it was purchased by the Freemasons.[22] Nos. 7, 9 and 11 the Vale were built in 1845 and provide an example of mid-nineteenth-century middle-class domestic architecture. The composition of brickwork, stonework and chimney detail are much to be admired. Towards the end of the nineteenth century more middle-class housing was erected. Detached or semi-detached, these were usually set back from the road with large gardens, and can be seen in Park Lane and Mossley.

The small workers' houses of the nineteenth century were, from a sanitary point of view, an improvement on earlier ones, which had relied on night soil tubs, and a bucket water supply. The newer dwellings had a limited communal usage of water closets and mains water taps, and later all houses had their water closets and mains water supply.

To meet growing housing needs after the first World War the first corporation housing estate was built at the Crescent in 1921, and similar estates erected by private builders followed. The speed of building the smaller workers' houses always fell behind growing demand. Since 1921 housing estates of substantial size have developed all round the fringes of the town.

Public buildings erected since the second World War include three large schools—in Box Lane, Jackson Road, the Girls' Grammar School in Holmes Chapel Road and the Quinta Primary School.

Important mid-twentieth-century commercial buildings include two supermarkets in Swan Bank designed on the open-plan system, both occupying prominent positions. Berisfords' Mill extension of 1962 is a fine example of contemporary commercial architecture.

Notes

1 This chapter does not cover the architecture of churches and chapels, descriptions of which are to be found in the religious sections. Use has been made here of a Ministry of Town and Country Planning List of Buildings in Congleton, 1947 (typescript). Many other noteworthy buildings then can be mentioned here exist in Congleton. A card catalogue of photos. and detailed descriptions is presently (1969) being compiled by the Cheshire Community Council (investigator, Joan P. Alcock).

2 White, *Dir. Ches.* (1860); *T.H.S.L.C.*, cvi, 107–8. For phot. see also *ibid.*, 105. Cf. *Cong. Chron.*, 7 September 1951.

3 See Ormerod, iii, 40–2 for Buglawton and Crossley manors.

4 See p. 140.

5 Cf. R. Fulford, *Votes for Women* (1957), 327; S. Pankhurst, *The Suffragette Movement* (1931), *passim*. J. Kamm, *Rapiers and Battleaxes* (1966), 117; R. Strachey, *The Cause* (1928), 274, 292. Another resident was Robert Hodgson, mayor 1803–4, whose wife was the grand-daughter of the Virginian settler who was the common ancestor of George Washington

and Claud Lyon-Bowes (later Bowes-Lyon), great-grandfather of Elizabeth II: *Cong. Chron.*, 14 January and 1 April 1966.

⁶ For a drawing see *Cong. Chron.*, 9 July 1966.
⁷ Built 1702 by a merchant: inf. from Mrs. S. Galbraith, present occupier.
⁸ A phot. of Mossley Hall is in R. Head, *Cheshire at Opening of the Twentieth Century*, 115. For Buglawton Hall see Ormerod, iii, 41.
⁹ Phots. exist in National Buildings Record files.
¹⁰ Yates, 52.
¹¹ *Ibid.*, 71.
¹² *Ibid.*
¹³ Post Office, *Dir. Ches.* (1857).
¹⁴ Yates, 61; Head, 137.
¹⁵ Yates, 72. Now Hightown Garage.
¹⁶ See pp. 138–9. See also plate in this vol.
¹⁷ For a phot. of the demolition see *Cong. Chron.*, 28 October 1966.
¹⁸ See p. 125.
¹⁹ Cf. D. M. Smith, *Industrial Archaeology of the East Midlands* (1965), 40.
²⁰ See religious sections of this volume.
²¹ B. Fletcher, *History of Architecture* (1954 edn.), 860. He also built Bristol Assize Courts. See also D. Harbon, *The Conscious Stone* (1949), 41, 49; Eastlake, *Gothic Revival* (1873), 358.
²² See *Cong. Chron.*, 21 October 1966, and *Eaton Lodge, Souvenir of Centenary Festival* (1946), for details of the history of this lodge.

IX *Place-names of Congleton*

by J Colin Jones

Celtic Place-names

The part of Cheshire in which Congleton is situated was thinly occupied from about 100 B.C. to A.D. 650 by Celts who spoke a language similar to, and the parent of, modern Welsh. They are remembered by a small group of place-names referring to natural features like rivers and hills. They called Congleton's river the *daven* a word meaning 'water' or 'stream', which survives in Davenport, Davenshaw, Dane-in-Shaw and Dane. Other Celtic names nearby are *minn* ('mountain' as in Bosley Minn), *chwilog* ('twisting' as in Wheelock) and *cryw* ('ford' as in Crewe). Within the borough of Congleton there is Peover Lane which, like its namesake Peover near Holmes Chapel, derives from *pefr* meaning 'glittering' (stream).

The name Congleton is particularly intriguing. The second element -*ton* is Anglo-Saxon for 'town' or 'settlement' but the first element is not Anglo-Saxon. Though there is a possibility that *congl-* is tenth-century Norwegian (and this will be discussed later) an earlier Celtic origin is far more likely. Two possibilities here present themselves. The first is that *congl* is a late Celtic word for 'bend', as in the Anglesey village-name Ty'n-y-gongl which means 'house on the bend'. The bend in Congleton's case is the sweep made by the River Dane as it goes round Lower Heath. The only objection to this theory is that the word *congl* has not so far been found in Welsh records before the thirteenth century.[1] The second possibility is that Congleton is a tribal place-name containing a reference to the Ceangli or

Deceangli tribe which during Roman times mined lead in Flintshire. If there were evidence that this tribe[2] settled this part of Cheshire or had dealings here, the theory would gain substantially.

However disappointing these two theories are, through lack of evidence from the Dark Ages, there is more support for the belief that the Celts were quite interested in this part of the Dane valley. A possible Celtic place-name within the borough is Buglawton. Here the -*lawton* element is Anglo-Saxon (meaning 'hillside settlement') but the *bug*- prefix is to be derived from *bug* meaning a 'ghost' or 'goblin', seen in our modern words 'bogey' and 'bugbear'. The idea is quite acceptable in a place-name, and one may quote another Cheshire example, that of Shocklach near Farndon, where *shock* means 'goblin' and *lach* means 'stream'. The Celtic element involved in *bug*- derives from the fact that *bug* in the sense of 'ghost' is generally held to come from the Celtic word *bwg* meaning 'ghost'. Whether the first element of Buglawton was affixed by Celt or by Anglo-Saxon therefore depends on when the name was first given. In the thirteenth and fourteenth centuries the prefix was not always used, and the use of Lawton Street instead of Buglawton Street in Congleton emphasizes this choice. Our first reference to Buglawton in 1287[3] is too late to help solve the problem.

Finally we come to the River Dare. A recent work gives it as the name of a stream running next to Moody Street.[4] As this is the Howty, it is assumed rather that the name refers to the stream originating at the foot of Silver Street and flowing behind Kinsey Street, then appearing in the North Rode timber yard and continuing to the river. The name is nowhere documented, but could conceivably be a shortened form of Darent or Derwent, the Celtic name for 'stream' or 'river'.

Thus the frequency of Celtic place-names as given above is rather greater than one would expect in so small an area, but the adherence of the Celts to dry and well-drained land close to running water is typical of their normal settlement pattern. The supposition that the words Congleton and Buglawton are both half-Celtic and half-Saxon would indicate that both hamlets were established about A.D. 650 when this part of Cheshire was overrun by the Anglo-Saxons.[5] If the establishment of these hamlets had been made later, their names would not have contained a Celtic prefix. When a group of men are the

Y

unquestioned masters, they make place-names in their own language.

Anglo-Saxon Place-names

For the Anglo-Saxon period ending at 1066 the evidence of place-names provides the sole information for Congleton's history. As far as is known no written record of the period mentions the town, yet place-names of Anglo-Saxon derivation indicate in surprising detail what communities, individuals and utilized land existed then.

Place-name evidence gives support to the possibility of a Roman camp overlooking Astbury, discussed above.[6] *East-burig* or Astbury can be interpreted as being 'east of the *burg* or camp', and the name Wallhill (first recorded in 1399)[7] may reflect the usual Anglo-Saxon name of *weal* or *wal* in imitation of the Roman word *vallum* referring to the earthworks of the camps.

Astbury was probably a community before the Norman Conquest. There was already a church there in 1086, and probably in 1066, and it is possible that Saxon fragments in the church belonged to the original building. At all events at the time of the Conquest it formed part of the large English estate, Newbold, which derives from the Anglo-Saxon *Niwebothl* in which *niwe* means 'new' and *bothl* means 'buildings'.[8]

Nearer Congleton, between West Heath and the River Dane, ran a little brook called the *Cross-lœcc* or 'crosswise stream' which has since become Crossledge. The stream itself is now straddled by the Forge Lane pumping station. The sixteenth- and seventeenth-century spellings Crosslytch and Croslitch bridge the gap.[9]

Buglawton certainly existed in Anglo-Saxon times, for *hlaw-tun* means 'hillside settlement'. The hill referred to is more likely to be the Cloud than Church Bank, as the nucleus of the village was in the Robin Hood area until the Industrial Revolution. The possible Celtic origin of the *Bug* of Buglawton has been referred to above and it remains only to say that the prefix *Bug-* was invoked in Norman times to allow the knight Hugo to differentiate between his two similarly named possessions Buglawton and Church Lawton. The name appears as Lawton in the 1086 Domesday survey and as Buggelawton in the Court Rolls of 1287. Adjacent to Buglawton is the small community of Under Rainow, and in this place-name, where the Anglo-Saxon *hrafn-hoh* means Raven Hill, we have one of several references to the wild life of the times.

In the middle of Congleton, under Bridge Street, runs the Howty Brook. It rises near the golf course, frolics through Priesty Fields, becomes subterranean at Bridge Street, gives Culvert Street its name, and then pours ignominiously into the Dane just above Mill Bridge. The earliest written references to it are *Houghteth* in 1443, *Heghtegh* in 1487 and *Houghtith* in 1507. These spellings[10] derive from the Anglo-Saxon *hiewet-ey*. A 'hewitt' was a place where trees were hewn, and an 'ey' or 'eye' was a riverside meadow. The *-gh-* sound was then pronounced *-w-* as in 'bough', so the Anglo-Saxon Congletonians of a thousand years ago pronounced their stream the 'Hewitty' or 'Hewty'. Next to the stream is Howey Hill which gets its name from the Holway or Holloway. This hole-way or hollow-way, noted in 1442 as 'in Holway'[11] is the deep channel gouged out by the Howty as it leaves Priesty Fields.

The Howty ends its short course by swirling through an iron pipe and pouring into the Dane. In earlier times it flowed gently into a small creek or 'fleet' on the bend immediately upstream from Mill Bridge. The Anglo-Saxons called a bend a *byge*, pronounced like a mixture of 'bee' and 'bye'. The place where the Howty joined the Dane was therefore known as the *byge-fleot* or Byfleet. A farmstead stood there in 1423[12] and was known as the Byflete. When it was washed away in the great flood of 1451[13] the name was still found useful for designating the area and it is occasionally heard today. It so happened that the flood levelled the bank of the Dane on the town side and, by a popular misunderstanding the name 'Byflat(s)' came into regular use instead.[14] By extension the name is now applied by some people for all the river bank from Mill Bridge to the weir.

The devastation caused by the flood indicates that in medieval times most of Congleton lay on the meadows and round its edges. Higher up than the farmsteads there was a public bird-trapping reserve known in Anglo-Saxon times as the *cocc-sceotas*, and now as the Cockshoot. In those days migrant fowl and game-birds were far more numerous and on the Cockshoot tame birds lured strange ones into the nets of the fowlers. These areas are always on hillocks ('shoots') and this explains why names like Cockshoot and Cockshutt are met with so frequently. Just outside the town were several places which we know today.

The word *mor* in Anglo-Saxon meant 'marsh' as well as 'moor'. At first called *mor-weg* and then *More Way*,[15] the present Moor Lane was in those days a twisting track which led to the marsh now called Green Island. The land is still pretty soggy, as the name Brook Street indicates. The route to Buglawton in these times lay across the *Bromleah* or *Bremel-leah*, the Broom Meadow now figuring in the name Bromley Road.

A mile south lay the turf and peat mosses of Mossley[16] and there could be seen a straight track, possibly Roman, leading from Wall Hill to the Bridestones. This dry solid track was used by the Anglo-Saxons especially at lambing-time. They called the section between Astbury and Mossley *Lambra Lane*, the Lane of Lambs. In Elizabethan times the district was used as a source of saplings and small trees, and in connection with this we come across variant spellings like Lamber Lane, Lamber Loon, Lambers Lane and the modern Lamberts Lane. The name is first recorded in ink in 1407 as Lambers Loone.[17]

Dane-in-Shaw (or Daneinshaw) is a place-name with a remarkable history. Really it is the name not of a hamlet but of that twisting valley which goes from the Castle Inn past Ward's Lane and Bath Vale to the foot of Church Bank in Buglawton. The first part of the name is *Danings* which means 'connecting with the Dane'. The second part is *healh* which is Anglo-Saxon for 'a twist' or 'a twisting valley'. The progressive forms of the word are, first, the Anglo-Saxon *Daningshealh* (unrecorded), then Danehynchill in 1407,[18] then Dane-ynsale in 1593,[19] then Dane-henshaw in 1825,[20] and finally Dane-in-Shaw today, pronounced Dane-enshaw. Beside all these forms there are the long versions which use *Daven* instead of *Dane* for their first syllable and give us Daveningshealh, Davenhynchill, Davenynsale and Davenshaw. Finally, there are the peculiar versions which were erroneously started by some seventeenth-century map-maker like Morden in 1695 who thought that the middle section of the word Danehynchill contained the Celtic word *inch* ('island' or 'water-meadow'). He gave us Dane Inch, which Harrison copied as late as 1789 in his Map of Cheshire, and which has led some to suppose erroneously that the old name for the Biddulph Brook is the River Inch. Another name offered is the 'River Bug', a genuine folk-given name some 1,500 years old. It derives from a superstition about a ghost (Celtic *bwg*) and is evidenced by Buglawton at one end of its course and the two Biddulph names River Bug and Bug's Lane (or Bogs Lane) near its source.

If the word Daveningshealh seems rather difficult to pronounce today, the same seems to have been true a thousand years ago. In those days people who journeyed to Buglawton called it merely 'the brook'. As the brook lay in the middle between Congleton and Buglawton it was known as 'the middle brook'. Speaking Anglo-Saxon to each other, they would say they were going 'to middes broces forde', that is, to the ford over the middle brook. In time this was shortened to 'to mids broc' and we ourselves miss out the fifth letter when we say 'Tommy's Brook'.

Another example of shortening occurs in the name Radnor. The red soil on the banks of the River Dane at this beauty spot led the Anglo-Saxons to call the site *readan ora* which means 'red banks'. In process of time these two words became fused into *radnora*, the final letter dropped off, and then the word Bank was needlessly added.

Three miles north-east of Radnor is another example of a fused name, the eminence where a certain Anglo-Saxon called Tida lived. Tida's *hoh* or hillock was, in those days, called *Tidan hoh*. This became fused into *Tidanoch* and now we have the shortened form Tidnock.

Moving from Tidnock proper to Tidnock House on the Manchester Road and then to Tidnock Avenue, we come to Lower Heath. It is interesting that the ancient eastern boundary of this satellite of Congleton was a little ditch which still exists today. It is an almost motionless stream which flows from the junction of the Manchester Road and Smithy Lane (one mile north of the Grove Inn) to the fields behind Midway House and then on to the new cattle market. From there it moves under Macclesfield Road and behind Jackson Road until it finds its way, mostly underground, to the Dane at Eaton Bank. The now-forgotten name of this stream is the Merlache[21] coming from the Anglo-Saxon *maer-læc* or 'boundary stream'.

No doubt there are several other Congleton place-names which go back to Anglo-Saxon times. West Street is such a one. We know that it was used in Anglo-Saxon times because a document of 1403 mentions a property called *Challercroft* which is Anglo-Saxon for 'Calves' Croft' lying on West Street, and a will of 1442 speaks of *Meerstall* ('Pond Farm') which stood where the Crescent is now. Without such chance references, West Street would have been allotted to the Norman period on the grounds that the first-known reference to it is in 1392. Other places with clear Anglo-Saxon ancestry include Moss Hey, Whateley Bank and Bagge Lane.[22] Bagge Lane appears first in 1264[23] as 'Bagge Lone'. It almost certainly represents Chapel Street at a time when there was no chapel-at-ease. The meaning is probably Back Lane (having nothing to do with the nineteenth-century Back Lane on West Heath) since it ran at the back of the main street. A meaning 'Bag Lane' is possible implying that leather bags were made there, but this would suggest Norwegian influence since the word 'bag' does not exist in Anglo-Saxon. The Norwegian word was *baggi*.

The frequency of Anglo-Saxon place-names in Congleton suggests, however tentatively, a population of several score at least so that the 30 or so inhabitants at the time of Domesday[24] may represent all that were left after William I's punitive expedition of 1069.

Norwegian Place-names

A large group of Norwegians was expelled from Ireland soon after A.D. 900. These, with a few Irish wives and adherents, landed on the banks of the Mersey. Toxteth (Toki's landing-place) was their place of entry and from there they spread inland as far as Knypersley ('Rocks Meadow'), Scholar Green ('shed on river-bend Green'), Lingards ('Flax Paddocks') and Macclesfield.[25] The incursion was violent on occasion, for in A.D. 920 King Sihtric 'broke into Davenport'[26] burnt it, and settled the neighbourhood. Signs of Norwegian settlement in Congleton are definite, but not so numerous as to lead us to believe that they took the town over. Hulme ('Meadow') was a small Norwegian settlement between Walfield and the Dane. It was still considered separate from Walfield in 1262 when record refers to 'Wallefelde et Hulm'[27] though Norwegian influence had already caused the Wellfield[28] people to pronounce their hamlet's name in the Norse fashion. Another site in Congleton which bore a Norwegian name till Elizabethan times at least was the long hollow which runs from Loachbrook Bridge behind the boys' secondary school to the crossroads on the Holmes Chapel Road where one branches off for Radnor. This hollow was called Babslack.[29] A slack is a dip in arable ground, known in Norwegian as a *slakki*. The first element supposes that a Scandinavian called Bæbbi owned it.

On the eastern side of Congleton is Earlsway, the extension of Leek Road running from Daneinshaw to the Bridestones and Rushton. Earl is a Scandinavian title, *jarl*, used by them where English people would use the word thane. Another Earlsway, known as High Earlsway, formed in medieval times that part of the Congleton–Manchester road which passes through Marton.

It has been suggested that there is strong evidence of Norwegian settlement in field-names containing *-eye* or *-flat* suffixes. The nationality of the *-eye* depends, however, on the type of field. If it is, or was, totally surrounded by water, the Norwegian *-ey* ('island') is a safe source for the name. But if the field rises gently from a brook or river, the Anglo-Saxon *eg* ('water-meadow') is a preferable ancestor. Several *-eye* field-names like Wheat Eye, Ash Eye, Plaister Eye and Bridge Eye are named in the 1691 deeds of Eaton Bank Farm, and here an Anglo-Saxon origin seems preferable. With the suffix *-flat*, however, Norwegian influence is certain because the word *flat* did not exist in Anglo-Saxon. Though no detailed survey of Congleton field-names has yet been made, the examination of many private deeds has not revealed any *-flats*. This is in contrast with the many examples existing in the Newbold Astbury area. Any Norwegian influence on the word Byflat must be rejected as all the early forms use the suffix *-flete*.

Finally we come to the possible Norwegian origin of the word Congleton. There is a Norwegian root, varying between *kongl-* and *kengl-*[30] but it is unlikely that the Norwegians would establish a township where so many Anglo-Saxons already lived. Further, one would expect to meet several Scandinavian personal names in the earliest charters and wills, but there are none.

Place-names since the Norman Conquest
Until medieval times there is no written evidence of place-names in Congleton. From the thirteenth century onwards, however, many of the names, which from their formation are known to have been Celtic or Anglo-Saxon in origin, appear on record for the first time, together with others probably dating only from the Middle Ages. The following list indicates some of

these.[31] Others are mentioned in the chapter on medieval Congleton above. In the list the form of the first-known reference is in some cases given in brackets. The names are arranged chronologically according to the date of the document in which they have been discovered. Many places here listed undoubtedly existed before these dates.

c. 1262	Hulme Walfield (*Wallefelde et Hulm*)[32]
1264	Bagge Lane (Bagge Lone)[33]
c. 1272–1307	Park at foot of Park Lane (*parcum de Congleton*, i.e. Congleton park)[34]. This could have been a small park or a paddock for wintering stock. It stood between the present Moor Street and Park Street, and gave its name to Park Lane, Park Street and Park House (demolished in late nineteenth century). The pond[35] has now gone, but a stream still flows parallel to Moor Street
c. 1272–1307	Mossley[36]
1287	Buglawton (Buggelawton)[37]
1295	Congleton Edge (*firma rupe*, i.e. the firm rock)[38]
1305	Dane Bank (*hul super davene*, i.e. hill above the Dane)[39]
1385	Town cross[40]
1386	Town Wood[41]
1386	Market Place (marketstede)[42]
1386	Whateley Bank (i.e. Wheat-meadow bank)[43]
1392	West Street (*le Weste Strete*)[44]
1393	Moor Lane (*le Moreway*). The use of the word 'way' suggests a beaten track. By 1520 it had become More Lawne (Lane) implying a more significant route. By 1593 it was a 'horse-waie' with stepping stones across Tommy's Brook.[45] In 1658 a 'horse-bridge' across the 'Davenshaw Ford' was constructed
1399	Wall Hill (*le Wallehul*)[46]
1405	Mill Street (le Mylnestrete)[47]
1407	Congleton Bridge[48]
1407	Dane-in-Shaw or Daneinshaw (Danehynchill)[49]
1413	Hertislip (at Park entrance)[50] (i.e. 'hart's leap', a common phrase for a short sharp slope or track). From later records it is clear it ran from Lower Heath down the top section of the present Hillfield Steps, down Wood Street, behind R. H. Lowe's Roldane Mill, and out at the Park entrance. A later form (1470) is 'horslyppe' or horse-leap. This became 'Horsley Bank' in the sixteenth century. The use of trees for this bank, noted by the records suggests that the steep slope to the mill was being made into large steps. The last reference to Horsley Bank is in 1702, its place probably being taken by the present Rood Hill (first written as Rode Lane in 1582) being widened[51]
1421	Overparke or Highcroft.[52] Overpark was the upper parrock

	as opposed to the park at the foot of Park Lane. Its site may be that of the Highcroft Hotel
1423	Mill Hill.[53] At this date the mill was still on the town side of the Dane, and the hill ran from Mill Street to the meadows till washed away in 1451. Solly's Steps indicates its course
1423	Byflat (*Byflete*)[54]
1442	Wellescroft (*Wellscroft*). Probably this was the same place mentioned as 'Wellacre' in 1407[55]
1442	Lamberts Lane (Lamberts Loone)[56]
1442	Meerstall.[57] In Anglo-Saxon this means 'pond farmstead'. The pond stood where the Crescent is now. Water still rises there and is led underground to pass under West Street, a few yards on the town side of the junction with Antrobus Street. It appears briefly in a garden and then proceeds underground until it reappears with the Howty at Brookside
1442	Holway.[58] This 'hollow way' was the channel gouged out by the Howty between the present Vale Crossing and Bridge Street
1443	Howty (*Houghteth*). This reference is not to the stream but to a piece of land beside the Dane. The original meaning is 'hewing place' so possibly the stream in Anglo-Saxon times passed through a small wood as it approached the Dane near the present gas works. In 1595 the stream 'that runneth down into the Howte Eye' is mentioned, so that the confluence of the two streams was still regarded as a place called the Howty[59]
1443	The Meadows. (*Davenhees*, i.e. Dane eyes or Meadows)[60]
1457	Park Lane. This existed as a way in 1421 but not by name[61]
1463	Dog Lane[62] (now Canal Street). This is probably comparable with Cathayes (which lay behind Daisy Bank) meaning 'wild-cat fields'. It is unlikely to be based on the Anglo-Saxon *dagg* (dew) because of its late appearance[63]
1511	Congleton Moss and Moss Farm[64]
1520	Dog Lane Brook.[65] This is the stream flowing under the present Silver Street and under the last few yards of Canal Street near Albert Place. In 1600 it still flowed over the road and there were stepping stones[66]

If these sites are plotted on a map it will be seen that Congleton was by 1500 a sizeable settlement. For a more detailed look at one section of the borough and its place-names, we will consider West Heath. In 1403 Richard Glede conveyed certain land in 'le West Strete'. It stretched from 'le Challercroft' along the highway. Challercroft is Anglo-Saxon for 'Calves' croft' and indicates that a paddock for raising cattle had existed beside West Street since before 1066. This would be in the present

Silk Street–Booth Street area. In 1442 Thomas Chell left land near Meerstall which is the Anglo-Saxon name for 'pond farmstead', indicating settlement on the Crescent site before the Conquest.

There is no record of holdings of this type further out of town than Booth Street. There began Westfield, common land extending to Crossledge. One parcel of land on this common which retained its identity from 1595 to 1818 is traceable (supposing the King's Butt on a map of 1818[67] is the same as the archery butts noted in the town accounts for 1595) but that is all. From a bequest of 1423[68] and Thomas Chelle's will, it is deduced that the Latham family owned the meadows on the Crossledge side of the Dane, known as Netherfield, and that Sir Lawrence Fyton held the high land from Crossledge to Windy Bank up to the Brownswolds, known as Overwestfield. The town had certain rights over part at least of Overwestfield, however, because in 1584 it forbade the foddering of cattle there overnight. The Brownswolds, between Windy Bank, Fol Hollow and Banky Fields were also common land.

Places found for the first time in the sixteenth century include[69] Crossledge (1555), the Black Lakes (formerly the 'Flaskes') (1582) (behind the present Girls' Grammar School on Holmes Chapel Road), Lawton Street (1592), Padgbridge Lane and the Brownswolds (1595), Howaye Lane (1599), and Radnor Bridge and the Cloud (1605). Roger Read of Daneinshaw, mentioned in 1593, may well have given his name to Reade's Lane. In that year too are recorded the Waters (the meadows opposite the present Castle Inn) and Moreton's Meadows.

In the seventeenth century only a few new names appear. There was Moody Street (1641), Chapel Street (1655), and the Kinsey family (1672) which may have given its name to Kinsey Street. A certain Thomas Higginbotham of Buglawton is referred to in the 1670s, and in 1682 Thomas Higginbotham from Shallcross appears. He was one of the first of many Derby men to move to Congleton. The presence of tinsmiths, silver makers and button moulders may explain the names Silver Street and Cole Hill Bank. Congleton points were properly the silver tips fitted to leather laces and thongs. It may be that the silver-work was done at the foot of Dog Lane. There is no actual mention, however, of Silver Street or Colehill Bank before 1789, so both sites are likely to be eighteenth-century foundations.

'Cole' meant 'charcoal' in pre-1750 times and Cole Hill Bank could possibly have this meaning, but there was a coal wharf at that very spot serving the Moss Road tram-road (see below) and this suggests that coal had been brought to Cole Hill Bank several years before by pack-horses.

With the coming of the great textile age in the mid-eighteenth century Reade's Cotton Shop Bank of 1785 gave its name to Shop Lane off Canal Street. The establishment of a coal-supply route from Gillow Heath over Mow and down to Moss Road led to the naming of Moss Road as Coal Pit Road in the late eighteenth century.[70] Up till 1802 packhorses carried the coal, but between 1802 and 1807 a railroad was in operation.

A gazeteer of 1789 gives the existing streets as Lawton Street, High Street, Swan Bank, Little Street, West Street, West Road, Mill Street, Duck Street, Bridge Street, Rood Hill, Rood Lane, Dog Lane, Park Lane, Moor Lane, Chapel Street, Moody Street, Mill Green, Wagg Street, Silver Street, Cole Hill Bank, Wood Street, Water Street (known also as Puddingbag Street and facing Kinsey Street), Howty Lane and Bramley Lane. Without further evidence it is impossible to say whether Swan Bank was named from the *Lion and Swan* inn or the other way round. The alternative name Clay Bank seems to imply that the Bank came first and so does the neighbouring name Duck Street, refined in the late nineteenth century to Duke Street. Little Street was in fact what its name implied, a little cul-de-sac on the level and leading to Wagg Street up a flight of steps. The line of roof and downstairs windows indicate this clearly. The site of the tyre depot opposite the gas works was used as a dye-house in 1741[71] and the old name Well Gutter for Ticklebelly Entry or Woodcock's Entry shows that it was built there because water was available. The route to the dye-house was down the entry, past one of the few wattle-and-daub houses now left standing in Congleton. Tickleberry Entry is a local term for a passage hardly wide enough for two persons to pass.

There are only a few other Congleton place-names which appear to originate in the eighteenth century. The building which was to become the *Castle Inn* is mentioned in 1779,[27] the Mount from 1731,[73] Windy Bank from 1775[74] and Havannah from 1762.[75]

In the nineteenth century some 65 streets were built in Congleton. There are one or two dating from 1820 but the majority were built between 1840 and 1865 to house mill-workers. Their names fall into three categories: those associated with the past, those indicating trades, and those recalling people. Historical associations are present in Chapelcroft, later called Milk Street, which was built in 1837 on land next to the Bridge Chapel property. Stonehouse Green, which is mentioned in 1860,[76] was built on Stonehouse Field noted in the tithe award of 1843 and recalls the Stonehall recorded in medieval times.[77] Similarly Peel Farm on the way to Astbury recalls the fortified mansions known as 'peels' and may be a re-building of the 'maner House' spoken of in the Newbold Astbury records of 1586.[78]

The streets associated with commerce include New Street which was new in 1820 and appears to be the first example of millworkers' cottages, Cooper Street where there was a cooper's yard, Booth Street where in 1820 booths were still being set up for cattle-fairs, Hatter Street where hats were made, Spragg Street where coachnails called 'spraggs' were forged, and Rope Walk where there was a rope-works in the 1830s. Bark Street and Tanner Street recall the nineteenth-century tannery and its stock of bark, and Silk Street perpetuates the memory of George Barlow's silk mill of 1840.

The place-names associated with people are of two types: those honouring important people, like Parnellscroft, recalling Sir Henry Brooke Parnell (later Lord Congleton), Albert Place, after the Prince Consort, Brunswick Street and the Leipsic Printing Office in Bridge Street, also honouring the Prince; and those bearing the name of the landowner, like Davenport Street, named after the owners of Prospect Hill, Antrobus Street, Hogg's Row, after Henry Hogg the silk-mill owner and mayor of Congleton. Bull's Bank (also called Eaton Bank because the lower part is in the parish of Eaton) and Bull's Lane (renamed Jackson Road after an alderman) owe their name to Samuel Bull who bought Eaton Bank Farm in 1814 and built the Bridge Silk Factory at the foot of the hill between then and 1820. At the top of Davenport Street[79] there was a mill called Bull's Shop, built in 1886 by Charles Bull for making silk and velvet. It was demolished in 1931. Between Parson Street and Astbury Street Bull made a reservoir which was later drained and became a rough playground known as the Razzer(voir).

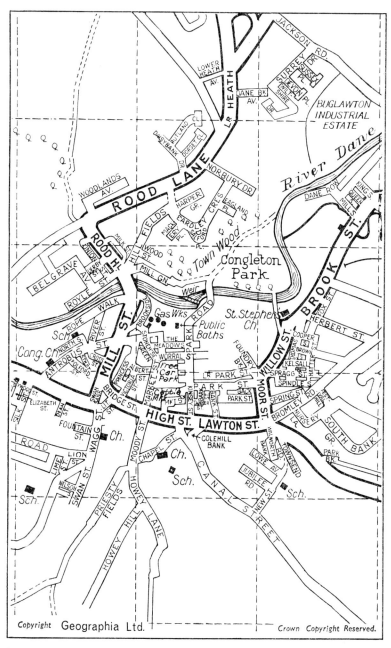

Congleton in the 1960s

One odd name is Roggin Row which occurs twice. The earliest one names a row of cottages built about 1820 on Flint Mill Lane and the second denotes a row built about 1840 on Prospect Street. The name derives from a purely Cheshire dialect word 'Rogging' which means 'shaking' or 'rattling'. Clearly the road-surface was as unsatisfactory as the one which gave Lumpy Street its name.

Apart from these visible records of the past, there are dozens of forgotten and half-forgotten place-names recorded in the deeds of local properties. The *Lion and Swan* deeds contain an 1857 map showing Banky Fields, Top Field, Swan Meadow and the Slang. The *Castle Inn* deeds give Piper's Bank (forgotten except as a house-name) and Barn Field, and mention the Revd. James Brierley of Mossley Hall, who is still remembered in the name Brierley Lane as applied to the main road where it passed his door. The voluminous deeds of Eaton Bank Farm[80] enumerate such lost fields as Wheat Eye, the Plaister Eye Meadow and the Bridge Eye.

Most of the twentieth-century place-names recall local dignitaries and picturesque parts of Britain. Certain roads commemorate the Festival of Britain, the Coronation, the war-ship *Woolston* which the town adopted during the last war, and the Royal Family. Others honour revered townsmen like Samuel Maskery, Dr. W. J. Fern, George Harold Eardley V.C., Fred. Barton and Charles Bradwell. The third group invokes Coniston Water, Dorset, Rutland, and Devon.

Congleton is richer than many towns in the variety of its place-names. They themselves tell almost 2,000 years of history.

Notes

1 Inf. from Prof. Melville Richards. The word *congl* derives from medieval Latin *concus* ('bend') with an added -l under the influence of Romano-Celtic *ongl* ('angle' or 'corner' from Latin *angulus*). For other Celtic place-names see E. Ekwall, *Concise Oxford Dict. of English Place-Names*, (1960).

2 For another argument concerning the presence of the Ceangli in this district see the *Cong. Chron.* 30 July 1965.

3 *Calendar of County Court, City Court and Eyre Roles of Chester, 1259–1297*, ed. R. S. Brown, Chetham Soc. NS., lxxxiv, 69.

4 Tom Taylor, *Concerning Congleton* (n.d. but *c.* 1940), 7.

5 P. H. Blair, *Roman Britain and Early England* (1963), 191.

6 See p. 14.

[7] SC 11/8.

[8] The name Astbury is first mentioned in 1093: Ormerod, iii, 21. Soon afterwards it appears as Esteburi *c.* 1100 and is Asteburi *c.* 1180 in *Chartulary or Register of the Abbey of St. Werburgh, Chester*, ed. J. Tait (Chetham Soc., lxxix, lxxxii).

[9] Borough accounts, *passim*.

[10] Duchy of Lancaster ministers' accounts (DL 29, DL 30). Much of the inf. on place-names for the thirteenth to the seventeenth century has been provided from the researches into these accounts by J. M. Dodgson, Esq., and J. B. Blake, Esq., to whom thanks are due.

[11] Borough charters, iii, will of Thos. Chell and charter to Hugh Grene.

[12] DL 29/5/58.

[13] Congleton town hall, Letter Patent of 29 June 1451 from Henry VI permitting the re-cutting of the course of the Dane speaks of 'a farm or piece of land of ours called Biflete' as if the farm was not then there.

[14] From 1600 onwards, when the Borough Order Bk., 1544–1699, mentions 'Byflatte' the *-flat* suffix becomes normal spelling.

[15] le Moreway 1393 and More Lawne (Lane) 1520: B. M. Add. Chs. 37004, 37023.

[16] Mossley occurs first in the reign of Edward I as Moseley in the John Rylands Library, Manchester, Charter No. 1266 and as Mosley in DL 29/4/30.

[17] Borough charters, i, charter of Thomas Hassall and will of Thomas Chell.

[18] Borough charters, i, charter of Thomas de Hassall.

[19] Congleton town hall, Perambulation of the Bounds of the Lordshyppe of Congleton, 1593.

[20] C.R.O., Macclesfield Canal Plan, 1825.

[21] Borough charters, i, charter of William de Pulford, temp. Edward I.

[22] le West Strete appears in 1392: BM. Add. Ch. 49890; Moss Hey appears in 1370: DL 29/4/30; Whateley Bank, Watley Bank and six alternative spellings are recorded in DL 29 various accounts, 1386 to 1514. The meaning in Anglo-Saxon is 'Wheat-meadow bank'.

[23] *E.P.N.S.* xxii, p. lxxix.

[24] See pp. 28–9.

[25] For Norwegian influence in Macclesfield see Davies, *Macclesfield*, 14.

[26] *Symeon of Durham: Omnia Opera* ed. Arnold (1885), ii, 93, 123, entry for A.D. 920.

[27] 'Wallefelde et Hulm' appears in 1262: John Rylands Library, Bromley-Davenport MSS., Box 55; Record Comm., *Inquisitiones Post Mortem* i, 101, 102; ii, 478.

[28] Wellfield gets its name from the welling-forth of the stream at Claphatch. It can be argued that the spelling *Wal-* is Anglian rather than Norwegian, but the existence of Wellacre in Thomas de Hassall's charter of 1407 and Wellcroft in Thomas Chell's will of 1442 suggest that the regular spelling in this district was *Well-*.

[29] Perambulation of the Bounds, 1593.

[30] Ekwall, *Concise Oxford Dictionary of English Place-Names*, under 'Congleton'.

[31] Unless otherwise indicated information of place-names between 1200 and 1550 is derived from the volumes of Borough charters, Congleton town hall and from duchy of Lancaster accounts, DL 29, DL 30.

[32] 'Wallefelde et Hulm' is found in John Rylands library, Bromley-Davenport MSS., Box 55.

[33] *E.P.N.S.* xxii, lxxix; see also above p. 324. In the eighteenth century cul-de-sacs were known as 'Pudding-bag lanes', as Water Street was in Congleton, but there is no evidence of earlier usage.

[34] John Rylands Library, Charter No. 1266.

[35] Borough Order Bk., 1599.

[36] John Rylands Library, Charter No. 1266.

[37] R. Stewart Brown, *Calendar of County Court, City Court and Eyre Rolls of Chester 1259–1297* (Chetham Soc. NS., lxxxiv), 69.

[38] P. A. Lyons, *Two Compoti of the Lancashire and Cheshire Manors of Henry de Lacy, Earl of Lincoln, 24–33 Edward I* (Chetham Soc., cxii), 54, 55, 61.

[39] *Ibid.*, 62.

[40] Borough charters, i.

[41] There is a certain difficulty here. The phrase 'milnestonbergh in Congleton Wood' (DL 29/4/40) means 'the millstone-grit hill in Congleton Wood' and this refers to Congleton Edge. By Elizabethan times the wood next to the present Park was being used and this, as the Borough Order Bk. for 1584 shows, was called 'the town wood' or 'the acre wood'.

[42] DL 29/4/40.

[43] *Ibid.*

[44] B.M., Add. Ch. 49890.

[45] *Ibid.*, 37004; 37023; Perambulation of the Bounds, 1593.

[46] See p. 320.

[47] B.M., Add. Ch. 37006.

[48] Borough charters, i, Thos. de Hassall's charter. See p. 20.

[49] Thos. de Hassall's charter.

[50] Borough charters, iii, will of Reginald de Brodok; *ibid.*, i, John Newton's indenture.

[51] Borough Order Bk., 1544–1699.

[52] Borough charters, i, will of Ric. Bronnesscherde.

[53] DL 29/5/58.

[54] See p. 321 above.

[55] Thos. Chell's will (1442) and Thos. de Hassall's charter (1407) both cited above. Land 'near Lamberts Lane, between the King's Way and 'Wellscroft' is mentioned. The King's Way to Astbury led along the landowner Richard Wagg's lane and met Lamberts Lane at Moreton Meadows Farm (a name first found *c.* 1593: Perambulation of the Bounds) when William Moreton held it. Probably Meadows and Farm replaced the names Wellscroft and Wellacre. 'Well' in Middle English still had the sense of 'spring' or 'stream' and such a stream rises close in front of the farm.

[56] Thos. Chell's will. See also p. 322.

[57] Thos. Chell's will.

[58] *Ibid.* See p. 321.

[59] DL 29/7/77; Borough Order Bk., 1595. Michael Drayton in his *Polyol*

bion (1612) speaks in his eleventh song of the stream called the Howty and this is the earliest example of the modern spelling.

[60] DL 29/7/77 where also '*les warthes*' again meaning 'the meadows'.
[61] B.M., Add. Chs. 37014–5; Borough charters, i, will of Ric. Bronnesscherde, 1421. See above (the Park).
[62] Borough charters, iii, charter of Hugh Green; John Rylands Library, Bromley-Davenport MSS., Box 34/1/6.
[63] *Cong. Chron.* 3 September 1965 where it is observed that the name is frequently met within the communities on edges of the Forest of Lyme; cf. Macclesfield where Stanley Street succeeded the Dog Lane which existed there after 1310: Davies, *Macclesfield*, 15.
[64] SC 12/1/2, 41.
[65] B.M., Add. Ch. 37023.
[66] Borough Order Bk., 1544–1699.
[67] Moorehouse, *Map of Congleton* (1818).
[68] Borough charters, iii.
[69] Borough accounts; Perambulation of the Bounds, 1593.
[70] C.R.O., Congleton Enclosure Map, 1795.
[71] Deeds of Congleton Tyre Service establishment, kindly shown by J. Charlton Esq.
[72] Deeds of *Castle Inn*, kindly shown by Greenall Whitley and Co.
[73] Astbury churchwarden's accounts, 1731.
[74] *Cong. Chron.* 26 April 1965.
[75] See pp. 154–5.
[76] White, *Dir. Ches.* (1860).
[77] See above pp. 19–20.
[78] SC 12/1/2, 37.
[79] C.R.O., Tithe Award, 1843.
[80] Kindly shown by R. Taylor, Esq.

z

Appendices

Appendix A: The Charter of Henry de Lacy[1]

Know all men present and future that we Henry Lacy, earl of
Lincoln and constable of Chester, have given conceded and by this
our present charter confirmed for us and our heirs to the free
burgesses of Congleton that the aforesaid town shall be a free borough
and that our burgesses of the same town have for evermore a
merchant gild with all liberties and free customs to a gild of this kind
belonging, they shall also have common pasture for all their animals
and herds everywhere in the territory of Congleton, and of digging,
drying, and taking turves and peats everywhere in the turbary of
Congleton, and they shall be quit of pannage, however many pigs
they may have within the bounds of Congleton, and that, by virtue
of a charter of grant and confirmation of liberties to our boroughs
which we have from our lord the king, they are absolved for ever
through all places of Cheshire whether by land or by water under
the guard and protection of us and our heirs with all their merchandise from toll, stallage, passage, pontage, lastage, and murage, and
from all other impediments which affect merchandise except from
reasonable fines if they do transgress, and that they shall not be
impleaded nor judged for any pleas concerning their lands or
tenements nor concerning any plea for trespass done within the
limits of the town aforesaid without their own proper borough, and
that if any of them incur an amercement before judgement by
default, twelve pence shall not be exceeded, and, after judgement,
a reasonable amercement according to the extent of the offence, and
that they grind their corn at our mill of Congleton, on payment of
the twentieth grain, so long as the mill is sufficient, and that our
burgesses aforesaid may elect for themselves henceforth a mayor and
catchpoll and ale-tasters and shall present them in the sitting of our
great court on the Tuesday next after the feast of St. Michael and
our bailiff shall administer to them an oath of faithful service to their
lord and community, also we will and concede for us and our heirs
and assigns that the aforesaid burgesses and their heirs and assigns
may have and hold peacefully and quietly for ever their burgages
and the lands belonging to their burgages and also the lands which
can be approved and let at rent within the lordship aforesaid by the
oath of the aforesaid burgesses without damage to their liberties and

336

their right of common aforesaid, namely, sixpence for each burgage and twelvepence for each acre at the usual rent terms of the said town, and that they make three appearances at our court yearly at fixed times but that if a writ of right is current in our court they shall make suit from fortnight to fortnight for all other services and demands, and that they may lawfully sell, give, and mortgage, or in any way alienate at their will their burgages and lands aforesaid except to men of religion, and that if the bailiffs of the said town take any felon they shall if they will keep him in the stocks for three days and afterwards they shall deliver him at our castle of Halton with the chattels found on him saving to them the fee pertaining to the sergeancy.

And we the aforesaid Henry and our heirs will warrant acquit and defend forever all the aforesaid liberties burgages lands and tenants with the appurtenances and with free usages of the town to the aforesaid burgesses their heirs and assigns against all men. In witness thereof to this chanter we have appended our seal. John Deyville, William de Vavasour, Robert de Stokeport, Geffry de Chedle, knights, Ranulph de Rode, Gralam de Tideby, Bertram de Saxeby, Vincent de Wombwell, Gervase the clerk, and others.

Note
[1] A copy of the original charter is in Congleton town hall; later copies include B.M., Harl. MSS. 2074, fol. 194; DL 7/1 no. 47; DL 42/25, p. 5. The charter is printed in Ormerod and in Head. See also A. Ballard and J. Tait, *British Borough Charters, 1216–1307* (1923).

Appendix B: Mayors of Congleton[1]

1318	Philip son of Richard[2]	1397–8	William Moreton
1341–2	William de Moreton[3]	1398–9	William Moreton
1346–7	Richard de Brodok[4]	1401–2	Robert del Yate
1348–9	Richard de Brodok	1402–3	Ralph Somerford
1358–9	Richard de Brodok	1404–5	William Moreton[8]
1367–8	Roger Moreton	1406–8	Hugh Lathom[9]
1369–70	Roger Moreton	1408–9	Philip del Green
1375–6	Roger Moreton	1409–10	Robert del Yate
1379–80	Richard de Brodok	1411–12	Ralph Somerford[10]
1381–2	John Brodok[5]	1412–13	Philip del Green
1384–5	Ralph Somerford	1414–15	Philip del Green[11]
1385–6	Ralph Somerford	1415–16	Hugh Lathom
1387–8	Roger Moreton	1416–17	Philip del Green[12]
1391–2	Richard del Yate[6]	1420–1	Robert del Yate
1394–5	Ralph Somerford[7]	1421–2	Philip del Green[13]

1422–3	Robert Arclide	1540–1	Robert Spencer
1423–4	Robert Arclide	1541–2	Richard Grene
1425–6	Richard Moreton[14]	1542–3	Robert Spencer
1427	Roger Moreton	1544	John Davenport
1428	John Spenser	1545	William Moreton
1432–3	John Spenser	1548–9	Richard Grene
1433–4	Peter Wilbram[15]	1549–50	Richard Grene
1434–5	Hugh Lathom	1552–3	James Rode
1435–6	Philip del Green	1553–4	James Rode
1436–7	John Spenser[16]	1554–5	James Rode
1437–8	Roger Moreton	1555–6	James Rode
1438–9	John Spenser	1556–7	Richard Grene
1440–1	Hugh Green	1557–8	Richard Grene
1441–2	Roger Moreton	1558–9	William Rode
1443–4	John Spenser	1559–60	Roger Grene
1444–5	John Spenser	1560–1	Richard Spencer
1445–6	Hugh Green	1561–2	William Thorley
1447–8	Alexander Lathom	1562–3	Roger Grene
1449–50	John Barker	1563–4	Roger Grene
1450–1	Alexander Lathom	1564–5	Richard Spencer
1452–3	Hugh Green	1565–6	John Hobson
1453–4	Hugh Moreton	1566–7	Thomas Comberbach
1454–5	John Barker	1567–8	Roger Grene
1456–7	Hugh Moreton[17]	1568–9	Randle Hankinson
1458–9	John Spenser	1569–70	William Thorley
1459–60	Hugh Green[18]	1570–1	Alexander Latham
1462–3	Hugh Green	1571–2	Roger Grene
1464–5	Roger Moreton	1572–3	John Hobson
1466–7	William Madeow	1573–4	John Rode
1467–8	Hugh Green	1574–5	Randle Hankinson
1468–9	Hugh Green	1575–6	Thomas Comberbach
1469–70	John Newton	1576–7	Roger Grene
1476–7	William Smith	1577–8	Alexander Latham
1483–4	William Madeow[19]	1578–9	Alexander Latham
1493	Thomas Grene	1579–80	John Scragge
1503–4	William Rode	1580–1	Thomas Joneson
1510	Hugh Wagge	1581	John Hobson
1511	Hugh Wagge	1582	John Somerford
1512–13	William Brereton	1582–3	Richard Spencer
1517–18	Robert Spencer	1583–4	Richard Grene
1518–19	Ralph Rode	1584–5	Richard Grene
1520–1	John Walker	1585–6	Richard Spencer
c.1521–2	Ralph Yardeley	1586–7	John Smythe
1527	William Moreton	1587–8	Richard Grene
1529	Richard Grene	1588–9	John Hobson, jun.
1534	John Hobson, jun.	1589–90	Matthew Moreton
1536	Geoffrey Rathebon	1590–1	John Woulfe
1537–8	Simon Foxholes	1591–2	Richard Grene
1539–40	Richard Grene	1592–3	William Drakeford

1593–4	John Cresswell	1641–2	George Ford
1594–5	William Stubbes	1642–3	John Henshaw
1595–6	Richard Spencer	1643–4	George Ford
1596–7	John Cresswell	1644–5	John Latham
1597–8	Richard Grene	1645–6	Thomas Spencer
1598–9	Matthew Moreton	1646–7	Robert Knight
1599	Roger Spencer	1647–8	Richard Parnell
1600	Roger Spencer	1648–9	Roger Hobson
1600–1	John Hobson, jun.	1649–50	John Holliday
1601–2	Roger Spencer	1650–1	John Holliday
1602–3	John Hobson, senr.	1651–2	John Buckley
1603–4	John Hobson, senr.	1652–3	John Henshaw
1604–5	Edward Drakeford	1653–4	Roger Poynton
1605–6	John Smyth, senr.	1654–5	John Latham
1606–7	Randle Rode	1655–6	Thomas Spencer
1607–8	Randle Rode	1656–7	Robert Knight
1608–9	Edward Drakeford	1657–8	Richard Parnell
1609–10	John Latham	1658–9	Richard Parnell
1610–11	William Drakeford	1659–60	John Buckley and
1611–12	William Drakeford		John Hobson
1612–13	Richard Grene	1660–1	George Forde
1613–14	Henry Haworth	1661–2	John Walker
1614–15	Henry Haworth	1662–3	Thomas Higginbotham
1615–16	John Hobson	1663–4	William Moreton
1616–17	John Brooke	1664–5	John Kent
1617–18	Matthew Holliday	1665–6	Ralph Hammersley
1618–19	Edward Drakeford	1666–7	John Latham
1619–20	Edward Drakeford	1667–8	Richard Hall
1620–1	Thomas Parnell	1668–9	John Walker, jun.
1621–2	Randle Rode	1669–70	William Knight
1622–3	Roger Poynton	1670–1	Richard Cotton
1623–4	William Newton	1671–2	William Newton
1624–5	Philip Oldfield	1672–3	William Harding
1625–6	James Lingard	1673–4	Robert Hobson
1626–7	William Knight	1674–5	Peter Lingard
1627–8	Richard Grene	1675–6	Thomas Spencer
1628–9	John Latham	1676–7	Thomas Butcher
1629–30	James Lingard	1677–8	John Walker
1630–1	Ralph Wagge	1678–9	John Smith
1631–2	Richard Grene	1679–80	Richard Hall
1632–3	Roger Hobson	1680–1	William Newton
1633–4	Randle Rode	1681–2	William Harding
1634–5	John Walker	1682–3	Robert Hobson
1635–6	Randle Rode	1683–4	Robert Knight
1636–7	William Newton	1684–5	Peter Lingard
1637–8	John Bradshaw	1685–6	Thomas Malbone
1638–9	Edward Drakeford	1686–7	Thomas Spencer
1639–40	William Knight	1687–8	Thomas Wolrich
1640–1	John Walker	1688–9	John Smith

1689–90	William Newton	1738–9	John Bostock
1690–91	John Shaw	1739–40	John Vardon, jun.
1691–2	Robert Hobson	1740–1	William Bayley
1692–3	Robert Knight	1741–2	Richard Throp
1693–4	Peter Lingard	1742–3	Richard Martin
1694–5	Thomas Malbone	1743–4	Richard Throp
1695–6	John Shaw	1744–5	John Smith
1696–7	Thomas Wolrich	1745–6	William Poynton
1697–8	John Vardon	1746–7	John Vardon
1698–9	John Cotton	1747–8	John Bostock
1699–1700	John Sydebotham	1748–9	John Drake
1700–1	Richard Jackson	1749–50	William Bayley
1701–2	John Markland	1750–1	Richard Martin
1702–3	William Bayley	1751–2	Richard Throp
1703–4	Thomas Beckett	1752–3	Joseph Bramhall
1704–5	Thomas Wolrich	1753–4	John Drake
1705–6	William Ferne	1754–5	John Clayton
1706–7	William Gorst	1755–6	William Bayley
1707–8	Thomas Malbon	1756–7	Joseph Bramhall
1708–9	John Shaw	1757–8	John Drake
1709–10	Thomas Wolrich	1758–9	Richard Martin
1710–11	William Ferne	1759–60	John Clayton
1711–12	Thomas Becket	1760–1	John Drake
1712–13	John Vardon	1761–2	James Vardon
1713–14	John Toft	1762–3	Joseph Hill
1714–15	Thomas Shaw	1763–4	Richard Webster
1715–16	John Jackson	1764–5	Philip Antrobus
1716–17	William Gorst	1765–6	William Bailey
1717–18	Thomas Wolrich	1766–7	John Drake
1718–19	Joseph Wood	1767–8	Joseph Hill
1719–20	John Vardon	1768–9	Thomas Yearsley
1720–1	Joseph Malbon	1769–70	Thomas Brooks
1721–2	William Amery	1770–1	James Vardon
1722–3	Joseph Malbon	1771–2	Richard Webster
1723–4	John Vardon	1772–3	John Whitfield
1724–5	Thomas Shaw	1773–4	William Ward
1725–6	John Barlowe	1774–5	Joseph Hill
1726–7	John Bostock	1775–6	Thomas Yearsley
1727–8	Samuel Brooke	1776–7	Thomas Vawdrey
1728–9	Thomas Kelsall	1777–8	Bowyer L. Wynne
1729–30	William Amery	1778–9	Thomas Brookes
1730–1	Thomas Bowyer	1779–80	William Read
1731–2	John Vardon, jun.	1780–1	Philip Antrobus
1732–3	John Bostock	1781–2	John Whitfield
1733–4	William Bayley	1782–3	Thomas Yearsley
1734–5	Richard Throp	1783–4	Bowyer L. Wynne
1735–6	John Barlow	1784–5	Thomas Brookes
1736–7	Richard Martin	1785–6	William Reade
1737–8	John Smith	1786–7	Nathaniel M. Pattison

1787–8	Bowyer L. Wynne	1836–7	Thomas Hall
1788–9	Richard Martin	1837–8	John F. Reade
1789–90	Robert Hodgson	1838–9	John F. Reade
1790–1	Thomas Vardon	1839–40	John Pickford
1791–2	George Reade	1840–1	John Andrew
1792–3	Thomas Garside	1841–2	William Warrington
1793–4	John Shaw Reade	1842–3	William Hadfield
1794–5	John Dean	1843–4	James Broadhurst
1795–6	Joseph Vardon	1844–5	John B. Johnson
1796–7	Nathaniel M. Pattison	1845–6	John Pickford
1797–8	John Whitfield	1846–7	Joseph Bullock
1798–9	Owen Lloyd	1847–8	William Warrington
1799–1800	Samuel Williamson	1848–9	John Andrew
1800–1	James Twemlow	1849–50	William Hadfield
1801–2	John Wilkinson	1850–1	Henry Hogg
1802–3	George Reade	1851–2	Henry Hogg
1803–4	Robert Hodgson	1852–3	Thomas Goode
1804–5	John Dean	1853–4	John Dakin
1805–6	John Johnson	1854–5	John Dakin
1806–7	Jonathan Broadhurst	1855–6	James Pearson
1807–8	John Wilkinson	1856–7	Richard L. Ginder
1808–9	Nathaniel M. Pattison	1857–8	Charles W. Barlow
1809–10	Holland Watson	1858–9	Edward H. Solly
1810–11	James Twemlow	1859–60	Edward H. Solly
1811–12	John Wilkinson	1860–1	Henry Hogg
1812–13	Samuel Wilkinson	1861–2	William Hadfield
1813–14	Jonathan Broadhurst	1862–3	Joseph C. Washington
1814–15	Thomas Bowers	1863–4	Joseph C. Washington
1815–16	Jonathan Broadhurst	1864–5	Benjamin Radley
1816–17	John Johnson	1865–6	Benjamin Radley
1817–18	John Skerratt	1866–7	John Latham
1818–19	Thomas Bowers	1867–8	John Latham
1819–20	Nathaniel M. Pattison	1868–9	Robert Beales
1820–1	Jonathan Broadhurst	1869–70	Robert Beales
1821–2	Thomas Bowers	1870–1	John Dakin
1822–3	George Reade	1871–2	James Pearson
1823–4	John Johnson	1872–3	James Pearson
1824–5	John Johnson	1873–4	John Kennerley
1825–6	Jonathan Broadhurst	1874–5	John Kennerley
1826–7	John Jackson	1875–6	Dennis Bradwell
1827–8	George Reade	1876–7	Dennis Bradwell
1828–9	William Lowndes	1877–8	Dennis Bradwell
1829–30	Charles Gent	1878–9	Charles Goode
1830–1	William Lowndes	1879–80	Charles Goode
1831–2	Thomas Hall	1880–1	Robert Beales
1832–3	Charles Barlow	1881–2	Thomas George Sheldon
1833–4	Charles Pedley		
1834–5	Charles Gent	1882–3	Thomas George Sheldon
1835–6	Samuel Pearson		

1883–4	Thomas Cooper	1927–8	Samuel Maskery
1884–5	Isaac Salt	1928–9	Samuel Maskery
1885–6	Isaac Salt	1929–30	Rea Albiston Daniel
1886–7	Joshuah Howard	1930–1	Rea Albiston Daniel
1887–8	Joshuah Howard	1931–2	Frederick William
1888–9	Hugh Moss		Gibson
1889–90	Hugh Moss	1932–3	Frederick William
1890–1	Hugh Moss		Gibson
1891–2	Samuel Maskery	1933–4	William Edward Gee
1892–3	Samuel Maskery	1934–5	Frederick Charles Pass
1893–4	Robert Shepherd	1935–6	Frederick Charles Pass
1894–5	Robert Shepherd	1936–7	Frederick Charles Pass
1895–6	Robert Shepherd	1937–8	Herbert Hackney
1896–7	Isaac Salt	1938–9	Herbert Hackney
1897–8	Isaac Salt	1939–40	Daniel Charlesworth
1898–9	William Worrall	1940–1	Daniel Charlesworth
1899–1900	William Worrall	1941–2	Frank Dale
1900–1	George Pedley	1942–3	Frank Dale
1901–2	George Pedley	1943–4	George Rowell
1902–3	Joseph Birks	1944–5	George Rowell
1903	George Pedley	1945–6	Jessie Burgess
1903–4	Robert Shepherd	1946–7	Jessie Burgess
1904–5	Samuel Maskery	1947–8	Samuel Moores
1905–6	James Thomas Lucas	1948–9	Samuel Moores
1906–7	James Thomas Lucas	1949–50	Samuel Moores
1907–8	Arthur John Solly	1950–1	Horace Woolley
1908–9	Arthur John Solly		Howard
1909–10	Alfred Barlow	1951–2	Horace Woolley
1910–11	Alfred Barlow		Howard
1911–12	William Isaac Fern	1952–3	Ernest Hancock
1912–13	William Isaac Fern	1953–4	Ernest Hancock
1913–14	James Thomas Lucas	1954–5	John Thomas Howarth
1914–15	James Thomas Lucas	1955–6	John Andrew Clayton
1915–16	James Thomas Lucas	1956–7	Wilfred Herbert
1916–17	James Thomas Lucas		Semper
1917–18	Fred Jackson	1957–8	Esme Owen
1918–19	Fred Jackson	1958–9	Ada Ethel Crayford
1919–20	Charles Dennis	1959–60	Frank Davenport
	Bradwell	1960–1	Ronald Foster
1920–1	Charles Dennis	1961–2	Frank Bailey
	Bradwell	1962–3	Roland Wilfred
1921–2	Samuel Maskery		Beardmore
1922–3	Samuel Maskery	1963–4	George Albert
1923–4	William Isaac Fern		Campbell
1924–5	William Isaac Fern	1964–5	George Harris
1925–6	Charles William	1965	Georgia Frances
	Whitter		Finger
1926–7	Charles William	1965–6	George Harris
	Whitter	1966–7	Fred Heapy

1967–8	Daniel Charlesworth	1969–70	George Albert
1968–9	Wilfred Herbert		Campbell
	Semper		

Notes

1 For the years 1358–9 to 1379–80; 1384–5; 1387–8; 1397–8 to 1401–2; 1408–9 to 1409–10; 1415–16; 1422–3; 1438–9 to 1443–4; 1445–6 to 1449–50 the source is DL 29, various accounts. For the years 1402–3; 1420–1; 1423–4; 1432–3; 1435–6; 1444–5; 1450–1 to 1454–5; 1458–9; 1462–3; 1466–7 to 1476–7 the source is Borough Charters, various volumes. For other years where no reference is given the only source is Head or town order books, accounts, and Council Minutes. In a very few cases Head's names are incorrect. The names of medieval mayors have been compiled by J. B. Blake, those for the Tudor and Stuart period by Miss Norah Fuidge, and the remainder by W. H. Semper.

2 B.M., Add. Ch. 37003.

3 *Ibid.*, 72344.

4 *Ibid.*, 37005.

5 *Ibid.*, 72345–6.

6 *Ibid.*, 49890.

7 SC 2/155/84.

8 B.M., Add. Ch. 37006.

9 *Ibid.*, 37007.

10 *Ibid.*, 37008.

11 *Catalogue of Ancient Deeds*, v, A11024.

12 B.M., Add. Ch. 37009.

13 *Ibid.*, 37010.

14 *Ibid.*, 37011.

15 *Ibid.*, 37012.

16 *Ibid.*, 49891.

17 Public Record Office, *Deputy Keeper's Report*, xxxvii, 186.

18 B.M., Add. Ch. 37015.

19 DL 42/20, 52.

Appendix C: Town Clerks of Congleton since 1835[1]

Christopher Moorhouse	(1814)–1842
John Latham	1842–1851
John Wilson	1851–1856
Christopher Moorhouse	1856–1867
John Wilson	1867–1894
A. Steele Sheldon	1894–1899
E. A. Plant	1899–1943
A. D. Vickerman	1943–1945
J. Mee	1945–1968
H. Lawton	1968

1 For earlier town clerks see Head, 55.

Appendix D: Honorary Freemen of Congleton[1]

Alderman S. Maskery	3 October 1927	*d.* 5 May 1932
Alderman W. I. Fern	14 May 1934	*d.* 29 December 1939
Alderman F. Jackson	2 August 1944	*d.* 11 July 1952
Mr. F. Barton	16 June 1947	*d.* 3 October 1950
Alderman F. Dale, M.B.E.	26 October 1953	*d.* 22 January 1966
Mr. H. Williams, J.P.	26 October 1953	
Dr. H. B. Davidson	17 March 1958	*d.* 16 February 1964
Dr. A. J. Pirie	2 May 1962	
Alderman D. Charlesworth, J.P.	22 May 1967	

[1] Conferred by the Town Council in recognition of eminent services to the town, pursuant to the Honorary Freedom of Borough Act, 1885, and the Local Government Act, 1933. For an earlier list see Head, 56–7.

Appendix E: High Stewards of Congleton since 1757[1]

1757–1796	Richard Bootle Wilbraham
1796–1798	Richard Lowndes
1798–1861	Randle Wilbraham
1861–1887	Randle Wilbraham
1887–1900	General Sir Richard Wilbraham, K.C.B.
1900–1912	Sir George Baker Wilbraham, Bt.
1912–1957	Sir Philip Baker Wilbraham, Bt.
1957–	Sir Randle Baker Wilbraham, Bt.

[1] For earlier High Stewards, see Head, 45–7. Dates omitted by Head include: Thomas Savage to 1635, Bradshaw to May 1656, Thomas Savage (Earl Rivers) 1657–1694, Richard Savage (Earl Rivers) to 1712 (not 1727), Earl of Barrymore to 1747, Furnival to 1749.

Appendix F: Population of Congleton and Buglawton, 1801–1961

	Congleton borough	Buglawton township	Total	Percentage Increase/ Decrease
1801	3,861	517	4,378	—
1811	4,616	584	5,200	+19
1821	6,405	948	7,353	+41
1831	9,352	2,087	11,439	+56
1841	9,222	1,864	11,086	−3
1851	10,520	2,052	12,572	+13
1861	12,344	2,014	14,358	+14
1871	11,344	1,629	12,973	−10
1881	11,116	1,550	12,666	−2
1891	10,744	1,382	12,126	−4
1901	10,707	1,452	12,159	—
1911	11,309	1,438	12,747	+5
1921	11,764	1,572	13,336	+5
1931	13,046	1,620	14,666	+10
1951	union of townships		15,492	+6
1961			16,210	+5

Appendix G:　The Arms of Congleton[1]

It was not until very recently that the corporation of Congleton obtained an official grant of arms. By the eighteenth century it had adopted the arms which it was to use without authority for so long.

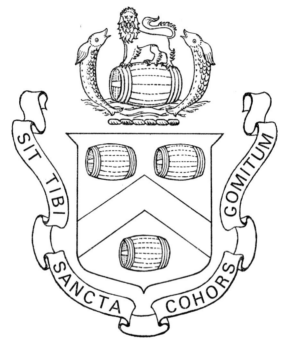

Arms: *Sable, a chevron between three tuns Argent*
Crest: *A Tun floating in water between two gold conger eels rising from the water, and on the Tun a Lion statant guardant gules*

The crest was derived from the device on a seal of fifteenth-century date, the congers and tun suggesting the syllables of the name Congleton. The lion may represent Henry de Lacy. The fact that this shield is identical with the arms of the Vintners Company of London, granted in 1447, led in 1966 to an application from the corporation to Garter King of Arms for an official grant of Arms and Supporters. This was obtained on 5 September 1967, and the new arms incorporate the de Lacy lion, the congers and tun, the Cheshire wheatsheaf, and the famous bear. The motto remains as before, and may be translated: 'To Thee be the band of Comrades dedicated'.[2]

Arms: *Sable on water in base Barry wavy Azure Argent a Tun between two conger eels Argent a Lion statant guardant Or on the Tun*
Crest: *On a wreath of the colours A Demi Bear muzzle proper with chain reflexed over the back and supporting a garb or*
Supporters: *On the dexter side A Wolf Argent and on the sinister side a Lion Purpure armed and Langued Or about the neck of each a chain pendent therefrom two keys in saltire*

Notes

[1] This appendix is based on C. W. Scott-Giles, *Civic Heraldry in England and Wales* (1953), 77–8, and information supplied by Alderman W. H. Semper, mayor, 1968.

[2] Based on Juvenal's Eighth Satire, line 127, where *cohors* is used for a provincial governor's staff, so that the motto is appropriate. The motto is differenced from the original only by the substitution of *sit* for *si*. Thanks are due to W. B. Thompson Esq., Leeds University, for these comments.

Index

NOTE: All personal names in the text are indexed, but those in Appendixes B, C, D, E are not. Thus, e.g., some listed in the index will be found, too, in the list of Mayors (App. B), but mayors only mentioned in App. B will not be found in the index.

The following abbreviations have been used: b., born; ch., church; D., Duke; d., died; E., Earl; fam., family; fl., flourished; fmly., formerly; La., Lane; m., married; R.C., Roman Catholic; Rd., Road; St., Street; w., wife.